Scott Foresman - Addison Wesley MIDDLE SCHOOL MATH

Practice Masters

Course 2

Scott Foresman - Addison Wesley

Editorial Offices: Menlo Park, California • Glenview, Illinois
Sales Offices: Reading, Massachusetts • Atlanta, Georgia • Glenview, Illinois
Carrollton, Texas • Menlo Park, California

http://www.sf.aw.com

Overview

Practice Masters provide additional exercises for students who have not mastered key skills and concepts covered in the student text. A Practice Master is provided for each regular lesson in the student text. In addition, a Practice Master is also provided for each Section Review and Cumulative Review lesson.

Lesson worksheets provide exercises similar to those in the Practice and Apply section of the student text.

Section Review worksheets review the student text section and include application problems that review previous material.

Cumulative Review worksheets cover important skills from the chapter at hand and from previous chapters. References to the applicable student text lessons are provided.

ISBN 0–201–31239–5

Printed in the United States of America

5 6 7 8 9 10 – BW – 01 00 99

Contents

Chapter 7: Proportion, Scale, and Similarity

Chapter 8: Percents

Chapter 9: Integers

Chapter 10: The Patterns of Algebra: Equations and Graphs

Chapter 11: Geometry: Solids, Circles, and Transformations

Chapter 12: Counting and Probability

Name ______________________________

Practice 1-1

Interpreting Graphs

Use the graph showing the three largest rice exporters for Exercises 1–3.

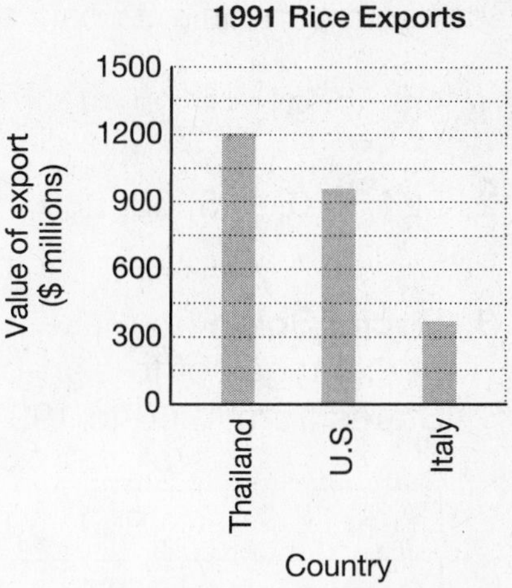

1. Use the graph to estimate the value of U.S. rice exports in 1991.

____

2. List the countries in order from the most exported rice to the least exported rice.

____

3. Thailand exports about how many times as much rice as Italy?

____

Career Use the graph showing reasons for unemployment in America for Exercises 4–6.

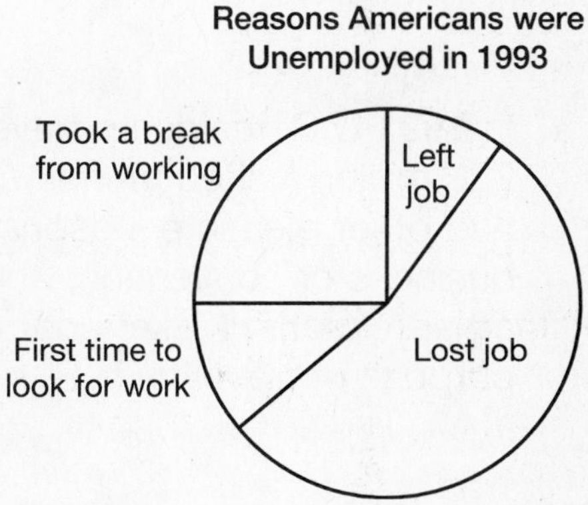

4. Which reason describes about $\frac{1}{4}$ of unemployed Americans?

____

5. What was the most common reason for unemployment?

____

6. About what percent of unemployed Americans were looking for a job for the first time?

____

Use the graph showing U.S. recycling habits for Exercises 7–8.

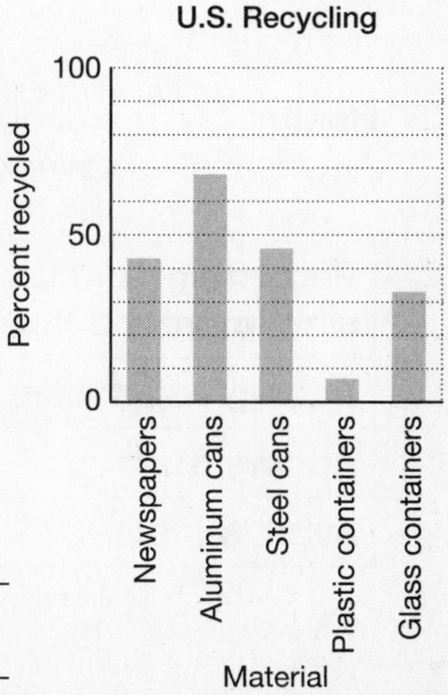

7. About what percent of steel cans are recycled?

____

8. List the five recyclables shown in order from the most likely to be recycled to the least likely to be recycled.

____

____

Name ______________________________

Practice 1-2

Making Bar Graphs

Choose a convenient scale and interval to use for graphing each set of data.

1. 85, 32, 91, 15, 24 scale ________ interval ____________

2. 324, 430, 125, 63, 260 scale ________ interval ____________

3. Social Science Make a bar graph to show the percentages of foreign-born people in the United States from 1960 to 1993.

Year	1960	1970	1980	1990	1993
Percentage	5.4%	4.7%	6.2%	7.9%	8.6%

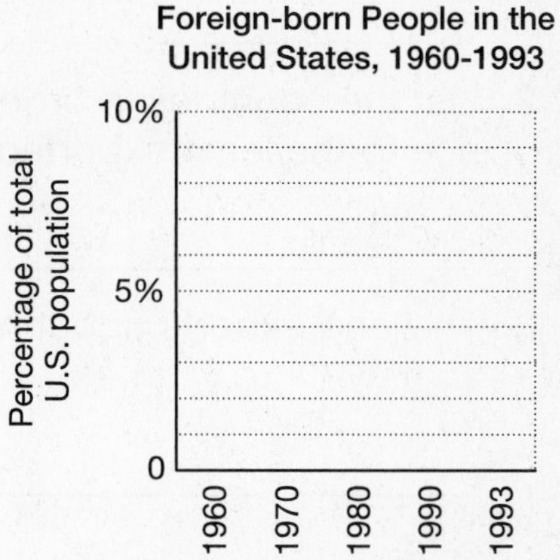

4. In 1991 U.S. residents traveled for many reasons–226 million visited friends and relatives, 240 million had other pleasure reasons, 153 million traveled for business or convention, and 46 million traveled for other reasons. Make a bar graph to show the purpose of travel by U.S. residents.

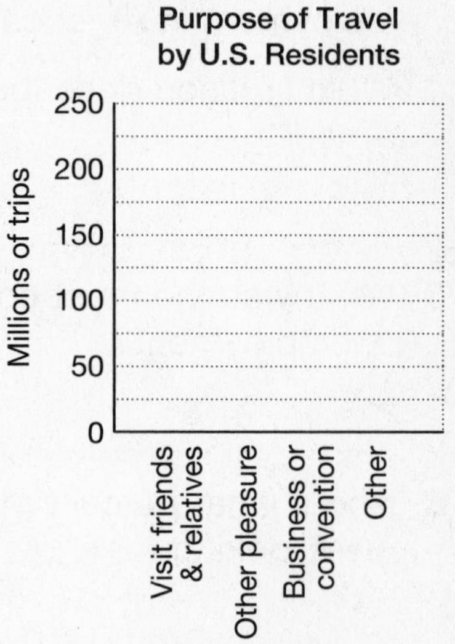

5. Health Make a double-bar graph showing how Americans improved their diets in 1991 and 1993.

Percentage of surveyed adults who improved their diet by:	1991	1993
Adding vegetables	40%	52%
Adding fruits	27%	36%
Avoiding fats	21%	29%

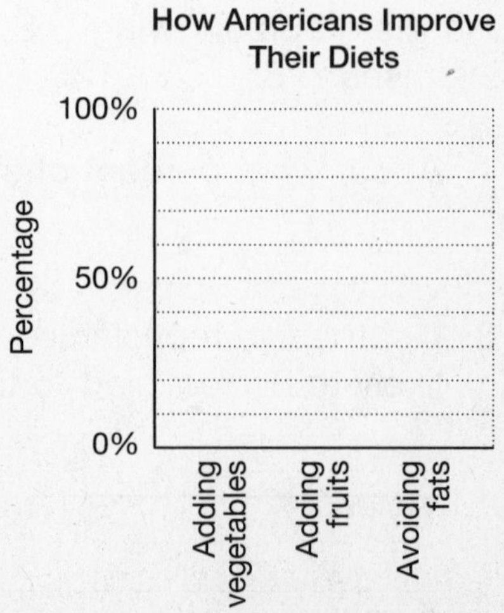

 Use with pages 11–15.

Name ______________________________

Practice 1-3

Line Plots and Stem-and-Leaf Diagrams

Make a line plot for each set of data and name any outliers.

1. 6, 9, 7, 9, 2, 8, 7, 9

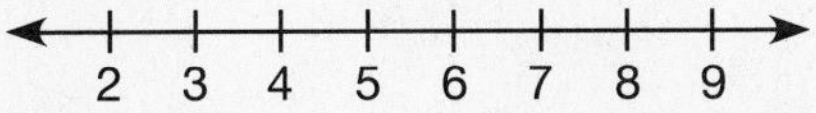

Outliers: ____________

2. 31, 29, 32, 30, 33, 32, 30, 32

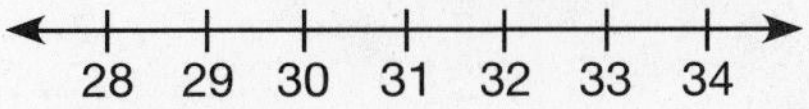

Outliers: ____________

Make a stem-and-leaf diagram for each set of data.

3. Number of musicians in local orchestras:

63, 41, 49, 34, 47, 62, 60, 38

What is the smallest number of musicians? ________

What is the largest number of musicians? ________

stem	leaf

4. Salaries (in thousands of dollars) at a local company:

36, 61, 42, 55, 39, 31, 47, 52, 33, 40, 39

stem	leaf

5. The stem-and-leaf plot shows the number of customers during different hours of the day at a local fast-food restaurant. How many customers arrived during the busiest hour?

stem	leaf
1	1 7 9
2	1 1 4 7 7
3	1 6 7 8
4	2 3 5 8 9

____

6. **Social Studies** The number of state senators in each of the southern states is given below. Make a stem-and-leaf diagram for the data.

stem	leaf

State	AL	AR	DE	FL	GA	KY	LA	MD	MS	NC	OK	SC	TN	TX	VA	WV
Senators	35	35	21	40	56	38	39	47	52	50	48	46	33	31	40	34

Name ________________________________

Practice 1-4

Mean, Median, Mode, and Range

Find the mean, median, mode(s), and range for each set of data.

1. 14, 16, 23, 18, 16, 16, 18, 21

mean ________

median ________

mode(s) ________

range ________

2. 3, 6, 12, 7, 9, 14, 8, 10

mean ________

median ________

mode(s) ________

range ________

3. 13, 12, 11, 12, 13, 11, 12, 11, 13, 12

mean ________

median ________

mode(s) ________

range ________

4. 3, 0, 15, 11, 7, 6, 14, 7, 9

mean ________

median ________

mode(s) ________

range ________

5. Social Science The table shows the number of congressional representatives for each of the 50 states.

Number of reps.	1	2	3	4	5	6	7	8	9	10	11	12	13	16	19	20	21	23	30	31	52
Number of states	7	6	4	2	3	6	2	2	4	2	2	1	1	1	1	1	1	1	1	1	1

a. Find the mean, median, and mode(s) for the number of representatives in a state.

mean ____________ median ____________ mode(s) ____________

b. Which of these measures best summarizes the data set? Explain.

____

c. After the next census, the number of representatives in most states will change, but the total number will stay the same. Assuming that there are 50 states, do you expect the mean number of representatives per state to change? Explain.

____

Name ____________________

Practice

Section 1A Review

The line plot shows the number of students in classes at Pike Elementary School. Use it for Exercises 1–3.

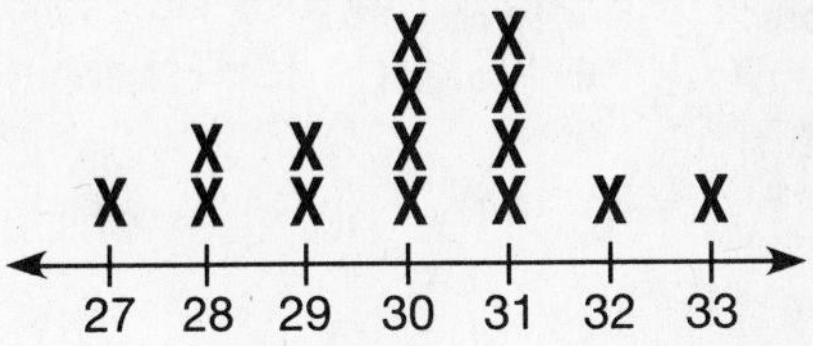

1. Name the outliers, if any. ____________

2. Find the mean, median, and mode(s) for the data.

mean ____________ median ____________ mode(s) ____________

3. Make a stem-and-leaf diagram of the data.

stem	leaf

The double bar graph shows the distribution of American hog farm sizes, as a percent of all hog farms. Use it for Exercises 4–5.

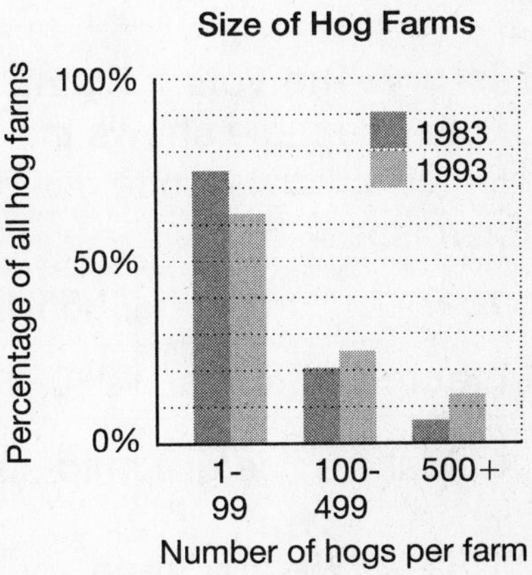

4. Would you say the average hog farm in 1993 was larger, smaller, or about the same size as the average hog farm in 1983?

____

5. How could circle graphs be used to display this information?

____

____

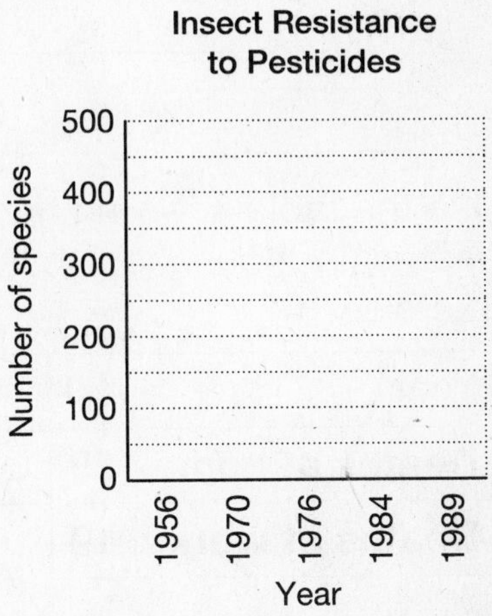

6. Science As more pesticides are used, they become less effective because insects become resistant to them. The table shows the number of insect species that were resistant to pesticides from 1956 to 1989. Make a vertical bar graph to show the data.

Year	1956	1970	1976	1984	1989
Number of species	69	224	364	447	504

7. Geography The summit of Mt. Whitney in California is 14,494 ft above sea level. A mountain climber is at a height of 11,677 ft above sea level. How much higher does the climber need to go in order to reach the summit of Mt. Whitney? *[Previous Course]*

____

Name ______________________

Practice 1-5

Line Graphs

Use the graph of the number of pieces of mail sent in the United States for Exercises 1–3.

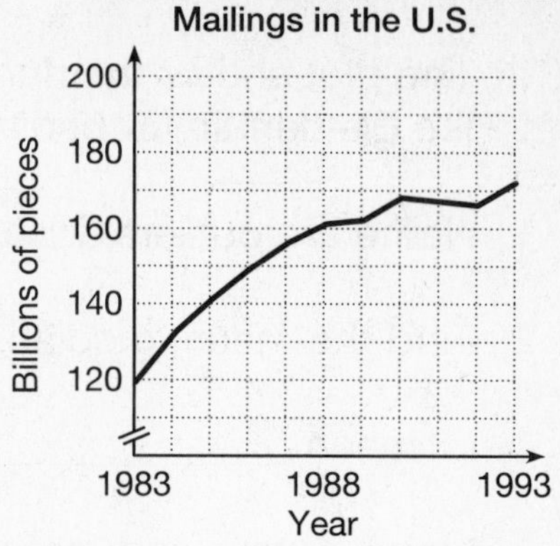

1. Predict the number of pieces of mail in 1997.

____

2. Describe any trend you see in the graph.

____

3. Describe how this graph would appear different if a scale from 0 to 200 billion pieces of mail were used.

____

History The Voting Rights Act was passed into law in 1965. The table shows the number of African-American elected officials since this time. Use this information in Exercises 4–5.

Year	1965	1970	1975	1980	1985	1990
Elected officials	280	1469	3503	4890	6016	7355

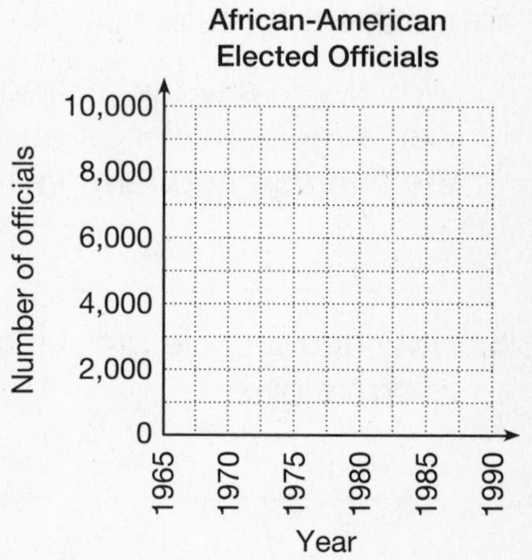

4. Make a line graph to display this information.

5. Describe any trend you see in the graph.

____

____

Use the table showing the number of accident-related deaths (in thousands) in the United States for Exercises 6–7.

Year	**'30**	**'40**	**'50**	**'60**	**'70**	**'80**	**'90**
Deaths at home	29	30	28	28	27	22	20
Deaths at work	19	18	16	14	13	12	9

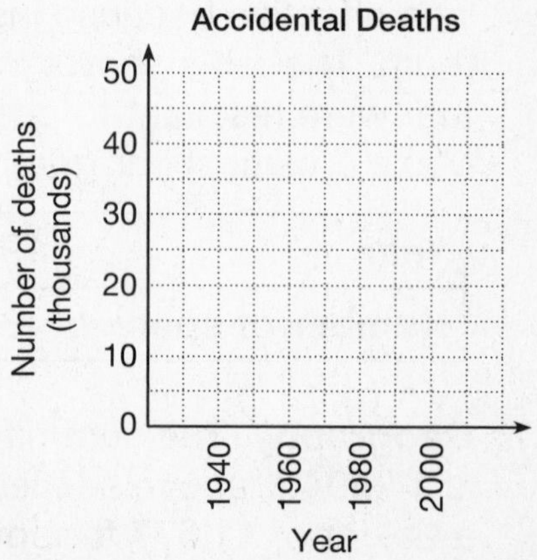

6. Use the data to make a double-line graph.

7. Describe any trend you see in the graph.

____

____

Name ____

Practice
1-6

Scatterplots and Relationships

Use the scatterplot showing weights and maximum speeds of animals for Exercises 1–3.

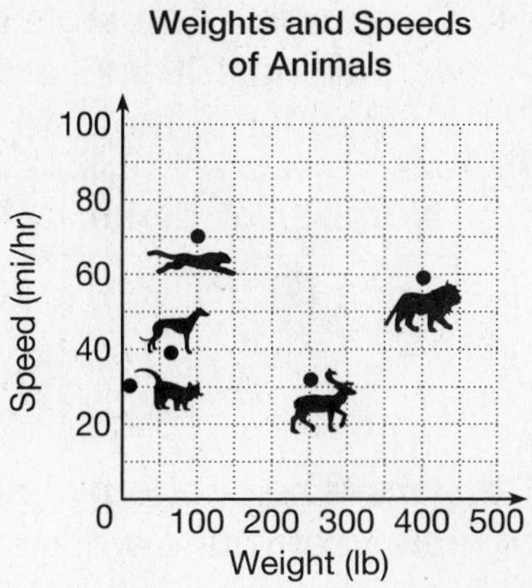

1. Which is the heaviest of these animals? ____________

the lightest? ____________

2. Which is the fastest of these animals? ____________

the slowest? ____________

3. What is the weight of a reindeer? ____________

the maximum speed of a cheetah? ____________

The table shows the number of passengers (millions) and the number of paid passenger-miles (billions) flown for the top 9 U.S. airlines in 1993. Use this information for Exercises 4–5.

Airline	**Delta**	**American**	**US Air**	**United**	**Northwest**
Passengers	84	83	70	54	44
Paid miles	82.9	99.0	101	35.3	58

Airline	**Southwest**	**Continental**	**TWA**	**America West**
Passengers	38	37	19	15
Paid miles	16.7	39.9	22.7	11.2

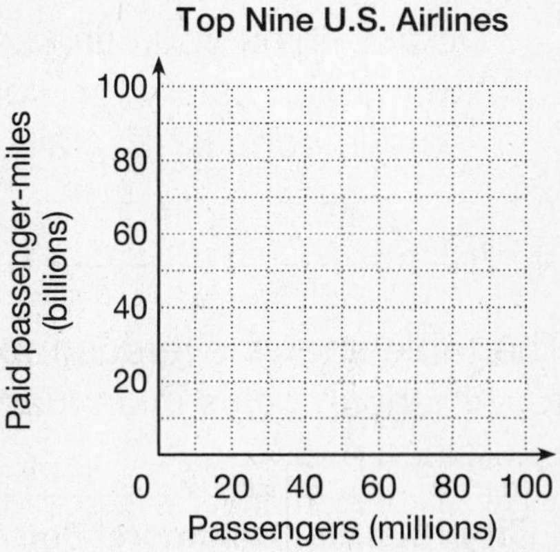

4. Make a scatterplot of the data.

5. What kind of relationship is shown? ____________

Describe whether the sets would show a positive relationship, a negative relationship, or no relationship.

6. The distance an airplane has to travel and the time it takes to make the flight. ____________

7. The number of a family's street address and their annual income. ____________

8. The number of songs on a compact disc and the average length of the songs. ____________

9. The number of bedrooms in a house and the price of the house. ____________

Name ____________________

Practice
1-7

Trend Lines

1. Consumer The table shows prices of packages containing 100-megabyte computer disks. Make a scatterplot of the data. Draw the trend line.

Number of disks	1	2	3	6	10
Price ($)	20	37	50	100	150

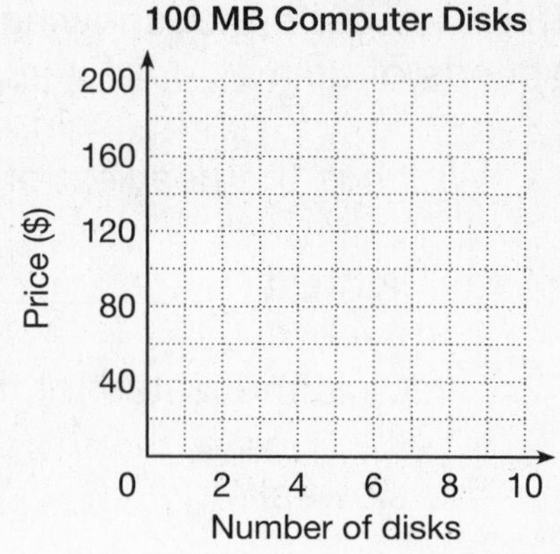

Careers The scatterplot shows the 1989 median income of male year-round workers and the number of years of school. The trend line is shown. Use this scatterplot for Exercises 2–3.

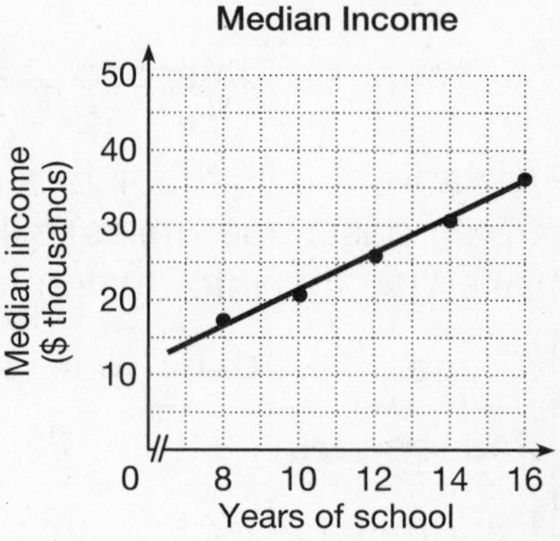

2. Predict the median income for men who have spent 20 years in school.

____

3. Do you think you can use this scatterplot to predict the median salary for women who have spent 20 years in school? Explain.

____

The table shows average monthly temperatures in degrees Fahrenheit for American cities in January and July. Use this information for Exercises 4–6.

City	Seattle	Baltimore	Boise	Chicago	Dallas	Miami	LA
Jan.	39.1	32.7	29.9	21.4	44.0	67.1	56.0
Jul.	64.8	76.8	74.6	73.0	86.3	82.5	69.0

City	Anchorage	Honolulu	New York	Portland	New Orleans
Jan.	13.0	72.6	31.8	21.5	52.4
Jul.	58.1	80.1	76.4	68.1	82.1

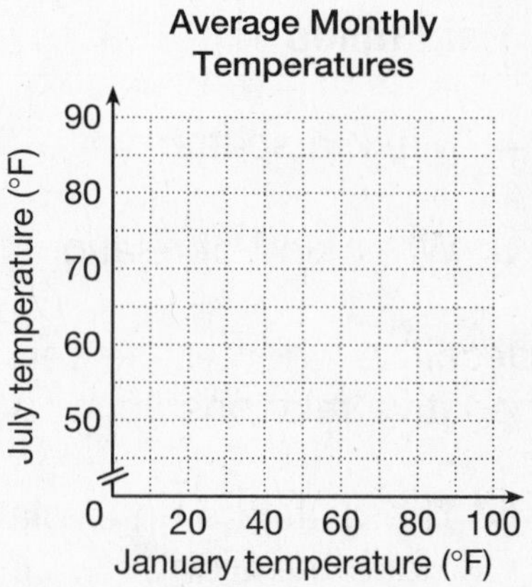

4. Make a scatterplot and draw a trend line.

5. Use your trend line to predict the July temperature of a city whose average January temperature is 10°F.

____

6. Use your trend line to predict the January temperature of a city whose average July temperature is 75°F.

____

Name ______________________________

Practice

Section 1B Review

Use the data in the table for Exercises 1–2.

Year	1994	1995	1996	July 1996
Unemployment rate	6.5%	5.3%	5.3%	5.1%

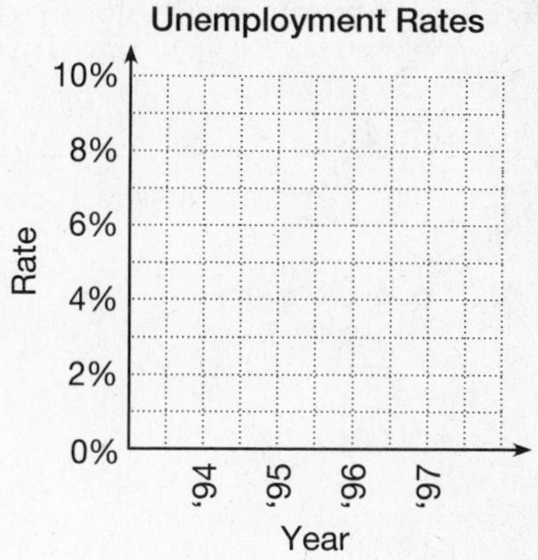

1. Make a line graph of the data in the table.

2. Use your line graph to predict the unemployment rate in 1997.

____

Ron's Bookstore is having a sale. The table shows the regular and sale prices for several books. Use the data for Exercises 3–5.

Regular price ($)	5.00	7.50	10.00	15.00	25.00	35.00
Sale price ($)	4.00	6.00	7.50	12.00	19.00	25.00

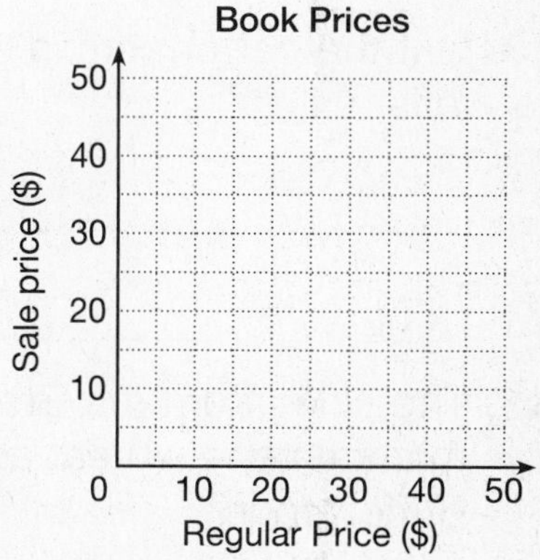

3. Make a scatterplot of the data.

4. Draw a trend line on your scatterplot.

5. Use your trend line to predict the sale price of a book whose regular price is $50.00.

____

The graph shows the top five largest-grossing movies from 1990–1995. Use this information for Exercises 6–7. *[Lesson 1-1]*

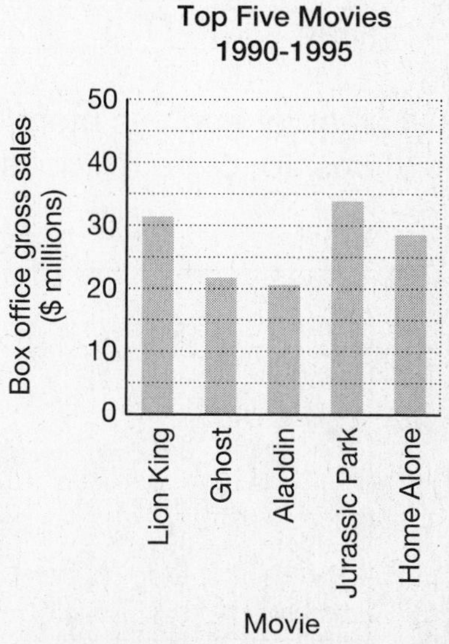

6. List these movies in order from the most sales to the least sales.

____

____

7. Give the dollar amount of ticket sales for *Home Alone*.

____

Name ______________________

Practice

Cumulative Review Chapter 1

Add, subtract, multiply, or divide. *[Previous Course]*

1. $385 + 649$

2. $964 - 129$

3. 643×81

4. 839×27

5. $638 + 416$

6. $429 - 57$

7. $14\overline{)2282}$

8. $37\overline{)26{,}418}$

9. $61\overline{)34{,}587}$

The graph shows the top five largest-grossing concert tours in 1993. Use this information for Exercises 10–11. *[Lesson 1-1]*

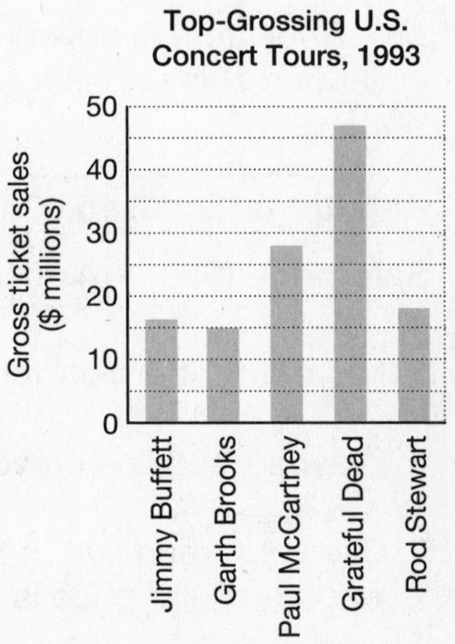

10. List the performers in order from the most sales to the least sales.

____

____

11. The sales from the Grateful Dead tour were about how many times as great as the sales from the Jimmy Buffett tour?

____

12. Find the mean, median, and mode(s) for the following data set. *[Lesson 1-4]*
37, 30, 39, 45, 39, 38, 47, 35

mean ____________ median ____________ mode(s) ____________

Tell whether each scatterplot shows a positive relationship, a negative relationship, or no relationship. *[Lesson 1-6]*

13. ____________

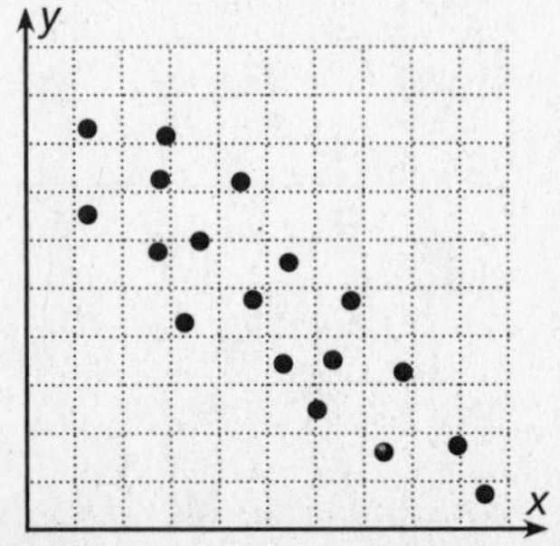

14. ____________

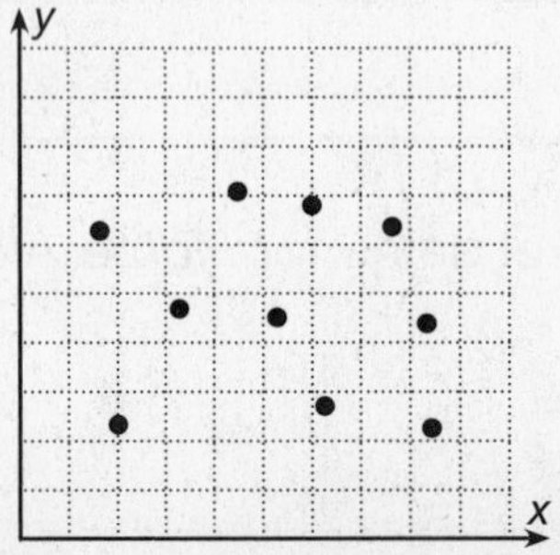

15. ____________

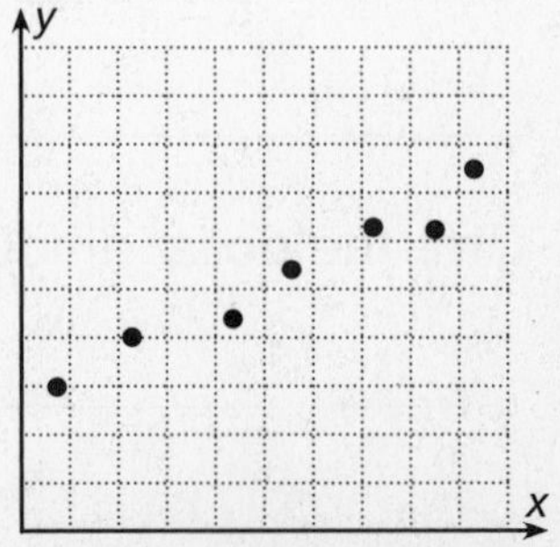

Name ______________________________

Practice 2-1

Formulas and Variables

Geometry You can use the formula $A = \frac{1}{2}bh$ to find the area of a triangle. Substitute the given values into the formula. Then use the formula to find A.

1. $b = 8$ in., $h = 5$ in., $A =$ __________

2. $b = 18$ cm, $h = 10$ cm, $A =$ __________

3. $b = 4$ m, $h = 3$ m, $A =$ __________

4. $b = 3$ ft, $h = 8$ ft, $A =$ __________

5. $b = 3$ mi, $h = 8$ mi, $A =$ __________

6. $b = 12$ km, $h = 3$ km, $A =$ __________

Science The formula $t = \frac{d}{v}$ is used to find t (time) when you know d (distance) and v (rate or average speed). Substitute the values for d and v into the formula. Then use the formula to find t.

7. $d = 465$ km, $v = 93$ km/hr

$t =$ __________

8. $d = 180$ mi, $v = 45$ mi/hr

$t =$ __________

9. $d = 200$ ft, $v = 25$ ft/sec

$t =$ __________

10. $d = 85$ km, $v = 85$ km/hr

$t =$ __________

Use the table for Exercises 11–12.

Street	Main St	Harbor Blvd	Oak Hwy	River Fwy
Speed Limit (mi/hr)	25	35	50	65

11. How far can you travel in 3 hours on Harbor Blvd? __________

On Oak Hwy? __________ On River Fwy? __________

12. How much farther can you travel in 5 hours on Harbor Blvd than on Main St? __________

13. Geometry You can use the formula $A = \frac{h}{2}(b_1 + b_2)$ to find the area of a trapezoid with bases b_1 and b_2 and height h. Find the area of a trapezoid with bases 9 cm and 13 cm, and height 7 cm. __________

14. Health Sheri's pulse rate is 150 beats per minute when she exercises. The formula $b = 150t$ relates the number of beats (b) to the time (t) in minutes. Find the number of beats in 8 minutes of exercise. __________

Name ____________________

Practice 2-2

Order of Operations

Does the expression contain grouping symbols? What are they?

1. $\dfrac{10+6}{7+1}$ ____________________

2. $8 \cdot 4 - 2 \cdot 3$ ____________________

3. $8 - 3 + 7$ ____________________

4. $17(3 + 5)$ ____________________

5. $(5 + 3) \div 4$ ____________________

6. $4 \div 2 - 5$ ____________________

Find the value of each expression.

7. $6 + 8 \times 9$ ________

8. $10(8 - 3)$ ________

9. $\dfrac{2 \cdot 3 + 8}{5 + 2}$ ________

10. $\dfrac{25}{5} + \dfrac{18}{3}$ ________

11. $4 + \dfrac{8 + 10}{2}$ ________

12. $\dfrac{15}{8 - 7} + 6$ ________

13. $5 \times \dfrac{4}{4 - 2}$ ________

14. $\dfrac{5 \cdot 10}{25} + 4 \div 2$ ________

Operation Sense Insert parentheses to make each sentence true.

15. $3 + 7 \times 4 - 2 = 20$

16. $10 - 3 + 7 + 4 = 4$

17. $300 \div 50 \div 2 \times 3 = 1$

18. $24 \div 2 + 30 \div 3 = 2$

19. $6 + 4 \div 2 \div 2 = 7$

20. $4 - 2 \times 9 - 4 = 10$

Which property is being shown?

21. $11 \cdot (12 \cdot 13) = (11 \cdot 12) \cdot 13$ ____________________

22. $8(3 + 7) = (8 \cdot 3) + (8 \cdot 7)$ ____________________

23. $13 + 18 = 18 + 13$ ____________________

24. $(3 + 5) + 8 = 3 + (5 + 8)$ ____________________

25. $11 \cdot (12 + 13) = (11 \cdot 12) + (11 \cdot 13)$ ____________________

26. To calculate a distance, Herb used the formula $d = rt$. Sal used the formula $d = tr$. What property assures that Herb and Sal should get the same answer?

____

Name ______________________________

Practice
2-3

Formulas and Tables

1. The formula $P = 4s$ gives the perimeter (P) of a square, where s is the length of a side. Use this formula to make a table of the perimeters of squares with sides of length 1, 2, 4, 6, 9, 12, and 18 cm.

Side (s)	1	2	4	6	9	12	18
Perimeter (P)							

Find a formula relating the variables.

2. Formula: ______________

x	2	3	4	5
y	8	12	16	20

3. Formula: ______________

s	4	5	6	7
t	12	13	14	15

4. Formula: ______________

h	11	12	13	14
r	7	8	9	10

5. Formula: ______________

u	5	6	7	8
v	15	16	17	18

6. Formula: ______________

x	2	3	4	5
z	14	21	28	35

7. Formula: ______________

a	8	9	10	11
b	3	4	5	6

8. For a given distance, the formula $i = 12f$ relates the number of inches (i) to the number of feet (f). Make a table that shows the number of inches equal to 1, 2, 5, 8, 10, 12, and 20 feet.

Number of feet (f)	1	2	5	8	10	12	20
Number of inches (i)							

9. Science The formula $d = 16 \cdot t \cdot t$ gives the distance (d) in feet that a ball has fallen t seconds after it has been dropped. Make a table to show the distance the ball has fallen after 0, 1, 2, 3, 4, 5, and 6 seconds.

Time (t), sec	0	1	2	3	4	5	6
Distance (d), ft							

Name ______________________________

Practice

Section 2A Review

Evaluate each expression.

1. $6 + 8 \div 2 - 4$ ______ **2.** $2 \times 3 + 4 \times 5$ ______ **3.** $7 + 3 \cdot 8 \div 6$ ______

4. $\frac{7 + 8}{5 - 2}$ ______ **5.** $3 + \frac{10 - 2}{4}$ ______ **6.** $2 \times 5 - \frac{3 + 9}{5 - 1}$ ______

Place parentheses to make each sentence true.

7. $4 + 6 \div 2 - 1 = 10$ **8.** $7 \times 7 - 7 \div 7 = 6$

9. $40 + 20 \div 10 - 5 = 44$ **10.** $7 \times 10 - 8 \div 2 = 7$

Evaluate each formula for the given values.

11. $A = \ell w$, $\ell = 3$, $w = 7$; $A =$ ______ **12.** $d = rt$, $r = 30$, $t = 2$; $d =$ ______

13. $P = 2\ell + 2w$, $\ell = 6$, $w = 5$; $P =$ ____ **14.** $r = \frac{d}{t}$, $d = 150$, $t = 3$; $r =$ ______

Find a formula relating the variables.

15. ____________

x	2	3	4	5
y	6	9	12	15

16. ____________

u	11	12	13	14
v	3	4	5	6

17. The formula $r = \frac{d}{t}$ gives the average speed of travel for a distance *d* and time *t*. New Orleans, Louisiana, is a 400-mile drive from Memphis, Tennessee. Complete the table to find the average speed if the trip from Memphis to New Orleans is made in different times.

Time (*t*) in hours	2	4	8	10	20
Speed (*r*) in mi/hr					

18. The per capita public debt (in thousands of dollars) of the United States for the years 1940 to 1990 appears below. Create a scatterplot and determine a trend line. Based on your scatterplot, what do you expect the per capita public debt to be in 2020? *[Lesson 1-7]*

Year	1940	1950	1960	1970	1980	1990
Amount ($)	325	1688	1572	1807	3970	12,823

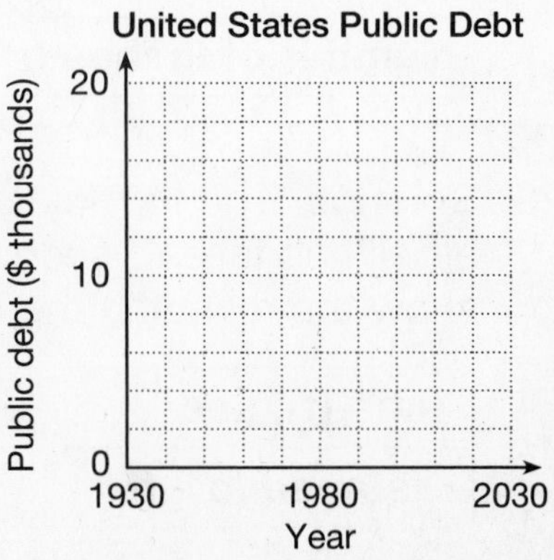

____

Name ______________________________

Practice 2-4

Inverse Operations

The machines below are inverse operation machines. What will be the result when the given number is entered into each machine? Record each step.

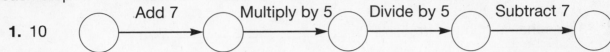

1. 10 ◯ → Add 7 → ◯ → Multiply by 5 → ◯ → Divide by 5 → ◯ → Subtract 7 → ◯

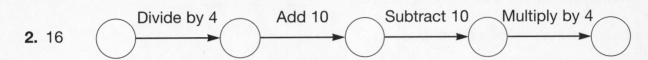

2. 16 ◯ → Divide by 4 → ◯ → Add 10 → ◯ → Subtract 10 → ◯ → Multiply by 4 → ◯

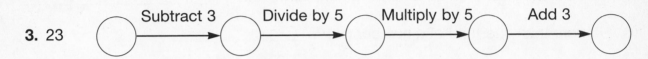

3. 23 ◯ → Subtract 3 → ◯ → Divide by 5 → ◯ → Multiply by 5 → ◯ → Add 3 → ◯

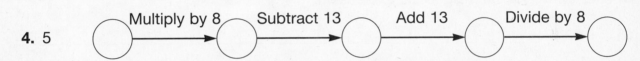

4. 5 ◯ → Multiply by 8 → ◯ → Subtract 13 → ◯ → Add 13 → ◯ → Divide by 8 → ◯

Add labels to each machine below so that the output will be the same as the input.

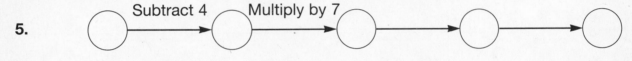

5. ◯ → Subtract 4 → ◯ → Multiply by 7 → ◯ → ____ → ◯ → ____ → ◯

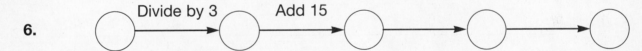

6. ◯ → Divide by 3 → ◯ → Add 15 → ◯ → ____ → ◯ → ____ → ◯

7. Maxine locked the door when she left her apartment. What will she need to do to get back inside?

____

8. At the mall, Tony went from his car to the shoe store, then the music store, then the card shop, and finally the video arcade. Suddenly he realized that he had lost his wallet, so he decided to retrace his steps back to his car. What route did he take going back?

____

____

Name ______________________________

Practice
2-5

Translating Words to Expressions

Write an algebraic expression for each phrase.

1. the product of a number (x) and 3 ____________

2. 13 less than a number (m) ____________

3. the quotient of a number (s) and 7 ____________

4. 7 less than twice a number (d) ____________

5. the difference between three times a number (k) and 4 ____________

6. 15 more than one-third of a number (m) ____________

Write a phrase for each algebraic expression.

7. $r + 12$ ____________

8. $3(x + 4)$ ____________

9. $c - 18$ ____________

10. $\frac{12}{u}$ ____________

11. $7z - 5$ ____________

12. $\frac{m}{n}$ ____________

13. Career Miguel earns $8.00 per hour at his job. Write an expression for the number of dollars he earns for working n hours. ____________

14. Thomas likes to paint bird houses in his garage on Saturday. He spends a total of one hour setting up and cleaning up, and during the rest of the day he can paint 3 bird houses every hour.

a. If Thomas spends n hours in his garage, how many hours can he spend actually painting? ____________

b. Write an expression for the number of bird houses Thomas can paint if he is in his garage for n hours. ____________

Name ______________________________

Practice
2-6

Solving Addition and Subtraction Equations

Tell if the given number is a solution to the equation.

1. $x + 18 = 99$; 80 _____ **2.** $u - 3 = 56$; 53 _____ **3.** $17 + t = 74$; 57 _____

4. $k - 12 = 84$; 96 _____ **5.** $r - 5 = 10$; 15 _____ **6.** $w + 15 = 40$; 20 _____

Solve each equation. Check your answer.

7. $y + 15 = 23$

$y =$ _____

8. $27 + s = 51$

$s =$ _____

9. $w - 31 = 25$

$w =$ _____

10. $64 + q = 123$

$q =$ _____

11. $41 = d - 28$

$d =$ _____

12. $37 = 11 + g$

$g =$ _____

Write an equation for each statement.

13. The number of students (x) decreased by 15 equals 81. _____________

14. The revenue (r) increased by $3,200 is $38,500. _____________

15. The number of hours (h) decreased by 12 equals 64. _____________

Estimate a solution to each equation.

16. $m - 483 = 1703$

$m \approx$ _____

17. $6309 = 4120 + p$

$p \approx$ _____

18. $3240 + y = 7735$

$y \approx$ _____

19. $v - 847 = 1256$

$v \approx$ _____

20. Career Xochitl is a real estate agent. This month she earned commissions of $6240, which is $3460 more than she earned last month. Write and solve an equation to find last month's commissions.

____

21. History Thomas Edison invented the phonograph in 1887, 98 years before the introduction of the compact disc (CD). Write and solve an equation to find the year (y) that CDs were introduced.

____

Name ____________________

Practice 2-7

Solving Multiplication and Division Equations

Tell if the given number is a solution to the equation.

1. $5x = 20$; 100 ______ **2.** $t \div 3 = 7$; 21 ______ **3.** $\frac{u}{9} = 36$; 4 ______

4. $8m = 88$; 11 ______ **5.** $\frac{b}{5} = 5$; 30 ______ **6.** $r \div 4 = 10$; 40 ______

7. $3x = 81$; 9 ______ **8.** $6c = 42$; 7 ______ **9.** $\frac{d}{11} = 1$; 11 ______

Solve each equation. Check your answer.

10. $12 = s \div 4$

$s =$ ______

11. $17x = 85$

$x =$ ______

12. $63 = p \cdot 3$

$p =$ ______

13. $6u = 222$

$u =$ ______

14. $\frac{w}{11} = 22$

$w =$ ______

15. $13 = \frac{z}{5}$

$z =$ ______

16. $38 = 19t$

$t =$ ______

17. $9q = 108$

$q =$ ______

18. $\frac{c}{5} = 35$

$c =$ ______

19. $\frac{k}{18} = 72$

$k =$ ______

20. $21j = 294$

$j =$ ______

21. $y \cdot 4 = 168$

$y =$ ______

Estimate a reasonable solution to each equation.

22. $210x = 4119$

$x \approx$ ______

23. $64{,}382 = 39y$

$y \approx$ ______

24. $\frac{m}{98} = 43$

$m \approx$ ______

25. $295 = \frac{r}{51}$

$r \approx$ ______

26. A 7-inch phonograph record turns at a rate of 45 revolutions per minute. Write and solve an equation to find the number of minutes to complete 315 revolutions.

____

27. Geometry A rectangle has area 50 in^2 and base 10 in. Write and solve an equation to find the height of the rectangle.

____

Name ______________________________

Practice 2-8

Problem Solving with Two-Step Equations

Solve each equation. Check your answer.

1. $3x + 7 = 37$ $x =$ ________

2. $31 = 7x - 11$ $x =$ ________

3. $11k - 84 = 92$ $k =$ ________

4. $4r + 13 = 57$ $r =$ ________

5. $\frac{z}{4} + 16 = 21$ $z =$ ________

6. $7 = \frac{t}{6} - 3$ $t =$ ________

7. $6q - 18 = 30$ $q =$ ________

8. $\frac{w}{15} + 26 = 42$ $w =$ ________

9. $15u + 18 = 18$ $u =$ ________

10. $9 = 7b - 12$ $b =$ ________

11. $\frac{x}{11} + 21 = 35$ $x =$ ________

12. $\frac{s}{7} - 11 = 17$ $s =$ ________

Explain what was done to the first equation to get the second equation.

13. $\frac{x}{5} - 3 = 12 \rightarrow x = 75$

____

14. $6x + 7 = 31 \rightarrow x = 4$

____

15. $\frac{x}{3} + 2 = 4 \rightarrow x = 6$

____

16. Hideki baked 41 cookies. He gave the same number of cookies to each of 5 friends, saving 11 cookies for himself. How many cookies did each friend receive? ________

17. **Consumer** Estelle is buying dresses by mail. She pays $65 for each dress, plus a shipping and handling charge of $8 for the entire order. If her order costs $268, how many dresses did she buy? ________

18. Ms. Juarez planted a 7-ft-tall tree. The height (h) of the tree, in feet, after n years is given by the equation $h = 4n + 7$. In how many years will the height be 39 feet? ________

Name ______________________

Practice

Section 2B Review

1. Before gym class, Scott takes off his boots, takes off his jeans, puts on his shorts, and puts on his shoes. Describe the inverse operations he would use after class.

____

Write an algebraic expression for each phrase.

2. Fourteen less than a number (g) __________

3. Eight more than the product of a number (k) and ten __________

Write a phrase for each algebraic expression.

4. $15x$ ______________________

5. $d + 17$ ______________________

Find the value of each expression.

6. $3 + 6 \times 4 =$ ________ 7. $\frac{23 - 5}{4 + 2} =$ ________ 8. $3 \times 4 - \frac{35}{5} =$ ________

Solve each equation.

9. $5s = 45$ 10. $y - 12 = 31$ 11. $2x + 8 = 46$ 12. $\frac{w}{7} - 3 = 10$

$s =$ ________ $y =$ ________ $x =$ ________ $w =$ ________

13. An online service charges $10.00 for the first 5 hours in a month, and $2.50 for each additional hour. If Seth's bill is $22.50, how many hours did he use the service?

____

14. Draw a bar graph to show the number of registered motorcycles (in thousands) in several states in 1990. *[Lesson 1-2]*

State	CA	FL	NY	TX	WA
Reg. motorcycles	627	206	196	175	216

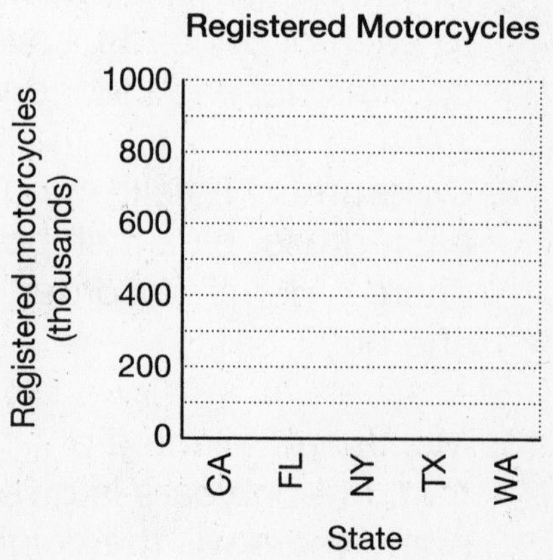

15. The formula $A = b \cdot h$ is used to find the area of a parallelogram with base b and height h. Find the area of a parallelogram with base 7 cm and height 5 cm. *[Lesson 2-1]*

____

Name ______________________

Practice

Cumulative Review Chapters 1–2

Use the circle graph to answer each question. *[Lesson 1-1]*

Kids Ages 14 and Under by Race and Ethnic Group 1994

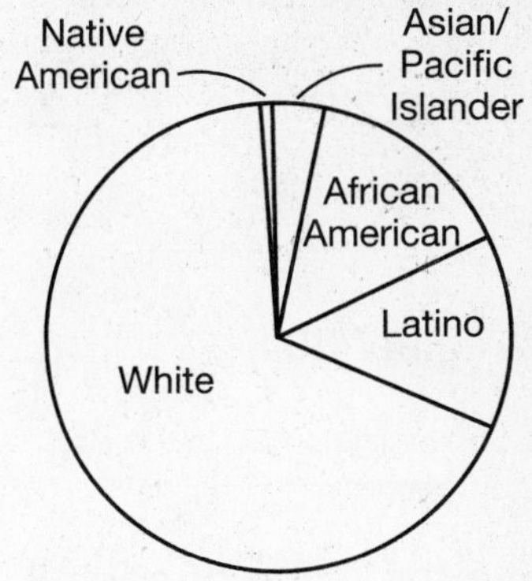

1. About what percent of American kids are white? ______

2. List the ethnic groups in order from the largest to the smallest. ______________________

____

Find the mean, median, and mode(s) for each set of data. *[Lesson 1-4]*

3. 35, 26, 28, 26, 31, 35, 29

Mean ________

Median ________

Mode(s) ________

4. 161, 163, 186, 163, 172, 193

Mean ________

Median ________

Mode(s) ________

Find the value of each expression. *[Lesson 2-2]*

5. $7 \times 4 - 6 \times 3$ ______

6. $7(6 - 5) + 2$ ________

7. $(8 - 3) \div (4 + 1)$ ________

8. $\frac{12}{3} - \frac{18}{9}$ ________

9. $\frac{20 + 10}{10 - 5}$ ________

10. $25 - 3 \cdot \frac{33}{11}$ ________

Write a phrase for each algebraic expression. *[Lesson 2-5]*

11. $2 + 7t$ ______________________

12. $\frac{4}{5 + x}$ ______________________

13. $3(8 + r)$ ______________________

Solve each equation. Check your answer. *[Lesson 2-8]*

14. $3x - 10 = 35$

$x =$ ________

15. $12 = 7c - 9$

$c =$ ________

16. $62 = 6g + 14$

$g =$ ________

17. $10k - 18 = 32$

$k =$ ________

18. $\frac{m}{6} + 5 = 21$

$m =$ ________

19. $11 = \frac{z}{4} - 10$

$z =$ ________

Name ____________________

Practice 3-1

Place Value: Comparing and Ordering Decimals

Give the value of each 1.

1. 316.24 ________
2. 587.13 ________
3. 201.473 ________
4. 17,364.9 ________
5. 8,447.301 ________
6. 8,139.64 ________
7. 9.4321 ________
8. 3,142,864.3 ________

Give the value of each 8.

9. 384.29 ________
10. 506.83 ________
11. 84,163.2 ________
12. 1841.67 ________

Give the value of each 3.

13. 1,203.7 ________
14. 382.87 ________
15. 610.731 ________
16. 53,042.75 ________

Use the symbols < or > to show which number is larger.

17. 387.65 ◯ 387.56
18. 72.83 ◯ 73.73
19. 0.005 ◯ 0.0005
20. 58.006 ◯ 58.060
21. 17.341 ◯ 17.3409
22. 312.745 ◯ 312.746

23. **Health** One cup of canned orange juice has 1.1 mg of iron. A 10-oz package of frozen peaches has 1.05 mg of iron. Which has more iron? ________

24. The table shows the top 5 earned-run averages in the history of major league baseball. Who had the highest of these averages? ________

    Who had the lowest of these averages? ________

Player	Mordecai Brown	Addie Joss	Christy Mathewson	Rube Waddel	Ed Walsh
Earned-run average	2.06	1.88	2.13	2.16	1.82

Name ______________________

Practice
3-2

Estimating by Rounding

Round each number to the nearest whole number.

1. 3.874 ________

2. 5.132 ________

3. 21.635 ________

4. 17.5 ________

5. 36.498 ________

6. 163.094 ________

7. 843.17 ________

8. 562.63 ________

Round each number to the nearest whole number and multiply.

9. 8.37×12.13 ________

10. 9.76×4.173 ________

11. 16.53×2.75 ________

12. 15.84×3.14 ________

13. 18.5×6.19 ________

14. 8.137×2.071 ________

15. 5.384×3.481 ________

16. 7.36×30.08 ________

Estimate.

17. 3.76×28.4 ________

18. $238.4 - 88.3$ ________

19. $19.47 + 3.21$ ________

20. $\frac{81.37}{8.65}$ ________

21. 6.83×98.6 ________

22. $361.238 - 23.7$ ________

23. $835.4 + 173.2$ ________

24. $157.3 \div 42.4$ ________

Round to (a) the nearest hundredth (b) the nearest tenth (c) the nearest thousandth

25. 81.3074 (a) ________ (b) ________ (c) ________

26. 123.6855 (a) ________ (b) ________ (c) ________

27. 3.41987 (a) ________ (b) ________ (c) ________

28. During the 1968 Olympic Games, Mamo Wolde of Ethiopia ran 26.21875 miles in 2.341 hours. Estimate the number of miles he ran each hour. ________

29. At the farmer's market, Saul bought 1.83 lb of broccoli, 0.84 lb of carrots, and 1.23 lb of onions. Estimate the total weight of his purchases. ________

Name ______________________________

Practice
3-3

Problem-Solving: Sums and Differences of Decimals

Estimate each sum or difference.

1. 63.7 + 24.3 ________

2. 841.63 − 124.8 ________

3. 364.78 − 37.2 ________

4. 53.87 + 81.3 ________

5. 738.2 − 18.37 ________

6. 98.76 − 21.3 ________

7. 8.7388 + 9.01 ________

8. 31.49 + 63.9 ________

9. 38.754 − 21.4 ________

10. 3.7 + 8.4 + 9.2 ________

11. 9.3 + 1.4 + 8.9 ________

12. 2.8 + 1.3 + 0.6 ________

13. 87.43 + 9.06 ________

14. 53.21 − 8.7 ________

15. 321.846 + 0.049 ________

16. 68.037 − 5.9 ________

Solve each equation.

17. $x + 0.37 = 9.42$ $x =$ ________

18. $x - 6.43 = 8.7$ $x =$ ________

19. $3.841 = x + 1.2$ $x =$ ________

20. $8.93 = x - 0.41$ $x =$ ________

21. $x + 2.75 = 11.3$ $x =$ ________

22. $x - 5.2 = 10.17$ $x =$ ________

23. $3.6 = x - 8.471$ $x =$ ________

24. $5.2 = x + 2.13$ $x =$ ________

25. $88.43 = x + 1.8$ $x =$ ________

26. $x - 12.87 = 3.6$ $x =$ ________

27. $x + 37.4 = 91.6$ $x =$ ________

28. $63.24 = x - 9.3$ $x =$ ________

29. Career A designer needs 4.83 yards of a certain fabric to make curtains. If the designer already has 1.9 yards of the fabric, how much additional fabric must be purchased? ________

30. The Lucky Seven Discount Store calculates the retail price (R) of every item using the formula $R = W + 7.77$, where W is the wholesale price. If a chair retails for $61.23, what is the wholesale price? ________

Name ______________________

Practice 3-4

Problem-Solving: Products and Quotients of Decimals

Estimate each product or quotient.

1. 0.05×0.86 ______

2. 0.809×1.2 ______

3. 3.54×0.07 ______

4. $\frac{21.44}{13.4}$ ______

5. $\frac{0.1944}{0.9}$ ______

6. $\frac{4.716}{3.6}$ ______

7. 13.9×0.35 ______

8. 7.5×0.41 ______

9. 0.348×0.3 ______

10. $\frac{64.32}{13.4}$ ______

11. $\frac{9.4325}{0.686}$ ______

12. $\frac{161.56}{8.8}$ ______

13. 0.009×80 ______

14. 2.9×0.1 ______

15. 14.58×0.2 ______

16. $\frac{0.1572}{0.4}$ ______

Solve each equation.

17. $8.5d = 112.2$ $d =$ ______

18. $\frac{a}{0.29} = 8.9$ $a =$ ______

19. $0.1n = 0.313$ $n =$ ______

20. $\frac{b}{0.7} = 8.953$ $b =$ ______

21. $\frac{s}{11.39} = 0.48$ $s =$ ______

22. $1.13f = 0.2712$ $f =$ ______

23. $\frac{k}{4.1} = 15$ $k =$ ______

24. $9.2d = 30.222$ $d =$ ______

25. $\frac{x}{8.5} = 9.378$ $x =$ ______

26. $2.1d = 6.3$ $d =$ ______

27. $\frac{m}{4.33} = 1.5$ $m =$ ______

28. $\frac{u}{15.5} = 4.79$ $u =$ ______

29. $4.7z = 19.458$ $z =$ ______

30. $\frac{u}{3.155} = 6.4$ $u =$ ______

31. $2.08m = 5.3456$ $m =$ ______

32. $\frac{v}{4.4} = 8.37$ $v =$ ______

33. **Measurement** The formula $p = 2.2k$ relates the mass (k) in kilograms and the weight (p) in pounds. Find the mass, in kilograms, of a casserole weighing 1.474 pounds. ______

34. Find the price of 1.83 lb of cauliflower costing \$0.63 per pound. Round your answer to the nearest cent. ______

Name ______________________

Practice 3-5

Powers of 10 and Scientific Notation

Evaluate.

1. 4^2 ______ **2.** 5^4 ______ **3.** 3^3 ______ **4.** 9^2 ______

Write each number in scientific notation.

5. 30 ______ **6.** 84,000 ______ **7.** 400 ______ **8.** 390 ______

9. 3,820 ______ **10.** 470 ______ **11.** 976,000 ______ **12.** 3,740,000 ______

Write each number in standard form.

13. 3.5×10^3 ______ **14.** 7.8×10^6 ______ **15.** 6.38×10^4 ______ **16.** 1.87×10^7 ______

17. 3.41×10^2 ______ **18.** 3.841×10^3 ______ **19.** 8.4×10^4 ______ **20.** 9.3×10^6 ______

21. 5.1×10^{11} ______ **22.** 9×10^{13} ______

23. Social Science The table shows estimated 1995 populations of some eastern Asian nations. List the populations, in standard form, in order from least to greatest.

Nation	China	Hong Kong	Japan	North Korea	South Korea	Mongolia
Population	1.22×10^9	5.9×10^6	1.25×10^8	2.39×10^7	4.5×10^7	2.4×10^6

____

____

24. The average person has about 1×10^4 taste buds. Use your calculator and the information in Exercise 23 to estimate the number of human taste buds in China. Give your answer in scientific notation. ______

Name ____________________

Practice

Section 3A Review

Put the correct symbol (<, >, or =) to make a true statement.

1. 17.651 ◯ 17.65 **2.** 2.940 ◯ 2.904 **3.** 37.84 ◯ 38.74

Estimate.

4. $143.74 - 31.2$ ______ **5.** 4.631×9.31 ______ **6.** $87.4 \div 10.9$ ______

Solve each equation. Estimate the solution first.

7. $2.83x = 13.301$ **8.** $x + 5.3 = 8.241$ **9.** $x - 8.972 = 7.6$ **10.** $\frac{x}{12.3} = 4.89$

$x =$ ______ $x =$ ______ $x =$ ______ $x =$ ______

Write in scientific notation.

11. 16,430 **12.** 370,000 **13.** 94,300,000

______ ______ ______

Write in standard form.

14. 4.91×10^3 **15.** 3×10^6 **16.** 1.8×10^8

______ ______ ______

17. Shagufta is going on a backpacking trip. She wants to carry no more than 30 lb. If her backpack weighs 4.87 lb, her food weighs 8.6 lb, and her clothing weighs 7.3 lb, find the maximum weight of other items she can bring. ______

18. Monte has $18.60. Can he buy 2 lb of shiitake mushrooms priced at $0.59 per ounce? Explain. (Hint: 1 lb = 16 oz)

______

The line graph shows the number of American newspapers being published from 1920 to 1990. Use the graph for Exercises 19–20.

19. Estimate the number of newspapers that were being published in 1940. ______

20. Predict the number of newspapers in 2010.

______

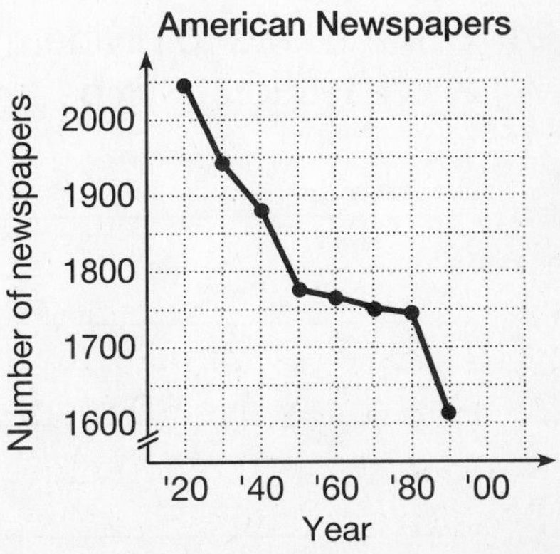

Name ______________________________

Practice
3-6

Divisibility and Prime Factorization

Test each number for divisibility by 2, 3, 4, 5, 6, 8, 9, and 10.

1. 7040 ____________ **2.** 4532 ____________ **3.** 250 ____________ **4.** 554 ____________

5. 2168 ____________ **6.** 1992 ____________ **7.** 3215 ____________ **8.** 2291 ____________

9. 2180 ____________ **10.** 2604 ____________ **11.** 1197 ____________ **12.** 873 ____________

Determine whether each of these numbers is composite or prime.

13. 181 ____________ **14.** 674 ____________ **15.** 373 ____________ **16.** 64 ____________

17. 377 ____________ **18.** 345 ____________ **19.** 569 ____________ **20.** 205 ____________

Use factor trees to find the prime factorization of the following numbers.

21. 144 = ____________ **22.** 385 = ____________ **23.** 90 = ____________

24. Zelda wants to divide a 96-inch-long plank into equal sections. If the length of each section is to be a whole number of inches, what lengths can she use?

____

____

25. Give the ways 30 students can be divided into groups of the same size.

____

Name ______________________________

Practice
3-7

GCF and LCM

Find the GCF by listing all the factors of each number.

1. 145, 100

Factors of 145 ______________________________

Factors of 100 ______________________________

GCF: ____________

Find the GCF by writing the prime factorization of each number.

2. 243, 54

243 = ______________________

54 = ______________________

GCF = ______________________

3. 150, 155

150 = ______________________

155 = ______________________

GCF = ______________________

4. 96, 84

96 = ______________________

84 = ______________________

GCF = ______________________

5. 57, 285

57 = ______________________

285 = ______________________

GCF = ______________________

Find the LCM of each pair of numbers.

6. 11, 5 ________ **7.** 5, 12 ________ **8.** 12, 7 ________ **9.** 5, 9 ________

10. 5, 18 ________ **11.** 5, 20 ________ **12.** 7, 10 ________ **13.** 17, 13 ________

14. 14, 8 ________ **15.** 11, 23 ________ **16.** 14, 5 ________ **17.** 16, 9 ________

18. Cameron is making bead necklaces. He has 90 green beads and 108 blue beads. What is the greatest number of identical necklaces he can make if he wants to use all of the beads? ________________

19. A radio station broadcasts a weather forecast every 18 minutes and a commercial every 15 minutes. If the station broadcasts both a weather forecast and a commercial at noon, when is the next time that both will be broadcast at the same time? ________________

Name ______________________________

Practice 3-8

Equivalent Fractions and Lowest Terms

Find an equivalent fraction with (a) a smaller and (b) a larger denominator.

1. $\frac{4}{28}$ (a) ________ (b) ________
2. $\frac{9}{69}$ (a) ________ (b) ________
3. $\frac{7}{35}$ (a) ________ (b) ________
4. $\frac{6}{30}$ (a) ________ (b) ________
5. $\frac{52}{86}$ (a) ________ (b) ________
6. $\frac{45}{75}$ (a) ________ (b) ________
7. $\frac{34}{56}$ (a) ________ (b) ________
8. $\frac{42}{52}$ (a) ________ (b) ________
9. $\frac{30}{38}$ (a) ________ (b) ________
10. $\frac{10}{18}$ (a) ________ (b) ________
11. $\frac{72}{81}$ (a) ________ (b) ________
12. $\frac{12}{22}$ (a) ________ (b) ________

Express each fraction in lowest terms.

13. $\frac{46}{62}$ ________
14. $\frac{5}{60}$ ________
15. $\frac{15}{24}$ ________
16. $\frac{20}{58}$ ________
17. $\frac{12}{14}$ ________
18. $\frac{26}{64}$ ________
19. $\frac{8}{342}$ ________
20. $\frac{30}{46}$ ________
21. $\frac{30}{64}$ ________
22. $\frac{6}{14}$ ________
23. $\frac{18}{98}$ ________
24. $\frac{24}{46}$ ________
25. $\frac{30}{45}$ ________
26. $\frac{14}{24}$ ________
27. $\frac{48}{80}$ ________
28. $\frac{49}{77}$ ________
29. $\frac{123}{171}$ ________
30. $\frac{38}{72}$ ________
31. $\frac{22}{60}$ ________
32. $\frac{8}{10}$ ________
33. $\frac{210}{304}$ ________
34. $\frac{18}{39}$ ________
35. $\frac{42}{104}$ ________
36. $\frac{40}{116}$ ________

37. The city of Austin, Texas, typically has 115 clear days out of the 365 days in a year. What fraction of Austin's days are clear? Write your answer in lowest terms. ________

38. In 1985, American education expenditures totaled \$247.7 billion, of which \$137 billion was spent on public elementary and secondary schools. About what fraction of education expenditures were spent on public elementary and secondary schools? ________

Name ______________________________

Practice 3-9

Comparing and Ordering Fractions

Compare.

1. $\frac{16}{21} \bigcirc \frac{28}{38}$
2. $\frac{12}{40} \bigcirc \frac{13}{44}$
3. $\frac{5}{22} \bigcirc \frac{8}{32}$
4. $\frac{12}{26} \bigcirc \frac{16}{36}$
5. $\frac{12}{35} \bigcirc \frac{7}{18}$
6. $\frac{7}{16} \bigcirc \frac{16}{35}$
7. $\frac{10}{20} \bigcirc \frac{20}{41}$
8. $\frac{4}{6} \bigcirc \frac{9}{12}$
9. $\frac{4}{9} \bigcirc \frac{19}{44}$
10. $\frac{4}{6} \bigcirc \frac{10}{15}$
11. $\frac{21}{25} \bigcirc \frac{18}{22}$
12. $\frac{20}{24} \bigcirc \frac{16}{20}$
13. $\frac{20}{25} \bigcirc \frac{10}{13}$
14. $\frac{4}{13} \bigcirc \frac{8}{25}$
15. $\frac{26}{45} \bigcirc \frac{3}{6}$
16. $\frac{23}{27} \bigcirc \frac{16}{18}$
17. $\frac{4}{12} \bigcirc \frac{13}{41}$
18. $\frac{4}{11} \bigcirc \frac{7}{21}$
19. $\frac{4}{8} \bigcirc \frac{25}{50}$
20. $\frac{6}{24} \bigcirc \frac{8}{31}$
21. $\frac{4}{6} \bigcirc \frac{12}{17}$
22. $\frac{22}{25} \bigcirc \frac{22}{26}$
23. $\frac{11}{26} \bigcirc \frac{14}{32}$
24. $\frac{7}{12} \bigcirc \frac{30}{50}$
25. $\frac{11}{20} \bigcirc \frac{25}{46}$
26. $\frac{13}{47} \bigcirc \frac{3}{9}$
27. $\frac{19}{21} \bigcirc \frac{32}{35}$
28. $\frac{16}{22} \bigcirc \frac{25}{35}$
29. $\frac{4}{6} \bigcirc \frac{22}{33}$
30. $\frac{4}{42} \bigcirc \frac{2}{19}$
31. $\frac{8}{38} \bigcirc \frac{8}{39}$
32. $\frac{4}{7} \bigcirc \frac{27}{47}$
33. $\frac{6}{32} \bigcirc \frac{4}{18}$
34. $\frac{22}{33} \bigcirc \frac{34}{50}$
35. $\frac{39}{48} \bigcirc \frac{38}{47}$
36. $\frac{4}{15} \bigcirc \frac{3}{11}$
37. $\frac{4}{6} \bigcirc \frac{9}{14}$
38. $\frac{38}{46} \bigcirc \frac{38}{45}$
39. $\frac{20}{48} \bigcirc \frac{16}{39}$
40. $\frac{9}{21} \bigcirc \frac{22}{50}$
41. $\frac{4}{18} \bigcirc \frac{4}{19}$
42. $\frac{15}{19} \bigcirc \frac{15}{20}$
43. $\frac{6}{18} \bigcirc \frac{13}{37}$
44. $\frac{15}{42} \bigcirc \frac{8}{21}$

45. Kenny estimates that the distance from his home to the library is between $\frac{1}{3}$ and $\frac{1}{2}$ mile. Find four fractions in that range and list them in order from least to greatest. Express the fractions in lowest terms.

____

46. The table shows the approximate fraction of new books and editions published in 1993 in each of several subjects. Order these fractions from least to greatest.

Art	Biography	Fiction	History	Technology
$\frac{3}{100}$	$\frac{21}{500}$	$\frac{1}{9}$	$\frac{2}{43}$	$\frac{7}{155}$

____

Name ______________________________

Practice 3-10

Converting Between Fractions and Decimals

Convert to a fraction in lowest terms.

1. 0.405 ________ **2.** 0.874 ________ **3.** 0.26 ________ **4.** 0.497 ________

5. 0.216 ________ **6.** 0.684 ________ **7.** 0.465 ________ **8.** 0.865 ________

9. 0.38 ________ **10.** 0.72 ________ **11.** 0.79 ________ **12.** 0.464 ________

13. 0.204 ________ **14.** 0.392 ________ **15.** 0.108 ________ **16.** 0.042 ________

Convert to a decimal. Tell if the decimal terminates or repeats.

17. $\frac{3}{5}$ ________ **18.** $\frac{8}{9}$ ________ **19.** $\frac{7}{8}$ ________

20. $\frac{5}{11}$ ________ **21.** $\frac{37}{50}$ ________ **22.** $\frac{3}{16}$ ________

23. $\frac{22}{55}$ ________ **24.** $\frac{4}{12}$ ________ **25.** $\frac{17}{34}$ ________

Use a calculator to convert each repeating decimal to a fraction.

26. $0.\overline{6}$ ________ **27.** $0.\overline{7}$ ________ **28.** $0.\overline{27}$ ________ **29.** $0.02\overline{27}$ ________

30. $0.1\overline{6}$ ________ **31.** $0.\overline{15}$ ________ **32.** $0.\overline{47}$ ________ **33.** $0.\overline{90}$ ________

34. About $\frac{7}{25}$ of the residents of Seattle, Washington, have attended 16 or more years of school. Convert $\frac{7}{25}$ to a decimal. ________

35. Geography The area of Brazil is about 0.908 of the area of the United States. Convert 0.908 to a fraction in lowest terms. ________

 Use with pages 153–156.

Name ____________________

Practice

Section 3B Review

Compare.

1. $\frac{11}{28} \bigcirc \frac{18}{44}$ 2. $\frac{6}{8} \bigcirc \frac{7}{10}$ 3. $\frac{4}{6} \bigcirc \frac{14}{21}$ 4. $\frac{7}{12} \bigcirc \frac{14}{25}$

5. $\frac{4}{7} \bigcirc \frac{28}{50}$ 6. $\frac{9}{22} \bigcirc \frac{13}{33}$ 7. $\frac{4}{7} \bigcirc \frac{29}{49}$ 8. $\frac{5}{7} \bigcirc \frac{36}{50}$

Find the prime factorization of each number.

9. 36 ____________ 10. 945 ____________ 11. 693 ____________

12. 100 ____________ 13. 539 ____________ 14. 117 ____________

Find the GCF and LCM.

15. 45, 36
GCF: ________
LCM: ________

16. 140, 28
GCF: ________
LCM: ________

17. 44, 55
GCF: ________
LCM: ________

18. 25, 30
GCF: ________
LCM: ________

19. A bottle contains 0.296 L of teriyaki sauce. Write 0.296 as a fraction in lowest terms. ____________

Convert each fraction to a decimal.

20. $\frac{3}{4}$ ________ 21. $\frac{18}{25}$ ________ 22. $\frac{5}{9}$ ________ 23. $\frac{8}{24}$ ________

24. $\frac{6}{11}$ ________ 25. $\frac{21}{80}$ ________ 26. $\frac{4}{7}$ ________ 27. $\frac{13}{250}$ ________

28. Life expectancies for people in eastern and southeastern Asian and African nations are 71, 78, 79, 71, 71, 64, 51, 63, 51, 71, 58, 65, 64, 69, and 64 years. Make a stem-and-leaf diagram to display the data. *[Lesson 1-3]*

stem	leaf

29. The table relates the number *m* of miles to the number *k* of kilometers. Write a formula relating these values. *[Lesson 2-3]* ____________

m	1	2	3	4	5
k	1.61	3.22	4.83	6.44	8.05

Name ______________________________

Practice

Cumulative Review Chapters 1–3

The bar graph shows how many American homes had access to electronic media in 1990. Use the graph for Exercises 1–2. *[Lesson 1-1]*

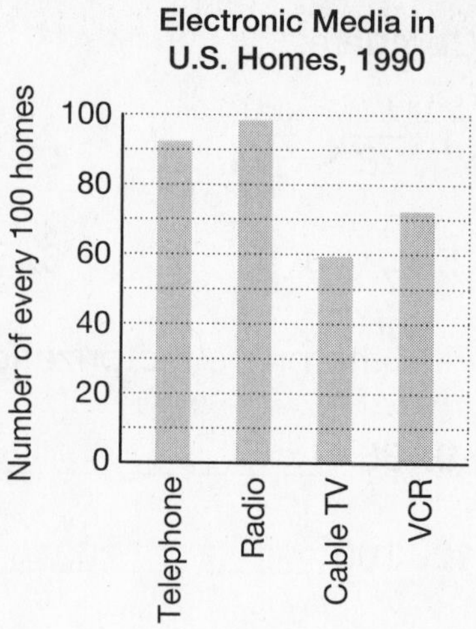

1. About how many of every 100 homes had a videocassette recorder (VCR)? __________

2. Which item was in the most homes? __________

The fewest homes? __________

Find the value of each expression. *[Lesson 2-2]*

3. $18 + 21 \div 3$ ______

4. $7 \times 2 + 5 \times 3$ ______

5. $3(8 - 2) + 4$ ______

6. $2 + \frac{10 - 2}{1 + 3}$ ______

7. $\frac{12}{3} - \frac{24}{6 + 2}$ ______

8. $30 - (10 - 7) \times 2$ ______

Use the given formula to complete each table. *[Lesson 2-3]*

9. $y = 2x - 5$

x	5	6	7	8
y				

10. $D = 25t$

t	3	4	5	6
D				

11. $t = 45 - 6s$

s	2	3	4	5
t				

12. $p = \frac{100}{n + 6}$

n	4	14	19	44
p				

Use the symbols > or < to show which number is larger. *[Lesson 3-1]*

13. 8.631 ◯ 8.63

14. 4.354 ◯ 4.356

15. 18.73 ◯ 17.83

16. 2.070 ◯ 2.007

17. 5.386 ◯ 5.376

18. 12.39 ◯ 12.3899

Solve each equation. *[Lessons 3-3, 3-4]*

19. $x + 1.7 = 8.63$

$x =$ ______

20. $y - 5.83 = 12.3$

$y =$ ______

21. $6.54 = j + 2.87$

$j =$ ______

22. $8.273 = q - 4.13$

$q =$ ______

23. $2.3x = 20.93$

$x =$ ______

24. $\frac{u}{1.49} = 3.65$

$u =$ ______

25. $18 = 4.8k$

$k =$ ______

26. $9.03 = \frac{c}{17.8}$

$c =$ ______

Name ______________________________

Practice 4-1

Estimating: Fractions and Mixed Numbers

Estimate each sum or difference.

1. $\frac{3}{8} + \frac{2}{3}$ ______ **2.** $\frac{7}{8} - \frac{1}{2}$ ______ **3.** $\frac{3}{16} + \frac{11}{12}$ ______ **4.** $\frac{9}{10} - \frac{3}{8}$ ______

5. $\frac{2}{3} - \frac{3}{8}$ ______ **6.** $\frac{5}{6} + \frac{1}{3}$ ______ **7.** $\frac{4}{5} - \frac{1}{7}$ ______ **8.** $\frac{1}{5} + \frac{7}{15}$ ______

Round each mixed number to the nearest whole number, then estimate each sum or difference.

9. $2\frac{7}{8} + 3\frac{1}{4}$ ______ **10.** $12\frac{5}{8} - 3\frac{4}{5}$ ______ **11.** $7\frac{5}{6} + 4\frac{1}{3}$ ______ **12.** $12\frac{2}{5} - 8\frac{3}{7}$ ______

13. $15\frac{2}{3} - 7\frac{1}{6}$ ______ **14.** $11\frac{1}{2} + 9\frac{3}{5}$ ______ **15.** $10\frac{1}{4} - 5\frac{1}{2}$ ______ **16.** $8\frac{1}{5} + 6\frac{5}{7}$ ______

17. $12\frac{7}{8} + 6\frac{4}{5}$ ______ **18.** $14\frac{1}{8} - 2\frac{3}{4}$ ______ **19.** $13\frac{3}{8} + 2\frac{1}{3}$ ______ **20.** $14\frac{2}{9} - 9\frac{9}{10}$ ______

Use compatible numbers to estimate each product or quotient.

21. $8\frac{1}{3} \times \frac{1}{2}$ ______ **22.** $23\frac{1}{6} \div 7\frac{1}{2}$ ______ **23.** $\frac{1}{6} \times 40\frac{2}{3}$ ______ **24.** $35\frac{2}{3} \div 4\frac{7}{8}$ ______

25. $43\frac{1}{2} \div 4\frac{1}{2}$ ______ **26.** $\frac{1}{3} \times 32\frac{1}{4}$ ______ **27.** $73\frac{4}{11} \div 6\frac{1}{4}$ ______ **28.** $62\frac{1}{2} \times \frac{1}{8}$ ______

29. $\frac{1}{4} \times 35\frac{1}{7}$ ______ **30.** $28\frac{6}{7} \div 5\frac{2}{3}$ ______ **31.** $41\frac{1}{7} \times \frac{1}{5}$ ______ **32.** $83\frac{3}{8} \div 11\frac{9}{16}$ ______

33. The hypsilophodon was about $2\frac{1}{3}$ m long, and the geranosaurus was about $1\frac{1}{5}$ m long. Use rounding to estimate the difference between the length of these dinosaurs. ______

34. Tim's bucket can hold up to $12\frac{1}{3}$ quarts of liquid. If it is $\frac{1}{3}$ full of water, estimate the number of quarts of water in the bucket. ______

Name ____________________

Practice 4-2

Adding and Subtracting Fractions

Find the least common denominator for each pair of fractions.

1. $\frac{2}{5}, \frac{3}{8}$ ________
2. $\frac{3}{4}, \frac{5}{8}$ ________
3. $\frac{2}{3}, \frac{1}{7}$ ________
4. $\frac{3}{5}, \frac{7}{10}$ ________
5. $\frac{5}{6}, \frac{1}{14}$ ________
6. $\frac{3}{8}, \frac{3}{10}$ ________
7. $\frac{5}{7}, \frac{1}{4}$ ________
8. $\frac{7}{8}, \frac{5}{12}$ ________

Find each sum or difference. Rewrite in lowest terms.

9. $\frac{9}{11} - \frac{5}{11}$ ________
10. $\frac{3}{4} + \frac{1}{14}$ ________
11. $\frac{19}{60} - \frac{1}{4}$ ________
12. $\frac{1}{2} + \frac{1}{3}$ ________
13. $\frac{7}{15} - \frac{1}{5}$ ________
14. $\frac{1}{3} + \frac{1}{25}$ ________
15. $\frac{7}{9} - \frac{1}{9}$ ________
16. $\frac{11}{25} - \frac{1}{5}$ ________

Solve each equation.

17. $m - \frac{4}{15} = \frac{3}{5}$ $m =$ ________
18. $q - \frac{1}{2} = \frac{1}{8}$ $q =$ ________
19. $h - \frac{1}{9} = \frac{1}{2}$ $h =$ ________
20. $z + \frac{3}{11} = \frac{10}{11}$ $z =$ ________
21. $s - \frac{2}{25} = \frac{2}{3}$ $s =$ ________
22. $s - \frac{1}{4} = \frac{4}{7}$ $s =$ ________
23. $g + \frac{1}{3} = \frac{8}{9}$ $g =$ ________
24. $s + \frac{2}{5} = \frac{9}{10}$ $s =$ ________
25. $a - \frac{14}{25} = \frac{1}{5}$ $a =$ ________
26. $j + \frac{1}{9} = \frac{34}{63}$ $j =$ ________
27. $q - \frac{5}{11} = \frac{1}{4}$ $q =$ ________
28. $y + \frac{11}{15} = \frac{14}{15}$ $y =$ ________

29. The price of Rolando's stock went up $\frac{7}{8}$ the day he bought it, but the next day it went down $\frac{3}{16}$. What was the total increase over the two days? ________

30. In 1994, about $\frac{3}{5}$ of the federal budget was spent on human resources, and $\frac{1}{20}$ of the federal budget was spent on physical resources. About what fraction of the federal budget was spent on human and physical resources combined? ________

Name ______________________________

Practice 4-3

Adding and Subtracting Mixed Numbers

Rewrite each mixed number as an improper fraction.

1. $4\frac{3}{8}$ ________ **2.** $7\frac{1}{9}$ ________ **3.** $2\frac{3}{5}$ ________ **4.** $3\frac{5}{6}$ ________

Find each sum or difference.

5. $27\frac{7}{10} - 15\frac{7}{10}$ **6.** $29\frac{8}{15} - 20\frac{1}{3}$ **7.** $7\frac{3}{10} + 23\frac{8}{25}$ **8.** $3\frac{1}{6} + 8\frac{5}{8}$

________ ________ ________ ________

9. $8\frac{13}{18} + 11\frac{11}{18}$ **10.** $24\frac{5}{7} + 23\frac{1}{8}$ **11.** $3\frac{4}{25} + 3\frac{4}{5}$ **12.** $32\frac{24}{25} - 14\frac{19}{25}$

________ ________ ________ ________

Solve each equation.

13. $k - 7\frac{1}{10} = 4\frac{5}{18}$ **14.** $q + 1\frac{1}{2} = 23\frac{2}{3}$ **15.** $f + 13\frac{1}{6} = 20\frac{17}{30}$

k = ________ q = ________ f = ________

16. $r - \frac{1}{5} = 7\frac{3}{7}$ **17.** $z - 17\frac{17}{20} = 11\frac{2}{15}$ **18.** $m - 19\frac{5}{9} = 4\frac{4}{7}$

r = ________ z = ________ m = ________

Geometry Find the perimeter of each figure.

19. ________________

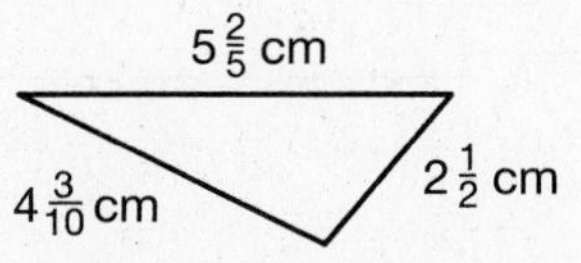

20. ________________

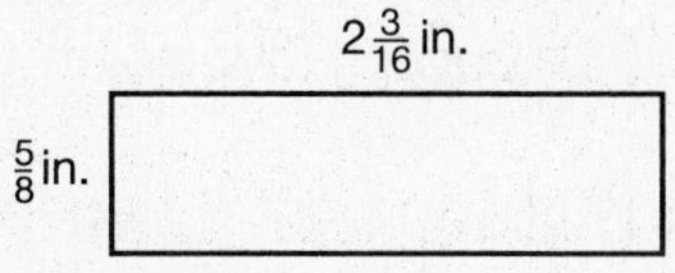

21. On May 21, 1996, Iomega stock was priced at $43\frac{3}{8}$. On May 22, it was priced at 54.

a. How much did the price go up on May 22? ________________

b. On May 23, the price went down $2\frac{3}{4}$. What was the closing price on May 23? ________________

Name ______________________

Practice

Section 4A Review

Round each addend to 0, $\frac{1}{2}$, or 1, then estimate each sum or difference.

1. $\frac{4}{5} - \frac{3}{8}$ ________ **2.** $\frac{1}{3} + \frac{9}{16}$ ________ **3.** $\frac{1}{7} + \frac{4}{9}$ ________ **4.** $\frac{8}{9} - \frac{3}{7}$ ________

Round each mixed number to the nearest whole number, then estimate each sum or difference.

5. $4\frac{1}{5} + 9\frac{7}{8}$ ________ **6.** $8\frac{3}{8} - 2\frac{3}{4}$ ________ **7.** $11\frac{4}{5} + 7\frac{2}{7}$ ________ **8.** $12\frac{4}{9} - 5\frac{1}{3}$ ________

Find each sum or difference.

9. $\frac{37}{40} - \frac{3}{10}$ ________ **10.** $\frac{23}{65} - \frac{1}{5}$ ________ **11.** $\frac{1}{24} + \frac{1}{16}$ ________ **12.** $\frac{13}{25} + \frac{1}{5}$ ________

Solve each equation.

13. $j + \frac{5}{8} = \frac{65}{72}$ $j =$ ________

14. $n - \frac{1}{10} = \frac{3}{8}$ $n =$ ________

15. $h + \frac{3}{4} = \frac{11}{12}$ $h =$ ________

16. $q - \frac{3}{16} = \frac{1}{3}$ $q =$ ________

17. $k + 2\frac{7}{20} = 8\frac{2}{5}$ $k =$ ________

18. $d - 9\frac{1}{12} = 10\frac{1}{4}$ $d =$ ________

19. $c - 17\frac{5}{7} = 5\frac{4}{21}$ $c =$ ________

20. $p + 11\frac{1}{2} = 20\frac{7}{10}$ $p =$ ________

21. A cake recipe calls for $\frac{3}{4}$ cup cocoa plus enough flour to make a total of $3\frac{1}{3}$ cups. How much flour is in the recipe? ________

22. A computer printer can print 8 pages per minute. *[Lesson 2-5]*

a. Write an expression for the number of pages that can be printed in *t* minutes. ________

b. How many pages can be printed in 9 minutes? ________

23. Science A male American toad can reach a length of 13.97 cm, which is 5.08 cm longer than the length of a female American toad. Write and solve an equation to find the length of a female American toad.

____

Name ________________________

Practice 4-4

Multiplying Fractions

Find each product. Rewrite in lowest terms.

1. $\frac{1}{8} \cdot \frac{2}{3}$ ______
2. $\frac{5}{9} \cdot \frac{3}{5}$ ______
3. $\frac{1}{2} \cdot \frac{4}{5}$ ______
4. $\frac{8}{9} \cdot \frac{5}{6}$ ______
5. $\frac{2}{9} \cdot \frac{3}{5}$ ______
6. $\frac{7}{9} \cdot \frac{9}{10}$ ______
7. $\frac{5}{6} \cdot \frac{4}{9}$ ______
8. $\frac{5}{8} \cdot \frac{4}{9}$ ______
9. $\frac{1}{8} \cdot \frac{6}{7}$ ______
10. $\frac{1}{2} \cdot \frac{4}{5}$ ______
11. $\frac{3}{4} \cdot \frac{5}{6}$ ______
12. $\frac{2}{5} \cdot \frac{3}{10}$ ______
13. $\frac{2}{7} \cdot \frac{3}{4}$ ______
14. $\frac{3}{10} \cdot \frac{1}{9}$ ______
15. $\frac{8}{9} \cdot \frac{3}{7}$ ______

Divide the numerator and the denominator of the following fractions by common factors *before* you multiply. Then multiply the fractions that remain.

16. $\frac{10}{17} \cdot \frac{7}{16}$ ______
17. $\frac{3}{40} \cdot \frac{5}{21}$ ______
18. $\frac{12}{35} \cdot \frac{10}{21}$ ______
19. $\frac{19}{36} \cdot \frac{9}{13}$ ______
20. $\frac{11}{32} \cdot \frac{9}{11}$ ______
21. $\frac{35}{72} \cdot \frac{36}{43}$ ______
22. $\frac{9}{28} \cdot \frac{8}{15}$ ______
23. $\frac{9}{11} \cdot \frac{25}{27}$ ______
24. $\frac{6}{19} \cdot \frac{19}{50}$ ______
25. $\frac{5}{36} \cdot \frac{16}{45}$ ______
26. $\frac{45}{91} \cdot \frac{13}{33}$ ______
27. $\frac{16}{51} \cdot \frac{63}{80}$ ______

Measurement Find the area of each rectangle.

28. ______

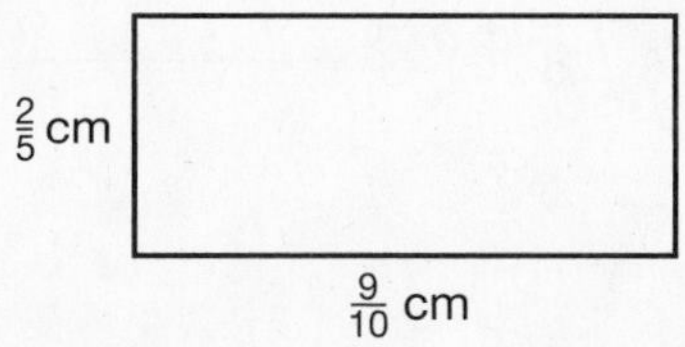

29. ______

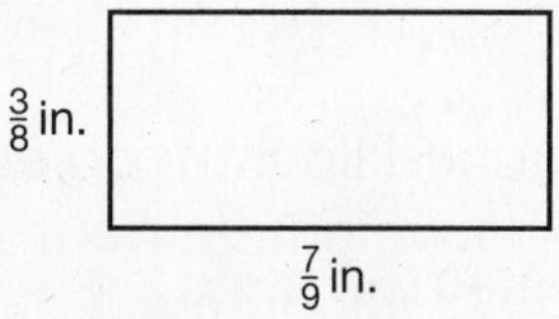

30. A sheet of plywood is $\frac{5}{8}$ in. thick. How tall is a stack of 21 sheets of plywood? ______

31. A poster measures 38 cm across. If a photocopy machine is used to make a copy that is $\frac{3}{5}$ of the original size, what is the width of the copy? ______

Name ______________________________

Practice
4-5

Multiplying Mixed Numbers

Use the distributive property to find each product mentally.

1. $6 \cdot 7\frac{3}{5}$ ________
2. $7 \cdot 2\frac{9}{10}$ ________
3. $3 \cdot 6\frac{3}{5}$ ________
4. $4\frac{1}{8} \cdot 7$ ________
5. $1\frac{2}{7} \cdot 7$ ________
6. $5 \cdot 5\frac{1}{6}$ ________
7. $6 \cdot 2\frac{4}{9}$ ________
8. $8 \cdot 3\frac{3}{4}$ ________
9. $6\frac{3}{5} \cdot 4$ ________
10. $4\frac{7}{9} \cdot 4$ ________
11. $4\frac{1}{6} \cdot 9$ ________
12. $2 \cdot 5\frac{6}{7}$ ________

Find each product.

13. $9\frac{1}{2} \cdot 1\frac{1}{2}$ ________
14. $8\frac{5}{8} \cdot 3\frac{3}{5}$ ________
15. $1\frac{5}{7} \cdot 4\frac{2}{3}$ ________
16. $7\frac{6}{7} \cdot 8\frac{1}{3}$ ________
17. $6\frac{1}{2} \cdot 5\frac{3}{4}$ ________
18. $9\frac{1}{3} \cdot 4\frac{3}{7}$ ________
19. $4\frac{9}{10} \cdot \frac{1}{2}$ ________
20. $4\frac{3}{5} \cdot 6\frac{1}{9}$ ________
21. $2\frac{1}{2} \cdot 6\frac{1}{3}$ ________
22. $6\frac{3}{4} \cdot 1\frac{2}{3}$ ________
23. $8\frac{1}{2} \cdot 3\frac{3}{4}$ ________
24. $6\frac{2}{3} \cdot 3\frac{2}{3}$ ________
25. $5\frac{5}{6} \cdot 3\frac{7}{10}$ ________
26. $8\frac{6}{7} \cdot 3\frac{1}{4}$ ________
27. $8\frac{2}{3} \cdot 7\frac{1}{3}$ ________
28. $2\frac{1}{7} \cdot 5\frac{5}{8}$ ________
29. $7\frac{2}{7} \cdot 2\frac{1}{7}$ ________
30. $7\frac{3}{4} \cdot 5\frac{2}{3}$ ________
31. $3\frac{1}{3} \cdot 2\frac{1}{10}$ ________
32. $5\frac{1}{2} \cdot 1\frac{3}{4}$ ________
33. $6\frac{5}{8} \cdot 4\frac{3}{5}$ ________
34. $2\frac{1}{2} \cdot 4\frac{2}{5}$ ________
35. $8\frac{1}{3} \cdot 5\frac{8}{9}$ ________
36. $7\frac{1}{8} \cdot 7\frac{1}{3}$ ________

37. **Measurement** A one-kilogram object weighs about $2\frac{1}{5}$ pounds. Find the weight, in pounds, of a computer monitor with mass $7\frac{3}{8}$ kilograms. ________

38. **Social Science** The population of Sweden is about $1\frac{11}{16}$ times as great as the population of Denmark. Find the population of Sweden if the population of Denmark is about 5,190,000. ________

Name ____________________

Practice 4-6

Dividing Fractions and Mixed Numbers

Change each mixed number to an improper fraction and write its reciprocal.

1. $1\frac{1}{5}$ ________ 2. $4\frac{5}{6}$ ________ 3. $3\frac{1}{4}$ ________

4. $5\frac{7}{9}$ ________ 5. $7\frac{3}{5}$ ________ 6. $2\frac{5}{7}$ ________

7. $6\frac{7}{8}$ ________ 8. $9\frac{3}{10}$ ________ 9. $3\frac{6}{7}$ ________

Rewrite each division expression as a multiplication expression to find the quotient.

10. $\frac{1}{9} \div \frac{5}{6}$ 11. $\frac{1}{2} \div \frac{4}{5}$ 12. $\frac{1}{2} \div \frac{2}{3}$ 13. $\frac{3}{5} \div \frac{4}{9}$

________ ________ ________ ________

14. $\frac{2}{3} \div \frac{5}{6}$ 15. $\frac{1}{2} \div 3\frac{1}{4}$ 16. $4\frac{2}{5} \div \frac{4}{5}$ 17. $6\frac{2}{3} \div \frac{3}{4}$

________ ________ ________ ________

18. $1\frac{3}{8} \div \frac{2}{3}$ 19. $3\frac{2}{9} \div 2\frac{1}{3}$ 20. $5\frac{1}{2} \div 1\frac{1}{2}$ 21. $11\frac{1}{2} \div 3\frac{1}{2}$

________ ________ ________ ________

Find each quotient. Rewrite in lowest terms.

22. $\frac{1}{2} \div \frac{6}{7}$ ________ 23. $\frac{1}{10} \div \frac{8}{9}$ ________ 24. $\frac{2}{7} \div \frac{3}{4}$ ________

25. $\frac{3}{4} \div \frac{3}{5}$ ________ 26. $5\frac{1}{3} \div \frac{5}{7}$ ________ 27. $2\frac{4}{5} \div \frac{1}{3}$ ________

28. $2\frac{1}{2} \div \frac{1}{10}$ ________ 29. $\frac{4}{5} \div 4\frac{2}{3}$ ________ 30. $1\frac{1}{8} \div 1\frac{4}{5}$ ________

31. $2\frac{1}{3} \div 1\frac{3}{4}$ ________ 32. $3\frac{3}{4} \div 4\frac{1}{2}$ ________ 33. $2\frac{5}{8} \div 2\frac{4}{5}$ ________

34. **Measurement** A mile is about $1\frac{3}{5}$ km. How many miles are in $6\frac{4}{5}$ km? ________

35. **Measurement** A 10-oz drinking glass holds $1\frac{1}{4}$ cups of liquid. How many drinking glasses are needed for 5 gallons (80 cups) of lemonade? ________

Name ______________________

Practice

Section 4B Review

Find each product. Rewrite in lowest terms.

1. $\frac{1}{3} \cdot \frac{1}{5}$ ________
2. $\frac{6}{7} \cdot \frac{1}{5}$ ________
3. $\frac{7}{10} \cdot \frac{2}{5}$ ________
4. $\frac{1}{8} \cdot \frac{3}{5}$ ________
5. $\frac{11}{14} \cdot \frac{7}{22}$ ________
6. $\frac{2}{45} \cdot \frac{9}{10}$ ________
7. $\frac{11}{26} \cdot \frac{8}{11}$ ________
8. $\frac{20}{21} \cdot \frac{15}{22}$ ________
9. $\frac{3}{4} \cdot 2\frac{6}{7}$ ________
10. $\frac{1}{2} \cdot 3\frac{5}{7}$ ________
11. $\frac{8}{9} \cdot 6\frac{1}{5}$ ________
12. $\frac{2}{5} \cdot 6\frac{2}{7}$ ________
13. $1\frac{1}{3} \cdot 3\frac{1}{2}$ ________
14. $6\frac{2}{3} \cdot 2\frac{3}{7}$ ________
15. $7\frac{2}{3} \cdot 9\frac{3}{4}$ ________
16. $4\frac{1}{5} \cdot 3\frac{2}{3}$ ________
17. $2\frac{2}{7} \cdot 1\frac{1}{5}$ ________
18. $\frac{7}{11} \cdot \frac{5}{13}$ ________

Find each quotient. Rewrite in lowest terms.

19. $\frac{1}{5} \div \frac{1}{3}$ ________
20. $\frac{7}{10} \div \frac{3}{4}$ ________
21. $\frac{1}{2} \div \frac{8}{9}$ ________
22. $\frac{1}{2} \div \frac{8}{9}$ ________
23. $2\frac{2}{3} \div 3$ ________
24. $11\frac{1}{2} \div \frac{1}{5}$ ________
25. $2 \div 3\frac{1}{3}$ ________
26. $1\frac{7}{9} \div 2\frac{2}{5}$ ________
27. $2\frac{4}{5} \div 1\frac{1}{2}$ ________
28. $5\frac{1}{3} \div 2\frac{4}{5}$ ________
29. $\frac{1}{4} \div \frac{9}{10}$ ________
30. $2\frac{1}{5} \div 5\frac{4}{5}$ ________

31. A recipe calls for $1\frac{2}{3}$ cups of flour. If Ron is making $1\frac{1}{2}$ times the recipe, how much flour should he use? ________

32. **Geometry** The table shows the relationship between the side length *x*, and the perimeter *P*, of a square. Find a formula relating the variables. *[Lesson 2-3]* ________

x	2	4	6	8
P	8	16	24	32

33. **Science** The spider *tegenaria atrica* can travel at speeds up to 1.17 mi/hr. How long will this spider take to travel 1.638 miles at that speed? *[Lesson 3-4]* ________

Name ____________________

Practice

Cumulative Review Chapters 1–4

The circle graph shows sources of funding for American public elementary and secondary schools. Use the graph to answer Exercises 1–3. *[Lesson 1-1]*

Public School Funding, 1992

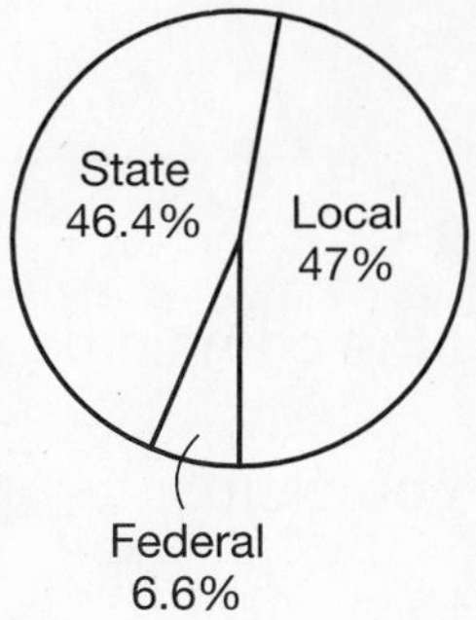

1. List the sources of funding in order of size from largest to smallest. ____________________

2. Which two sources provide about the same amount of funding? ____________________

3. Which source provides about 6.6% of public school funding? ____________________

Write an algebraic expression for each phrase. *[Lesson 2-5]*

4. one-fifth of a number (w) __________

5. seven more than a number (k) __________

6. three times the difference of a number (g) and 8 ____________________

Solve each equation. *[Lessons 3-3, 3-4]*

7. $3.16 = x - 5.23$ $x =$ __________

8. $n + 8.3 = 12.147$ $n =$ __________

9. $7.1 = j + 1.85$ $j =$ __________

10. $p - 2.1 = 8.99$ $p =$ __________

11. $3.21s = 17.013$ $s =$ __________

12. $0.9s = 13.86$ $s =$ __________

13. $\frac{m}{2.36} = 5.9$ $m =$ __________

14. $\frac{z}{3.72} = 1.54$ $z =$ __________

Find each sum or difference. *[Lesson 4-3]*

15. $15\frac{10}{11} + 14\frac{2}{3}$ __________

16. $15\frac{20}{21} - 2\frac{2}{7}$ __________

17. $37\frac{68}{75} - 22\frac{21}{25}$ __________

18. $13\frac{3}{35} - \frac{4}{5}$ __________

19. $19\frac{1}{3} + 11\frac{9}{20}$ __________

20. $28\frac{9}{10} - 16\frac{2}{5}$ __________

Find each product. *[Lesson 4-5]*

21. $3\frac{1}{2} \cdot 7\frac{7}{8}$ __________

22. $3\frac{7}{10} \cdot 5\frac{3}{4}$ __________

23. $7\frac{2}{5} \cdot 4\frac{1}{2}$ __________

24. $7\frac{1}{6} \cdot 6\frac{4}{5}$ __________

25. $4\frac{4}{9} \cdot 7\frac{5}{8}$ __________

26. $5\frac{1}{2} \cdot 2\frac{4}{9}$ __________

Name ______________________________

Practice 5-1

Angles

Name each angle and give its measure.

1. ____________

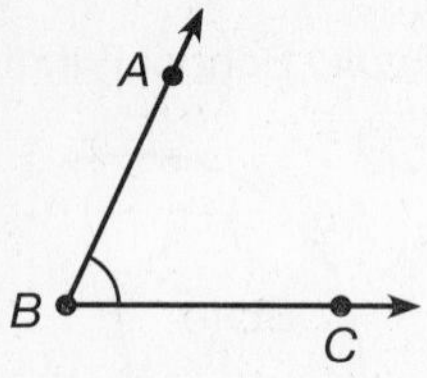

2. ____________

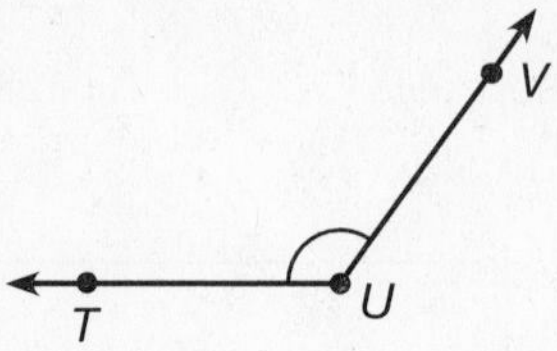

3. ____________

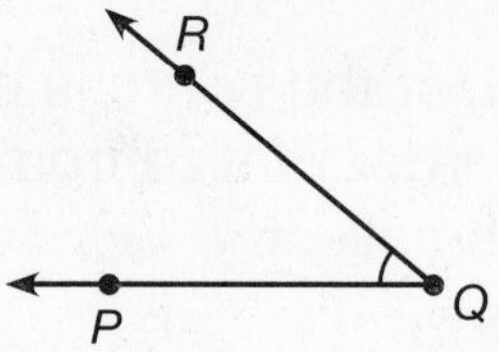

Find the complement and the supplement of $\angle P$.

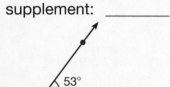

4. complement: ________

supplement: ________

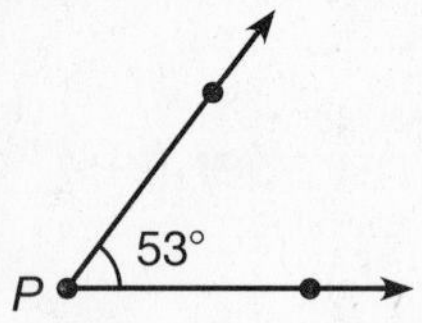

5. complement: ________

supplement: ________

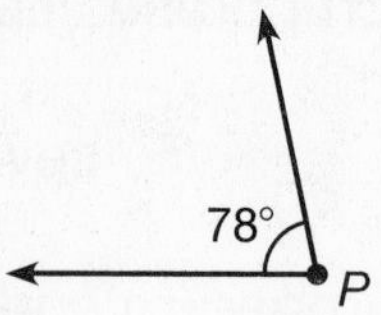

6. complement: ________

supplement: ________

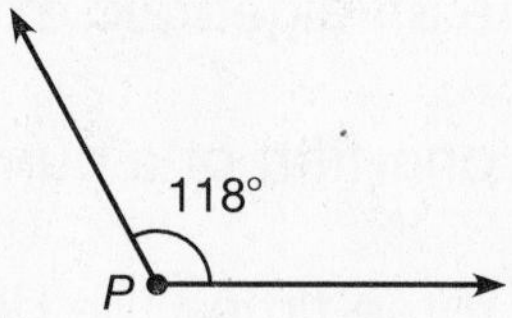

Measure each angle using a protractor.

7. ____________

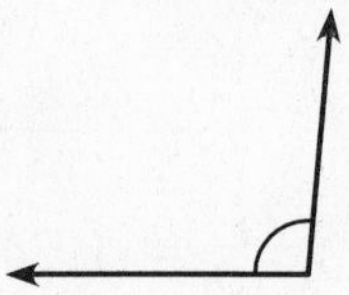

8. ____________

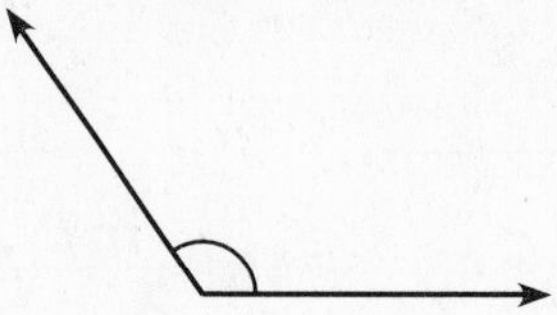

9. ____________

Classify each angle.

10. ____________

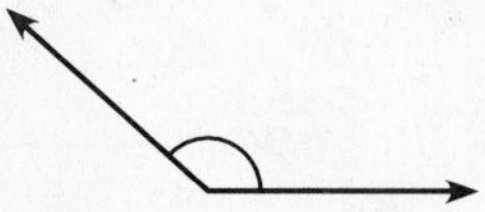

11. ____________

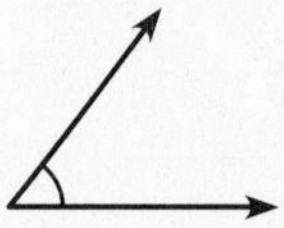

12. ____________

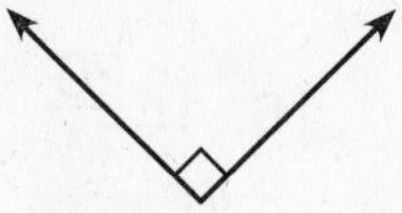

13. ____________

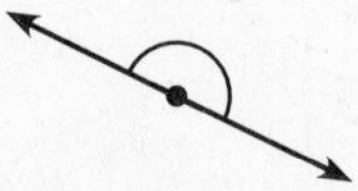

14. Science When a beam of light strikes a flat mirror, the light reflects at the same angle at which it hits the mirror's surface.

a. If light strikes a mirror at 63°, at what angle will the light reflect? ________

b. What is the measure of the angle between the angle at which the light strikes the mirror (63°), and the angle at which the light reflects? ________

Name ______________________________

Practice
5-2

Parallel and Perpendicular Lines

Write the word that describes the lines or line segments.

1. the strings on a guitar __________

2. the marks left by a skidding car __________

3. sidewalks on opposite sides a street __________

4. the segments that make up a + sign __________

5. the wires suspended between telephone poles __________

6. the hands of a clock at 9:00 P.M. __________

7. two palm trees in Los Angeles __________

Use the figure to name each pair of angles or lines.

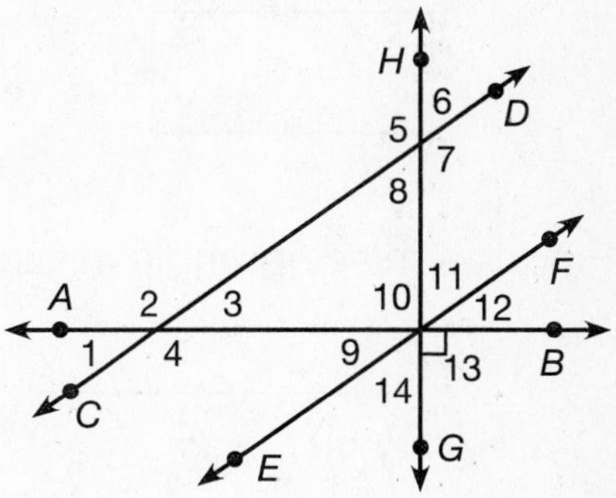

8. a pair of parallel lines __________

9. a pair of perpendicular lines __________

10. a pair of supplementary angles __________

11. a pair of corresponding angles __________

12. a pair of alternate interior angles __________

13. a pair of complementary angles __________

14. a pair of vertical angles __________

15. In the figure above, name three angles that are congruent to $\angle 6$.

____

16. Use a ruler to draw a segment bisector of $\overline{UV}$.

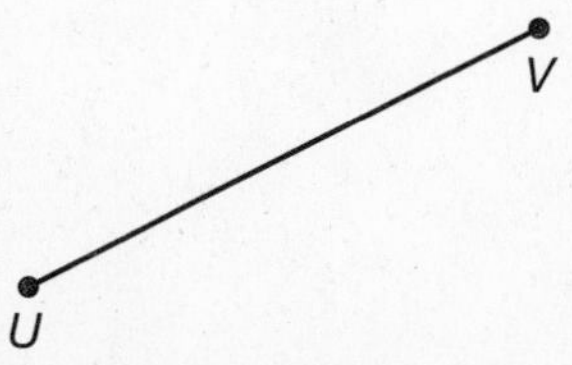

17. Use a ruler and a protractor to draw a perpendicular bisector of $\overline{XY}$.

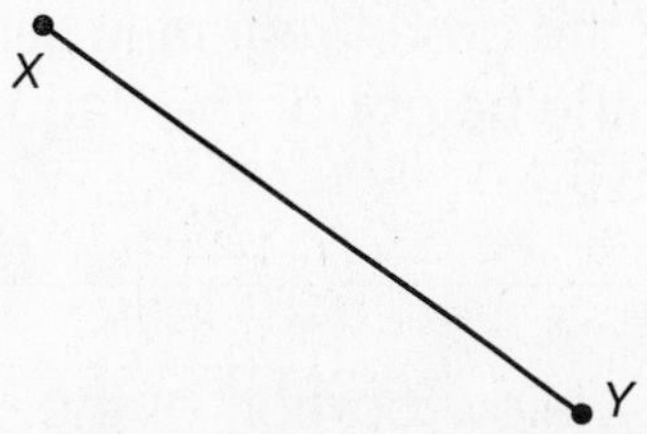

Name ______________________

Practice 5-3

Triangles and Quadrilaterals

Classify each triangle by its sides and by its angles.

1. ______________ **2.** ______________ **3.** ______________

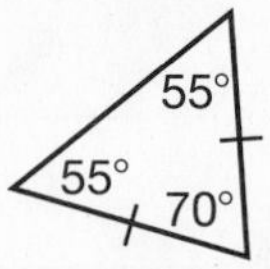

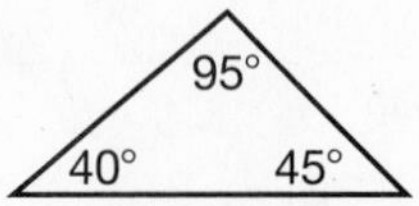

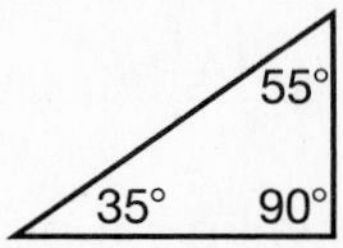

Classify each quadrilateral in as many ways as you can.

4. ______________ **5.** ______________ **6.** ______________

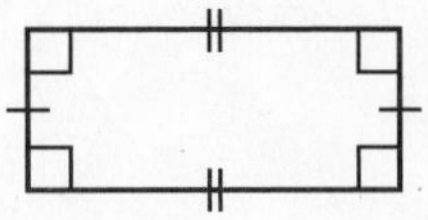

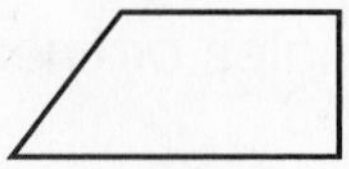

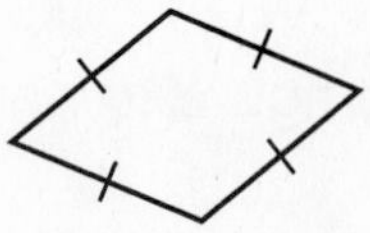

Find the missing angle in each triangle or quadrilateral.

7. $x =$ ______________ **8.** $n =$ ______________ **9.** $u =$ ______________

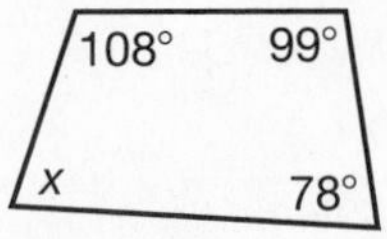

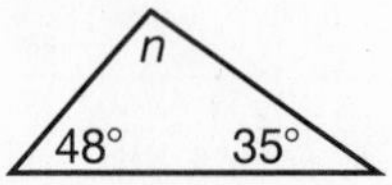

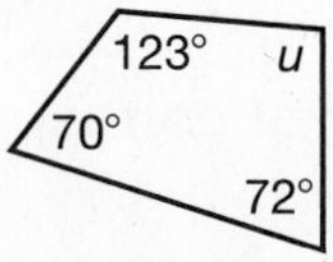

Fill in each blank with *always, sometimes,* or *never.*

10. A trapezoid is ______________ a parallelogram.

11. A rectangle is ______________ a rhombus.

12. Social Science The flag of the Congo is shown at the right.

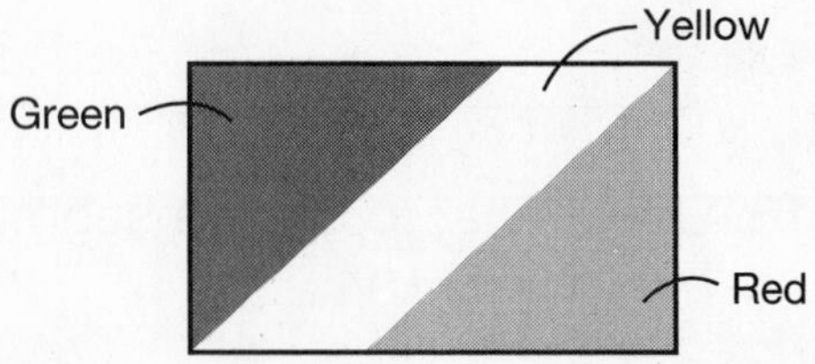

a. Classify the red and green portions of the flag in as many ways as you can. (Hint: The top edge of the green region is slightly longer than the height of the flag.)

____

b. Classify the yellow portion of the flag in as many ways as you can. ______________

Name ______________________________

Practice 5-4

Polygons

Tell why each polygon is not a regular polygon.

1. ______________________
____

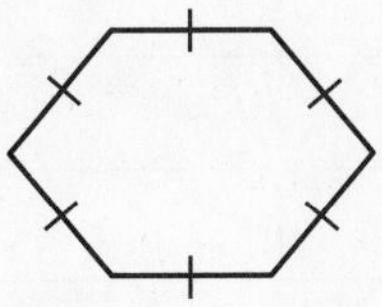

2. ______________________
____

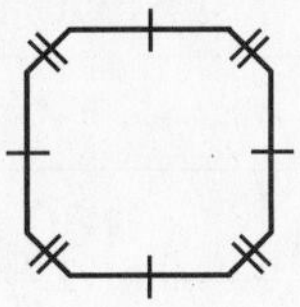

3. ______________________
____

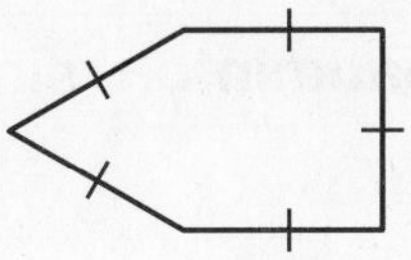

In each design, identify as many polygons as you can.

4. ______________________
____

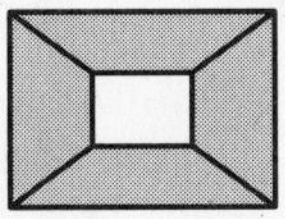

5. ______________________
____

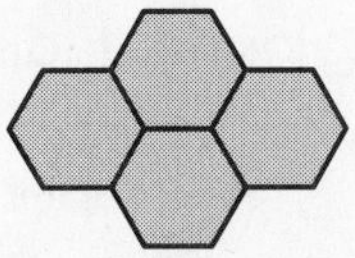

6. ______________________
____

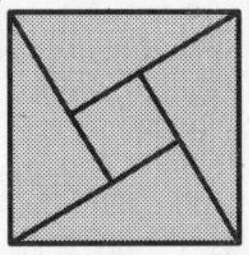

7. ______________________
____

8. ______________________
____

9. ______________________
____

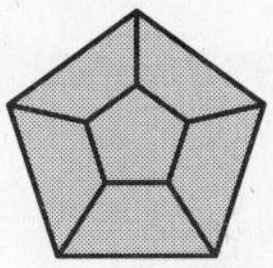

Find the sum of the measures of the angles of each polygon.

10. pentagon ______________________

11. 10-sided polygon ______________________

12. 32-sided polygon ______________________

13. Recall that an equilateral polygon has all sides congruent, and an equiangular polygon has all angles congruent. Draw each of the following, if possible.

a. equiangular hexagon that is not regular

b. equilateral quadrilateral that is not regular

c. equiangular triangle that is not equilateral

Name ______________________________

Practice
5-5

Perimeter and Area

Find the perimeter and area of each playing area.

Game	Base (length)	Height (width)	Perimeter	Area
1. tennis, singles	26 yd	9 yd		
2. volleyball	60 ft	30 ft		
3. badminton, singles	44 ft	17 ft		
4. cricket	170 m	160 m		
5. racquetball	40 ft	20 ft		
6. ice hockey	61 m	30 m		

Find the area and the perimeter of each bridge or canal. Assume that each has the shape of a rectangle.

7. Busiest bridge: Howrah Bridge, Calcutta, India—1500 ft by 72 ft

area: ______________________ perimeter: ______________________

8. Widest bridge: Sydney Harbor Bridge, Australia—49 m by 503 m

area: ______________________ perimeter: ______________________

9. Longest canal: Erie Barge Canal, New York—0.028 mi by 365 mi

area: ______________________ perimeter: ______________________

10. Largest lock: Berendrecht lock, Antwerp, Belgium—1640 ft by 223 ft

area: ______________________ perimeter: ______________________

11. Largest cut: Corinth Canal, Greece—6917 yd by 27 yd

area: ______________________ perimeter: ______________________

12. Geography The state of Wyoming is shaped like a rectangle, with a base measuring about 350 miles and a height of about 280 miles. Find the approximate area and perimeter of Wyoming.

area: ______________________ perimeter: ______________________

13. Orlando painted a mural measuring 3.7 m by 4.6 m. Find the area and perimeter of the mural.

area: ______________________ perimeter: ______________________

Name ______________________

Practice

Section 5A Review

Name each angle and find its measure. Classify it as acute, right, or obtuse.

1. ______________________ ______________________

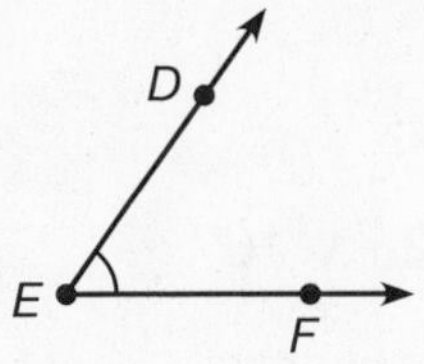

2. ______________________ ______________________

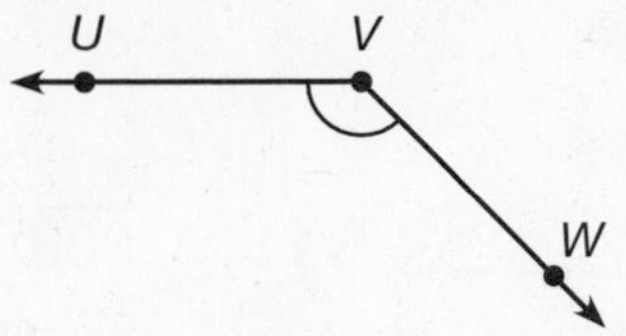

3. ______________________ ______________________

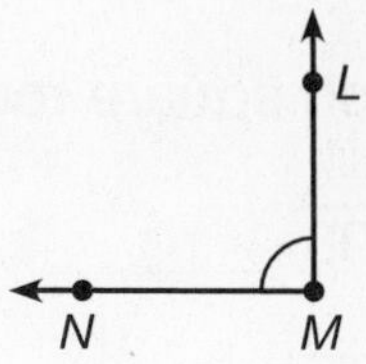

Find the missing angle in each quadrilateral.

4. $k =$ ______________________

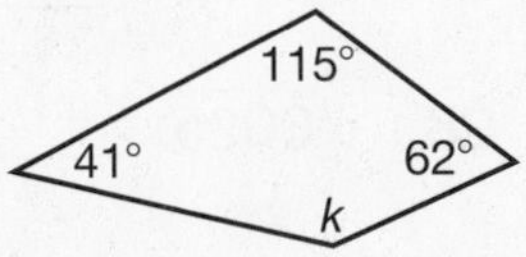

5. $x =$ ______________________

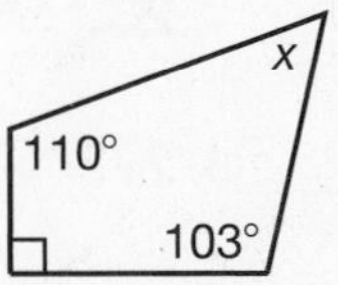

6. $c =$ ______________________

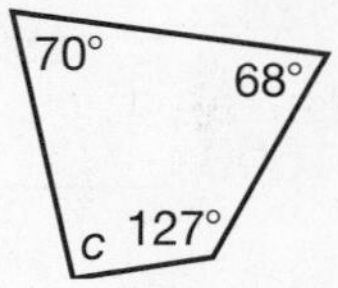

Classify each figure in as many ways as you can.

7. ______________________ ______________________

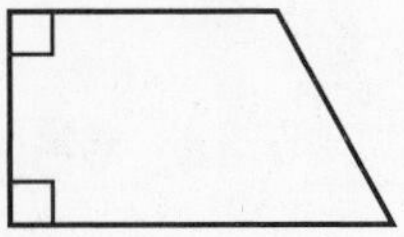

8. ______________________ ______________________

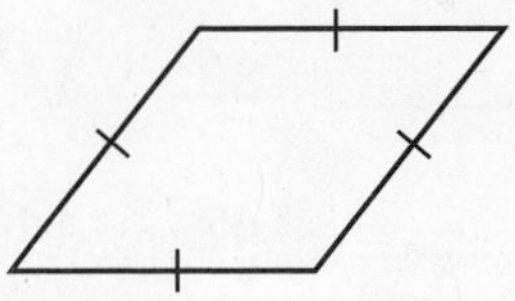

Find the sum of the measures of the angles of each polygon.

9. octagon ______________________ **10.** 14-sided polygon ______________________

11. A door measures 30 in. by 96 in. Find the perimeter and the area of the door.

perimeter: ______________________ area: ______________________

12. Heather and Denise are running laps. They start together at the same starting point. Heather completes a lap every 120 sec, and Denise completes a lap every 96 sec. In how many seconds will they again meet at the starting point? *[Lesson 3-7]* ______________________

13. On October 15, 1996, shares of Chips and Technologies stock increased $\$4\frac{7}{8}$ to $\$19\frac{3}{4}$. What was the original price? *[Lesson 4-3]* ______________________

Name ____________________

Practice 5-6

Squares and Square Roots

Determine if each number is a perfect square.

1. 90 ______ **2.** 225 ______ **3.** 49 ______ **4.** 28 ______

5. 289 ______ **6.** 144 ______ **7.** 240 ______ **8.** 1000 ______

Find each square root.

9. $\sqrt{196}$ ______ **10.** $\sqrt{4}$ ______ **11.** $\sqrt{289}$ ______ **12.** $\sqrt{16}$ ______

13. $\sqrt{361}$ ______ **14.** $\sqrt{64}$ ______ **15.** $\sqrt{1}$ ______ **16.** $\sqrt{25}$ ______

17. $\sqrt{9}$ ______ **18.** $\sqrt{484}$ ______ **19.** $\sqrt{256}$ ______ **20.** $\sqrt{400}$ ______

21. $\sqrt{324}$ ______ **22.** $\sqrt{729}$ ______ **23.** $\sqrt{36}$ ______ **24.** $\sqrt{1296}$ ______

25. $\sqrt{1600}$ ______ **26.** $\sqrt{49}$ ______ **27.** $\sqrt{22{,}500}$ ______ **28.** $\sqrt{3025}$ ______

Use a calculator to find each square root. Round the answer to two decimal places.

29. $\sqrt{10}$ ______ **30.** $\sqrt{48}$ ______ **31.** $\sqrt{28}$ ______ **32.** $\sqrt{55}$ ______

33. $\sqrt{72}$ ______ **34.** $\sqrt{37}$ ______ **35.** $\sqrt{86}$ ______ **36.** $\sqrt{98}$ ______

37. $\sqrt{946}$ ______ **38.** $\sqrt{14}$ ______ **39.** $\sqrt{62}$ ______ **40.** $\sqrt{316}$ ______

41. $\sqrt{68}$ ______ **42.** $\sqrt{146}$ ______ **43.** $\sqrt{76}$ ______ **44.** $\sqrt{521}$ ______

45. $\sqrt{813}$ ______ **46.** $\sqrt{83}$ ______ **47.** $\sqrt{23}$ ______ **48.** $\sqrt{617}$ ______

49. $\sqrt{35}$ ______ **50.** $\sqrt{123}$ ______ **51.** $\sqrt{51}$ ______ **52.** $\sqrt{463}$ ______

53. $\sqrt{583}$ ______ **54.** $\sqrt{96}$ ______ **55.** $\sqrt{203}$ ______ **56.** $\sqrt{1200}$ ______

57. $\sqrt{278}$ ______ **58.** $\sqrt{43}$ ______ **59.** $\sqrt{401}$ ______ **60.** $\sqrt{328}$ ______

61. $\sqrt{1365}$ ______ **62.** $\sqrt{785}$ ______ **63.** $\sqrt{635}$ ______ **64.** $\sqrt{2424}$ ______

65. The largest pyramid in Egypt, built almost 5000 years ago, covers an area of about 63,300 yd^2. Find the length of each side of the square base. ____________

66. Square floor tiles frequently have an area of 929 cm^2. Find the length of a side of one of these tiles. ____________

 Use with pages 240–243.

Name ______________________________

Practice 5-7

The Pythagorean Theorem

Use the Pythagorean Theorem to write an equation expressing the relationship between the legs and the hypotenuse for each triangle.

1. ____________

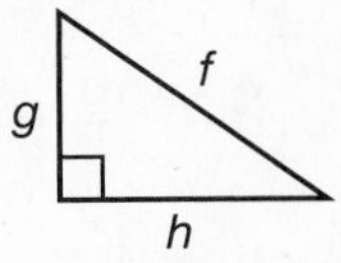

2. ____________

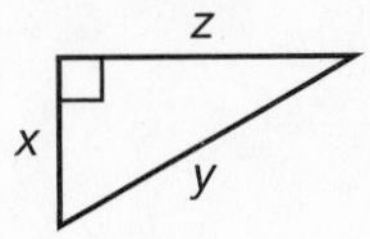

3. ____________

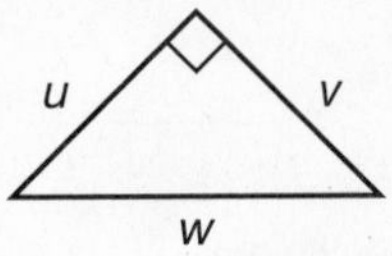

Determine if each triangle is a right triangle.

4. ____________

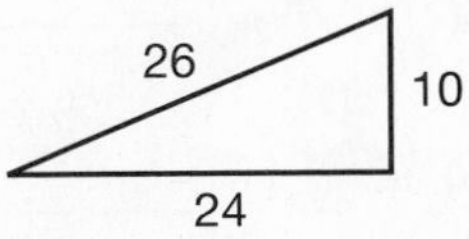

5. ____________

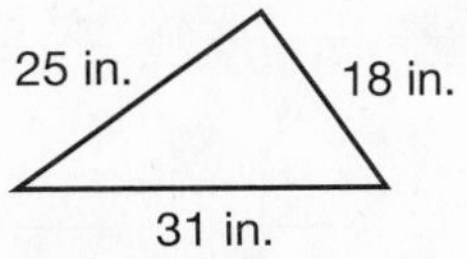

6. ____________

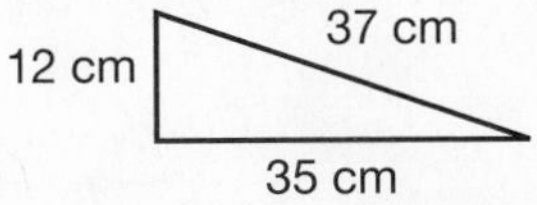

Find the missing length in each right triangle.

7. $t =$ ____________

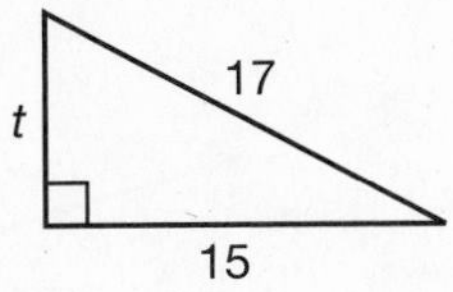

8. $d =$ ____________

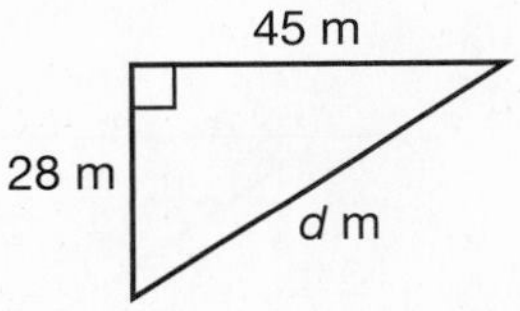

9. $m =$ ____________

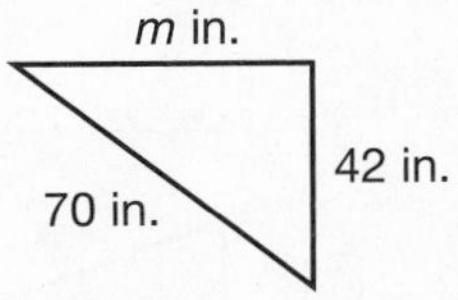

10. $x =$ ____________

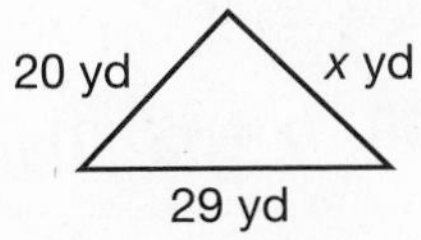

11. $u =$ ____________

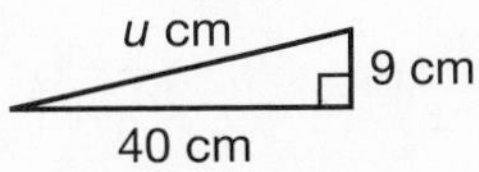

12. $r =$ ____________

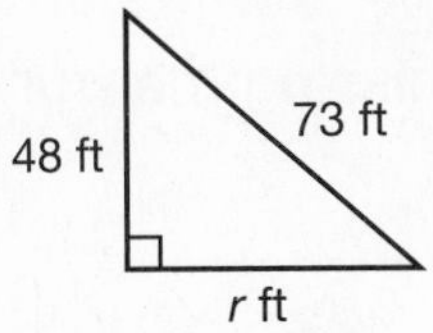

13. Geography The state of Colorado is shaped like a rectangle, with a base measuring about 385 mi and a height of about 275 mi. About how far is it from the northwest corner to the southeast corner of Colorado? ____________

14. A drawing tool is shaped like a right triangle. One leg measures about 14.48 cm, and the hypotenuse measures 20.48 cm. What is the length of the other leg? Round your answer to the nearest hundredth of a centimeter. ____________

15. An 8-foot ladder is leaned against a high wall from 4 feet away. How high up the wall does the ladder reach? Round your answer to the nearest tenth of a foot. ____________

Name ____________________

Practice 5-8

Area of Triangles

Find the area of each triangle.

1. $b = 3$ m
$h = 8$ m

$A =$ ________

2. $b = 12$ mi
$h = 5$ mi

$A =$ ________

3. $b = 7$ in.
$h = 14$ in.

$A =$ ________

4. $b = 21$ cm
$h = 16$ cm

$A =$ ________

5. $b = 6.8$ km
$h = 11.0$ km

$A =$ ________

6. $b = 3\frac{1}{4}$ yd
$h = 8\frac{1}{2}$ yd

$A =$ ________

7. $b = 5.7$ m
$h = 2.4$ m

$A =$ ________

8. $b = \frac{1}{4}$ ft
$h = \frac{3}{5}$ ft

$A =$ ________

9. $A =$ ________

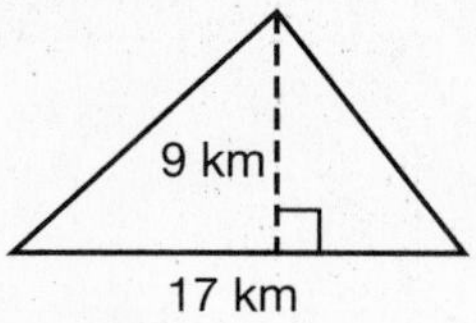

10. $A =$ ________

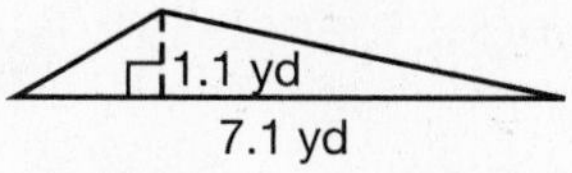

11. $A =$ ________

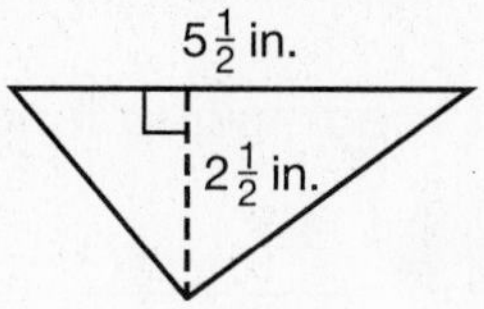

12. $A =$ ________

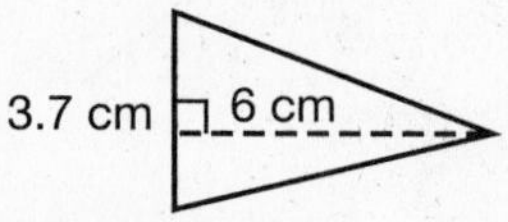

13. $A =$ ________

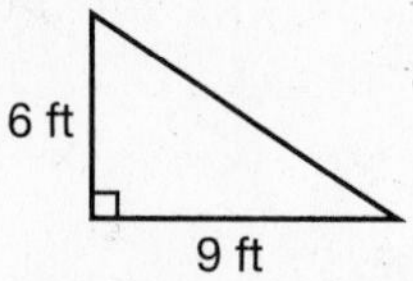

14. $A =$ ________

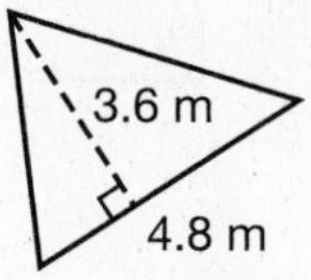

Find the missing measurements of the following triangles.

15. $b =$ ________
$h = 81$ mi
$A = 2592$ mi^2

16. $b = 46$ cm
$h =$ ________
$A = 368$ cm^2

17. $b =$ ________
$h = 35$ in.
$A = 700$ in^2

18. $b = 63$ m
$h =$ ________
$A = 1071$ m^2

19. $b =$ ________
$h = 24$ km
$A = 468$ km^2

20. $b = 10$ yd
$h =$ ________
$A = 415$ yd^2

21. $b = 68$ cm
$h =$ ________
$A = 748$ cm^2

22. $b =$ ________
$h = 25$ ft
$A = 925$ ft^2

23. Social Studies The flag of Puerto Rico features three red stripes and a blue triangle with a white star inside. Find the area of the triangle (including the star). ________

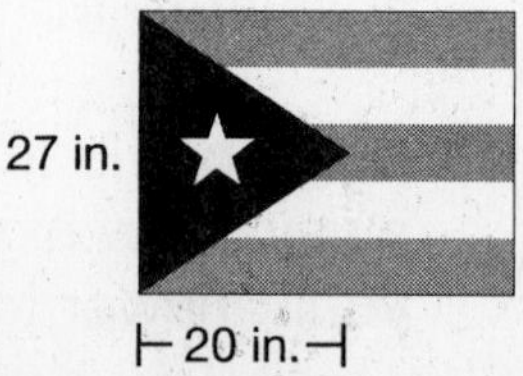

 Use with pages 248–252.

Name ______________________

Practice
5-9

Area of Parallelograms and Trapezoids

Which formula would you use to find the area of each figure, $A = bh$ or $A = \frac{1}{2}h(b_1 + b_2)$?

1. ______________

2. ______________

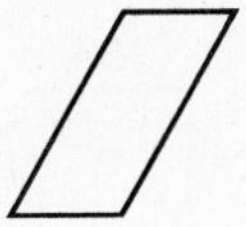

3. ______________

Find the area of each parallelogram.

4. ______________

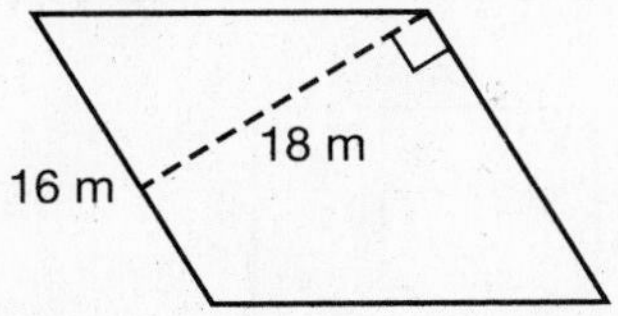

5. ______________

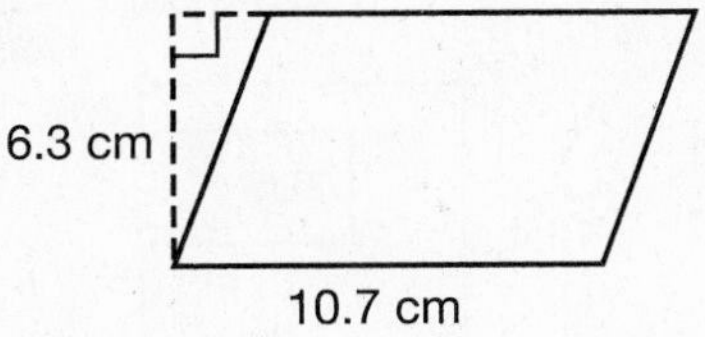

6. ______________

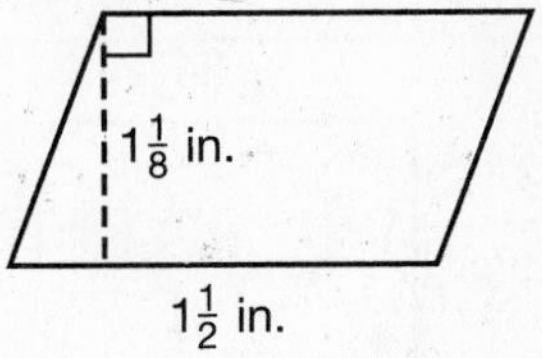

Find the area of each trapezoid.

7. ______________

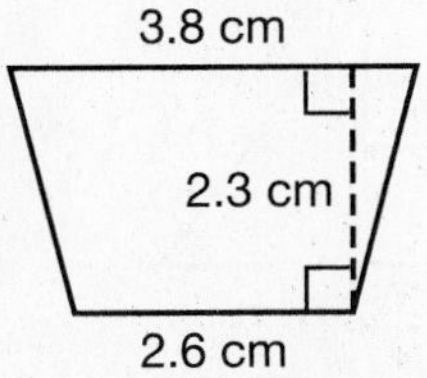

8. ______________

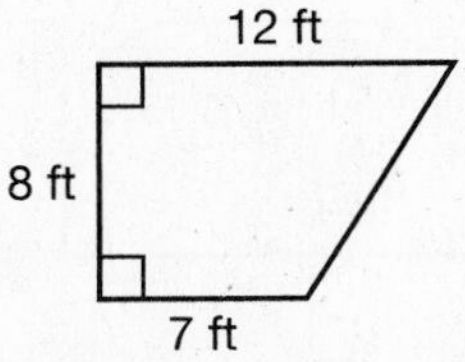

9. ______________

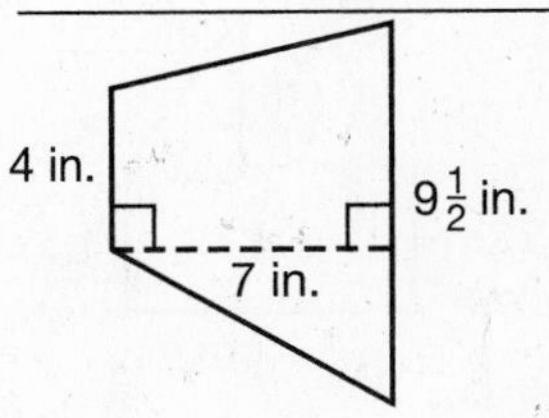

10. A 2-ft wide swing is suspended from a horizontal branch by 8-ft long ropes. Find the area that is formed when the swing is pushed sideways so that it is only $7\frac{1}{2}$ ft below the branch, as shown.

____

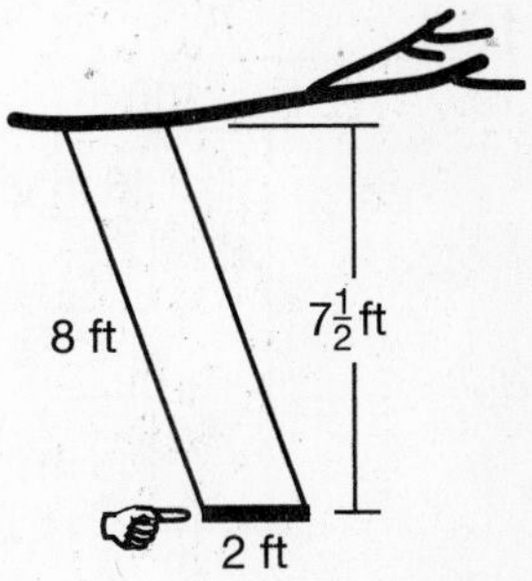

11. Social Science The flag of Kuwait is shown at the right. Find each area.

a. Black region ______________

b. Green region (top stripe) ______________

c. White region ______________

d. Red region (bottom stripe) ______________

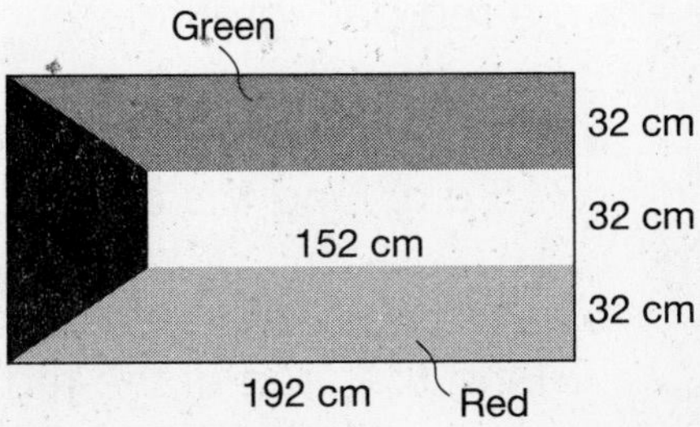

Name ______________________

Practice 5-10

Problem-Solving: Areas of Irregular Figures

Find the area of each figure.

1. ____________

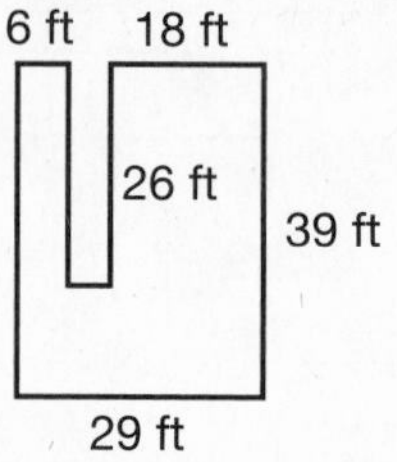

2. ____________

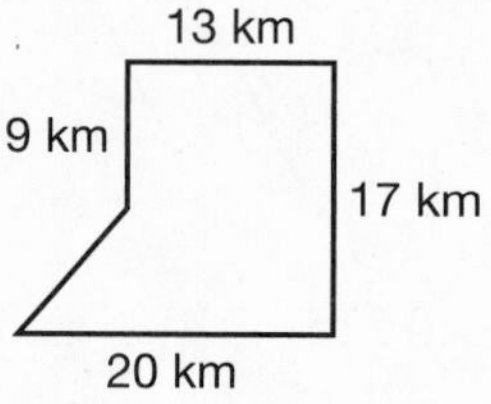

3. ____________

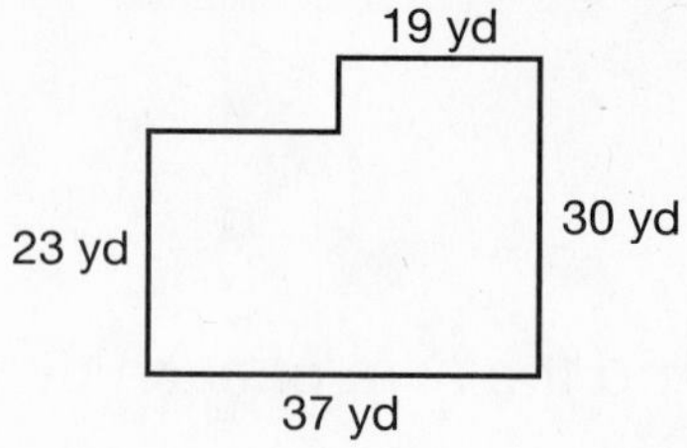

4. ____________

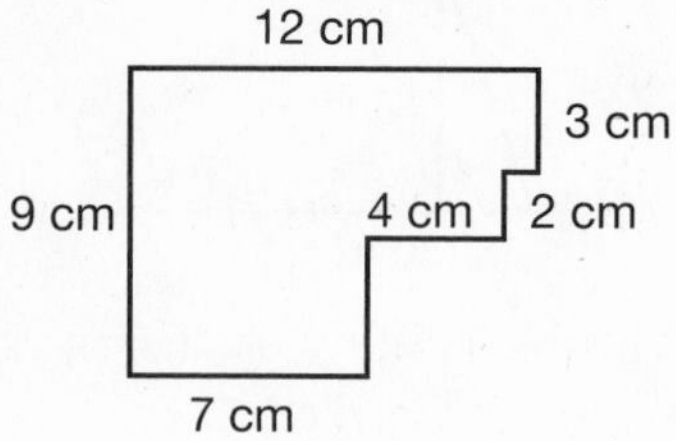

5. ____________

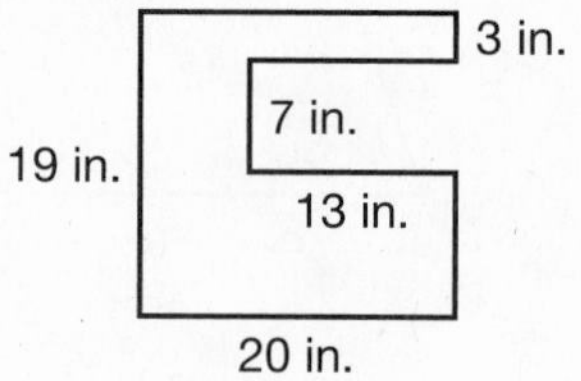

6. ____________

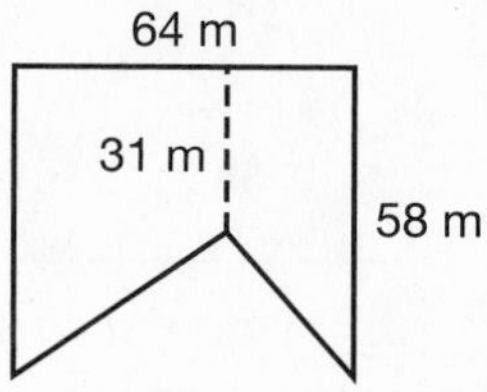

7. ____________

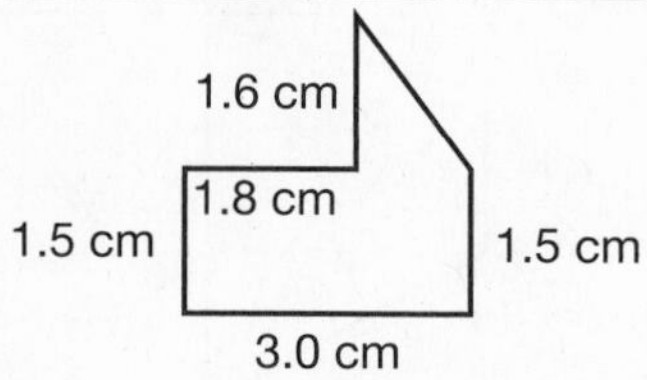

8. ____________

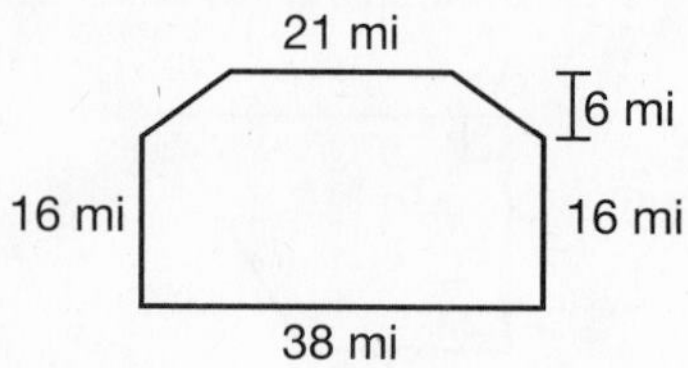

9. ____________

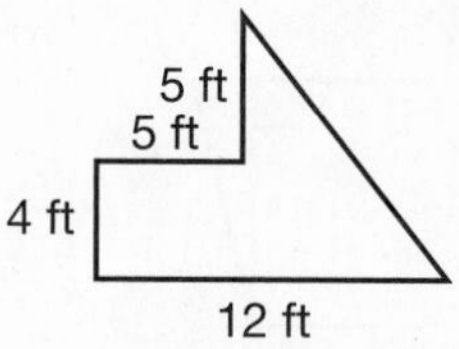

10. ____________

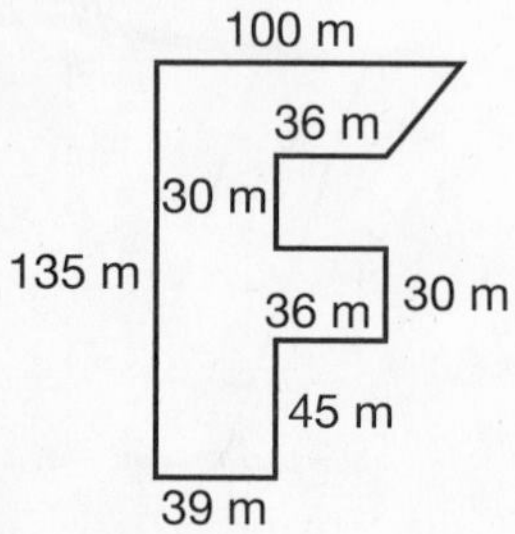

11. ____________

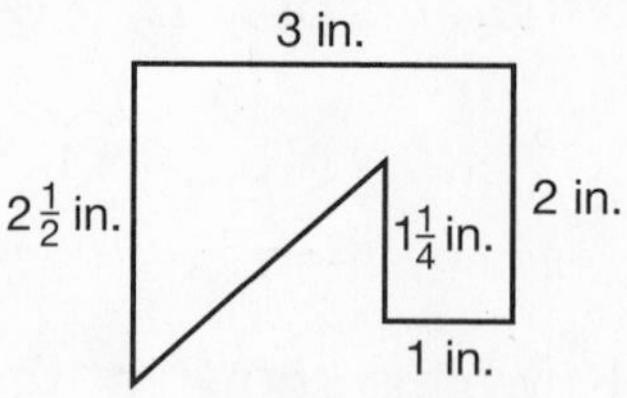

12. ____________

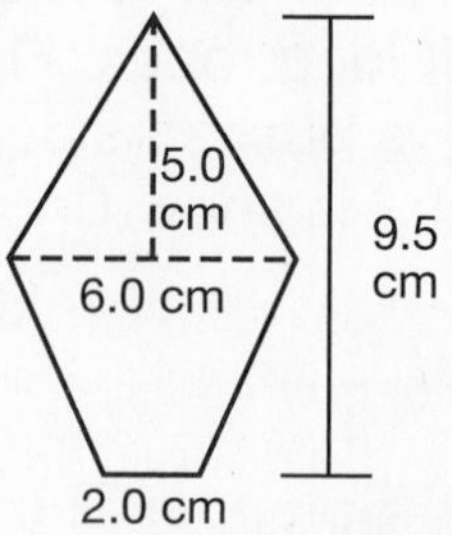

13. The flag of Switzerland features a white cross on a red background.

a. Each of the 12 sides of the cross has length 15 cm. Find the area of the white cross. ____________

b. The flag has dimensions 60 cm by 60 cm. Find the area of the red region. ____________

Name ______________________________

Practice

Section 5B Review

Find the value of each expression.

1. $\sqrt{81}$ ________ **2.** 7^2 ________ **3.** $\sqrt{625}$ ________ **4.** 14^2 ________

5. 3.8^2 ________ **6.** $\sqrt{144}$ ________ **7.** $\left(\frac{8}{11}\right)^2$ ________ **8.** $\sqrt{225}$ ________

Find the missing length in each right triangle.

9. ________________

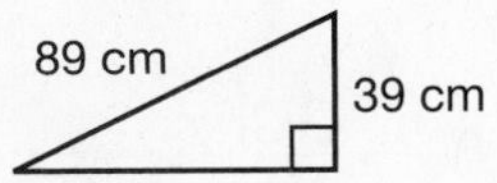

10. ________________

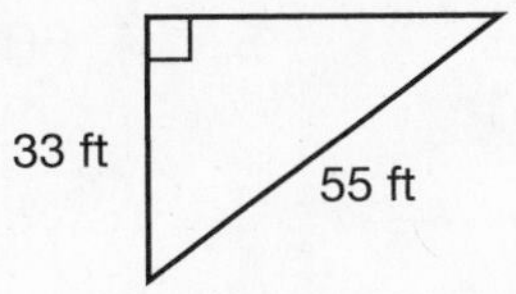

11. ________________

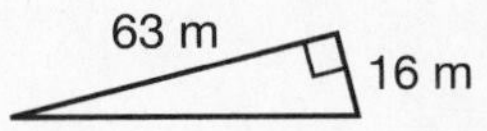

Find the area of each figure.

12. ________________

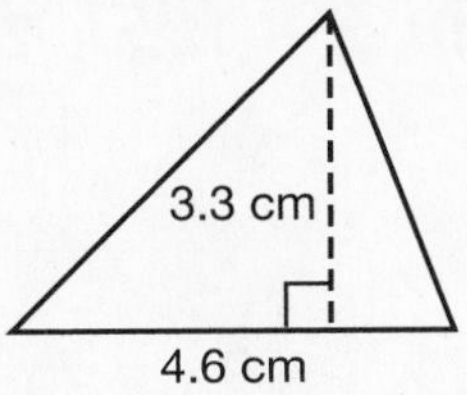

13. ________________

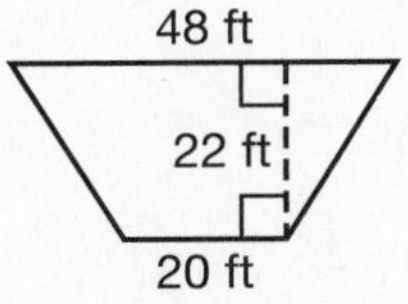

14. ________________

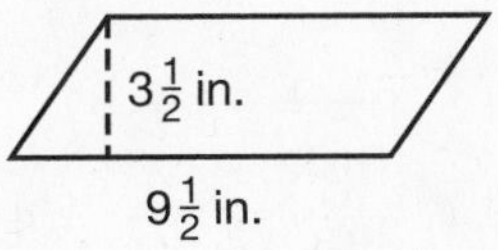

15. ________________

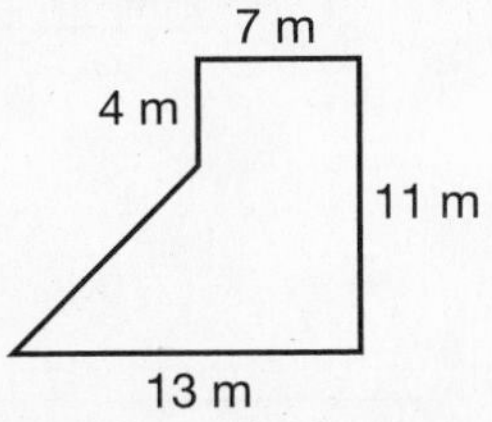

16. ________________

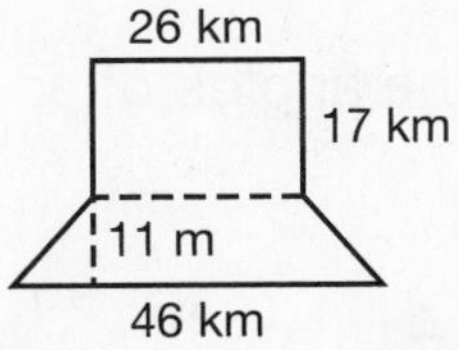

17. ________________

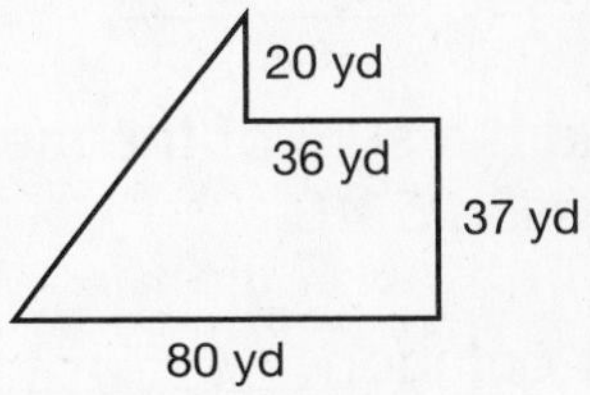

18. Measurement The Johnsons' living room measures 14 ft by 23 ft, and their kitchen measures 9 ft by 13 ft. How much greater is the living room area than the kitchen area? ________________

19. The element carbon makes up $\frac{9}{50}$ of the matter in your body. Convert $\frac{9}{50}$ to a decimal. *[Lesson 3-10]* ________________

20. The population of Asia is about $7\frac{8}{13}$ times as great as the population of North America. If the population of North America was 436,000,000 in 1992, what was the population of Asia? ________________

Name ______________________________

Practice

Cumulative Review Chapters 1–5

Use the given formula to complete each table. *[Lesson 2-3]*

1. $y = 5x + 8$

x	4	5	6	7
y				

2. $D = 60t$

D	3	4	5	6
t				

Find the GCF and LCM of each pair of numbers. *[Lesson 3-7]*

3. 14, 49

GCF: ________

LCM: ________

4. 65, 26

GCF: ________

LCM: ________

5. 24, 60

GCF: ________

LCM: ________

6. 32, 45

GCF: ________

LCM: ________

Solve each equation. *[Lesson 4-3]*

7. $5\frac{7}{8} + x = 10\frac{1}{4}$

$x =$ ________

8. $p - 12\frac{1}{3} = 6\frac{5}{6}$

$p =$ ________

9. $z + 3\frac{1}{4} = 10$

$z =$ ________

10. $c - 12\frac{1}{2} = 2\frac{1}{3}$

$c =$ ________

11. $k + 5\frac{3}{11} = 8\frac{1}{2}$

$k =$ ________

12. $d - 7\frac{3}{10} = 4\frac{1}{5}$

$d =$ ________

13. $4\frac{2}{3} + u = 6\frac{4}{15}$

$u =$ ________

14. $t - 9\frac{1}{8} = 7\frac{5}{12}$

$t =$ ________

Find the sum of the measures of the angles of each polygon. *[Lesson 5-4]*

15. octagon ______________

16. 14-sided polygon ______________

17. 18-sided polygon ______________

18. 29-sided polygon ______________

19. 36-sided polygon ______________

20. 57-sided polygon ______________

Find the missing length in each right triangle. *[Lesson 5-7]*

21. $n =$ ______________

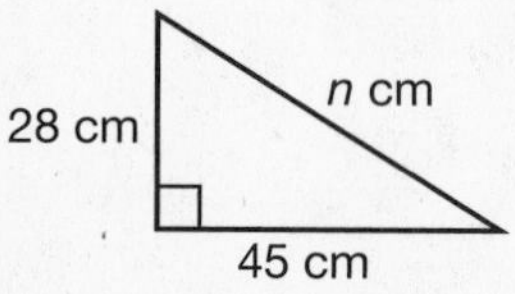

22. $u =$ ______________

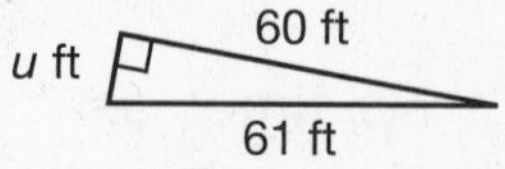

23. $p =$ ______________

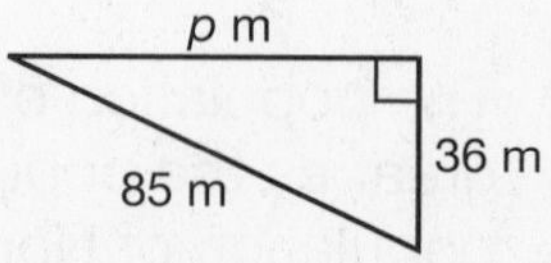

Name ______________________

Practice 6-1

Exploring and Estimating Ratios

Write each ratio in three ways. Write in lowest terms if possible.

1. 8 jazz CDs to 14 rock CDs ______

2. 25 oranges to 45 apples ______

3. $12 for 8 sandwiches ______

4. 8 dentists out of 10 dentists ______

5. 32 points in 18 games ______

6. 21 boys to 24 girls ______

A bag contains 5 red, 6 yellow, 8 green, 10 blue, and 15 clear marbles. Write each of the following ratios in lowest terms.

7. yellow to blue ______

8. green to yellow ______

9. blue to clear ______

10. blue to red ______

11. yellow to clear ______

12. red to clear ______

The table shows several popular TV programs and the number of years that each was produced. Write each of the following ratios in lowest terms.

Program	Number of Years
Walt Disney	33
Ed Sullivan	24
Gunsmoke	20
Meet the Press	18
Lassie	17

13. *Lassie* to *Gunsmoke* ______

14. *Walt Disney* to *Meet the Press* ______

15. *Ed Sullivan* to *Walt Disney* ______

16. A vase of flowers is shown. Estimate the ratio of the width of the vase to the total height of the vase and flowers. ______

Name ______________________________

Practice 6-2

Exploring and Estimating Rates

Find each rate. Remember to include units in your rates.

1. 60 students for 3 teachers

____

2. $8 for 4 books

____

3. 200 sit-ups in 5 minutes

____

4. $36.00 paid for 6 hours work

____

Express each rate as a unit rate.

5. 48 inches in 4 feet

____

6. $15 for 5 keychains

____

7. 80 pages in 5 hours

____

Consumer Use unit prices to find the better buy. Underline the correct choice.

8. Peaches: 87¢ for 3 peaches or $1.12 for 4 peaches

9. Video game tokens: $1.00 for 5 tokens or $5.00 for 30 tokens

10. Facial tissue: $3.50 for 2 boxes or $9.00 for 5 boxes

Determine whether each ratio is a rate. Explain.

11. $\frac{\$5}{\text{20 oranges}}$ ______________________________

____

12. $\frac{14}{21}$ ______________________________

13. $\frac{\text{32 ounces}}{\text{1 pint}}$ ______________________________

____

14. Science A black-billed cuckoo bird can eat 48 caterpillars in 6 minutes. Find the unit rate. ______________

15. The population of Stockton, California increased by 62,660 people during the 10 years from 1980 to 1990. Find the unit rate. ______________

Name ____________________

Practice 6-3

Equivalent Ratios and Rates

Multiply and divide to find two ratios equivalent to each ratio.

1. $\frac{12}{15}$ ______	**2.** $\frac{6}{9}$ ______	**3.** $\frac{8}{14}$ ______	**4.** $\frac{6}{12}$ ______
5. $\frac{10}{12}$ ______	**6.** $\frac{6}{8}$ ______	**7.** $\frac{5}{10}$ ______	**8.** $\frac{16}{22}$ ______
9. $\frac{6}{12}$ ______	**10.** $\frac{8}{30}$ ______	**11.** $\frac{20}{34}$ ______	**12.** $\frac{15}{18}$ ______
13. $\frac{16}{36}$ ______	**14.** $\frac{9}{12}$ ______	**15.** $\frac{24}{27}$ ______	**16.** $\frac{6}{10}$ ______
17. $\frac{6}{33}$ ______	**18.** $\frac{30}{42}$ ______	**19.** $\frac{10}{16}$ ______	**20.** $\frac{24}{28}$ ______
21. $\frac{16}{18}$ ______	**22.** $\frac{6}{15}$ ______	**23.** $\frac{14}{16}$ ______	**24.** $\frac{8}{10}$ ______
25. $\frac{20}{50}$ ______	**26.** $\frac{15}{30}$ ______	**27.** $\frac{19}{38}$ ______	**28.** $\frac{28}{30}$ ______
29. $\frac{10}{18}$ ______	**30.** $\frac{8}{12}$ ______	**31.** $\frac{12}{57}$ ______	**32.** $\frac{16}{20}$ ______
33. $\frac{26}{44}$ ______	**34.** $\frac{14}{24}$ ______	**35.** $\frac{35}{42}$ ______	**36.** $\frac{28}{34}$ ______
37. $\frac{13}{65}$ ______	**38.** $\frac{52}{78}$ ______	**39.** $\frac{10}{52}$ ______	**40.** $\frac{12}{18}$ ______
41. $\frac{6}{82}$ ______	**42.** $\frac{24}{48}$ ______	**43.** $\frac{25}{45}$ ______	**44.** $\frac{12}{68}$ ______
45. $\frac{20}{30}$ ______	**46.** $\frac{24}{39}$ ______	**47.** $\frac{12}{36}$ ______	**48.** $\frac{33}{44}$ ______
49. $\frac{46}{72}$ ______	**50.** $\frac{14}{54}$ ______	**51.** $\frac{18}{27}$ ______	**52.** $\frac{10}{15}$ ______
53. $\frac{6}{38}$ ______	**54.** $\frac{24}{26}$ ______	**55.** $\frac{18}{28}$ ______	**56.** $\frac{8}{56}$ ______
57. $\frac{6}{14}$ ______	**58.** $\frac{26}{32}$ ______	**59.** $\frac{35}{40}$ ______	**60.** $\frac{30}{96}$ ______

61. Science Neptune rotates 12 times in 18 Earth days. How many times will Neptune rotate in 6 Earth days? ______

62. Measurement There are 8 pints in a gallon. How many pints are in 7 gallons? ______

Name ______________________________

Practice 6-4

Using Tables to Explore Ratios and Rates

1. Using multiplication, complete the table to find 5 ratios equivalent to $\frac{3}{11}$.

3	6	9	12	15	18
11					

Ratios: ______________________

2. Using division, complete the table to find 5 ratios equivalent to $\frac{90}{225}$.

90	30	18	10	6	2
225					

Ratios: ______________________

Fill in each table to find four ratios equal to the ratio in the first column.

3.

5				40
8		24		

Ratios: ______________________

4.

21	7			
36			108	

Ratios: ______________________

5. In 1946, Stella Pajunas set a record by typing 216 words in a minute on an electric typewriter. Use the table to estimate how long it took her to type 100 words. ______________

Number of words	36	72	108	144	180	216
Number of seconds	10	20	30	40	50	60

Use a table to find two rates equivalent to each rate.

6. $15 per CD

Rates: ______________________

7. 16 pages typed in 4 hours

Rates: ______________________

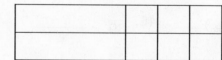

8. A walrus can swim at a rate of 24 kilometers per hour. Make a table to find five rates equivalent to this unit rate.

Rates: ______________________________

 Use with pages 286–290.

Name ____________________

Practice

Section 6A Review

Write each ratio in lowest terms.

1. $\frac{8}{10}$ ________ **2.** 36 to 48 ________ **3.** 16 : 20 ________

Express each rate as a unit rate.

4. baked 72 cookies in 3 hours ________

5. played 6 games in 2 hours ________

6. \$45 to 5 hours work ________

7. 60 students for 12 computers ________

8. Which price is better, \$4.32 for 2 pounds of granola or \$6.51 for 3 pounds? ________

Multiply and divide to find two ratios equivalent to each ratio.

9. $\frac{18}{24}$ ________ **10.** $\frac{22}{36}$ ________ **11.** $\frac{12}{15}$ ________

12. Consumer When buying a car, it is important to consider fuel efficiency. A more efficient car will travel a greater distance per gallon of gas. Make a table for each car to find five rates equivalent to each unit rate.

a. Yachtomobile: 13 miles per gallon

Rates: ________

____

b. Pepster: 45 miles per gallon

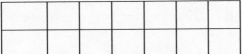

Rates: ________

____

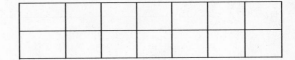

13. The Tremendous T-shirt Co. sells T-shirts by mail for \$7.00 each. Since there is a \$5.00 shipping charge, the price for n T-shirts is given by the formula $P = 7n + 5$. If Maria paid \$47, how many T-shirts did she order? *[Lesson 2-8]* ________

14. Science A typical male elk weighs about $\frac{7}{20}$ of a ton. How many elk would weigh 21 tons altogether? *[Lesson 4-6]* ________

Name ______________________________

Practice 6-5

Creating Proportions

Complete each table. Then write four proportions involving ratios in the table.

1.

3	6	9	12
5			

2.

4	8	20	32
11			

______________________ ______________________

______________________ ______________________

For each ratio, make a table and create three equal ratios. Then use your ratios to write three proportions.

3. $\frac{5}{7}$

4. $\frac{11}{15}$

______________________ ______________________

5. $\frac{16}{20}$

6. $\frac{8}{6}$

______________________ ______________________

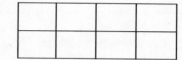

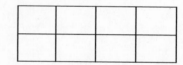

Use each proportion to write two other proportions.

7. $\frac{5}{8} = \frac{15}{24}$ ______________________

8. $\frac{4}{18} = \frac{6}{27}$ ______________________

9. $\frac{\$2}{7\text{ apples}} = \frac{\$6}{21\text{ apples}}$ ______________________

10. $\frac{80\text{ miles}}{15\text{ hours}} = \frac{32\text{ miles}}{6\text{ hours}}$ ______________________

11. An electronics kit contains 7 resistors, 3 capacitors, and 2 transistors. Tell how many of each part would be in 2, 3, and 4 kits.

2 kits: ______________________

3 kits: ______________________

4 kits: ______________________

Name ____________________

Practice
6-6

Testing for Proportionality

Decide if each pair of ratios is proportional.

1. $\frac{14}{10} \stackrel{?}{=} \frac{9}{7}$ ____________
2. $\frac{18}{8} \stackrel{?}{=} \frac{36}{16}$ ____________
3. $\frac{6}{10} \stackrel{?}{=} \frac{15}{25}$ ____________
4. $\frac{7}{16} \stackrel{?}{=} \frac{4}{9}$ ____________
5. $\frac{6}{4} \stackrel{?}{=} \frac{12}{8}$ ____________
6. $\frac{19}{3} \stackrel{?}{=} \frac{114}{18}$ ____________
7. $\frac{5}{14} \stackrel{?}{=} \frac{6}{15}$ ____________
8. $\frac{6}{27} \stackrel{?}{=} \frac{8}{36}$ ____________
9. $\frac{27}{15} \stackrel{?}{=} \frac{45}{25}$ ____________
10. $\frac{3}{18} \stackrel{?}{=} \frac{4}{20}$ ____________
11. $\frac{5}{2} \stackrel{?}{=} \frac{15}{6}$ ____________
12. $\frac{20}{15} \stackrel{?}{=} \frac{4}{3}$ ____________

Make a scatterplot to see if each relationship is proportional.

13.

Oranges	2	4	6	8
Price ($)	0.50	1.00	1.50	2.00

____

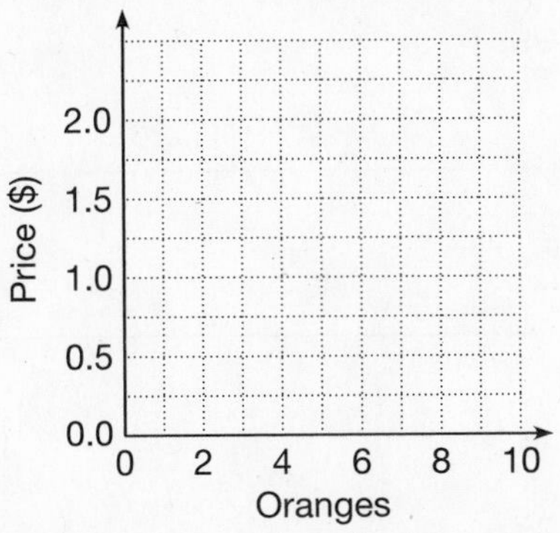

14.

Oats (cups)	0.50	1	2	3
Water (cups)	1	1.75	3.5	5

____

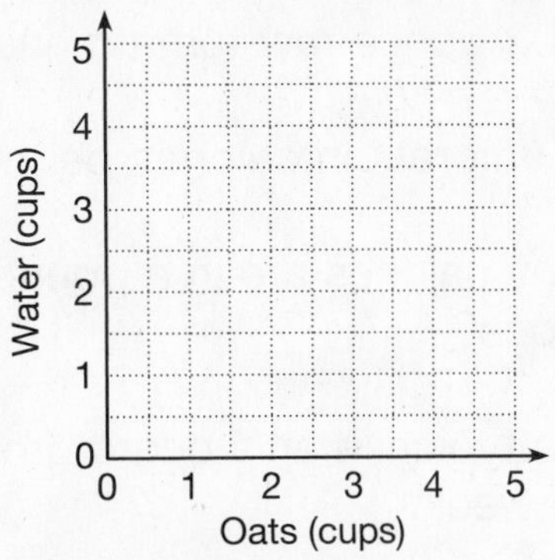

15. During the breaststroke competitions of the 1992 Olympics, Nelson Diebel swam 100 meters in 62 seconds, and Mike Bowerman swam 200 meters in 130 seconds. Are the rates proportional? ________

16. During a vacation, the Vasquez family traveled 174 miles in 3 hours on Monday, and 290 miles in 5 hours on Tuesday. Are the rates proportional? ________

Name ______________________

Practice 6-7

Solving Proportions Using Unit Rates

1. Bananas are on sale at 8 for $0.96.

   a. Find the cost of 1 banana. ______

   b. Find the cost of 7 bananas. ______

2. Sylvia earned $199.20 for 24 hours of work.

   a. Find her hourly rate. ______

   b. Find her earnings for 15 hours of work. ______

3. **History** In 1927, Charles Lindbergh flew 3600 miles from New York to Paris in $33\frac{2}{3}$ hours.

   a. Find Lindbergh's rate in miles per hour. Round to the nearest tenth. ______

   b. At this rate, how far did Lindbergh fly in 24 hours? ______

   c. Find Lindbergh's rate in hours per mile. ______

   d. How long did it take Lindbergh to travel 1600 miles? ______

4. **Health** A 4.3-ounce raw tomato has about 24 calories.

   a. Find the unit rate in calories per ounce. ______

   b. How many calories are in a pound (16 oz) of tomatoes? ______

5. The hair in a typical man's beard grows about 3.5 mm per week.

   a. Find the unit rate in mm per day. ______

   b. October has 31 days. How long will the hair grow in October? ______

6. In 1993, President Clinton received an average of 25,000 letters per day. How many letters did he receive during the entire year? ______

 Use with pages 304–307.

Name ______________________________

Practice 6-8

Cross Multiplication

Find the cross products for each proposition.

1. $\frac{6}{16} = \frac{9}{24}$ ______ ______

2. $\frac{21}{49} = \frac{3}{7}$ ______ ______

3. $\frac{4}{3} = \frac{16}{12}$ ______ ______

Decide whether each pair of ratios forms a proportion.

4. $\frac{2}{10} \stackrel{?}{=} \frac{4}{16}$ ______

5. $\frac{12}{7} \stackrel{?}{=} \frac{34}{20}$ ______

6. $\frac{20}{18} \stackrel{?}{=} \frac{30}{27}$ ______

7. $\frac{40}{45} \stackrel{?}{=} \frac{8}{9}$ ______

8. $\frac{7}{14} \stackrel{?}{=} \frac{3}{7}$ ______

9. $\frac{2}{6} \stackrel{?}{=} \frac{3}{9}$ ______

10. $\frac{10}{11} \stackrel{?}{=} \frac{18}{20}$ ______

11. $\frac{5}{13} \stackrel{?}{=} \frac{2}{6}$ ______

12. $\frac{4}{28} \stackrel{?}{=} \frac{2}{14}$ ______

13. $\frac{12}{9} \stackrel{?}{=} \frac{4}{3}$ ______

14. $\frac{18}{16} \stackrel{?}{=} \frac{45}{40}$ ______

15. $\frac{19}{18} \stackrel{?}{=} \frac{9}{8}$ ______

Solve each proportion.

16. $\frac{k}{8} = \frac{14}{4}$ $k =$ ______

17. $\frac{u}{3} = \frac{10}{5}$ $u =$ ______

18. $\frac{14}{6} = \frac{d}{15}$ $d =$ ______

19. $\frac{5}{1} = \frac{m}{4}$ $m =$ ______

20. $\frac{36}{32} = \frac{n}{8}$ $n =$ ______

21. $\frac{5}{30} = \frac{1}{x}$ $x =$ ______

22. $\frac{t}{4} = \frac{5}{10}$ $t =$ ______

23. $\frac{9}{2} = \frac{v}{4}$ $v =$ ______

24. $\frac{x}{10} = \frac{6}{4}$ $x =$ ______

25. $\frac{8}{12} = \frac{2}{b}$ $b =$ ______

26. $\frac{v}{15} = \frac{4}{6}$ $v =$ ______

27. $\frac{3}{18} = \frac{2}{s}$ $s =$ ______

28. The 1991 income for a typical 8-acre cotton farm was \$3040. Estimate the income for a 13-acre cotton farm. ______

29. A 150-pound person contains about 97.5 pounds of the element oxygen. Estimate the amount of oxygen in a 216-pound person. ______

Name ______________________________

Practice

Section 6B Review

1. Complete the table with equivalent ratios. Then write four proportions using ratios in the table.

8	16	24			
11					

____

____

Decide whether each pair of ratios forms a proportion.

2. $\frac{14}{2} \stackrel{?}{=} \frac{35}{5}$ ______________

3. $\frac{2}{6} \stackrel{?}{=} \frac{7}{18}$ ______________

Solve each proportion.

4. $\frac{35}{30} = \frac{28}{j}$ $j =$ ______

5. $\frac{8}{20} = \frac{d}{5}$ $d =$ ______

6. $\frac{1}{x} = \frac{5}{10}$ $x =$ ______

7. $\frac{16}{n} = \frac{40}{15}$ $n =$ ______

8. Make a scatterplot to see if the relationship is proportional.

Boys	5	9	13	17
Girls	4	7	10	13

____

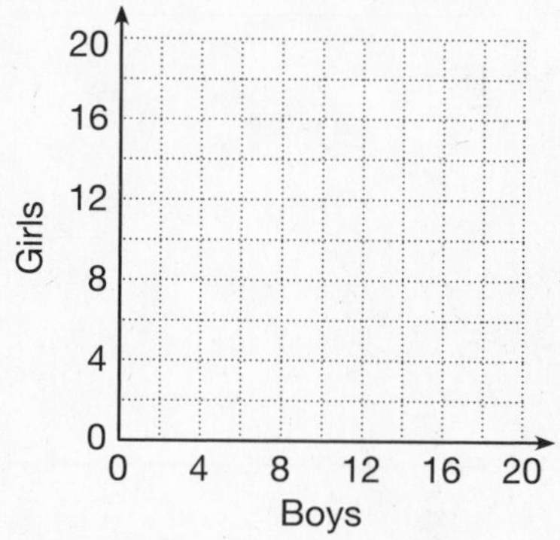

9. A certain brand of pen is priced at 5 for \$2.90. Find the unit price. Then tell how many pens you can buy for \$10.44. ______________

10. In 1991, the average household received 10 mail-order catalogs every 26 days. How many catalogs did the average household receive in 91 days? ______________

For Exercises 11–12, use the picture showing the approximate shape of Samuel Crawford Memorial Park in Dallas, Texas.

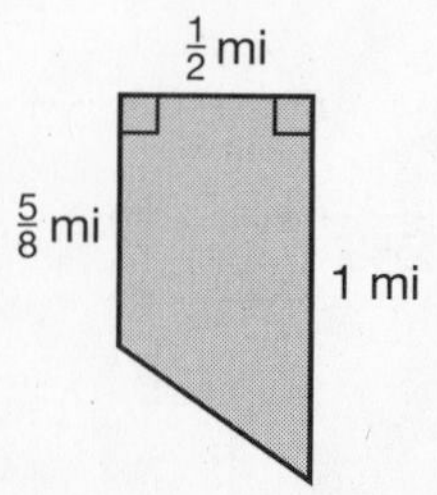

11. The perimeter of the polygon is $2\frac{3}{4}$ mi. Write and solve an equation to find the length of the unknown side. *[Lesson 4-3]*

____

12. Classify the polygon in as many ways as you can. *[Lesson 5-3]*

____

Name ______________________

Practice

Cumulative Review Chapters 1–6

Express each fraction in lowest terms. *[Lesson 3-8]*

1. $\frac{27}{72}$ ________ **2.** $\frac{12}{18}$ ________ **3.** $\frac{20}{28}$ ________ **4.** $\frac{21}{70}$ ________

5. $\frac{24}{52}$ ________ **6.** $\frac{32}{88}$ ________ **7.** $\frac{45}{90}$ ________ **8.** $\frac{48}{120}$ ________

Find each sum or difference. *[Lesson 4-3]*

9. $2\frac{1}{2} + 7\frac{3}{4}$ ________ **10.** $8\frac{2}{3} - 5\frac{1}{9}$ ________ **11.** $7\frac{1}{6} + 4\frac{1}{2}$ ________

12. $7\frac{3}{8} - 1\frac{3}{4}$ ________ **13.** $6\frac{4}{7} + 9\frac{5}{7}$ ________ **14.** $4\frac{2}{5} - 2\frac{7}{10}$ ________

15. $\frac{15}{16} + 3\frac{5}{8}$ ________ **16.** $14\frac{5}{7} - 8\frac{1}{2}$ ________ **17.** $6\frac{5}{9} + 3\frac{7}{11}$ ________

Use the figure to name each pair of angles or lines if it is possible. *[Lesson 5-2]*

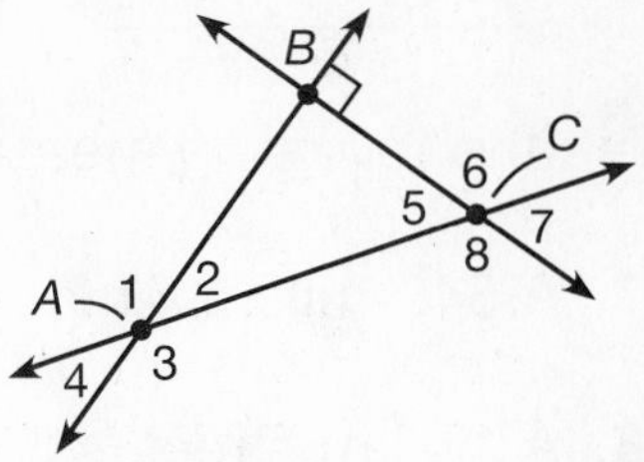

18. a pair of parallel lines ________

19. a pair of perpendicular lines ________

20. a pair of vertical angles ________

21. a pair of supplementary angles ________

Consumer Use unit prices to find the better buy. Underline the correct choice. *[Lesson 6-2]*

22. Used books: $1.00 for 5 books or $1.47 for 7 books

23. Candied apples: $9.60 for 8 apples or $7.32 for 6 apples

24. Ribbon: $2.82 for 60 ft or $3.68 for 80 ft

25. Baseball cards: $8.19 for 7 cards or $12.98 for 11 cards

Solve each proportion. *[Lesson 6-8]*

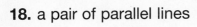

26. $\frac{3}{7} = \frac{x}{21}$ $x =$ ________ **27.** $\frac{n}{16} = \frac{15}{24}$ $n =$ ________ **28.** $\frac{6}{u} = \frac{14}{35}$ $u =$ ________ **29.** $\frac{42}{24} = \frac{28}{r}$ $r =$ ________

Name ______________________________

Practice
7-1

Measurement: Estimating Actual and Scale Distances

Write each scale in two other ways.

1. 1 in. : 25 mi ______________________

2. 3 cm = 100 km ______________________

3. $\frac{\text{2 in.}}{\text{17 mi}}$ ______________________

4. 5 cm : 8 km ______________________

5. 4 in. = 21 mi ______________________

6. $\frac{\text{1 cm}}{\text{85 km}}$ ______________________

Use the following measurements to find the scale of each map.

7. A 540-mile river is 10 inches long. ______________

8. A 15-km street is 3 cm long. ______________

9. A 2-mile-wide park is 5 inches wide. ______________

10. A 390-km freeway is 13 cm long. ______________

11. A 375-km railroad route is 15 cm long. ______________

Geography Estimate each map distance.

12. Dallas, Texas, is 803 miles from Chicago, Illinois. About how far apart will these cities appear on a map with scale 1 in. = 40 mi? ______________

13. Shanghai, China, is 1229 km from Hong Kong. About how far apart will these cities appear on a map with scale 1 cm : 500 km? ______________

14. **Science** The largest scale model of our solar system features a "Sun" at the Lakeview Museum in Peoria, Illinois. "Jupiter" is located about 20,600 feet away from the museum. The actual distance between the Sun and Jupiter is about 480,000,000 miles. Estimate the scale of the model solar system. ______________

 Use with pages 324–327.

Name ____________________

Practice 7-2

Calculating with Scales

Measure the scale drawing and find the length of the locomotive for each scale.

1. 1 cm = 1 m ________

2. 1 cm = 0.7 m ________

3. 2 cm = 1 m ________

4. 4 cm = 5 m ________

5. 5 cm = 4 m ________

A scale drawing of a house is 5 in. long. Use each scale to find the actual length of the house.

6. 1 in. = 8 ft ________ **7.** 1 in. = $9\frac{1}{2}$ ft ________ **8.** 1 in. = 18 ft ________

9. 1 in. = 15 ft ________ **10.** 1 in. = $6\frac{1}{4}$ ft ________ **11.** 1 in. = 14.3 ft ________

12. 2 in. = 17 ft ________ **13.** 1 in. = $12\frac{3}{4}$ ft ________ **14.** 4 in. = 35 ft ________

Solve for *x* in each proportion.

15. $\frac{3\text{ in.}}{5\text{ft}} = \frac{x}{10\text{ ft}}$ $x =$ ________

16. $\frac{8\text{ cm}}{20\text{ m}} = \frac{2\text{ cm}}{x}$ $x =$ ________

17. $\frac{9\text{ in.}}{6\text{ mi}} = \frac{x}{2\text{ mi}}$ $x =$ ________

18. $\frac{15\text{ cm}}{3\text{ km}} = \frac{20\text{ cm}}{x}$ $x =$ ________

19. $\frac{3\text{ cm}}{9\text{ m}} = \frac{4\text{ cm}}{x}$ $x =$ ________

20. $\frac{9\text{ in.}}{10\text{ ft}} = \frac{27\text{ in.}}{x}$ $x =$ ________

21. $\frac{30\text{ cm}}{9\text{ km}} = \frac{x}{12\text{ km}}$ $x =$ ________

22. $\frac{8\text{ in.}}{x} = \frac{12\text{ in.}}{3\text{ mi}}$ $x =$ ________

23. $\frac{x}{40\text{ ft}} = \frac{20\text{ in.}}{32\text{ ft}}$ $x =$ ________

24. $\frac{9\text{ cm}}{12\text{ km}} = \frac{15\text{ cm}}{x}$ $x =$ ________

25. $\frac{x}{21\text{ mi}} = \frac{81\text{ in.}}{7\text{ mi}}$ $x =$ ________

26. $\frac{45\text{ cm}}{x} = \frac{27\text{ cm}}{30\text{ m}}$ $x =$ ________

27. Science For a science project, Lucinda built a model of Hawaii's Hualalai volcano using a scale of 3 in. : 1000 ft. If the model was $24\frac{3}{4}$ in. high, how high is the actual volcano? ________

28. Geography Thomas has a map of Europe that uses a scale of 1 cm = 50 km. He has found that London, England, and Berlin, Germany, are 18.6 cm apart on this map. What is the actual distance between these cities? ________

Name ______________________________

Practice 7-3

Problem Solving Using Maps

Margaret left home at 8:00 A.M. and traveled 120 miles. Find her arrival time for each of the following speeds.

1. 30 mi/hr ________ **2.** 45 mi/hr ________ **3.** 72 mi/hr ________

4. 40 mi/hr ________ **5.** 60 mi/hr ________ **6.** 50 mi/hr ________

7. After a camping trip, Anh drove 75 miles home at a rate of 60 mi/hr. If he arrived home at 8:30 P.M., what time did he begin his drive? ________

8. Scott drove 115 miles from Cleveland, Ohio to Pittsburgh, Pennsylvania, at a rate of 69 mi/hr. If he arrived in Pittsburgh at 11:30 A.M., what time did he leave Cleveland? ________

9. Carol and Mike have decided to go see a movie that is playing tonight at 9:00 P.M. at both Cinema Six and Acme Theater. Cinema Six is 20 miles away on the freeway, where the speed limit is 60 mi/hr. Acme Theater is only 10 miles away, but the speed limit on the road to Acme Theater is 25 mi/hr.

a. Which theater should they choose if they want to get there in the shortest time? Explain how you decided.

____

____

b. What time do they need to leave to get to the theater you chose in part a? ________

10. The Yamada family plans to go to a ball game at 7:30 P.M. They drive 45 mi/hr on Atlantic Parkway.

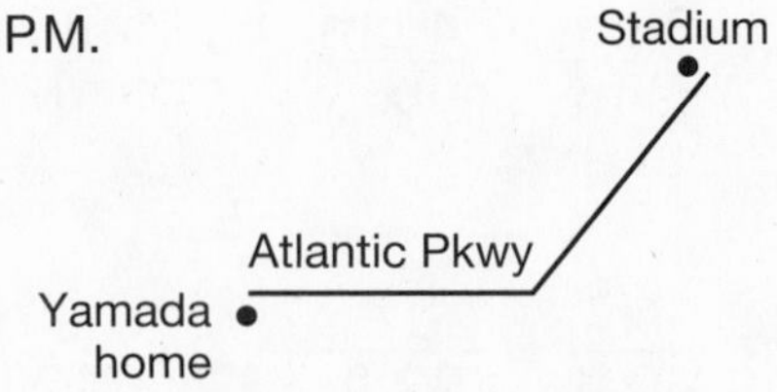

Scale: 1 in. = 16 mi

a. What is the distance from home to the stadium?

____

b. How long will it take them to get from home to the stadium? ________

c. When do they need to leave to get to the stadium at 7:30 P.M.? ________

11. Howard plans to drive from Seattle, Washington, to Portland, Oregon, a road distance of 172 miles. He needs to be in Portland by 11:45 A.M. If he drives at a rate of 60 mi/hr, what is the latest time he can leave Seattle? ________

Name ________________________________

Practice
7-4

Creating Scale Drawings and Scale Models

The Statue of Liberty is 152 ft tall. Find the maximum scale you can use for a model of the Statue of Liberty if the model must fit in a:

1. room with an 8-foot ceiling ________

2. 4-inch tall toy box ________

3. 12-foot-tall crate ________

4. hotel lobby with a 38-ft ceiling ________

5. Determine an appropriate scale to make a scale drawing of this figure on an $8\frac{1}{2}$-in. × 11-in. sheet of paper. Then make the scale drawing on a separate sheet of paper.

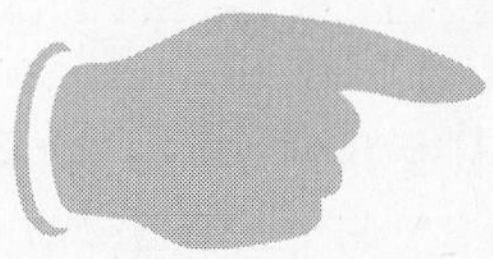

____

6. Geography Utah is approximately 275 miles from east to west and 350 miles from north to south. What is the largest scale that can be used to fit a map of Utah on an $8\frac{1}{2}$-in. × 11-in. sheet of paper, if:

a. the 11-in. side runs north-south

____

b. the $8\frac{1}{2}$-in. side runs north-south

____

7. A $3\frac{1}{2}$-in. × 5-in. photograph is enlarged to a 28-in. × 40 in. poster. What is the scale of the poster? ________

8. A painting measures 45 cm × 55 cm. What is the largest scale that can be used to create a print of this painting if the print must fit in a 20-cm × 25-cm frame? ________

9. Estimate the scale of the map whose scale of miles is shown.

____

10. A postage stamp measures $\frac{7}{8}$ in. × 1 in. Find the largest scale that can be used to make an enlargement of the stamp on a 3-in. × 5-in. note card. ________

11. Determine an appropriate scale to make a scale drawing of this figure on a 4-in. × 6-in. note card. Then make the scale drawing on a separate sheet of paper.

____

Name ______________________________

Practice

Section 7A Review

Give two other ways to write each scale.

1. 2 cm : 5 km

2. 3 in. = 40 mi

3. $\frac{1 \text{ cm}}{250 \text{ km}}$

4. 4 in. : 50 mi

Use the following measurements to find the scale of each map.

5. A 15-mi road is 4 in. long. ______________

6. A 120-km river is 6 cm long. ______________

7. Measure the height of the gingerbread man shown. Find the height of the actual cookie for each of the following scales.

a. 1 in. = 2 in. ________ **b.** 1 in. = 5 in. ________

c. 1 in. = $6\frac{1}{2}$ in. ________ **d.** 3 in. = 2 ft ________

8. The Transamerica Pyramid in San Francisco, California, is 260 m tall. If a model of this building uses a scale of 5 cm = 13 m, how tall is the model? ______________

9. Peter has both an LP and a CD copy of his favorite album. The LP cover art measures $12\frac{3}{8}$ in. on each side. The CD insert measures $4\frac{3}{4}$ in. on each side.

a. Estimate the scale if the LP cover is viewed as an enlarged copy of the CD insert. ______________

b. Estimate the scale if the CD insert is viewed as a reduced copy of the LP cover. ______________

10. A tree trunk makes an angle of 72° with the ground. A pole making an angle of 55° with the ground is used to support the tree. What angle does the pole make with the tree? *[Lesson 5-3]*

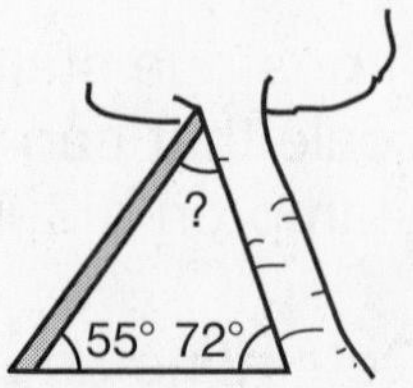

____

11. Health The average secretary burns 88 calories every 60 minutes while working. How many calories are burned in 21 minutes? *[Lesson 6-3]* ______________

Name ____________________

Practice 7-5

Choosing Appropriate Rates and Units

Suggest appropriate units for each rate.
You may use the same units more than once.

1. The speed of a roller coaster ________

2. The rate at which water comes out of a hose ________

3. The rate at which a child grows ________

4. The amount of music a radio station plays ________

Give a unit rate that describes each situation.

5. 200 miles in 4 hours ________

6. 80 students for 16 computers ________

7. $96.00 for 12 hours of work ________

8. 42 books shared by 14 people ________

Do the rates in each pair have the same meaning? Write *yes* or *no*.

9. $\frac{15\text{ mi}}{\text{hr}}, \frac{15\text{ hr}}{\text{mi}}$ ________

10. $\frac{\$5.00}{\text{hr}}, \frac{0.2\text{ hr}}{\text{dollar}}$ ________

11. $\frac{3\text{ cats}}{\text{dog}}, \frac{\frac{1}{3}\text{ dog}}{\text{cat}}$ ________

12. $\frac{12\text{ in.}}{\text{ft}}, \frac{\frac{1}{12}\text{ ft}}{\text{in.}}$ ________

13. $\frac{2\text{ oz}}{\text{cookie}}, \frac{\frac{1}{2}\text{ oz}}{\text{cookie}}$ ________

14. $\frac{1\text{ ft}}{\text{sec}}, \frac{1\text{ sec}}{\text{ft}}$ ________

For each rate, give a reciprocal unit rate that has the same meaning.

15. $\frac{4\text{ tomatoes}}{\text{lb}}$ ________

16. $\frac{100\text{ beats}}{\text{min}}$ ________

17. $\frac{20\text{ mi}}{\text{hr}}$ ________

18. $\frac{0.08\text{ hr}}{\text{dollar}}$ ________

19. $\frac{\frac{1}{8}\text{ teacher}}{\text{student}}$ ________

20. $\frac{40\text{ gal}}{\text{min}}$ ________

21. The average American worker needs to work about $\frac{1}{2}$ hour to earn enough money to buy a Barbie doll. Is this rate equivalent to 2 Barbie dolls per hour? ________

22. In 1990, there were, on the average, about 2.5 persons per American household. Find the number of households per person. ________

Name ______________________________

Practice 7-6

Converting Units

Write two conversion factors involving each pair of units. (Use the chart on page 346 of your textbook if you do not remember how some of these units compare.)

1. feet, yards ____________
2. minutes, seconds ____________
3. meters, kilometers ____________
4. fluid ounces, cups ____________
5. weeks, days ____________
6. tons, pounds ____________
7. ounces, pounds ____________
8. minutes, hours ____________
9. gallons, quarts ____________
10. miles, feet ____________

Convert each quantity to the given units. (Use the chart on page 346 of your textbook if you do not remember how some of these units compare.)

11. 5.8 meters to centimeters ________
12. 21 days to hours ________
13. 63 feet to inches ________
14. 45 kilometers to meters ________
15. 150 hours to minutes ________
16. 487 grams to kilograms ________
17. 93 yards to feet ________
18. 360 hours to days ________
19. 24 fluid ounces to cups ________
20. 21 gallons to quarts ________
21. 1500 pounds to tons ________
22. 78 inches to feet ________
23. 2.5 kilograms to grams ________
24. 165 centimeters to meters ________
25. 49 days to weeks ________
26. 64 gallons to fluid ounces ________
27. United States farms produced 2,460,000,000 bushels of soybeans in 1994. How many quarts is this? (A bushel is 32 quarts.) ________
28. In 1994, Brian Berg set a record by building an 81-story "house" using standard playing cards. The house was $15\frac{2}{3}$ ft tall. How many inches is this? ________

Name ____________________

Practice 7-7

Problem Solving: Converting Rates

Convert each rate to an equivalent rate.

1. 35 pounds per minute to pounds per hour ____________
2. $72.00 per hour to dollars per minute ____________
3. 75 feet per second to feet per minute ____________
4. 2.54 centimeters per inch to meters per inch ____________
5. 90 quarts per hour to quarts per minute ____________
6. 28.35 grams per ounce to grams per pound ____________
7. 7.2 inches per second to feet per second ____________
8. $1.44 per gallon to cents per quart ____________
9. $8.00 per pound to dollars per ounce ____________

Science Use conversion factors to complete the table.

	Name of Animal	Maximum Speed (mi/hr)	Maximum Speed (ft/sec)
10.	Elk	45	
11.	Grizzly bear		44
12.	Spider	1.17	
13.	Three-toed sloth		0.22
14.	Squirrel	12	

15. The average North American consumes about 26 barrels of petroleum per year, and the average African consumes about one barrel of petroleum per year. Convert these rates to gallons per day. (One barrel is 42 gallons.)

North America: ____________

Africa: ____________

16. In 1994, American farmers produced 133.8 bushels of corn per acre of corn crops. Convert this rate to pecks per square foot. (A bushel is equal to 4 pecks, and an acre is equal to 43,560 square feet.)

____

Name ______________________________

Practice

Section 7B Review

Suggest appropriate units for each rate.

1. The rate at which someone mows a lawn ____________

2. The rate of pay for a secretary ____________

3. A craftsman made 18 flower pots in 6 days. Write two unit rates that describe this situation. Is one of your rates more useful?

____

Do the rates in each pair have the same meaning? Write *yes* or *no*.

4. $\frac{25\text{ gal}}{\text{min}}, \frac{25\text{ min}}{\text{gal}}$ ______

5. $\frac{\$1.60}{\text{hr}}, \frac{0.625\text{ hr}}{\text{dollar}}$ ______

6. $\frac{100\text{ L}}{\text{day}}, \frac{0.01\text{ day}}{\text{L}}$ ______

7. $\frac{40\text{ mi}}{\text{hr}}, \frac{0.025\text{ hr}}{\text{mi}}$ ______

8. $\frac{5\text{ tons}}{\text{week}}, \frac{\frac{1}{5}\text{ ton}}{\text{week}}$ ______

9. $\frac{\$4.00}{\text{ft}}, \frac{\frac{1}{4}\text{ ft}}{\text{dollar}}$ ______

Convert each quantity to the given units.

10. 6.42 kilograms to grams ______

11. 12 centimeters to meters ______

12. 64 fluid ounces to quarts ______

13. 45 hours to seconds ______

Convert each rate to an equivalent rate.

14. 24 ounces per minute to pounds per minute ____________

15. $2.50 per minute to dollars per hour ____________

16. 21 pounds per foot to pounds per inch ____________

17. The average American eats 150 pounds of canned food per year. Convert this rate to ounces per day. ____________

18. A steel shelving unit uses a diagonal brace to prevent wobbling. Find the length of the brace. *[Lesson 5-7]* ____________

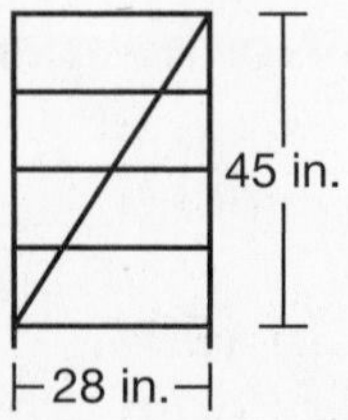

19. Fine Arts Pablo Picasso produced about 13,500 paintings during his 78-year career. Assuming that he painted at a consistent rate for his entire career, estimate the number of paintings he produced during the last 12 years. *[Lesson 6-7]* ____________

Name ______________________________

Practice 7-8

Creating and Exploring Similar Figures

Tell if the figures are similar. If they are, write a similarity statement using ~ and give the scale factor. If they're not, explain why not.

1. ______________________

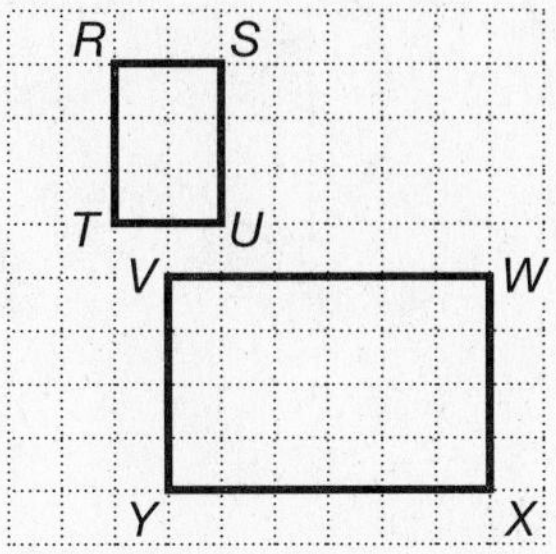

2. ______________________

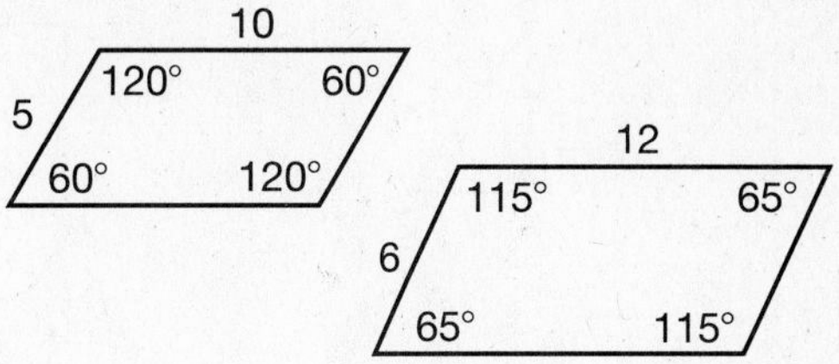

3. ______________________

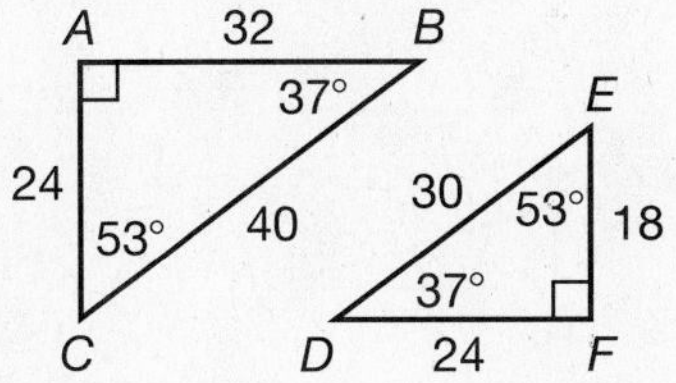

4. ______________________

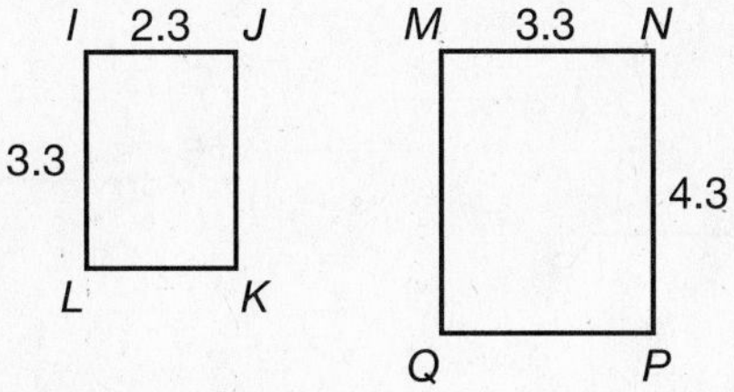

5. Draw two rhombuses that are similar and two that are not similar.

Similar: Not Similar:

6. Suppose $ABCD \sim FEHG$. If $m\angle A = 86°$, $m\angle B = 113°$, $m\angle C = 90°$, and $m\angle D = 71°$, find the measures of $\angle E$, $\angle F$, $\angle G$, and $\angle H$.

$m\angle E =$ ______ $m\angle F =$ ______ $m\angle G =$ ______ $m\angle H =$ ______

7. The One Liberty Place building in Philadelphia, Pennsylvania, is 945 feet tall. A model of this building used in a movie set is 18 inches tall. Find the scale factor of the model to the real building.

____

8. Fine Arts Leonardo da Vinci's famous painting, the *Mona Lisa*, measures 53 cm × 77.5 cm. Suppose a postcard reproduction of the painting measures 12 cm × 17 cm. Is the postcard similar to the original? Explain.

____

Name ____________________

Practice 7-9

Finding Measures of Similar Figures

Find x in each pair of similar figures.

1. $\triangle UVW \sim \triangle XYZ$

$x =$ ________

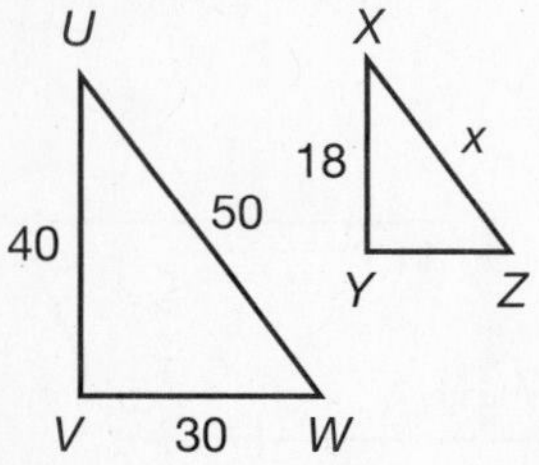

2. $JKLM \sim QRST$

$x =$ ________

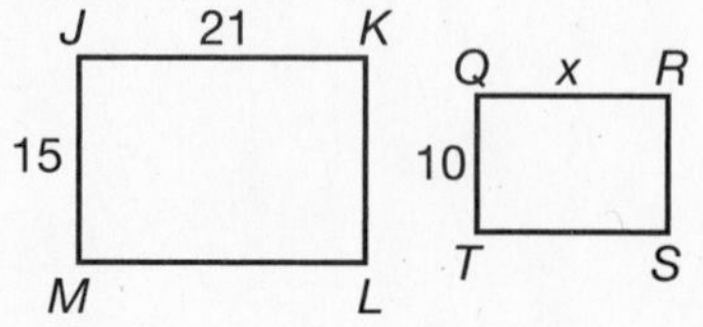

3. $\triangle DEF \sim \triangle GHI$

$x =$ ________

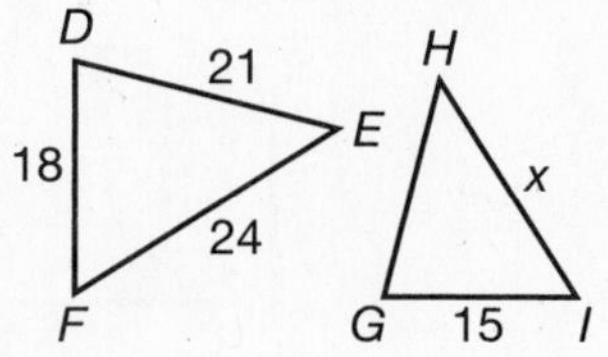

Find the missing side lengths in each pair of similar figures.

4. $\triangle PQR \sim \triangle STU$

$a =$ ______ $b =$ ______

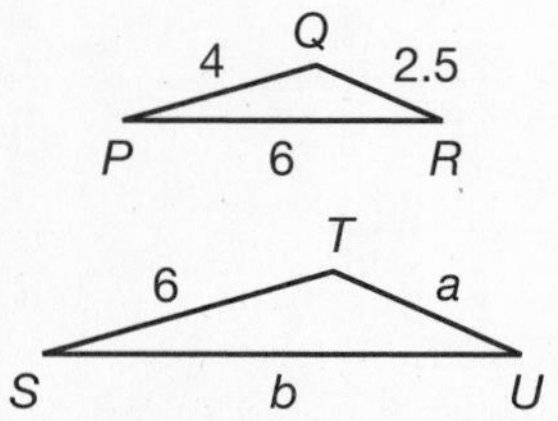

5. $EFGH \sim QRST$

$c =$ ____ $d =$ ____ $e =$ ____

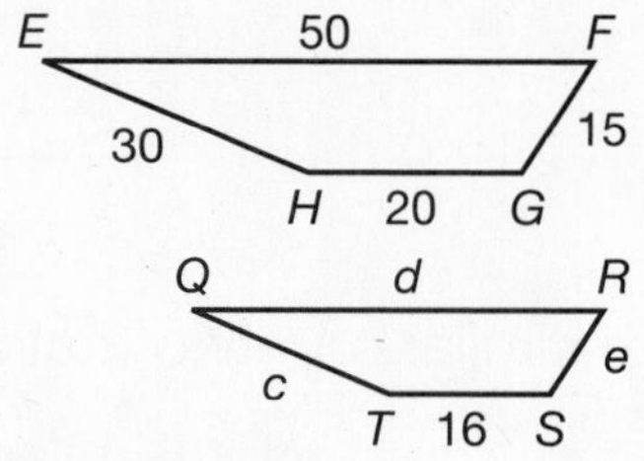

6. $\triangle ABC \sim \triangle DEF$

$m =$ ______ $n =$ ______

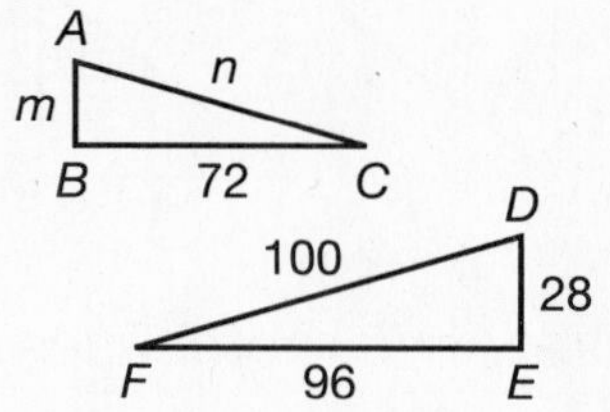

7. $ABCD \sim WXYZ$

$k =$ ______

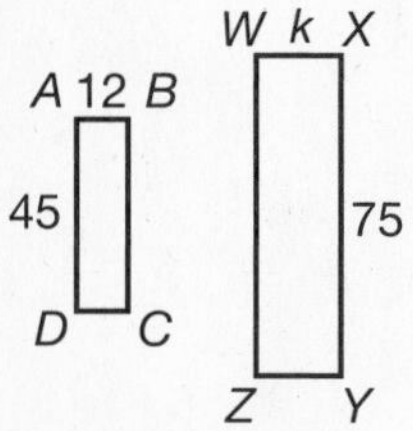

8. $GHIJ \sim KLMN$

$r =$ ____ $s =$ ____ $t =$ ____

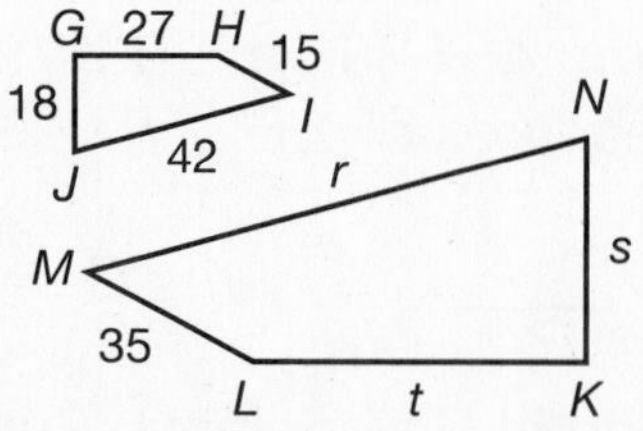

9. $\triangle JKL \sim \triangle UVW$

$x =$ ______ $y =$ ______

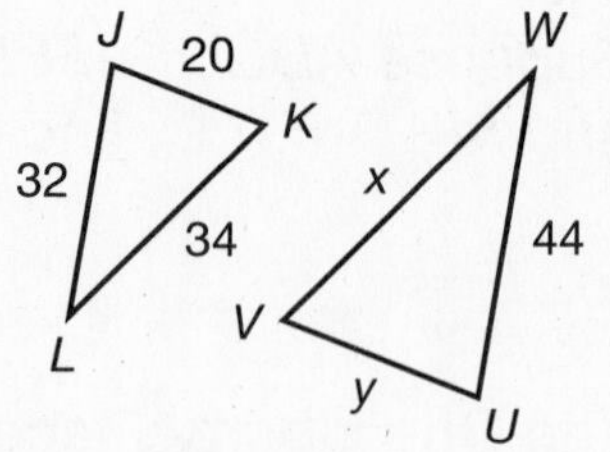

10. On a sunny day, if a 36-inch yardstick casts a 21-inch shadow, how tall is a building whose shadow is 168 ft? ____________

11. Geography Oregon is about 400 miles from west to east, and 300 miles from north to south. If a map of Oregon is 15 inches tall (from north to south), about how wide is the map? ____________

12. The Grand Coulee Dam on the Columbia River, Washington, is 4173 ft long and 550 ft high. If a scale model of the dam used in a movie is 16 ft high, how long is the model? ____________

Name ______________________________

Practice
7-10

Perimeters and Areas of Similar Figures

Predict the ratio of the areas of each pair of similar figures. Check your predictions by calculating the areas.

1. scale factor 3

area ratio = ________

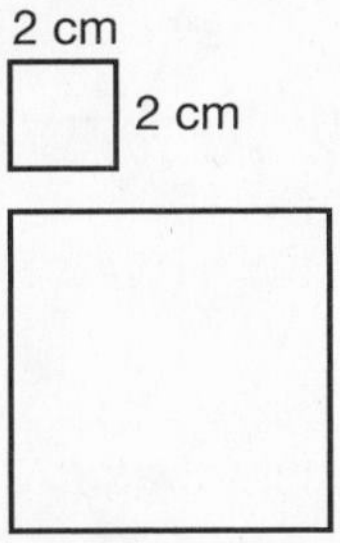

2. scale factor $\frac{1}{2}$

area ratio = ________

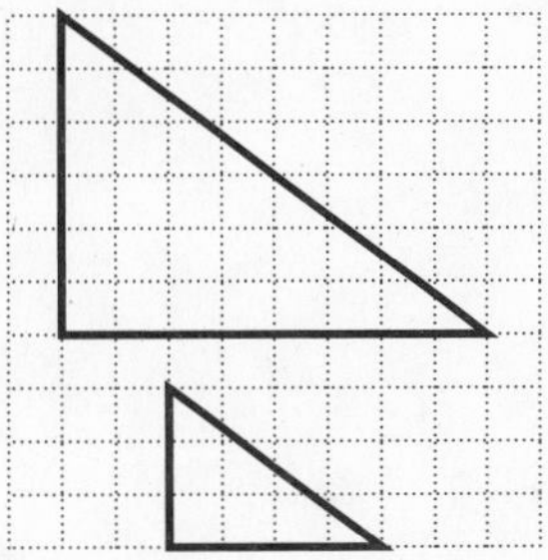

3. scale factor $\frac{4}{3}$

area ratio = ________

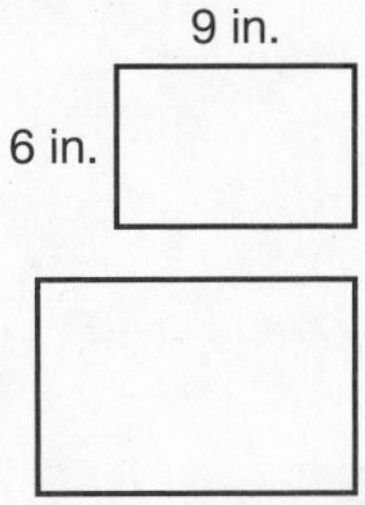

Suppose two figures are similar.

4. scale factor = 4, perimeter of smaller = 30 in.; area of smaller = 22 in^2
Find the perimeter and area of the larger figure.

perimeter = ______________ area = ______________

5. scale factor = $\frac{5}{3}$, perimeter of larger = 24 m; area of larger = 20 m^2
Find the perimeter and area of the smaller figure.

perimeter = ______________ area = ______________

Perimeter and area ratios of similar figures are given. Find each scale factor.

6. perimeter ratio = 81

scale factor = ________

7. area ratio = 16

scale factor = ________

8. perimeter ratio = 100

scale factor = ________

9. A common postage stamp has perimeter $3\frac{3}{4}$ in. and area $\frac{7}{8}$ in. Find the perimeter and area of a scale drawing of this stamp if the scale factor is 8.

perimeter = ______________ area = ______________

10. All circles are similar. The diameter of a long-playing record is about $\frac{5}{2}$ times the diameter of a compact disc. If the area of a compact disc is about 115 cm^2, estimate the area of a record.

____

Name ______________________________

Practice

Section 7C Review

Tell if the figures are similar. If they are, write a similarity statement using ~ and give the scale factor. If they're not, explain why not.

1. ______________________

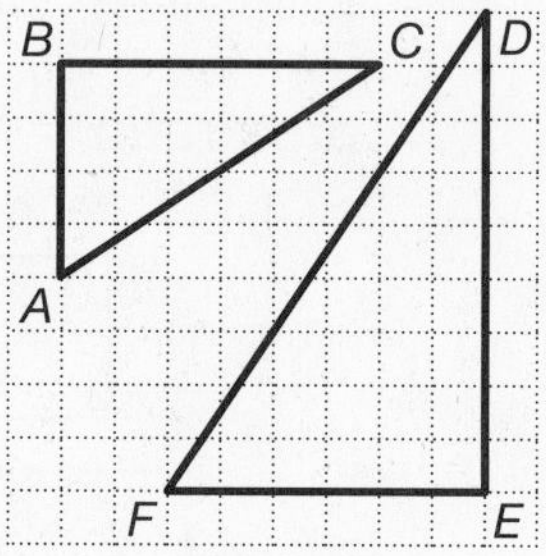

2. ______________________

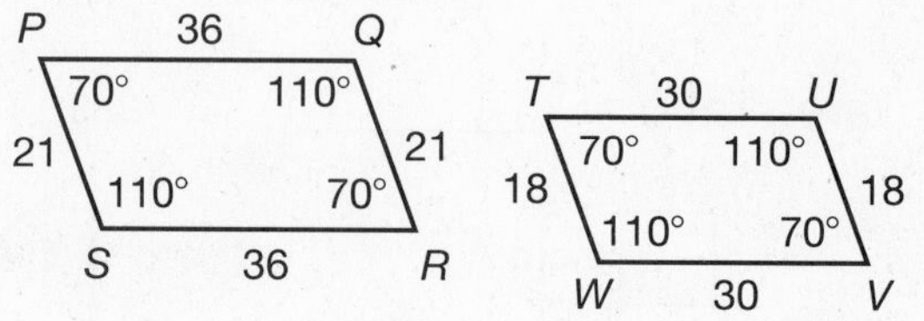

Find x in each pair of similar figures.

3. $DEFG \sim HIJK$; x = ______________

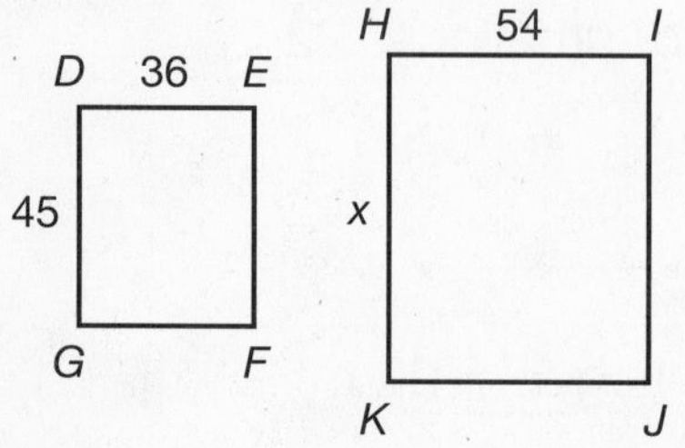

4. $PQRS \sim TUVW$; x = ______________

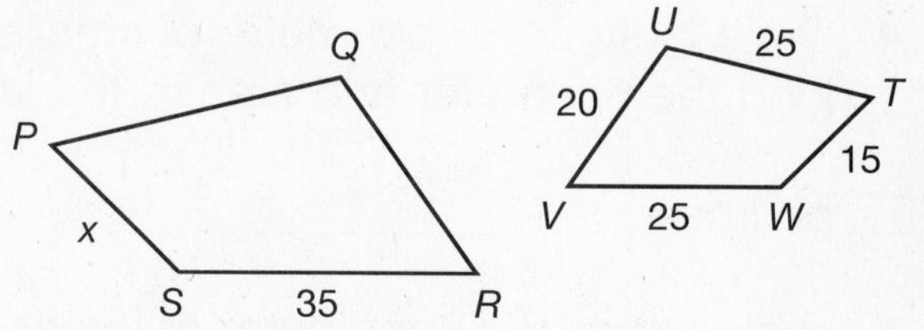

5. Two triangles are similar, and the scale factor is $\frac{3}{7}$. The perimeter of the larger triangle is 210 m, and its area is 2940 m^2. Find the perimeter and area of the smaller triangle.

perimeter = ______________ area = ______________

6. **Health** An ounce of garbanzo beans contains about 0.835 mg of iron. Write and solve an equation to find the number of ounces of garbanzo beans you would need to eat to obtain the recommended daily allowance of 18 mg. *[Lesson 3-4]*

____

7. The figure at the right shows the approximate shape of Nebraska. Use the figure to find the approximate area of Nebraska. *[Lesson 5-10]*

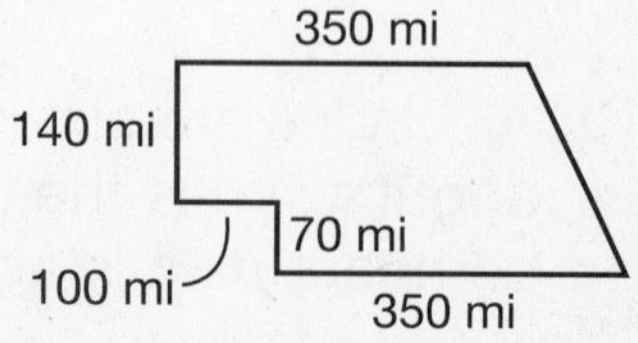

____

Name ______________________________

Practice

Cumulative Review Chapters 1–7

Find the GCF and LCM. *[Lesson 3-7]*

1. 57, 76 GCF: _____ LCM: _____

2. 60, 100 GCF: _____ LCM: _____

3. 84,144 GCF: _____ LCM: _____

4. 25, 35 GCF: _____ LCM: _____

5. 64, 112 GCF: _____ LCM: _____

6. 126, 56 GCF: _____ LCM: _____

Solve each equation. *[Lesson 4-3]*

7. $t - 4\frac{6}{7} = 3\frac{2}{7}$

$t =$ _______

8. $c - 2\frac{1}{2} = 5\frac{3}{7}$

$c =$ _______

9. $p - 3\frac{2}{9} = 21\frac{4}{9}$

$p =$ _______

10. $u + 12\frac{1}{6} = 21\frac{19}{24}$

$u =$ _______

Classify each figure in as many ways as you can. *[Lesson 5-3]*

11. ____________________
____

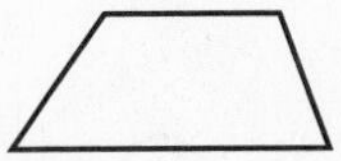

12. ____________________
____

13. ____________________
____

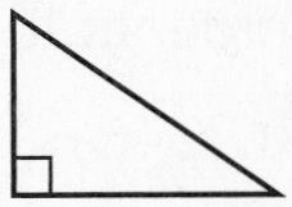

A model train is 30 in. long. Use each scale to find the length of the actual train. *[Lesson 7-2]*

14. scale: 1 in. = 8 ft

actual length: _______

15. scale: 1 in. = 12 ft

actual length: _______

16. scale: 2 in. = 15 ft

actual length: _______

Find the missing side lengths in each pair of similar figures. *[Lesson 7-9]*

17. *ABCD* ~ *EFGH*

$x =$ _______

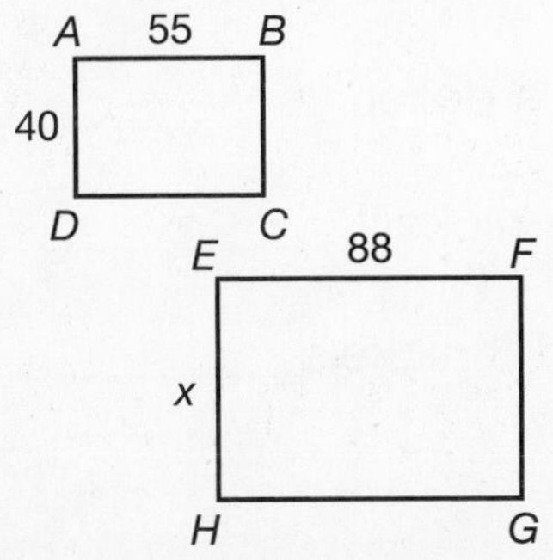

18. $\triangle IJK \sim \triangle LMN$

$p =$ ____ $q =$ ____

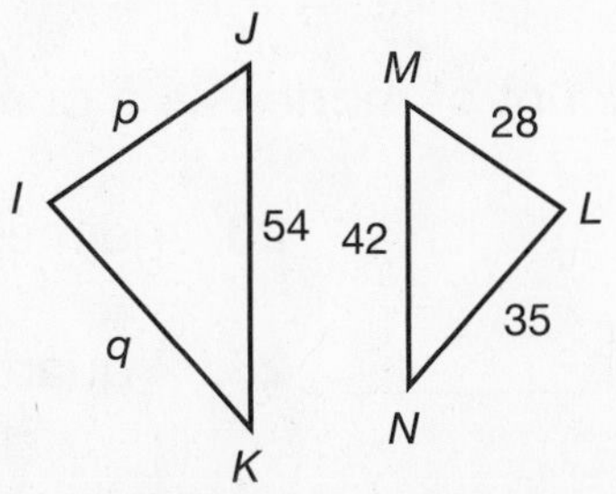

19. *PQRS* ~ *TUVW*

$a =$ ___ $b =$ ___ $c =$ ___

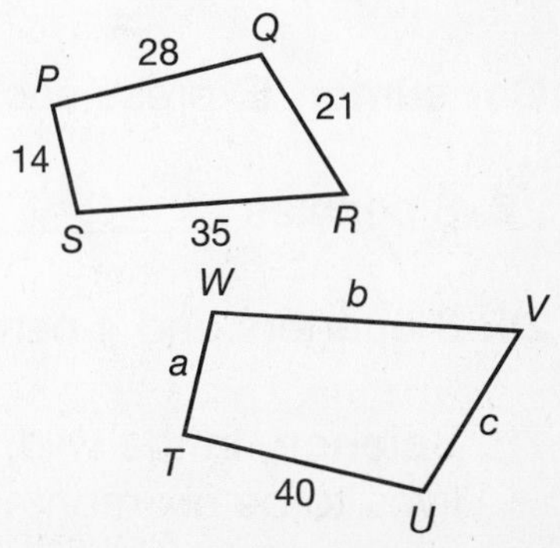

Name ______________________________

Practice 8-1

Understanding Percents

Express each fraction as a percent.

1. $\frac{21}{100}$ ________ 2. $\frac{38}{100}$ ________ 3. $\frac{7}{10}$ ________ 4. $\frac{11}{20}$ ________

5. $\frac{9}{25}$ ________ 6. $\frac{21}{50}$ ________ 7. $\frac{3.7}{25}$ ________ 8. $\frac{18.2}{25}$ ________

Use percents to compare.

9. $\frac{1}{4}$ and $\frac{1}{5}$

____% ◯ ____%

10. $\frac{17}{20}$ and $\frac{22}{25}$

____% ◯ ____%

11. $\frac{3}{10}$ and $\frac{17}{50}$

____% ◯ ____ %

12. $\frac{7}{25}$ and $\frac{13}{50}$

____% ◯ ____%

13. $\frac{3}{4}$ and $\frac{19}{25}$

____% ◯ ____%

14. $\frac{13}{20}$ and $\frac{6}{10}$

____% ◯ ____ %

Use percents to compare the shaded areas on each grid.

15. ____% ◯ ____%

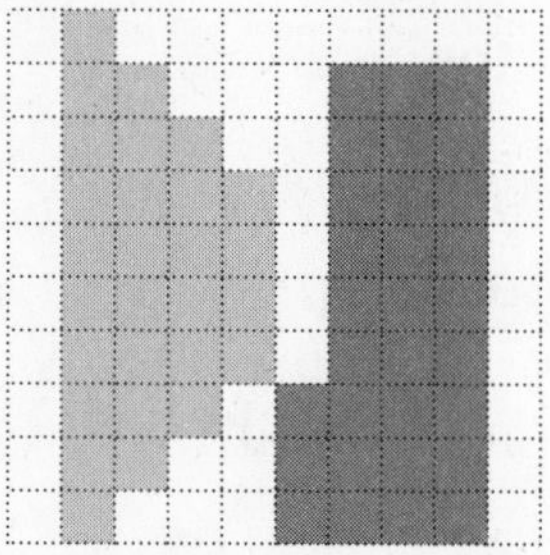

16. ____% ◯ ____%

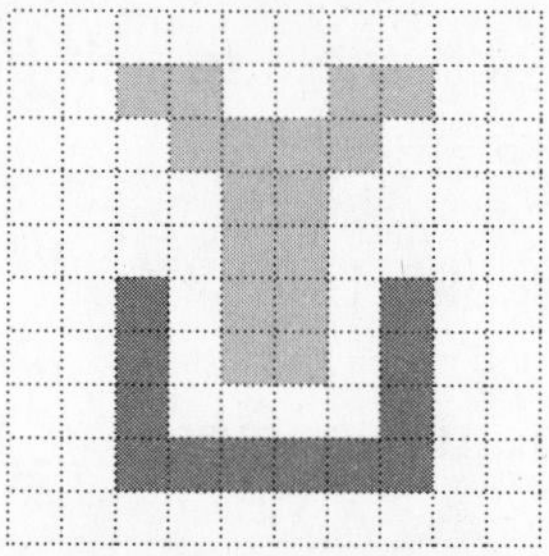

17. ____% ◯ ____ %

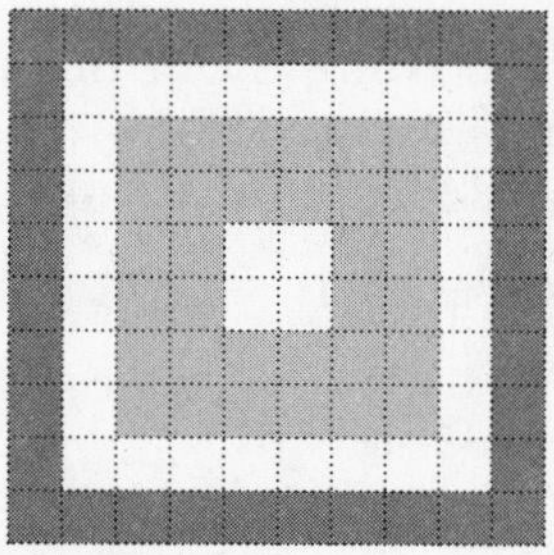

Measurement There are 100 cm in a meter. Express each length as a percent of a meter.

18. 5 cm ________ 19. 70 cm ________ 20. 48.5 cm ________ 21. 2.8 cm ________

Consumer Express each amount of money as a percent of a dollar.

22. 8 pennies ____________

23. 4 dimes and a nickel ____________

24. 3 quarters and 4 pennies ____________

25. 2 quarters and 3 nickels ____________

26. **Science** In the wild, only 1 out of 5 cottontail rabbits lives to be six months old. What percent is this? ____________

 Use with pages 386–389.

Name ______________________

Practice 8-2

Linking Fractions, Decimals, and Percents

Write each percent as a decimal.

1. 83% ______ **2.** 65% ______ **3.** 24% ______ **4.** 7% ______

5. 12.7% ______ **6.** 8.75% ______ **7.** $62\frac{1}{2}\%$ ______ **8.** $33\frac{1}{3}\%$ ______

9. 2.9% ______ **10.** 18.3% ______ **11.** 99% ______ **12.** $23\frac{1}{4}\%$ ______

Write each percent as a fraction in lowest terms.

13. 93% ______ **14.** 45% ______ **15.** 62% ______ **16.** 44% ______

17. 10% ______ **18.** 62.5% ______ **19.** 94% ______ **20.** 40% ______

21. 32% ______ **22.** 25% ______ **23.** 70% ______ **24.** 87.5% ______

Write each decimal as a percent.

25. 0.47 ______ **26.** 0.41 ______ **27.** 0.34 ______ **28.** 0.215 ______

29. 0.3 ______ **30.** 0.07 ______ **31.** 0.999 ______ **32.** 0.085 ______

Write each fraction as a percent. Where necessary, use a repeating decimal to help express your percent.

33. $\frac{2}{5}$ ______ **34.** $\frac{14}{25}$ ______ **35.** $\frac{11}{20}$ ______ **36.** $\frac{19}{50}$ ______

37. $\frac{17}{100}$ ______ **38.** $\frac{2}{3}$ ______ **39.** $\frac{7}{10}$ ______ **40.** $\frac{3}{5}$ ______

41. In 1994, there were 10,057 commercial radio stations in the United States. Of these, 926 stations were devoted to talk (including news, business, or sports). What percent of commercial radio stations were devoted to talk? ______

42. Geography The table lists the percent of the world's land in each continent. Express each percent as a fraction and a decimal.

Continent	Africa	Antarctica	Asia	Australia	Europe	N. America	S. America
Percent of total	20	9	30	5	7	16	9
Fraction							
Decimal							

Name ____________________

Practice 8-3

Percents Greater Than 100 or Less Than 1

Classify each of the following as: (A) less than 1%, (B) greater than 100%, or (C) between 1% and 100%.

1. $\frac{1}{2}$ ______ **2.** $\frac{4}{3}$ ______ **3.** $\frac{2}{300}$ ______ **4.** $\frac{3}{10}$ ______

5. 10.8 ______ **6.** 0.7 ______ **7.** 1.4 ______ **8.** 0.06 ______

9. 1.03 ______ **10.** 0.009 ______ **11.** 0.635 ______ **12.** 0.0053 ______

Use >, <, or = to compare the numbers in each pair.

13. $\frac{1}{4}$ ◯ 20% **14.** $\frac{1}{2}$% ◯ 50 **15.** 0.008 ◯ 8% **16.** 35% ◯ $\frac{3}{8}$

17. 150% ◯ $\frac{5}{4}$ **18.** 3 ◯ 300% **19.** $\frac{7}{250}$ ◯ 0.3% **20.** 650% ◯ 7

Write each fraction as a percent.

21. $\frac{7}{5}$ ______ **22.** $\frac{137}{100}$ ______ **23.** $\frac{0.8}{100}$ ______

24. $\frac{21}{4}$ ______ **25.** $\frac{17}{10}$ ______ **26.** $\frac{65}{40}$ ______

27. $\frac{37}{20}$ ______ **28.** $\frac{7}{500}$ ______ **29.** $\frac{9}{8}$ ______

Write each decimal as a percent.

30. 0.003 ______ **31.** 1.8 ______ **32.** 0.0025 ______

33. 5.3 ______ **34.** 0.0041 ______ **35.** 0.083 ______

36. 0.0009 ______ **37.** 0.83 ______ **38.** 20 ______

Write each percent as a decimal.

39. 175% ______ **40.** 120% ______ **41.** $\frac{2}{5}$% ______

42. $\frac{5}{8}$% ______ **43.** 750% ______ **44.** $8\frac{1}{4}$% ______

45. Social Science In 1990, the population of Kansas was 2,477,574, which included 21,965 Native Americans. What percent of the people living in Kansas were Native Americans? ______

46. Science The mass of Earth is $\frac{1}{318}$ of the mass of Jupiter. What percent is this? ______

 Use with pages 394–398.

Name ______________________

Practice
8-4

Finding a Percent of a Number

Find 50%, 10%, and 1% of each number.

1. 2,400 ______

2. 36 ______

3. 580 ______

4. 60 ______

5. 14,000 ______

6. 620 ______

7. 21 ______

8. 122 ______

Use mental math to find each percent of 4800.

9. 10% ______

10. 40% ______

11. 25% ______

12. 20% ______

13. 5% ______

14. 75% ______

15. 15% ______

16. 90% ______

Use mental math to find each percent.

17. 5% of 300 ______

18. 75% of 6000 ______

19. 20% of 800 ______

20. 60% of 700 ______

21. 40% of $90 ______

22. 10% of 450 ______

23. 50% of 28 ______

24. 30% of 200 ______

Estimate each answer.

25. 30% of 808 ______

26. 11% of 128 ______

27. 44% of 764 ______

28. 10% of 382 ______

29. 49% of 1737 ______

30. 62% of 923 ______

31. 71% of 416 ______

32. 15% of 620 ______

33. Social Science In 1993, 904,292 people immigrated to the United States. 7.3% of the immigrants came from mainland China. How many people immigrated to the U.S. from mainland China in 1993? ______

34. Science It is estimated that there are about 20,000 native plant species in the United States. About 21% of these species are threatened with extinction. How many native plant species are threatened with extinction? ______

Name ______________________

Practice

Section 8A Review

Write each fraction or decimal as a percent.

1. 0.38 ________ **2.** $\frac{2}{5}$ ________ **3.** $\frac{36}{40}$ ________ **4.** $\frac{3}{20}$ ________

5. $\frac{13}{250}$ ________ **6.** $\frac{63}{50}$ ________ **7.** 0.423 ________ **8.** 5.5 ________

9. Carolyn correctly answered 43 out of 50 problems on a multiple choice test.

What percent of the problems did she answer correctly? ________

What percent did she answer incorrectly? ________

Write each percent as a decimal.

10. 42% ________ **11.** 25% ________ **12.** 160% ________ **13.** 0.05% ________

14. 0.12% ________ **15.** 9.5% ________ **16.** 850% ________ **17.** 0.4% ________

Write each percent as a fraction in lowest terms.

18. 67% ________ **19.** 125% ________ **20.** 0.2% ________ **21.** 28% ________

22. 65% ________ **23.** 70% ________ **24.** 0.68% ________ **25.** 230% ________

Use mental math to find each percent.

26. 20% of 65 ________ **27.** 40% of 120 ________ **28.** 65% of 700 ________ **29.** 90% of 400 ________

30. A drug manufacturer claims that 512 out of 633 doctors who were surveyed recommend using the manufacturer's product. Estimate the percent of surveyed doctors who recommend using this product. ________

31. The average American ate 12.3 pounds of cookies and crackers in 1993. How many ounces is this? *[Lesson 7-6]* ________

32. Hans drove from Buffalo, New York, to Pittsburgh, Pennsylvania, a road distance of 219 miles. His average speed was 50 mi/hr, and he arrived in Pittsburgh at 6:30 P.M. What time did he leave Buffalo? *[Lesson 7-3]* ________

Name ______________________

Practice 8-5

Using Equations to Solve Percent Problems

Solve each problem. If necessary, round answers to the nearest tenth.

1. What percent of 64 is 48? ________

2. 16% of 130 is what number? ________

3. 25% of what number is 24? ________

4. What percent of 18 is 12? ________

5. 48% of 83 is what number? ________

6. 40% of what number is 136? ________

7. What percent of 530 is 107? ________

8. 74% of 643 is what number? ________

9. 62% of what number is 84? ________

10. What percent of 84 is 50? ________

11. 37% of 245 is what number? ________

12. 12% of what number is 105? ________

13. What percent of 42 is 7.5? ________

14. 98% of 880 is what number? ________

15. 7% of what number is 63? ________

16. What percent of 95 is 74? ________

17. Cafe Mediocre offers senior citizens a 15% discount off its regular price of $8.95 for the dinner buffet.

a. What percent of the regular price is the price for senior citizens? ________

b. What is the price for senior citizens? ________

18. In 1990, 12.5% of the people in Oregon did not have health insurance. If the population of Oregon was 2,880,000, how many people were uninsured? ________

Name ______________________

Practice 8-6

Solving Percent Problems with Proportions

Write a proportion and solve each problem. If necessary, round answers to the nearest tenth.

1. What number is 18% of 95? ______

2. 37 is what percent of 50? ______

3. 12 is 20% of what number? ______

4. What number is 54% of 82? ______

5. 89 is what percent of 395? ______

6. 33 is 16% of what number? ______

7. What number is 90% of 84? ______

8. 108 is what percent of 647? ______

9. 64 is 178% of what number? ______

10. What number is 46% of 835? ______

11. 861 is what percent of 513? ______

12. 19 is 0.7% of what number? ______

13. A store that normally sells a compact stereo system for $128 is having a sale. Everything is discounted 35%. How much can you save by buying the stereo during the sale? ______

14. In 1990, 17,339,000 Americans spoke Spanish at home. If 54.4% of non-English speakers spoke Spanish, find the number of non-English speakers. ______

15. **Measurement** An acre is 4,840 square yards. A hectare is 11,960 square yards. What percent of a hectare is an acre? ______

Name ______________________________

Practice
8-7

Problem Solving: Percent Increase and Decrease

Find each percent of increase or decrease. If necessary, round answers to the nearest tenth.

1. 12 is increased to 18. __________

2. 36 is decreased to 24. __________

3. 175 is increased to 208. __________

4. 642 is decreased to 499. __________

Find each amount of increase or decrease. If necessary, round answers to the nearest tenth.

5. 63 is increased by 40% __________

6. 93 is decreased by 17%. __________

7. 817 is increased by 62%. __________

8. 539 is decreased by 38%. __________

Find the new amount after each increase or decrease. If necessary, round answers to the nearest tenth.

9. 103 is increased by 28%. __________

10. $21 is decreased by 40%. __________

11. $65 is increased by 182%. __________

12. 417 is decreased by 8%. __________

Consumer Sales tax is an amount of increase. Find the amount of sales tax and the total price (including sales tax) for each of the following. If necessary, round answers to the nearest cent.

13. $17.50; 7% sales tax

tax: ________ total: ________

14. $21.95; 4.25% sales tax

tax: ________ total: ________

Geometry For each pair of similar figures, find the percent increase or decrease in area from figure A to figure B.

15. ____________________

A.

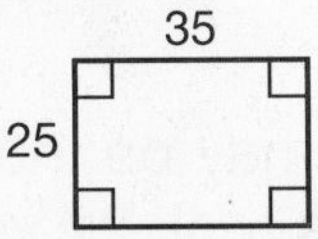

B.

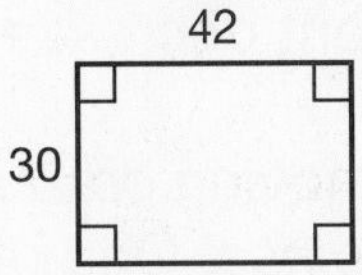

16. ____________________

A.

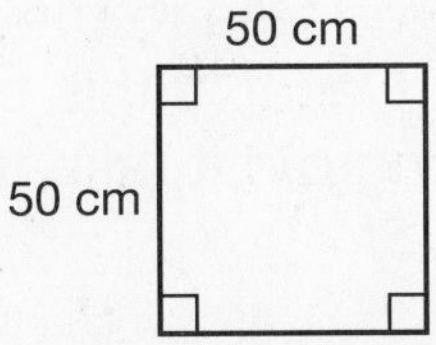

B.

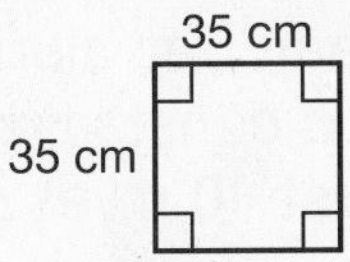

17. Social Science In 1990, there were 31,224,000 Americans of age 65-and-over. This population is expected to increase 71% by 2020. What is the expected 65-and-over population in 2020? ____________________

Name ______________________

Practice

Section 8B Review

Solve each problem. If necessary, round answers to the nearest tenth.

1. What percent of 95 is 18? ______
2. 68% of 68 is what number? ______
3. 43% of what number is 26? ______
4. What percent of 72 is 65? ______
5. 27% of 582 is what number? ______
6. 59% of what number is 222? ______
7. What percent of 803 is 719? ______
8. 215% of 78 is what number? ______
9. 77% of what number is 213? ______
10. What percent of 643 is 4.5? ______
11. 85% of 468 is what number? ______
12. 93% of what number is 745? ______
13. What percent of 37 is 5? ______
14. 4% of 890 is what number? ______
15. **Consumer** The Better Sweater Store sells a wool sweater for $37.95, plus 6.5% state sales tax. If you buy this sweater, how much will you pay? ______
16. A new top-selling compact disc is marked 25% off at Raspy Music, where the disc normally sells for $16.97. The same disc sells for $14.47 at Broken Records, where you have a coupon for 10% off anything in the store. Where would you buy the CD? Explain how you decided.

    ____

    ____
17. The number of Americans who speak Yiddish at home decreased from 320,380 in 1980 to 213,064 in 1990. Find the percent decrease. ______
18. The slowest-moving crab in the world may be the *Neptune pelagines.* One of these crabs took 29 years to travel the 101.5 miles from the Red Sea to the Mediterranean Sea along the Suez Canal. If this crab maintained a constant rate, how long did it take to travel the first 40 miles? *[Lesson 6-3]* ______
19. In 1935, Amelia Earhart made history by being the first woman to fly alone from Honolulu, Hawaii, to the U.S. mainland. Her average speed was about 133 miles per hour. Convert this rate to feet per second. *[Lesson 7-7]* ______

Name ______________________

Practice

Cumulative Review Chapters 1–8

Express each fraction in lowest terms. *[Lesson 3-8]*

1. $\frac{8}{12}$ ______ **2.** $\frac{24}{28}$ ______ **3.** $\frac{55}{75}$ ______ **4.** $\frac{21}{96}$ ______

5. $\frac{30}{84}$ ______ **6.** $\frac{32}{144}$ ______ **7.** $\frac{15}{75}$ ______ **8.** $\frac{42}{108}$ ______

Find each product or quotient. Reduce to lowest terms. *[Lessons 4-5 and 4-6]*

9. $3\frac{1}{3} \cdot 1\frac{1}{2}$ ______ **10.** $13 \div 4\frac{2}{7}$ ______ **11.** $6\frac{3}{10} \cdot \frac{1}{3}$ ______ **12.** $2\frac{1}{3} \div 1\frac{8}{9}$ ______

13. $1\frac{5}{9} \div 3\frac{3}{5}$ ______ **14.** $2\frac{3}{4} \cdot 3\frac{1}{2}$ ______ **15.** $19\frac{1}{6} \div 3\frac{5}{6}$ ______ **16.** $4 \cdot 6\frac{3}{8}$ ______

Find the sum of the measures of the angles in each polygon. *[Lesson 5-4]*

17. trapezoid ______ **18.** hexagon ______

19. 9-sided polygon ______ **20.** 17-sided polygon ______

Convert each rate to an equivalent rate. *[Lesson 7-7]*

21. 27 pounds per day to ounces per day ______

22. 45 kilograms per hour to grams per hour ______

23. 63 quarts per week to quarts per day ______

24. 154 feet per second to miles per hour ______

Write each percent as a fraction in lowest terms. *[Lesson 8-2]*

25. 12% ______ **26.** 50% ______ **27.** 38% ______ **28.** 45% ______

29. $66\frac{2}{3}\%$ ______ **30.** 27% ______ **31.** $12\frac{1}{2}\%$ ______ **32.** 4% ______

Solve each problem. If necessary, round answers to the nearest tenth. *[Lesson 8-6]*

33. What number is 26% of 83? ______ **34.** 4.3 is what percent of 738? ______

35. 69 is 17% of what number? ______ **36.** What number is 135% of 216? ______

37. 57 is what percent of 188? ______ **38.** 817 is 93% of what number? ______

Name ______________________

Practice 9-1

Using Integers to Represent Quantities

Tell whether each number is an integer. Write *Yes* or *No*.

1. 64 ________ **2.** -9.31 ________ **3.** $-2\frac{1}{2}$ ________ **4.** 16.7 ________

5. -37 ________ **6.** $\frac{27}{3}$ ________ **7.** 10.01 ________ **8.** $\frac{3}{8}$ ________

Use signs to write each number.

9. Spent $23 ________ **10.** Gained 12 yards ________

11. 14 degrees below zero ________ **12.** Profit of $640 ________

13. The distance from 0 to -4 on a number line ________

14. 7 units below the origin on a vertical number line ________

Write the opposite of each integer.

15. 42 ________ **16.** -163 ________ **17.** -24 ________ **18.** 69 ________

19. -39 ________ **20.** 7 ________ **21.** -572 ________ **22.** 18 ________

Find each absolute value.

23. $|-12|$ ________ **24.** $|23|$ ________ **25.** $|-42|$ ________ **26.** $|-58|$ ________

27. $|937|$ ________ **28.** $|-37|$ ________ **29.** $|2640|$ ________ **30.** $|1329|$ ________

31. Science The table gives the deepest recorded underwater dives of animals, as reported in the 1997 *Guinness Book of World Records*. Use an integer to represent the height of each animal during its dive. (The height at sea level is 0 ft.)

Animal	Depth (ft)	Height (ft)
Elephant Seal	5017	
Leatherback Turtle	3973	
Emperor Penguin	1584	
Human (without equipment)	428	

32. Science The average surface temperature on Mercury is 332°F. On Pluto, it is -355°F.

a. Find the absolute value of each temperature. ________

b. Which temperature is closer to 0°F? ________

Name ______________________________

Practice 9-2

Comparing and Ordering Integers

Using the number line, write an inequality to tell which number is greater.

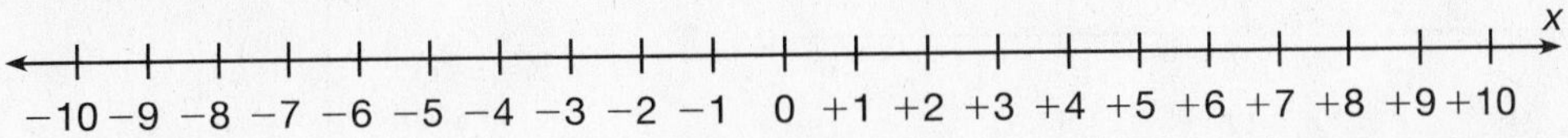

1. −3, 8 ________ **2.** 7, 5 ________ **3.** −9, −1 ________

4. −3, 0 ________ **5.** 9, −4 ________ **6.** 3, 4 ________

7. −4, −2 ________ **8.** −5, −6 ________ **9.** −7, 7 ________

Use >, <, or = to compare each pair of numbers.

10. −12 ◯ 17 **11.** −64 ◯ −46 **12.** 367 ◯ −376 **13.** −23 ◯ −32

14. −123 ◯ −321 **15.** 14 ◯ −15 **16.** 37 ◯ 73 **17.** 265 ◯ −265

18. 412 ◯ 421 **19.** −98 ◯ −89 **20.** −21 ◯ 21 **21.** −482 ◯ −284

22. $|-65|$ ◯ $|64|$ **23.** $|15|$ ◯ $|-14|$ **24.** $|18|$ ◯ $|-18|$ **25.** $|-84|$ ◯ $|-86|$

Order each set of numbers from greatest to least.

26. −42, 24, 58, −16, 44, −46 ________________

27. −\$8, \$11, −\$12, \$7, −\$10, \$9 ________________

28. 0°, 6°, −16°, −26°, −36°, 46° ________________

29. The chart shows the daily average minimum temperatures for fall and winter in McGrath, Alaska.

Month	Ave. Min. Temp. (°F)	Integer Temp. (°F)
October	18 above zero	
November	4 below zero	
December	15 below zero	
January	18 below zero	
February	14 below zero	
March	3 below zero	

a. Complete the table by representing each temperature as an integer.

b. Order the integers in **a** from least to greatest.

____

Name ______________________________

Practice 9-3

The Coordinate Plane

Find the coordinates of each point.

1. *S* ______________ **2.** *T* ______________

3. *U* ______________ **4.** *V* ______________

5. *W* ______________ **6.** *X* ______________

7. *Y* ______________ **8.** *Z* ______________

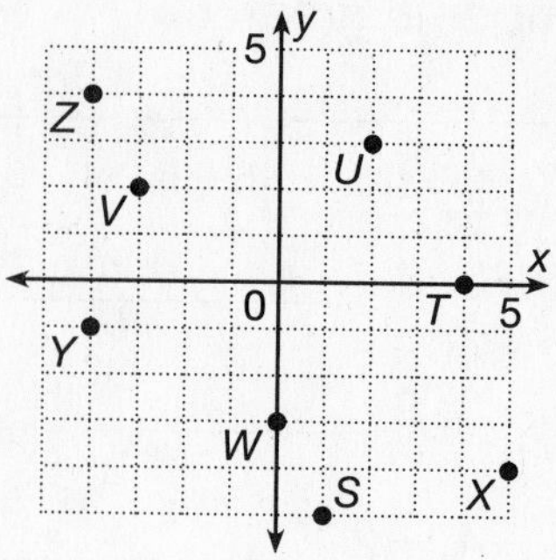

Plot each point on the same coordinate plane.

9. (2, −4) **10.** (0, 4)

11. (−3, 2) **12.** (0, 0)

13. (−2, 0) **14.** (−1, −3)

15. (5, 3) **16.** (4, −1)

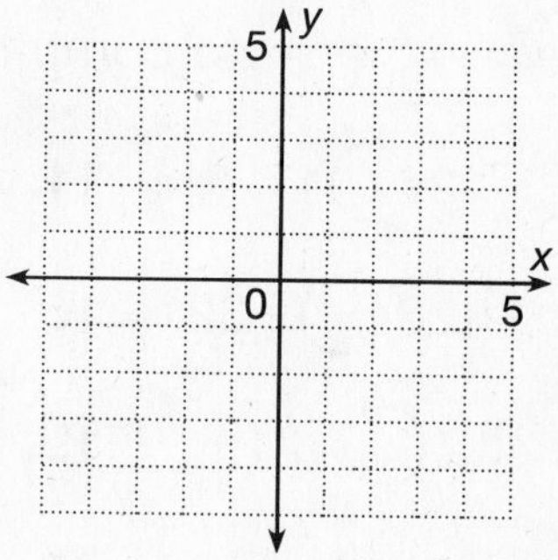

Plot each point on the same coordinate plane.

17. (8, 10) **18.** (−14, 6)

19. (0, −12) **20.** (2, −16)

21. (−5, 16) **22.** (−12, −14)

23. (−18, −4) **24.** (10, −13)

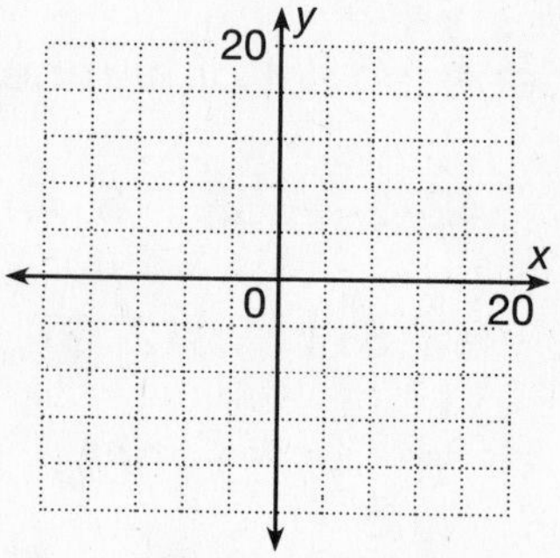

Name the quadrant or axis that contains each point.

25. (7, −12) ____ **26.** (16, 21) ____ **27.** (−83, 12) ____ **28.** (−61, −35) ____

29. (−31, 24) ____ **30.** (0, 3) ____ **31.** (−18, −25) ____ **32.** (47, −38) ____

33. (16, −18) ____ **34.** (−7, 23) ____ **35.** (−7, 0) ____ **36.** (17, 35) ____

37. Plot the points (2, −2), (3, 4), (−1, 2), and (−2, −4) on the coordinate plane. Connect the points, in order, to form a polygon. What kind of polygon is formed? Be as specific as possible.

____

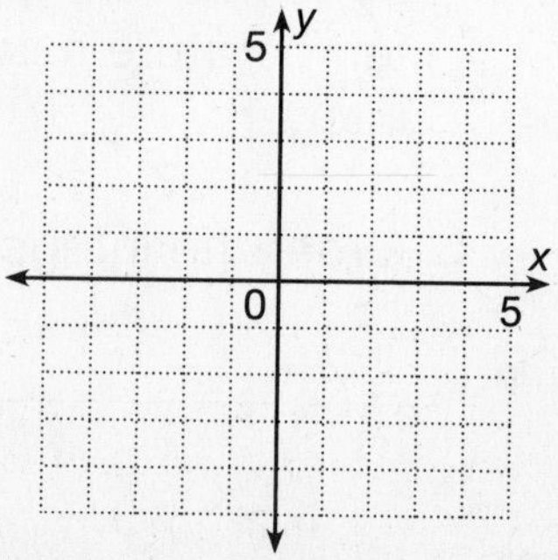

Name ______________________________

Practice

Section 9A Review

Write the opposite of each integer.

1. 15 ________ **2.** −8 ________ **3.** 27 ________ **4.** −58 ________

5. −367 ________ **6.** 222 ________ **7.** 638 ________ **8.** −412 ________

Find each absolute value.

9. $|37|$ ________ **10.** $|-41|$ ________ **11.** $|86|$ ________ **12.** $|-101|$ ________

13. $|-648|$ ________ **14.** $|-3841|$ ________ **15.** $|2163|$ ________ **16.** $|-484|$ ________

Use >, <, or = to compare each pair of numbers.

17. 38 ◯ −83 **18.** −47 ◯ −52 **19.** −85 ◯ −95 **20.** 637 ◯ 763

21. −321 ◯ −312 **22.** 418 ◯ −481 **23.** $|18|$ ◯ $|-21|$ **24.** $|-17|$ ◯ $|-15|$

Plot each point on the same coordinate plane.

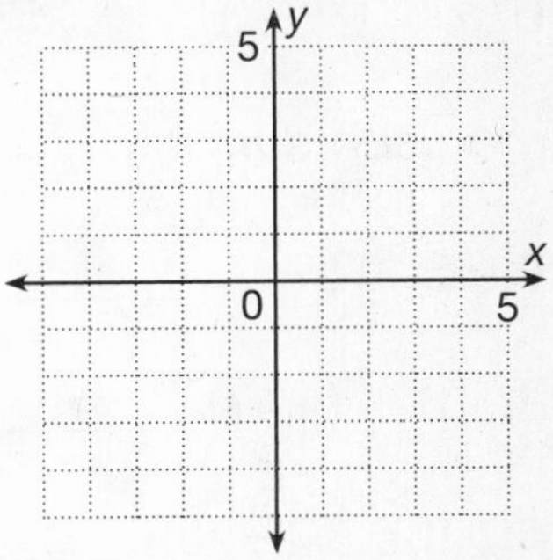

25. (−4, −2) **26.** (3, −3)

27. (3, 1) **28.** (−1, 4)

29. (0, −2) **30.** (2, 3)

31. In 1968, John Gruener and R. Neal Watson used scuba equipment to dive to a depth of 437 ft below sea level. Use an integer to represent their height during the dive. ________________

32. During its first half-year, Anita's business earned monthly profits of −\$3285, −\$680, \$329, \$567, −\$240, and \$980. (A negative number represents a loss.) Order the dollar amounts from lowest to highest.

____

33. Geography The area of Peru is about $3\frac{4}{25}$ times the area of Paraguay. If Paraguay has an area of 157,000 mi^2, what is the area of Peru? *[Lesson 4-5]* ________________

34. In 1964, Steve's Cheese of Denmark, Wisconsin, made a cheddar cheese weighing $17\frac{1}{2}$ tons. The milk used to make the cheese equalled the daily production of 16,000 cows. How many tons of cheddar cheese could be made using the daily production of milk from 3,200 cows? *[Lesson 6-8]* ________________

Name ______________________________

Practice
9-4

Adding Integers

Write the addition problem and the sum for each model. The lighter tiles represent positive numbers.

1. ________________

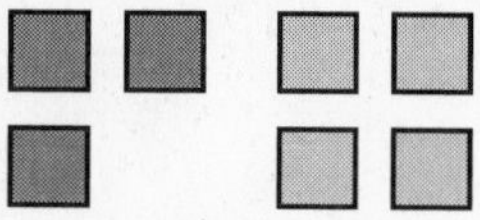

2. ________________

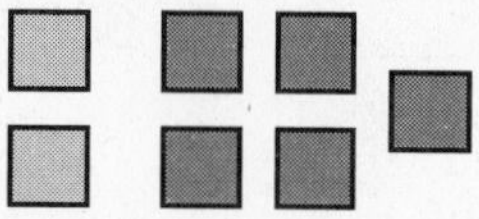

3. ________________

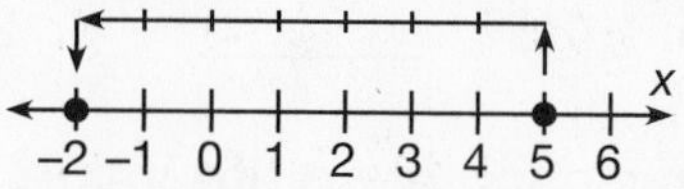

Find the additive inverse of each integer.

4. 7 ________ **5.** −9 ________ **6.** 37 ________ **7.** 14 ________

8. −16 ________ **9.** −23 ________ **10.** 41 ________ **11.** −28 ________

Use algebra tiles or a number line to find each sum.

12. 7 + (−4) ____ **13.** −1 + (−3) ___ **14.** 3 + 2 ______ **15.** −7 + 8 _____

16. −6 + (−1) ___ **17.** −1 + (−2) ___ **18.** −4 + 9 _____ **19.** −8 + 6 _____

Find each sum.

20. 58 + 57 ________ **21.** −110 + 19 ________ **22.** −49 + (−106) ________

23. 16 + (−47) ________ **24.** −40 + 16 ________ **25.** 35 + (−40) ________

26. −36 + (−58) ________ **27.** −17 + 13 ________ **28.** −146 + 16 ________

29. 10 + (−30) ________ **30.** −25 + (−21) ________ **31.** −66 + (−13) ________

Write the next integer in each pattern.

32. −12, −9, −6, ______ **33.** 6, −2, −10, ______ **34.** −20, −16, −12, ______

35. 10, 5, 0, ______ **36.** −11, −16, −21, ______ **37.** −11, −7, −3, ______

38. A diver is at a depth of 14 ft below sea level. If she is lifted to 10 ft above her present position, will she be above or below sea level? Write an addition problem and the sum to explain your answer.

____

39. The average daily minimum temperature in International Falls, Minnesota, is 38°F warmer in March than in January. If the temperature in January is −10°F, what is the temperature in March?

____

Name ______________________________

Practice 9-5

Subtracting Integers

Use algebra tiles to find each difference.

1. $-7 - 2$ ______ **2.** $7 - (-3)$ ______ **3.** $-4 - (-3)$ ______ **4.** $3 - (-4)$ ______

5. $-4 - (-1)$ ______ **6.** $-4 - 5$ ______ **7.** $3 - 7$ ______ **8.** $-3 - (-7)$ ______

Use a number line to find each difference.

9. $1 - (-6)$ ______ **10.** $2 - 4$ ______ **11.** $8 - 3$ ______ **12.** $-6 - 1$ ______

13. $-1 - (-1)$ ______ **14.** $4 - 7$ ______ **15.** $8 - (-1)$ ______ **16.** $0 - 2$ ______

Find each difference.

17. $-38 - 50$ ______ **18.** $-110 - 118$ ______ **19.** $-16 - (-34)$ ______

20. $10 - 73$ ______ **21.** $10 - (-78)$ ______ **22.** $-12 - 15$ ______

23. $-24 - (-56)$ ______ **24.** $-56 - 42$ ______ **25.** $13 - 100$ ______

Write the next integer in each pattern.

26. 15, 3 −9, ______ **27.** −8, −11, −14, ______ **28.** 17, 12, 7, ______

29. 12, 5, −2, ______ **30.** 4, −6, −16, ______ **31.** 18, 10, 2, ______

Find the unknown number in each difference.

32. $9 - y = 12$ ______ **33.** $-34 + x = -23$ ______ **34.** $32 + z = -13$ ______

35. Geography The table shows the highest and lowest elevations of each continent. Find the range of elevations for each continent by subtracting the low elevation from the high elevation.

Continent	Africa	Antarctica	Asia	Europe	N. America	S. America	Australia
High el. (m)	5895	4897	8848	5642	6194	6960	2228
Low el. (m)	−156	−2538	−400	−28	−86	−40	−16
Range (m)							

Which continent has the widest range? ______________

Which continent has the narrowest range? ______________

Name ______________________

Practice 9-6

Multiplying Integers

Find each product.

1. $-2 \cdot (-16)$ ________
2. $-29 \cdot 3$ ________
3. $-11 \cdot 21$ ________
4. $3 \cdot 19$ ________
5. $-2 \cdot 16$ ________
6. $-10 \cdot 12$ ________
7. $-2 \cdot (-6)$ ________
8. $-8 \cdot (-18)$ ________
9. $13 \cdot (-26)$ ________
10. $-2 \cdot 6$ ________
11. $-3 \cdot 28$ ________
12. $-2 \cdot (-2)$ ________
13. $-27 \cdot 28$ ________
14. $2 \cdot (-3)$ ________
15. $-2 \cdot (-5)$ ________
16. $2 \cdot (-6)$ ________
17. $12 \cdot (-14)$ ________
18. $-14 \cdot (-10)$ ________
19. $46 \cdot (-6)$ ________
20. $-4 \cdot 4$ ________
21. $-13 \cdot 2$ ________
22. $-17 \cdot (-4)$ ________
23. $19 \cdot 5$ ________
24. $16 \cdot (-14)$ ________
25. $-11 \cdot (-34)$ ________
26. $2 \cdot (-34)$ ________
27. $-17 \cdot (-5)$ ________
28. $9 \cdot (-10)$ ________
29. $2 \cdot (-13)$ ________
30. $-16 \cdot 3$ ________
31. $-17 \cdot 19$ ________
32. $-17 \cdot (-36)$ ________
33. $-22 \cdot 4$ ________
34. $-9 \cdot (-19)$ ________
35. $4 \cdot (-8)$ ________
36. $-14 \cdot (-2)$ ________
37. $-6 \cdot (-23)$ ________
38. $-9 \cdot 3$ ________
39. $-18 \cdot 9$ ________
40. $-16 \cdot 7$ ________
41. $-38 \cdot 18$ ________
42. $-32 \cdot (-6)$ ________
43. $-25 \cdot (-10)$ ________
44. $-13 \cdot 20$ ________
45. $2 \cdot (-9)$ ________
46. $-9 \cdot 11$ ________
47. $-4 \cdot (-2)$ ________
48. $-11 \cdot (-24)$ ________

49. In 1995, Nigeria was losing its forest cover at the rate of 4000 km^2 per year.

    a. Write the deforestation rate as a negative integer. ________

    b. Calculate the change in the amount of forest in a 5-year period. ________

50. Tabitha withdrew $85 a month from her savings account for seven months. What was the change in her balance? ________

 Use with pages 461–465.

Name ____________________

Practice 9-7

Dividing Integers

Use the given product to find each quotient.

1. $11 \cdot (-7) = -77$; $-77 \div (-7) =$ ____
2. $7 \cdot 14 = 98$; $98 \div 7 =$ ____
3. $-5 \cdot 10 = -50$; $-50 \div 10 =$ ____
4. $3 \cdot (-6) = -18$; $-18 \div (-6) =$ ____

Find each quotient.

5. $56 \div (-8)$ ____
6. $-196 \div (-14)$ ____
7. $-10 \div (-10)$ ____
8. $-117 \div (-9)$ ____
9. $-49 \div (-7)$ ____
10. $-63 \div 7$ ____
11. $-40 \div 4$ ____
12. $-18 \div (-3)$ ____
13. $7 \div (-7)$ ____
14. $-120 \div (-8)$ ____
15. $-4 \div (-1)$ ____
16. $-50 \div (-10)$ ____
17. $-40 \div (-8)$ ____
18. $-99 \div 9$ ____
19. $-117 \div 9$ ____
20. $44 \div (-4)$ ____
21. $-24 \div 8$ ____
22. $-40 \div 10$ ____
23. $18 \div (-6)$ ____
24. $180 \div 15$ ____
25. $-48 \div (-8)$ ____
26. $-84 \div (-14)$ ____
27. $-84 \div 7$ ____
28. $-91 \div (-7)$ ____
29. $9 \div (-3)$ ____
30. $-144 \div 12$ ____
31. $10 \div (-10)$ ____
32. $-70 \div 10$ ____
33. $117 \div (-13)$ ____
34. $-36 \div 9$ ____
35. $-3 \div (-1)$ ____
36. $120 \div (-10)$ ____
37. $-24 \div (-4)$ ____
38. $8 \div (-8)$ ____
39. $-28 \div (-4)$ ____
40. $-112 \div (-8)$ ____
41. $-36 \div 6$ ____
42. $-126 \div (-14)$ ____
43. $-77 \div (-11)$ ____
44. $-143 \div 11$ ____
45. $-22 \div (-11)$ ____
46. $-48 \div 8$ ____
47. $-44 \div 4$ ____
48. $-117 \div (-13)$ ____
49. $-112 \div 8$ ____

50. Some typical daily low temperatures for Alaska cities in February are: Anchorage, 12°F; Fairbanks, −14°F; Kotzebue, −12°F; Gulkana, −7°F; and Nome, −4°F. What is the average of these temperatures? ____

51. Over a 6-year period, a business reported annual profits of \$8 million, −\$5 million, −\$9 million, \$3 million, and −\$7 million, and −\$2 million. What was the mean annual profit? ____

Name ______________________

Practice

Section 9B Review

Find each sum, difference, product, or quotient.

1. $-135 \div 15$ ________
2. $-57 + 29$ ________
3. $3 \cdot (-5)$ ________

4. $21 - (-137)$ ________
5. $64 \div (-8)$ ________
6. $-76 + (-84)$ ________

7. $-20 \cdot (-16)$ ________
8. $-40 - 28$ ________
9. $-30 \div 3$ ________

10. $-26 + (-31)$ ________
11. $-5 \cdot 2$ ________
12. $38 - 59$ ________

13. $96 \div 8$ ________
14. $30 + (-60)$ ________
15. $8 \cdot (-2)$ ________

Evaluate each expression.

16. $6 + (-4) - (-8)$ ________
17. $3 \cdot (-5) \cdot 7$ ________
18. $-6 \cdot 10 \div (-15)$ ________

19. $-3 + (-7) \cdot (-4)$ ________
20. $64 \div (-4) + 12$ ________
21. $-28 \div (-7) \cdot (-4)$ ________

22. $4 \cdot (-9) - (-25)$ ________
23. $-2 + (-9) - (-15)$ ________
24. $36 \div (-12) + (-6)$ ________

25. Science Temperatures on the moon can be as high as 273°F (134°C) and as low as −274°F (−170°C). Find the difference between these extreme temperatures in °F and °C. ________

26. Stephan is playing a card game. He started out with 100 points, and then he scored +20, −15, +30, −5, and −40 points. Then his score was tripled because he held all the aces. What was his final score? ________

27. The population of Buffalo, New York, was about 580,000 in 1950 and 328,000 in 1990. Find the average rate of change of the population (in people per year) from 1950 to 1990.

____

28. Rebecca is buying new carpet for the section of her home that is shown. How many square feet of carpet will she need? *[Lesson 5-10]* ________

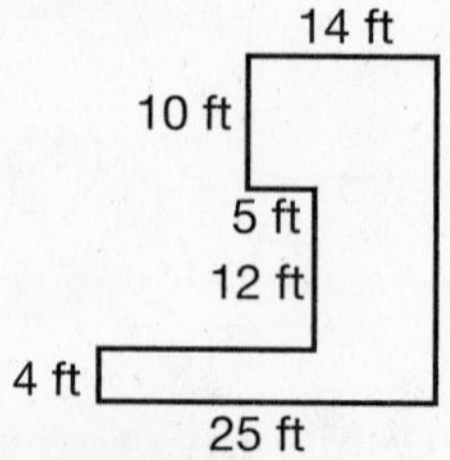

29. In 1980, independent presidential candidate John Anderson won 6.6% of the popular vote. He received about 5,720,000 votes. How many people voted in this election? *[Lesson 8-6]*

____

Name ______________________________

Practice

Cumulative Review Chapters 1–9

Convert to a fraction in lowest terms. *[Lesson 3-10]*

1. 0.63 ________ **2.** 0.75 ________ **3.** 0.56 ________ **4.** 0.45 ________

5. 0.6 ________ **6.** 0.375 ________ **7.** 0.124 ________ **8.** 0.36 ________

9. 0.888 ________ **10.** 0.98 ________ **11.** 0.413 ________ **12.** 0.175 ________

Find the missing length in each right triangle. *[Lesson 5-7]*

13. t = ________

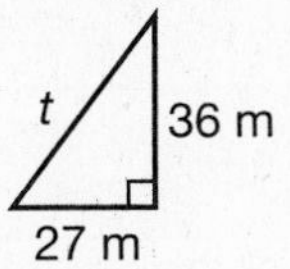

14. x = ________

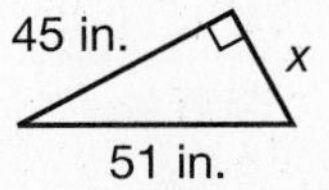

15. m = ________

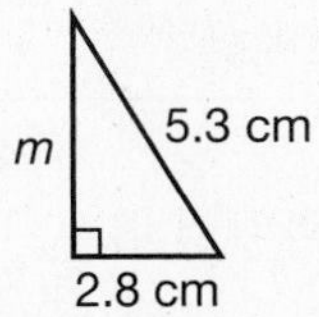

16. q = ________

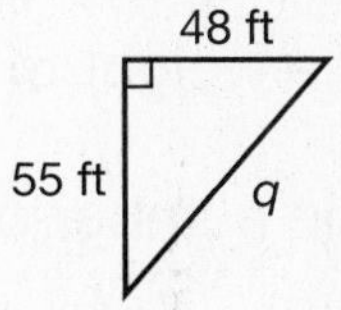

Consumer Use unit prices to find the better buy. Underline the correct choice. *[Lesson 6-2]*

17. Oranges: $1.44 for 3 lb or $2.50 for 5 lb

18. Granola cereal: $1.68 for 12 oz or $2.47 for 19 oz

19. Magazines: $21 for 12 issues or $44 for 24 issues

20. Blueberries: $2.98 for 2 baskets or $3.98 for 3 baskets

Perimeter and area ratios of similar figures are given. Find each scale factor. *[Lesson 7-10]*

21. Perimeter ratio $= \frac{49}{25}$

Scale factor = ______

22. Area ratio = 16

Scale factor = ______

23. Perimeter ratio = 0.36

Scale factor = ______

24. Perimeter ratio = 81

Scale factor = ______

25. Area ratio $= \frac{9}{100}$

Scale factor = ______

26. Area ratio = 2.25

Scale factor = ______

Find each sum, difference, product, or quotient. *[Lessons 9-4 to 9-7]*

27. $-21 + (-168)$ ________ **28.** $-41 - (-51)$ ________ **29.** $126 + (-146)$ ________

30. $30 \div (-6)$ ________ **31.** $53 + (-12)$ ________ **32.** $37 - (-44)$ ________

Name ______________________

Practice 10-1

Quantities, Constants, and Variables

Tell whether each quantity is a variable or a constant.

1. The number of ounces in a pound ________
2. The population of Memphis, Tennessee ________
3. The height of the Eiffel Tower ________

For each quantity, define a variable and give a reasonable range of values.

4. The width of a desk ________
5. The weight of a dog ________
6. The number of bathrooms in a house ________
7. The number of staples in a stapler ________

Measurement Give an appropriate unit of measurement for each quantity. You may use metric or customary units.

8. The amount of time it takes to run a mile ________
9. The height of a tree ________
10. The distance between two cities ________
11. You are managing an apartment complex with 65 units. In a typical month, several people move in or out of the complex.

    a. Name two variable quantities related to the apartment complex.

    ____

    b. Name two constant quantities related to the apartment complex.

    ____

12. The formula for the circumference of a circle is $C = 2\pi r$.

    a. Name all variable quantities in the formula. ________

    b. Name all constant quantities in the formula. ________

 Use with pages 482–485.

Name ____________________

Practice 10-2

Relating Graphs to Stories

Name another quantity that each given quantity might depend on.

1. The number of houses on a city block ____________________

2. The volume of a cube ____________________

3. The amount of a paycheck ____________________

4. A student's score on a test ____________________

In Exercises 5 and 6, choose the graph that best shows the story.

5. You catch the flu, so your temperature increases. As you regain your health, your temperature returns to normal.

a.

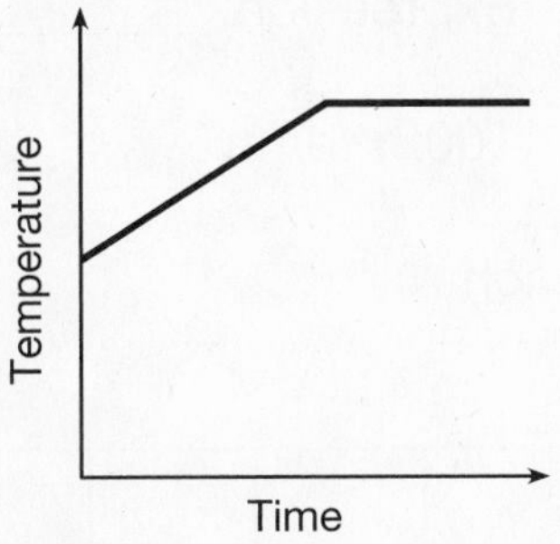

b.

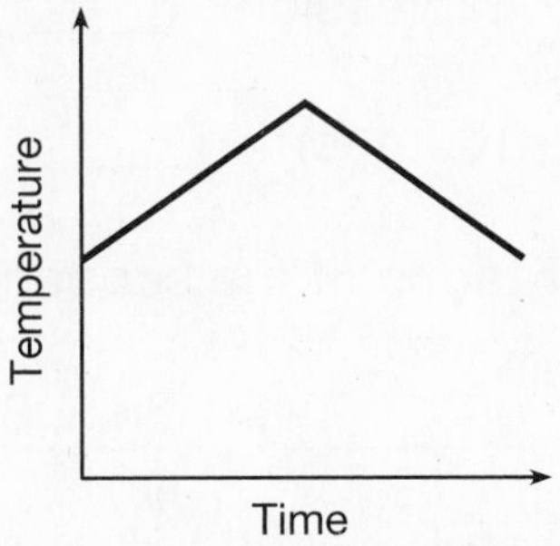

c.

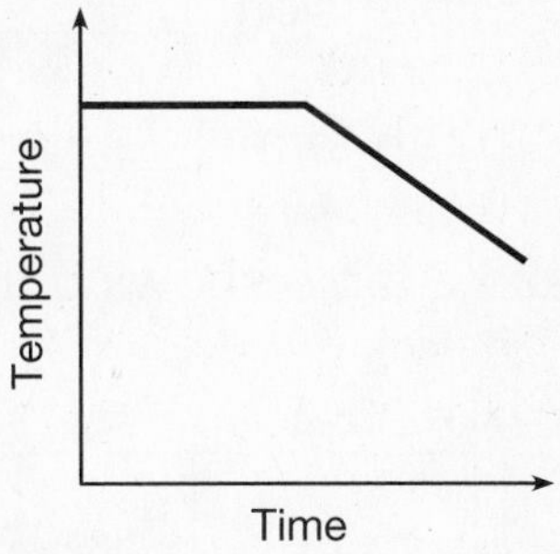

6. You leave for school in the morning. When you get halfway to school, you suddenly realize that you've left an important paper at home. You return home, and then go to school.

a.

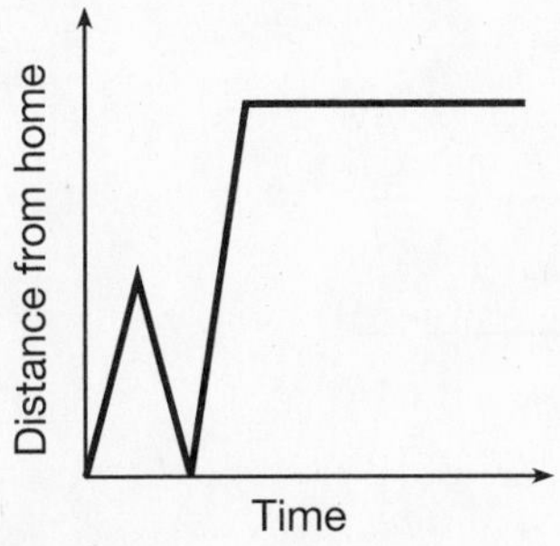

b.

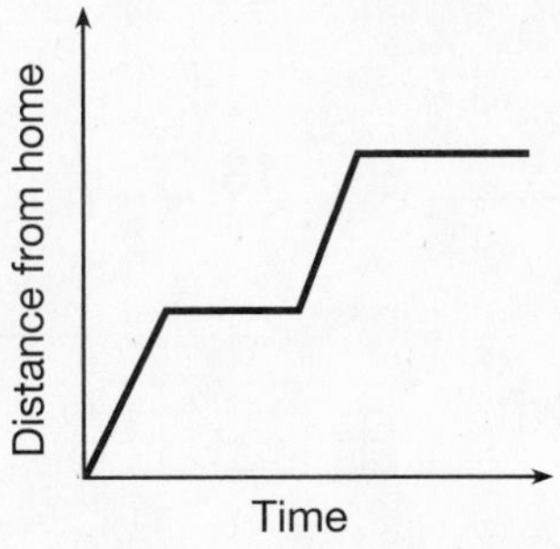

c.

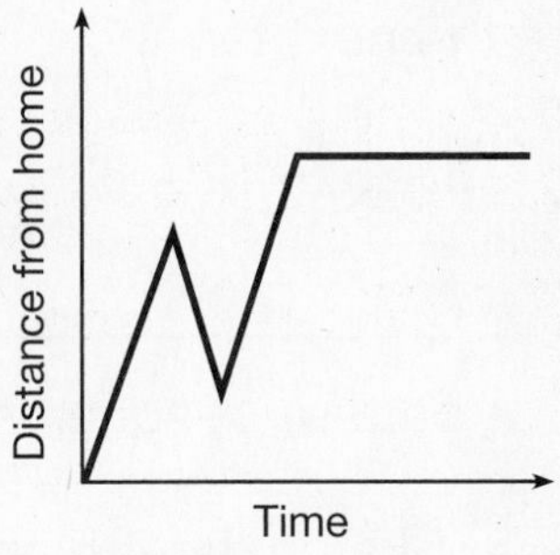

7. Tell a story that fits the graph.

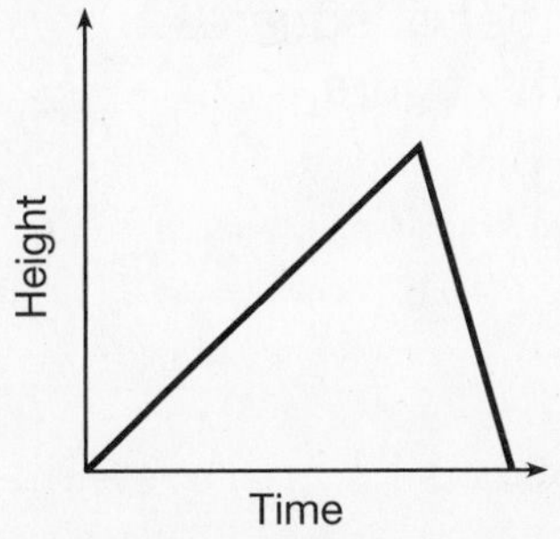

____

____

____

Name ______________________

Practice 10-3

Tables and Expressions

Give the next term in each sequence or the next picture in each pattern.

1. 4, 8, 12, 16, ____, ...

2. −20, −18, −16, −14, ____, ...

3. 8, −8, 8, −8, ____, ...

4. 3, 6, 12, 24, ____, ...

5. 

6. 

Write an expression describing the rule for each sequence. Then give the 100th term for the sequence.

7. 35, 36, 37, 38, ...

Expression: ________

100th term: ________

8. 8, 10, 12, 14, ...

Expression: ________

100th term: ________

9. 1.5, 3, 4.5, 6, ...

Expression: ________

100th term: ________

Make a table showing the first 4 terms of the sequence for each rule.

10. $n + 20$

11. $3n - 5$

Tell whether each sequence is arithmetic, geometric, or neither. Then give the next term.

12. −5, 25, −125, 625, ________, ...

____

13. $\frac{1}{3}, \frac{1}{6}, \frac{1}{9}, \frac{1}{12},$ ________, ...

____

14. A pattern of squares is shown. 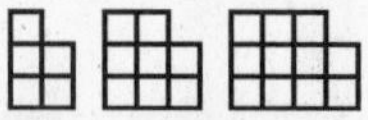

a. Sketch the 4th and 5th figure in this pattern.

b. Make a table comparing the figure number to the number of squares. Write an expression for the number of squares in the nth figure. ________

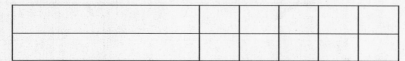

c. How many squares would there be in the 80th figure? ________

Name ________________________

Practice
10-4

Understanding and Writing Equations

For each table, write an equation to show the relationship between x and y. Use the equation to find y when $x = 7$.

1. ________________________

x	1	2	3	4	7
y	8	16	24	32	

2. ________________________

x	1	2	3	4	7
y	−3	−2	−1	0	

Complete each table, and write an equation to show the relationship between the variables.

3. ________________________

s	3	5	7	15	50
t	18	20	22		

4. ________________________

a	10	20	30	80	100
b	70	140	210		

5. ________________________

d	1	2	3	7	12
c	3.14	6.28	9.42		

6. ________________________

p	0	2	4	9	20
q	0	24	48		

Make a table of five pairs of values for each equation.

7. $y = x - 12$

8. $y = 0.7x$

9. $p = 5m - 3$

10. $v = \frac{u}{5} + 7$

11. Science The relationship between the amount of time a zebra runs at maximum speed and the distance it covers is shown.

Time (min)	3	6	9	12	15
Distance (mi)	2	4	6	8	10

a. Write an equation to describe this relationship. ________________________

b. Use the equation to find the distance the zebra would travel in 48 minutes. ________________________

Name ______________________________

Practice 10-5

Equations and Graphs

In Exercises 1–2, a table of points is given for each equation. Graph each equation on a coordinate plane.

1. $y = -2x$

x	-2	-1	0	1	2
y	4	2	0	-2	-4

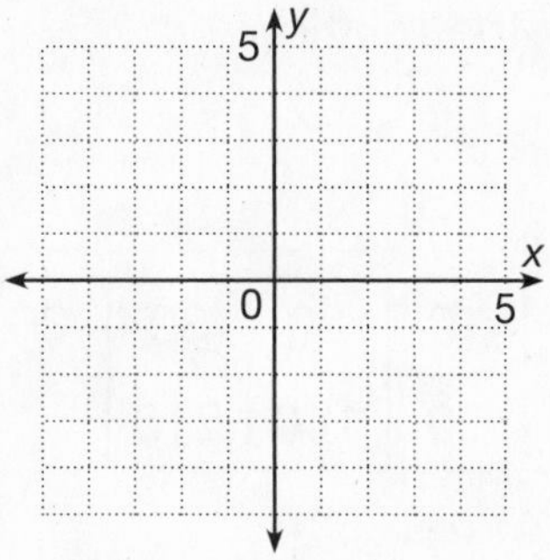

2. $y = x - 3$

x	-2	-1	0	2	4
y	-5	-4	-3	-1	1

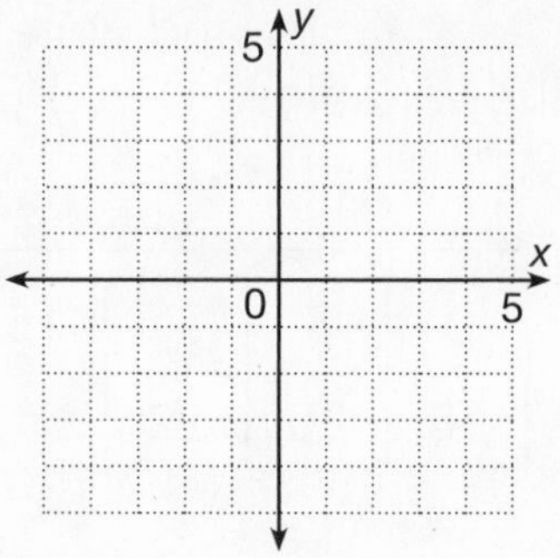

Graph each equation on a coordinate plane.

3. $y = x + 4$

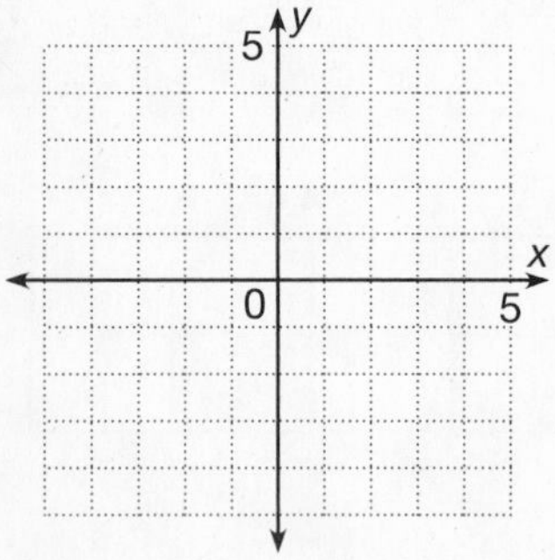

4. $y = 2x + 3$

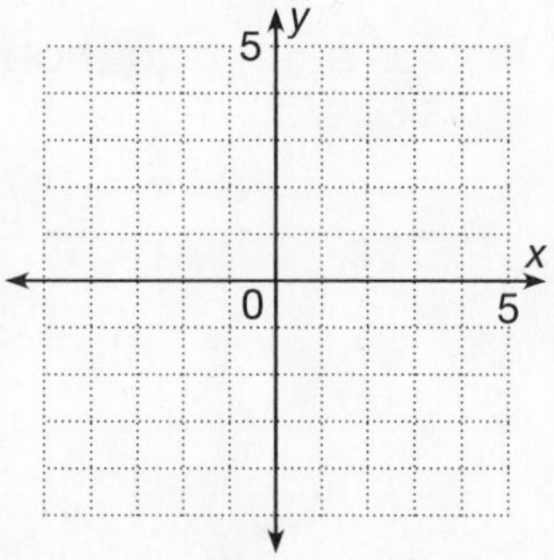

5. $y = x^2 - 2$

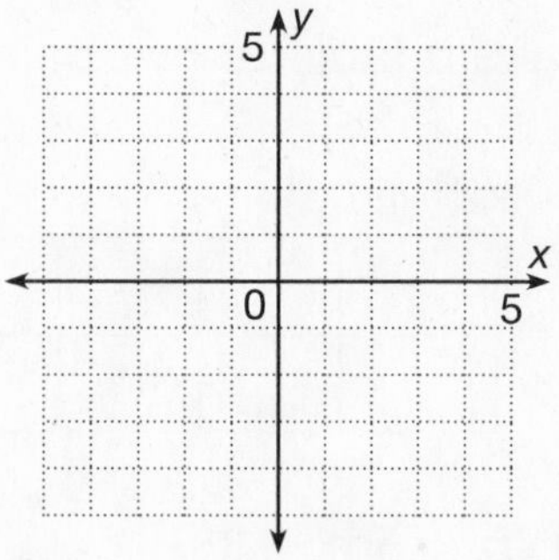

6. Health A typical slice of apple pie contains about 18 g of fat. An equation to represent the fat in several slices is $f = 18n$, where f represents the amount of fat in grams and n represents the number of slices. Graph this equation on a coordinate plane.

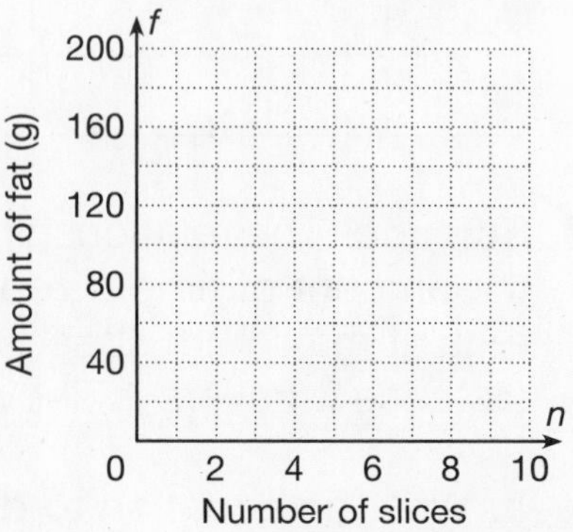

Name ______________________

Practice

Section 10A Review

1. Tell whether the depth of water in a bathtub is a variable or a constant. __________

2. A person making deliveries rode an elevator from the lobby to the 17th floor to deliver a package. She then rode to the 9th floor to make another delivery, and then she returned to the lobby. Which graph could represent this story?

a.

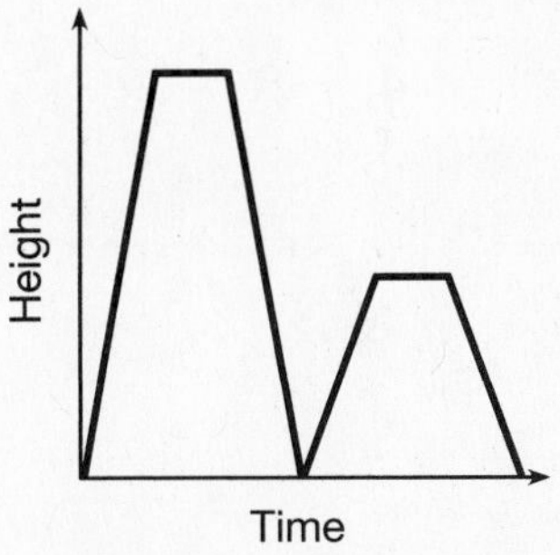

b.

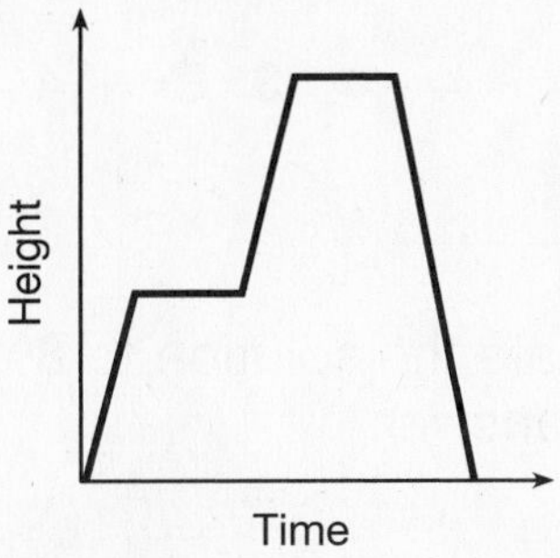

c.

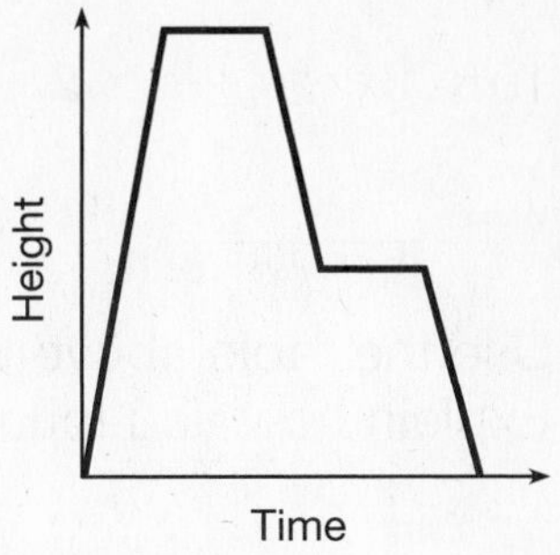

Write an expression describing the rule for each sequence.
Then give the 100th term for the sequence.

3. $-6, -12, -18, -24, \cdots$

Expression: ____ 100th term: _____

4. $-8, -7, -6, -5, \cdots$

Expression: _______ 100th term: _____

5. Write an equation to show the relationship between *x* and *y*. Use the equation to find *y* when $x = 9$.

x	1	2	3	4	9
y	7	8	9	10	

____

Graph each equation on a coordinate plane.

6. $y = -4x$

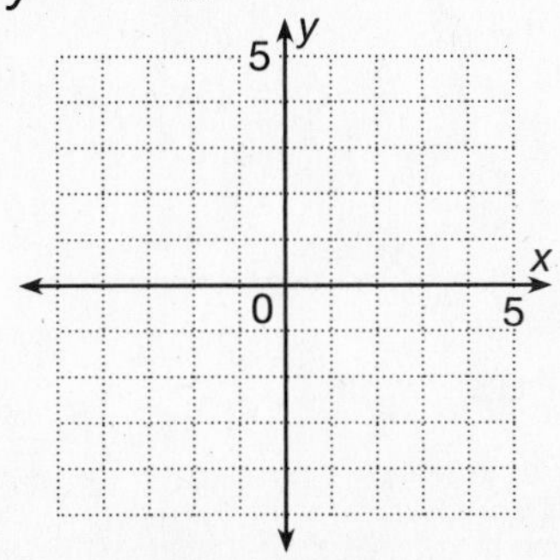

7. $y = x - 3$

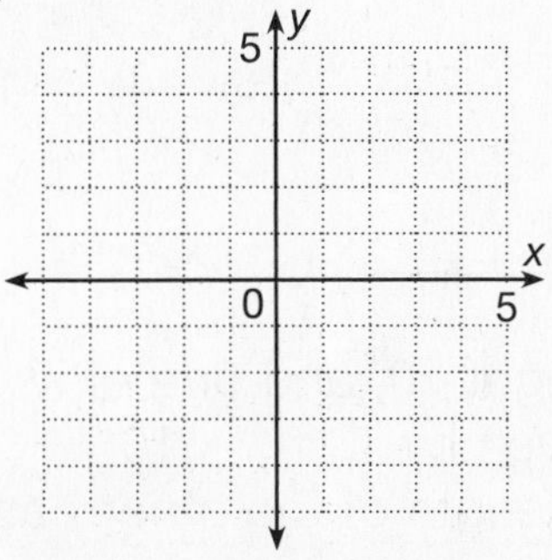

8. $y = -2x + 4$

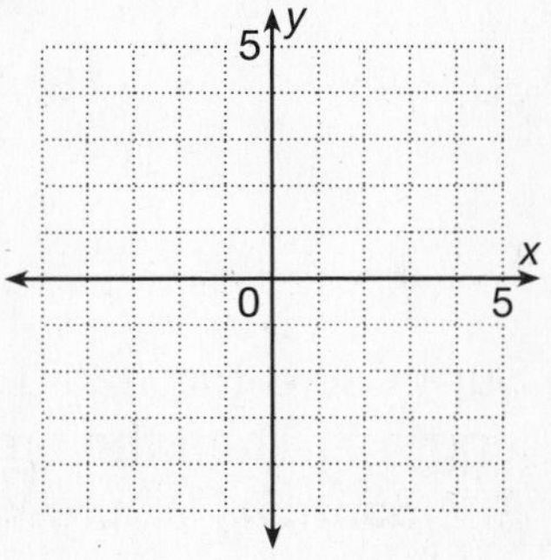

9. Dave traveled 271 mi from Philadelphia to Boston. He left at 10:00 A.M. and drove at 60 mi/hr. What time did he arrive? *[Lesson 7-3]* __________

10. Science Ice melts at 32°F. If the temperature of a block of ice increases 35°F from −10°F, does the ice melt? Explain your answer. *[Lesson 9-4]*

____

Name ______________________

Practice 10-6

Solving Equations Using Tables

The table below represents the equation $y = 3x + 4$. Use it to solve the related equations below the table.

x	−4	−3	−2	−1	0	1	2	3	4
y	−8	−5	−2	1	4	7	10	13	16

1. $10 = 3x + 4$ $x =$ ______

2. $-5 = 3x + 4$ $x =$ ______

3. $3x + 4 = 16$ $x =$ ______

4. $-8 = 3x + 4$ $x =$ ______

5. Use the table above to estimate the solution to $8 = 3x + 4$. Explain how you found your answer.

____

____

Make and use a table to solve each equation.

6. $20 = 5x$ $x =$ ______

7. $19 = x + 12$ $x =$ ______

8. $-6 = -3x$ $x =$ ______

9. $-5 = -2x + 5$ $x =$ ______

10. $-54 = 7x - 12$ $x =$ ______

11. $8 = -8x$ $x =$ ______

12. $3 = x - 5$ $x =$ ______

13. $2x - 3 = 9$ $x =$ ______

Make and use a table to estimate the solution to each equation.

14. $30 = 7x$ $x \approx$ ______

15. $35 = 5x + 7$ $x \approx$ ______

16. $-4x = 10\frac{1}{2}$ $x \approx$ ______

17. $-18 = 3x - 4$ $x \approx$ ______

18. Suppose a trapezoid has height 10, and one of its bases has length 7. Then the area is given by $A = \frac{1}{2} \cdot 10(7 + x)$, or $A = 35 + 5x$, where x is the length of the other base.

a. Make a table of values for $A = 35 + 5x$.

b. Use your table to estimate the value of x for one of these trapezoids with area 78. ______

Name ______________________________

Practice 10-7

Solving Equations Using Graphs

1. Follow the steps to solve $1 = -2x + 3$ by graphing.

a. Write the related equation for $1 = -2x + 3$ by replacing 1 with y. ____________

b. Make a table of values for the related equation.

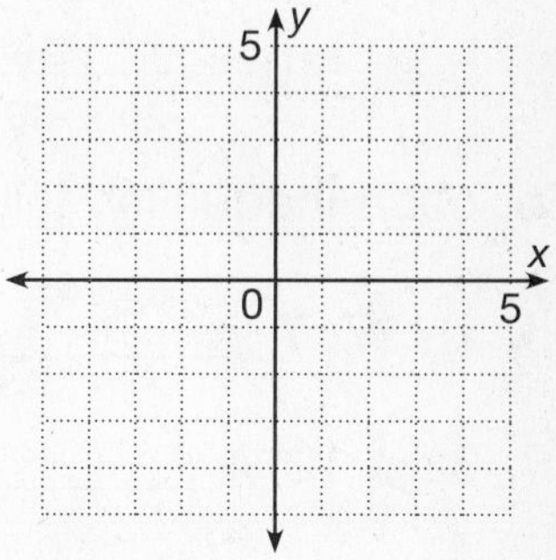

c. Plot the points in your table on a coordinate plane. Connect the points.

d. Start at 1 on the y-axis of your coordinate plane. Go across until you reach the graph. Then, drop vertically to the x-axis, and read the solution.

$x =$ ________

2. Use your graph above to estimate the solution to $-3\frac{1}{2} = -2x + 3$.

____

Use a graph to solve each equation.

3. $-4x = 12$ $x =$ ________

4. $17 = -2x + 9$ $x =$ ________

5. $-15 = 3x - 6$ $x =$ ________

6. $11 = -5x - 4$ $x =$ ________

7. $10 = 2k - 4$ $k =$ ________

8. $p + 6 = 11$ $p =$ ________

9. $-13 = 5h - 3$ $h =$ ________

10. $-5 = -4m + 7$ $m =$ ________

Use a graph to estimate the solution to each equation.

11. $6 = 4x + 17$ $x \approx$ ________

12. $15 = -3u + 8$ $u \approx$ ________

13. $-10 = 7p - 5$ $p \approx$ ________

14. $15 = -5b + 8$ $b \approx$ ________

15. The MaxiTaxi Company charges \$1.00 per mile, plus a base charge of \$2.50 per trip. The cost, c, to travel d miles is given by $c = d + 2.5$.

a. Graph this equation.

b. Melinda paid \$8.00 for her taxi ride. How far did she go? ________

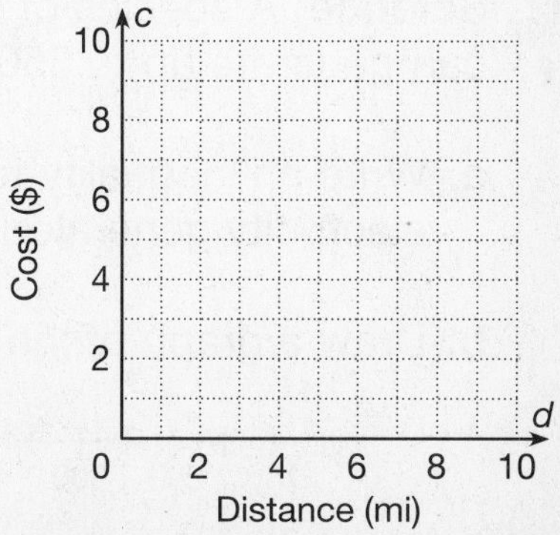

Name ______________________________

Practice 10-8

Relating Equations and Inequalities

Graph each inequality on a number line.

1. $x \le 3$

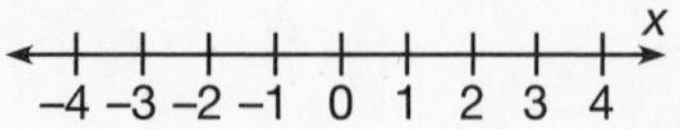

2. $t > 1$

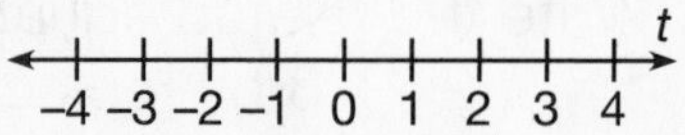

3. $q \ge -10$

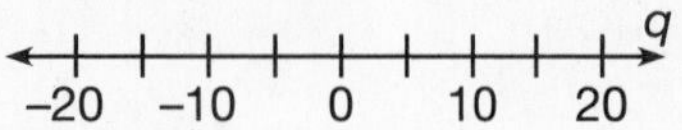

4. $m < 50$

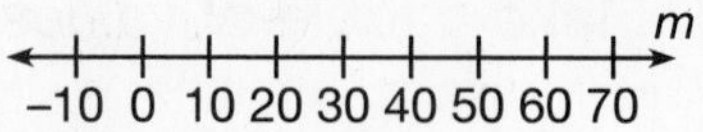

For each inequality, tell whether the number in bold is a solution.

5. $x < 7$; **7** __________

6. $p > -3$; **3** __________

7. $k \ge 5$; **0** __________

8. $3z \le 12$; **4** __________

9. $n - 5 > 3$; **6** __________

10. $2g + 8 \ge 3$; **–1** __________

Write an inequality for each graph.

11. ______________________________

12. ______________________________

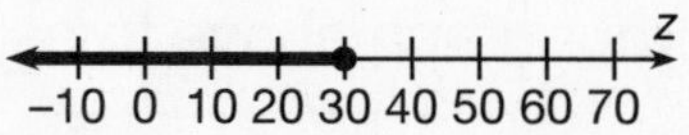

Write a real-world statement for each inequality.

13. $d \ge 60$

____

14. $p < 200$

____

Write and graph an inequality for each statement.

15. You can walk there in 20 minutes or less.

____

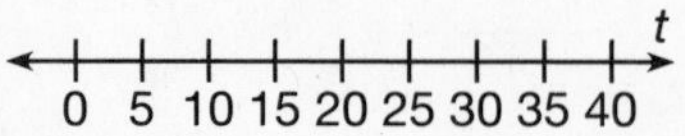

16. Each prize is worth over $150.

____

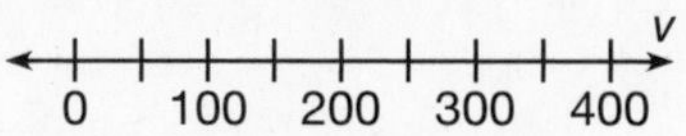

17. Science A species of catfish, *malapterurus electricus,* can generate up to 350 volts of electricity.

a. Write an inequality to represent the amount of electricity generated by the catfish. __________

b. Draw a graph of the inequality you wrote in **a**.

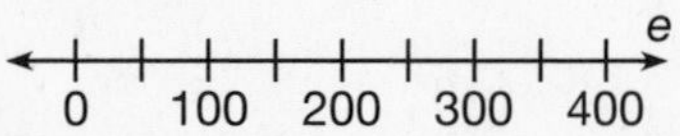

Name ______________________________

Practice

Section 10B Review

The table represents the equation $y = 6x - 8$. Use it to solve the related equations beneath the table.

x	-3	-2	-1	0	1	2	3	4	5
y	-26	-20	-14	-8	-2	4	10	16	22

1. $-14 = 6x - 8$ $x =$ ________

2. $6x - 8 = -26$ $x =$ ________

3. $16 = 6x - 8$ $x =$ ________

4. $6x - 8 = -2$ $x =$ ________

The graph of $y = -2x - 2$ is shown at right. Use it to solve the related equations.

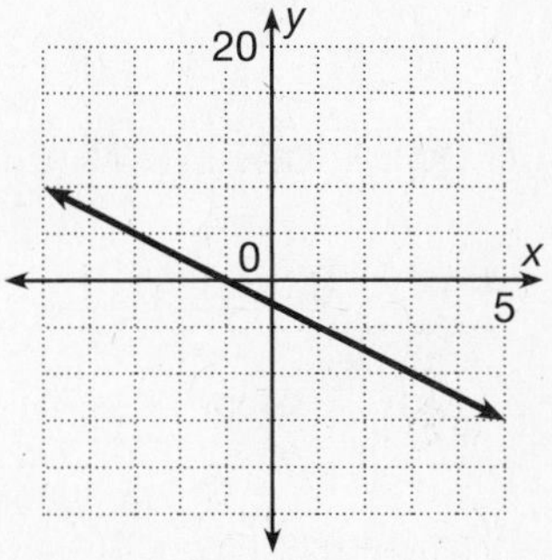

5. $-2x - 2 = 4$ $x =$ ________

6. $-4 = -2x - 2$ $x =$ ________

7. Use the graph to estimate the solution to $-9.5 = -2x - 2$. $x \approx$ ______

8. Dolphins can swim at rates up to 25 mi/hr. Write and graph an inequality for this statement. ____________

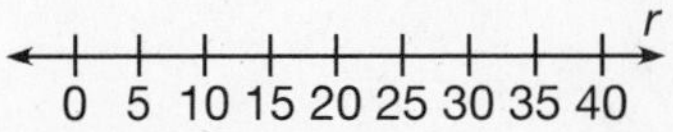

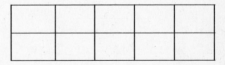

9. The Kitty Catalog offers T-shirts with kitten designs for \$12.00 each. A shipping charge of \$5.00 is added to the entire order.

a. Write an equation for the amount of money, *m*, that you would pay if you bought *t* T-shirts. ____________

b. Make a table of values for your equation in **a**.

c. Amy wants to buy as many shirts as she can. She has \$50 to spend. How many shirts can she buy? ____________

10. A typical credit card has an area of 7.17 in^2. A billboard artist draws a scale drawing of the credit card using a scale factor of 50. What is the area of the drawing? *[Lesson 7-10]* ____________

11. **Social Science** The population of Americans who speak a language other than English at home increased 6.5% from 1980 to 1990. If this population was 216 million in 1980, what was it in 1990? *[Lesson 8-7]* ____________

Name ________________________________

Practice 10-9

Integer Addition and Subtraction Equations

Write the equation represented by each equation box. Then solve the equation. The lighter tiles represent positive integers.

1. ________________

$x =$ ________________

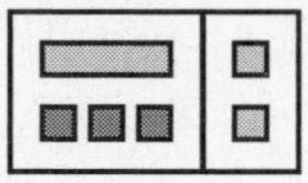

2. ________________

$x =$ ________________

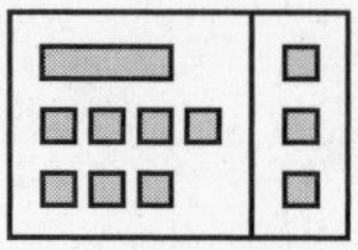

3. ________________

$x =$ ________________

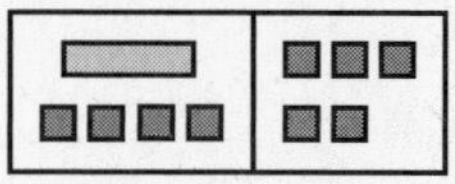

For each equation, tell whether the number in bold is a solution.

4. $x - 4 = 0$; **6** ________

5. $h + (-3) = -13$; **16** ___

6. $b - 1 = -4$; **−3** ________

7. $m + (-6) = 8$; **2** _____

8. $d - 7 = 6$; **13** ________

9. $p + (-8) = -35$; **43** ____

Solve each equation. Check your solutions.

10. $a - (-4) = -2$

$a =$ ________

11. $q + 2 = -47$

$q =$ ________

12. $s - (-5) = -7$

$s =$ ________

13. $t + 6 = 3$

$t =$ ________

14. $k + 8 = 2$

$k =$ ________

15. $f - (-7) = -24$

$f =$ ________

16. $c + (-2) = 51$

$c =$ ________

17. $y - 9 = 4$

$y =$ ________

18. $j + 15 = -9$

$j =$ ________

19. $u + (-21) = 18$

$u =$ ________

20. $g - 5 = 3$

$g =$ ________

21. $x - 31 = 74$

$x =$ ________

22. $w + (-45) = 11$

$w =$ ________

23. $r - 60 = -38$

$r =$ ________

24. $n + 3 = 26$

$n =$ ________

25. $z - (-72) = 62$

$z =$ ________

26. Yesterday's high temperature was 24°F. This was 33° higher than last night's low temperature. What was last night's low temperature?

____

27. The U.S. Postal Service handled 35.8 million pieces of library rate mail in 1994. This is 2.9 million pieces fewer than in 1993. How many library rate packages were mailed in 1993?

____

Name ____________________

Practice 10-10

Integer Multiplication and Division Equations

Write the equation represented by each equation box. Then solve the equation. The lighter tiles represent positive integers.

1. ____________ $x =$ ____________

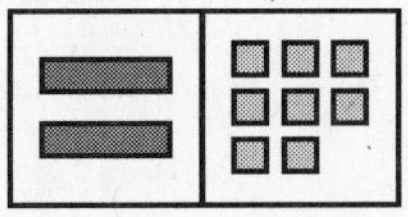

2. ____________ $x =$ ____________

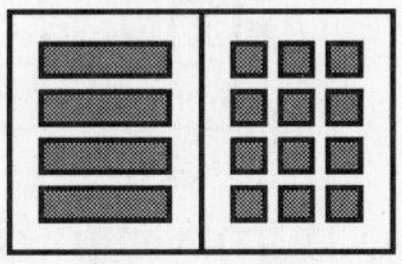

3. ____________ $x =$ ____________

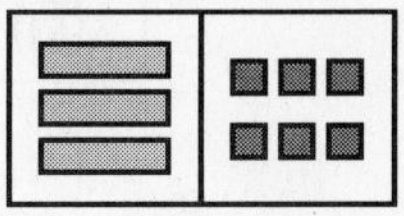

For each equation, tell whether the number in bold is a solution.

4. $\frac{x}{7} = 15$; **105** ________

5. $3x = 21$; **63** ________

6. $\frac{t}{-2} = 8$; **−4** ________

7. $-5z = -34$; **7** ________

8. $\frac{m}{4} = -9$; **−36** ________

9. $-6t = -24$; **4** ________

Solve each equation. Check your solutions.

10. $7n = 77$ $n =$ ________

11. $\frac{r}{-5} = 12$ $r =$ ________

12. $-2b = 34$ $b =$ ________

13. $\frac{g}{3} = 8$ $g =$ ________

14. $-8d = -64$ $d =$ ________

15. $-5k = 0$ $k =$ ________

16. $\frac{x}{10} = -6$ $x =$ ________

17. $\frac{u}{-8} = 15$ $u =$ ________

18. $-4a = 40$ $a =$ ________

19. $\frac{h}{-64} = 1$ $h =$ ________

20. $-7c = -56$ $c =$ ________

21. $\frac{f}{2} = -16$ $f =$ ________

22. $\frac{p}{-11} = -88$ $p =$ ________

23. $6t = -42$ $t =$ ________

24. $-12z = -96$ $z =$ ________

25. $\frac{y}{-18} = 3$ $y =$ ________

26. Computer Jerry recently bought a new modem for his computer. Yesterday, his new modem took 7 minutes to download a file. This is $\frac{1}{12}$ of the time it would have taken using his old modem. How long would it take to download the file using the old modem? ____________

27. Geography In 1994, the population of Argentina was about 34,000,000 people This was about 170 times as great as the population of Belize. What was the population of Belize? ____________

Name ______________________________

Practice
10-11

Solving Two-Step Equations

Write the equation represented by each equation box. Then solve the equation.

1. ______________ x = ______________

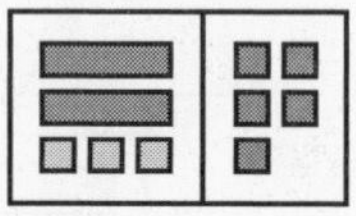

2. ______________ x = ______________

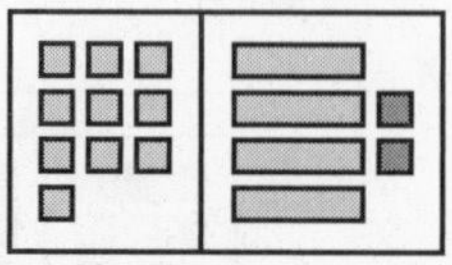

3. ______________ x = ______________

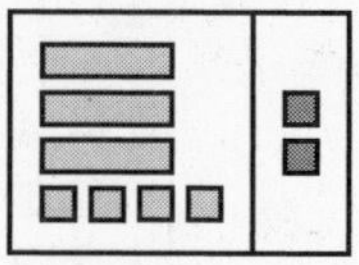

For each equation, tell whether the number in bold is a solution.

4. $\frac{p}{7} = -14$; **−98** ______

5. $-2x + 3 = 5$; **2** ______

6. $\frac{a}{-8} - 5 = -3$; **−16** ______

7. $\frac{u}{-5} + 7 = 12$; **30** ______

8. $4x + (-3) = 9$; **3** ______

9. $\frac{q}{3} + (-4) = 11$; **−15** ______

Solve each equation. Check your solutions.

10. $3b + (-7) = -25$ b = ______

11. $\frac{n}{-4} + (-3) = 8$ n = ______

12. $16 = 4h - 12$ h = ______

13. $\frac{x}{6} - (-10) = 3$ x = ______

14. $8w - 17 = -89$ w = ______

15. $\frac{c}{7} - 12 = -4$ c = ______

16. $\frac{p}{-5} + 12 = 20$ p = ______

17. $5j + (-16) = -76$ j = ______

18. $\frac{k}{-3} + (-8) = -8$ k = ______

19. $-11z + 42 = 86$ z = ______

20. $15 = \frac{d}{2} - (-12)$ d = ______

21. $13r - (-12) = 103$ r = ______

22. $\frac{g}{12} + (-8) = -5$ g = ______

23. $24 = \frac{m}{-5} + 17$ m = ______

24. $42 = 7t - 42$ t = ______

25. $-18y + 14 = -166$ y = ______

26. The area of a trapezoid is 32 cm^2. Its height is 8 cm and one base has length 3 cm. Write and solve an equation to find the length of the other base.

____

27. Science Gorillas and chimpanzees can learn sign language to communicate with humans. By 1982, a gorilla named Koko had learned 700 words. This is 50 fewer than 5 times as many words as a chimp named Washoe knew a decade earlier. How many words did Washoe know? ______________

Name ______________________________

Practice
10-12

Problem-Solving with Integer Equations

1. Suppose the temperature increases 8° to −7°F. What was the starting temperature? ____________

2. **Science** A typical giant squid is about 240 in. long, which is 16 times the diameter of one of its eyes. What is the diameter of the eye? ____________

3. **Consumer** James went to the store to return a defective $45 tape recorder for a refund. At the same time, he bought some batteries for $3 per package. If he received $33 of his refund, how many packages of batteries did he buy? ____________

4. The Rugyong Hotel in Pyongyang, North Korea, has 105 stories. This is 9 more than twice the number of stories of the Transamerica Pyramid in San Francisco, California. How many stories does the Transamerica Pyramid have? ____________

5. Rome, Italy, gets an average of 2 in. of rain in April. This is about $\frac{1}{4}$ the average April rainfall in Nairobi, Kenya. How much rain falls in Nairobi in April? ____________

6. **Science** Neptune has 8 known moons. This is 2 more than $\frac{1}{3}$ of the number of known moons of Saturn. How many moons is Saturn known to have? ____________

7. **Science** Ohm's Law states that the electrical current, I, through a resistor is given by the formula $I = \frac{V}{R}$, where V is the voltage in volts and R is the resistance in ohms. If the current is 6 amperes and the resistance is 18 ohms, what is the voltage? ____________

8. During Super Bowl XX in 1986, the Chicago Bears scored 46 points against the New England Patriots. This was 24 less than 7 times the Patriots score. How many points did the Patriots score? ____________

9. Fahrenheit and Celsius temperatures are related by the formula $F = \frac{9C}{5} + 32$. What is the Celsius temperature if

   a. the temperature is 77°F? ____________

   b. the temperature is −22°F? ____________

Name ____________________

Practice

Section 10C Review

Write the equation represented by each equation box. Then solve the equation.

1. ____________________

$x =$ ____________________

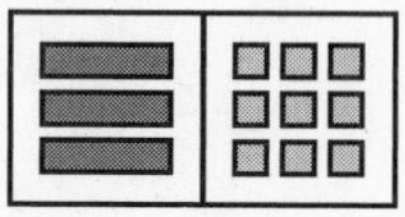

2. ____________________

$x =$ ____________________

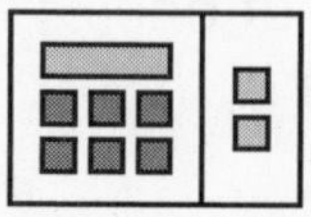

3. ____________________

$x =$ ____________________

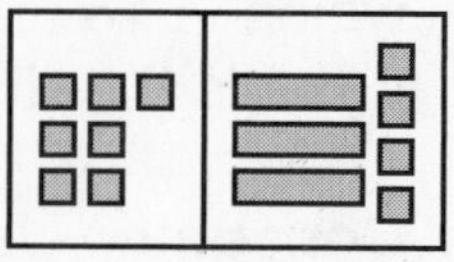

For each equation, tell whether the number in bold is a solution.

4. $k + (-16) = 4$; **20** ____

5. $8z = -24$; **−3** ____

6. $\frac{p}{-7} = 3$; **21** ____

7. $\frac{w}{7} + (-4) = 10$; **2** ____

8. $\frac{t}{5} - 12 = -2$; **50** ____

9. $-4s + 16 = -12$; **7** ____

Solve each equation. Check your solutions.

10. $b - 24 = -17$ $b =$ ______

11. $-7n = 49$ $n =$ ______

12. $\frac{h}{-3} + (-8) = -3$ $h =$ ______

13. $\frac{d}{5} = -8$ $d =$ ______

14. $8k + 4 = -20$ $k =$ ______

15. $c + 8 = -4$ $c =$ ______

16. $-6q = -78$ $q =$ ______

17. $\frac{s}{6} - 21 = -14$ $s =$ ______

18. $\frac{f}{-10} = 20$ $f =$ ______

19. $\frac{w}{7} = -17$ $w =$ ______

20. $y - (-12) = 43$ $y =$ ______

21. $4r + (-60) = -108$ $r =$ ______

22. A business lost \$38,000 in 1996. This is the same as a profit of −\$38,000, which is \$85,000 less than the 1995 profit. What was the profit in 1995? ____________

23. Fine Arts A mountain painting created by Kao K'o-kung in about 1300 is 32 in. wide and 48 in. tall. A reproduction of this painting in a book is 5 in. tall. How wide is the reproduction? *[Lesson 7-9]* ____________

24. Geography Temperatures in Siberia average about −35°F during the coldest months of the year. Temperatures in the arctic region of North America are about 10° warmer than this. Find the North American temperature. *[Lesson 9-4]* ____________

 Use with page 544.

Name ______________________________

Practice

Cumulative Review Chapters 1–10

Solve each proportion. *[Lesson 6-8]*

1. $\frac{y}{16} = \frac{7}{8}$ $y =$ ________

2. $\frac{8}{18} = \frac{20}{b}$ $b =$ ________

3. $\frac{3}{m} = \frac{15}{20}$ $m =$ ________

4. $\frac{25}{10} = \frac{j}{2}$ $j =$ ________

5. $\frac{6}{2} = \frac{9}{p}$ $p =$ ________

6. $\frac{8}{12} = \frac{r}{3}$ $r =$ ________

7. $\frac{7}{a} = \frac{28}{36}$ $a =$ ________

8. $\frac{n}{15} = \frac{30}{9}$ $n =$ ________

A model of a building is 8 in. tall. Use each scale to find the height of the actual building. *[Lesson 7-2]*

9. Scale: 1 in. = 3 ft

Actual height: ________

10. Scale: 1 in. = 5 ft

Actual height: ________

11. Scale: 1 in. = $1\frac{1}{2}$ ft

Actual height: ________

12. Scale: 1 in. = $8\frac{1}{4}$ ft

Actual height: ________

13. Scale: 2 in. = 11 ft

Actual height: ________

14. Scale: 3 in. = 25 ft

Actual height: ________

Find each sum, difference, product, or quotient. *[Lessons 9-4 to 9-7]*

15. $3 + (-16)$ ________

16. $7 \cdot (-5)$ ________

17. $-64 \div 4$ ________

18. $-8 - (-12)$ ________

19. $-14 \div (-7)$ ________

20. $-9 + (-32)$ ________

Graph each equation on a coordinate plane. *[Lesson 10-5]*

21. $y = -x + 4$

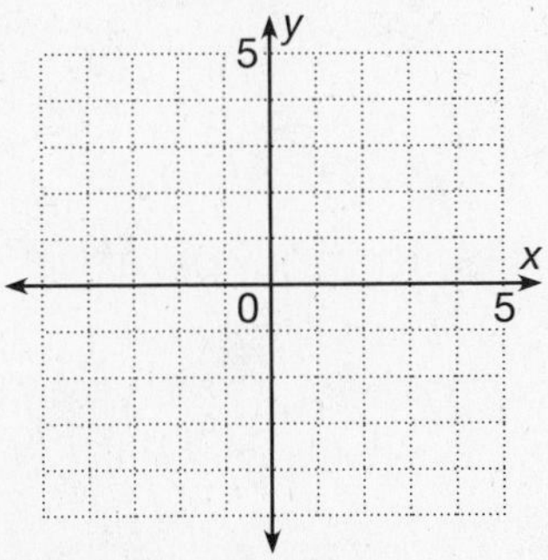

22. $y = 4x$

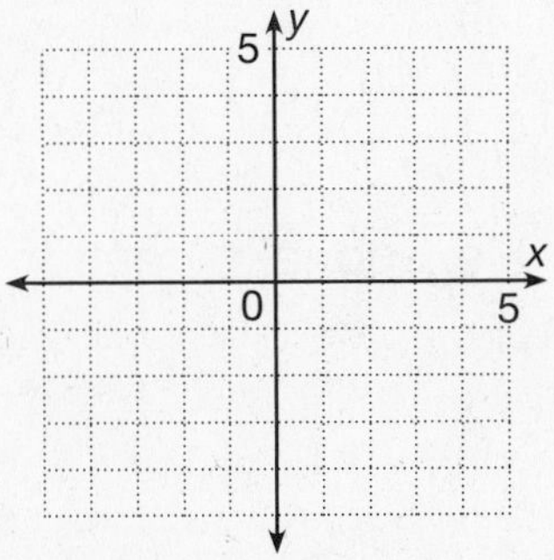

23. $y = 2x - 3$

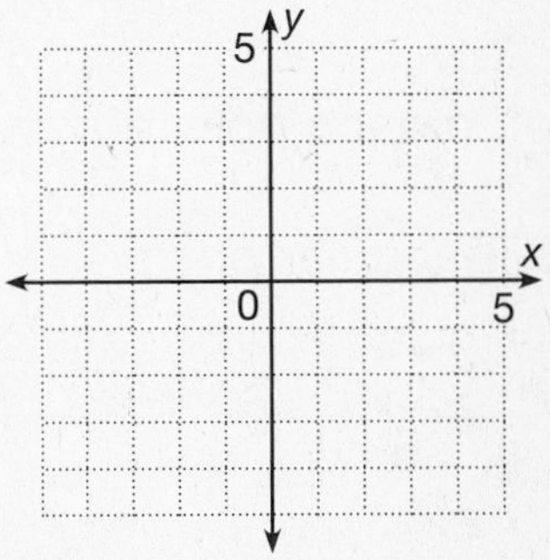

Solve each equation. Check your solutions. *[Lesson 10-12]*

24. $x + (-7) = 12$ $x =$ ________

25. $-4p = 28$ $p =$ ________

26. $\frac{t}{-5} + 8 = 13$ $t =$ ________

27. $-6n + 3 = 45$ $n =$ ________

Name ______________________________

Practice 11-1

Exploring Polyhedrons

Use the sketch of the polyhedron to answer each question.

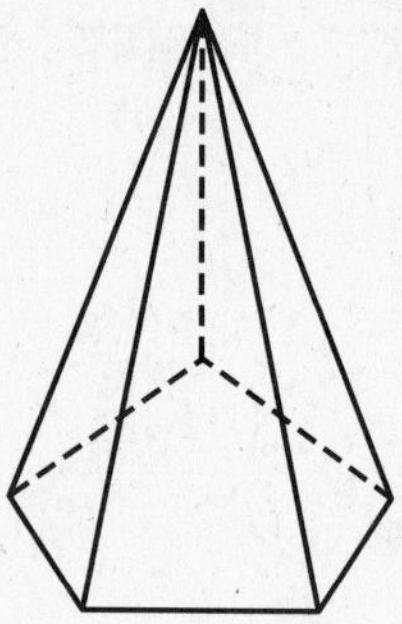

1. Name the polyhedron. ______________________

2. Name the polygons that are the faces of the polyhedron. How many of each type of polygon are there?

   ____

3. How many edges, faces, and vertices does the polyhedron have?

   Edges: __________ Faces: __________ Vertices: __________

Name each polyhedron.

4. ______________________

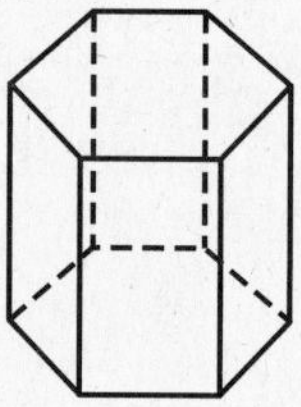

5. ______________________

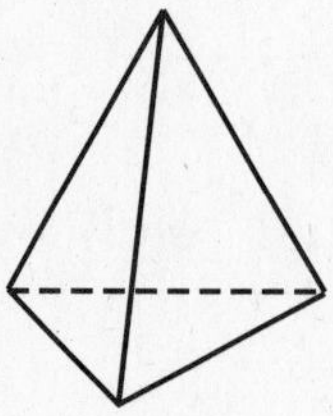

6. ______________________

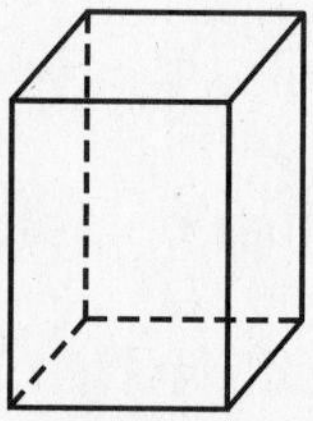

7. ______________________

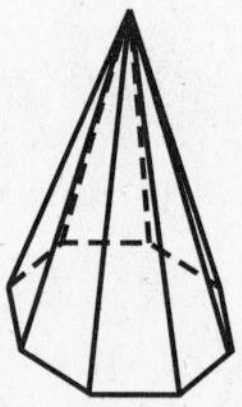

8. ______________________

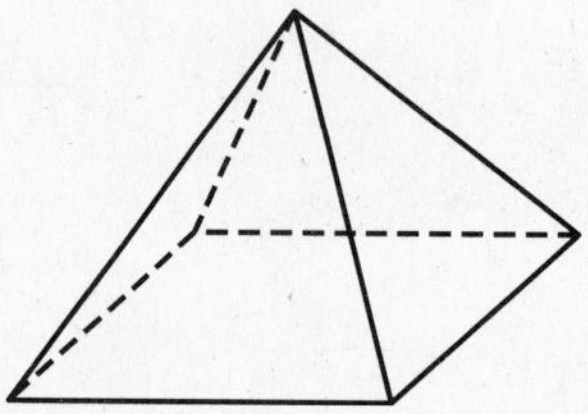

9. ______________________

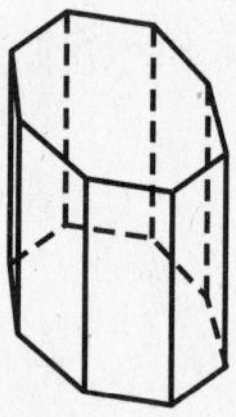

Sketch each polyhedron.

10. Triangular prism

11. Hexagonal pyramid

12. Pentagonal pyramid

Name ______________________________

Isometric and Orthographic Drawing

Find the number of cubes in each figure. Assume all cubes are visible.

1. ____________
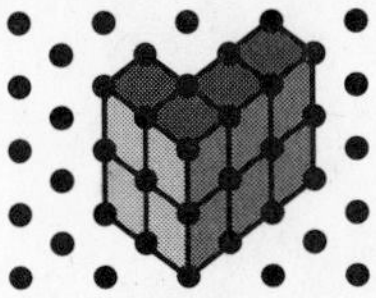

2. ____________
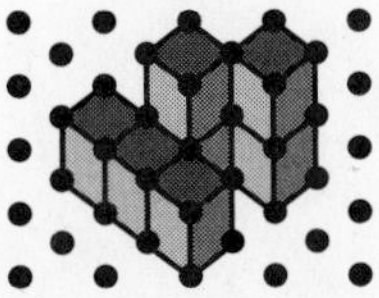

3. ____________
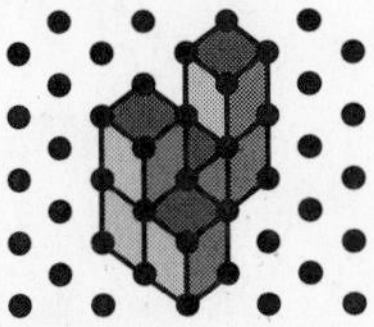

4. ____________
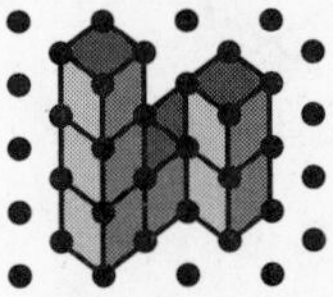

Match each isometric drawing with a set of orthographic views.

5. ____________
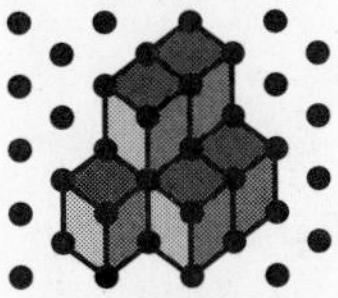

6. ____________
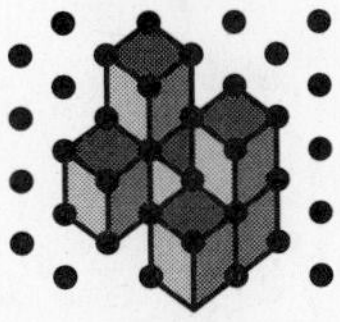

7. ____________
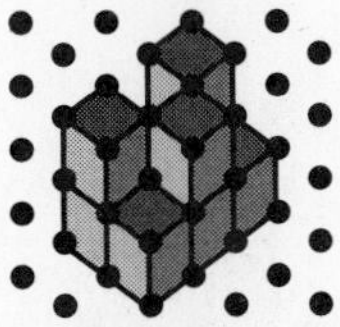

8. ____________

A.
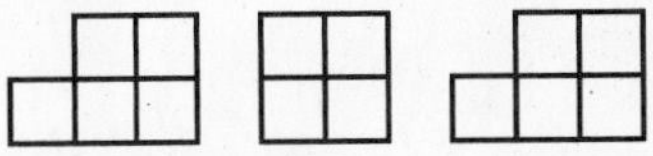
front side top

B.
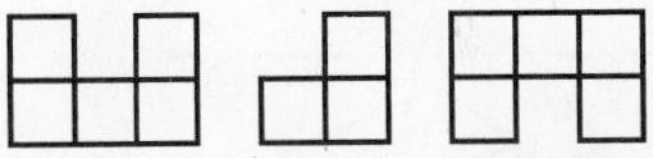
front side top

C.
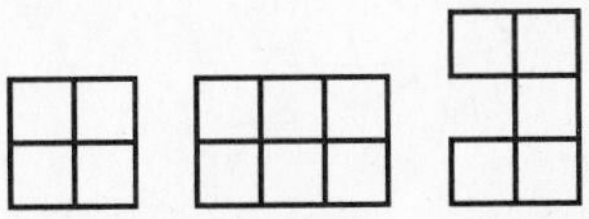
front side top

D.
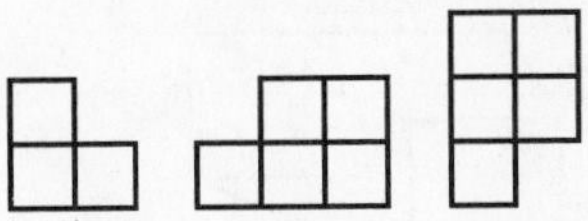
front side top

9. Sketch front, side, and top views of the object.

10. Make a perspective sketch of the object.

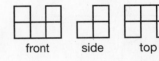

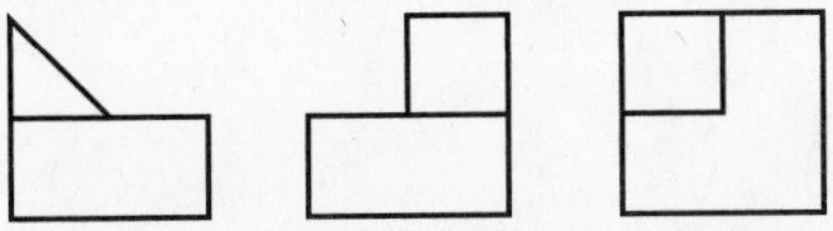
front side top

Name ______________________________

Practice
11-3

Polyhedron Nets and Surface Areas

Sketch a net for each polyhedron.

1.

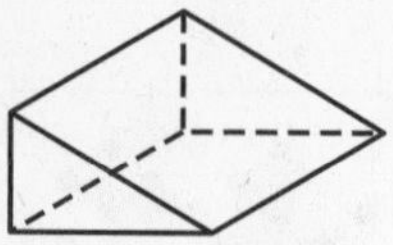

2.

3.

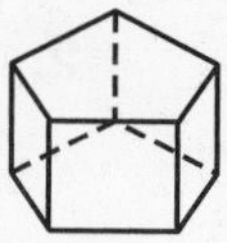

Sketch a net for each polyhedron, then find its surface area.

4. ______________

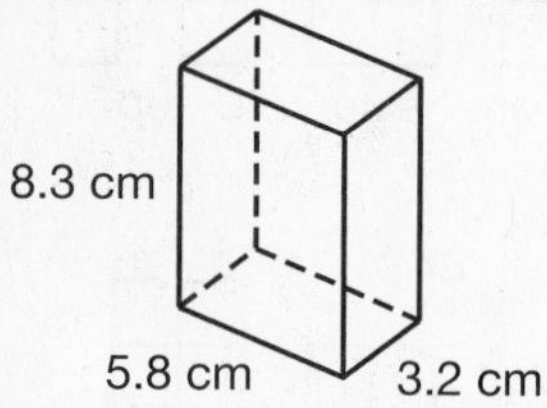

5. ______________

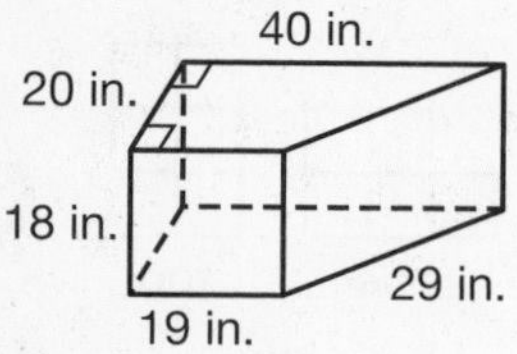

6. ______________

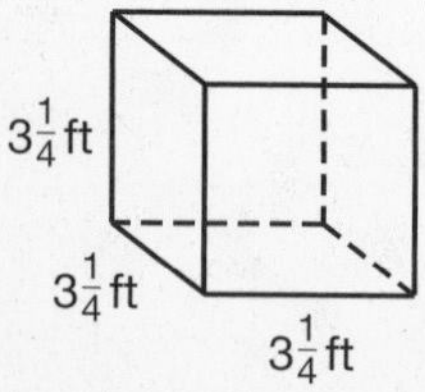

7. A box of facial tissue measures $9\frac{3}{8}$ in. by $4\frac{5}{8}$ in. by $3\frac{1}{4}$ in. Assuming no overlaps, how much cardboard was used to make the box? ______________

Name ____________________

Practice 11-4

Volumes of Prisms

Find the volume of each prism.

1. ____________

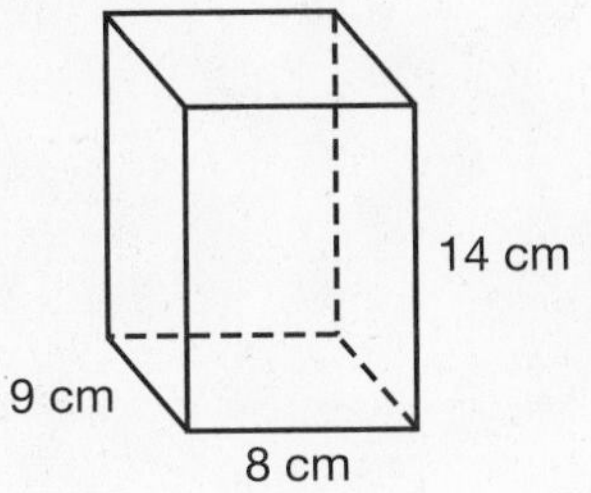

2. ____________

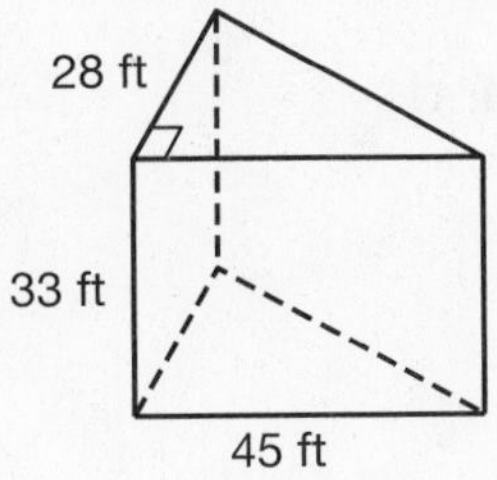

3. ____________

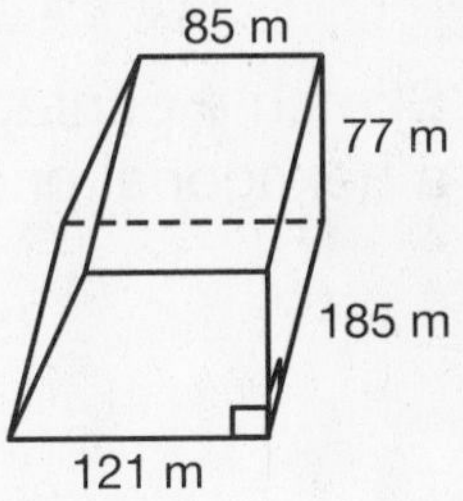

4. ____________

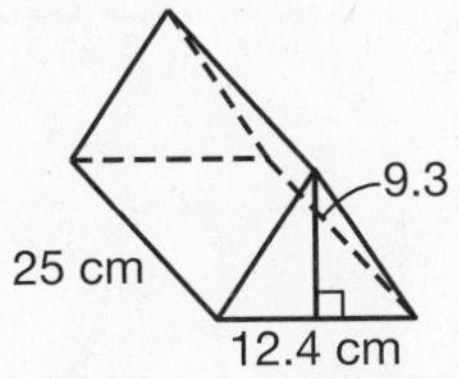

5. ____________

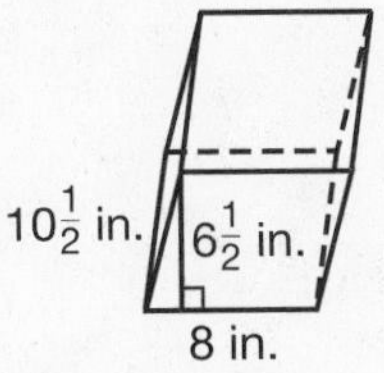

6. ____________

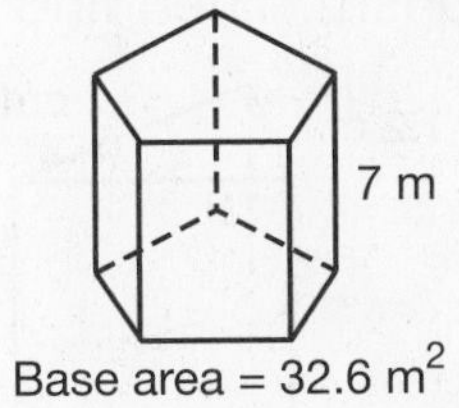

7. ____________

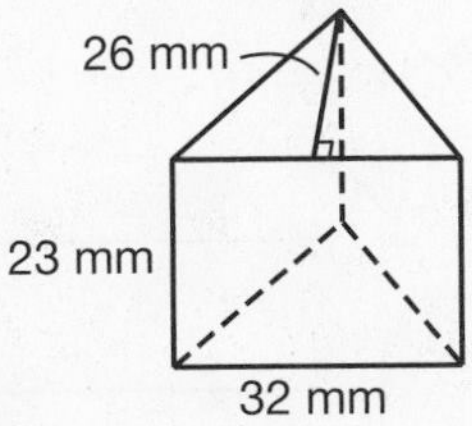

8. ____________

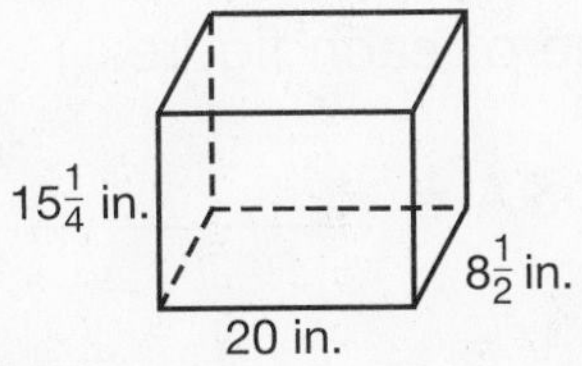

9. ____________

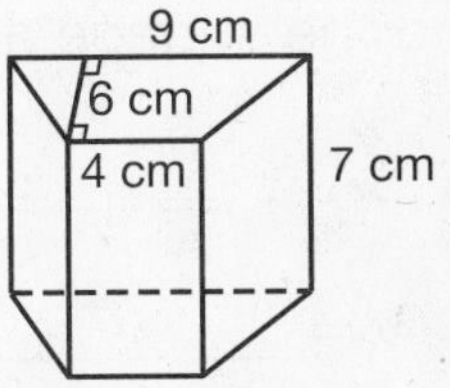

10. ____________

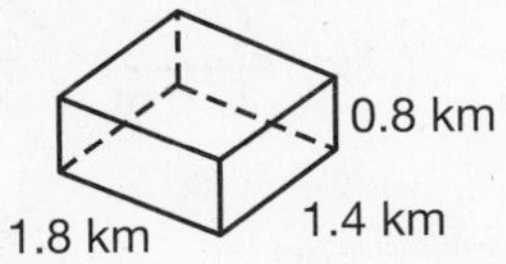

11. ____________

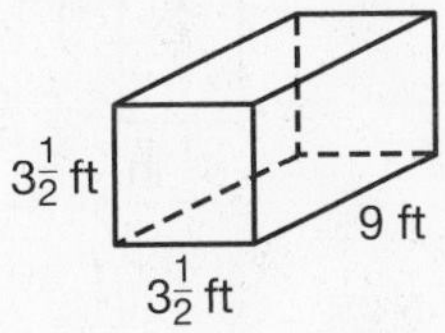

12. ____________

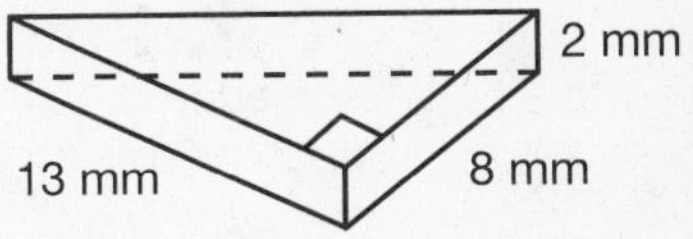

13. An asphalt speed bump has the shape of a trapezoidal prism. The prism is 450 cm long and each base has the dimensions shown. What is the volume of the speed bump?

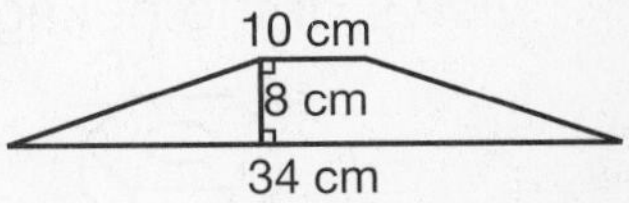

____

14. The tunnel on Yerba Buena Island near San Francisco, California, is about 78 ft wide, 56 ft tall, and 540 ft long. Estimate the amount of air in the tunnel by assuming that the tunnel has the shape of a rectangular prism.

____

Name ______________________________

Practice

Section 11A Review

Tell whether each statement is true or false.

1. A cube has 8 faces. ____________

2. All prisms are polyhedrons. ____________

3. Sketch a pentagonal pyramid and a hexagonal prism.

4. Sketch a net for the right triangular prism. Then find its surface area. ____________

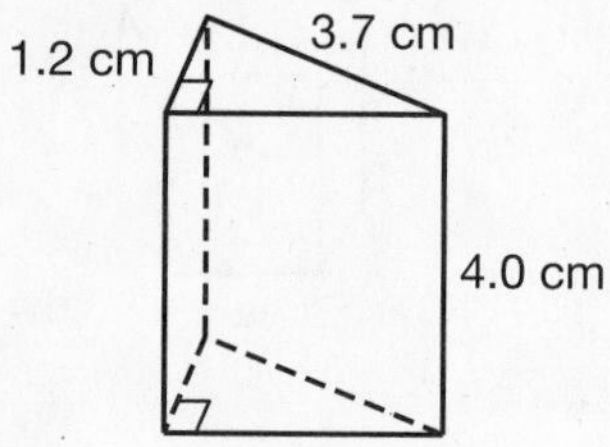

Find the surface area and volume of each figure.

5. *SA* = ____________

V = ____________

Each edge is 1 cm long

6. *SA* = ____________

V = ____________

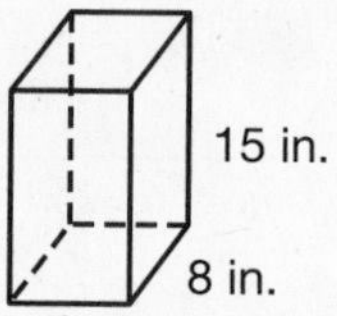

7. *SA* = ____________

V = ____________

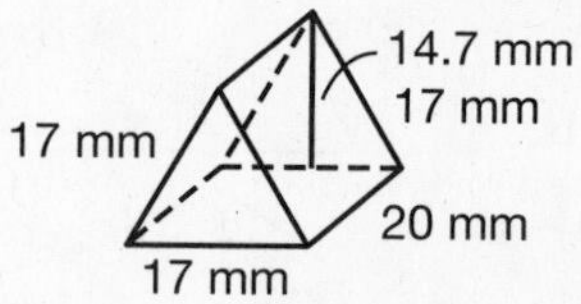

8. Sketch front, side, and top views of the hexagonal nut.

9. The floor plan of Andrea's home has the shape shown. What is the area of the floor? *[Lesson 5-10]*

____

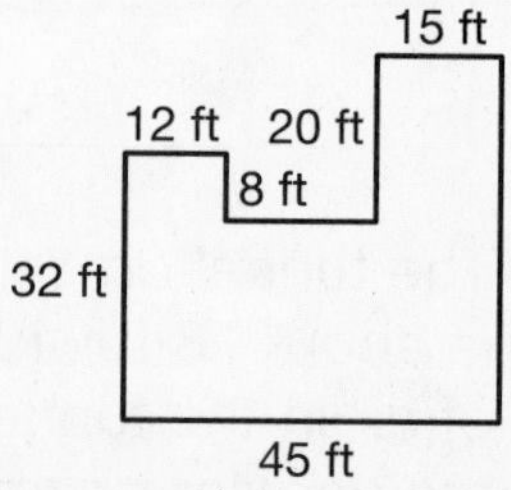

10. A group of people pulled a 747 aircraft 328 ft in 61 seconds in London, England, in 1995. Use a unit rate to estimate how far they pulled the plane during the first 17 seconds. ____________

Name ______________________________

Practice
11-5

Circles and Circle Graphs

Geography Use the circle graph to answer Exercises 1 and 2.

1. Estimate the percent of Cameroon's land in each category.

Arable land and crops ________

Meadows and pastures ________

Forest and woodland ________

Other ________

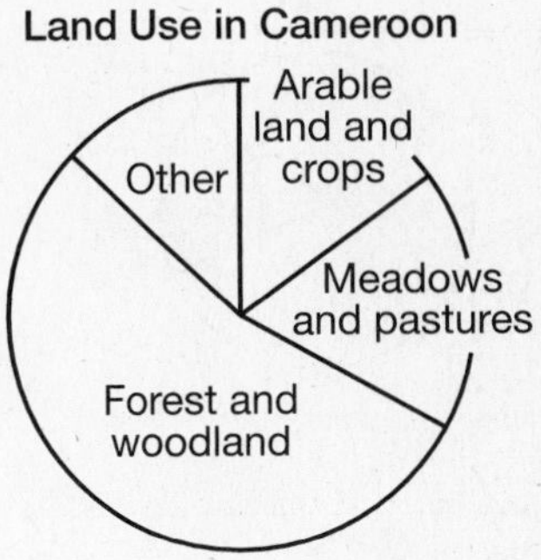

2. Identify any sectors that have central angles greater than 180°. ________________

Sketch a circle graph to show the data. (Do *not* calculate or measure the central angles.)

3. Social Science About 50% of Djibouti's exports go to other African nations. About 40% go to the Middle East, and 10% go to other places.

4. Social Science

Ethnic Groups in the Congo

Kongo	Sangha	Teke	M'Bochi	Other
48%	20%	17%	12%	3%

5. Geography

Areas of the Great Lakes (mi^2)

Ontario	Erie	Michigan	Huron	Superior
7,540	9,940	22,400	23,010	31,820

Name ______________________________

Practice
11-6

Pi and Circumference

Find the circumference of each circle given its diameter or radius. Use $\pi \approx 3.14$, and round answers to the nearest tenth.

1. ____________

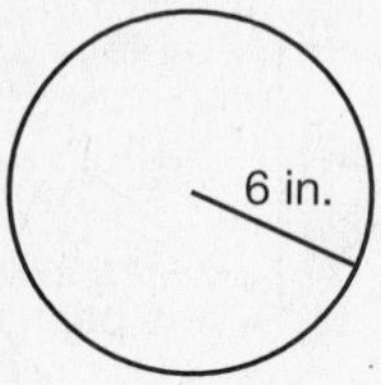

2. ____________

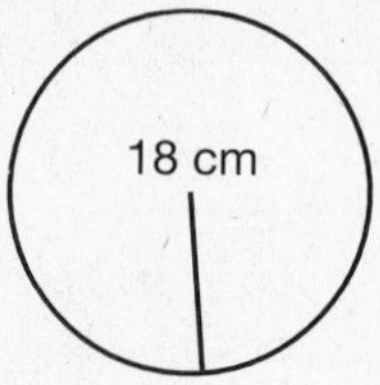

3. ____________

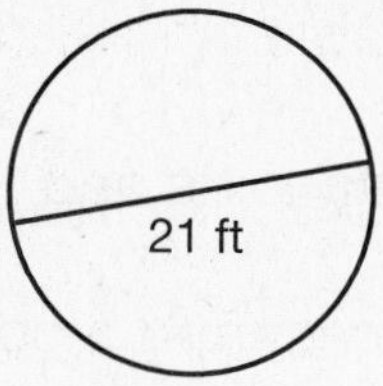

4. ____________

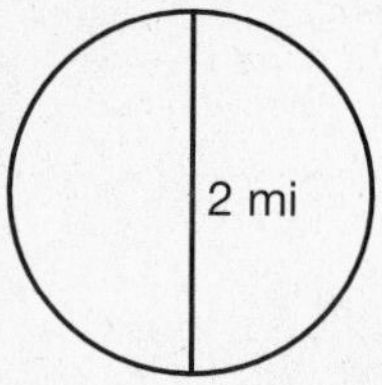

5. ____________

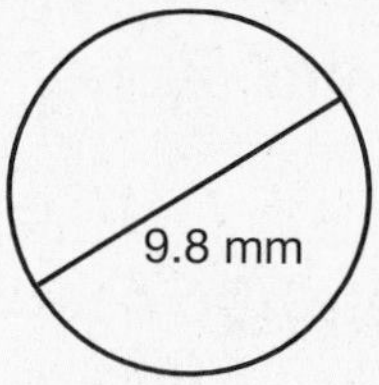

6. ____________

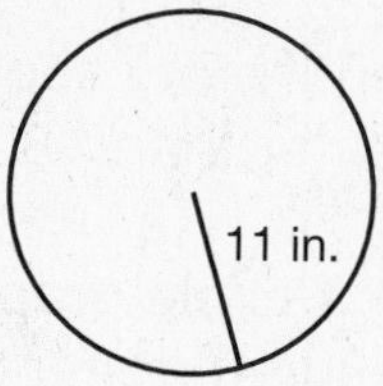

Find the circumference of each circle given its diameter or radius. Use $\pi \approx \frac{22}{7}$, and express answers in lowest terms.

7. ____________

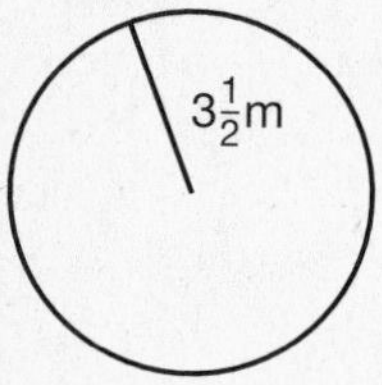

8. ____________

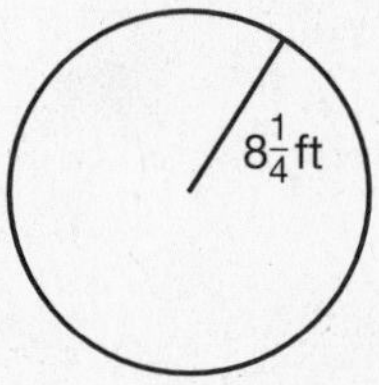

9. ____________

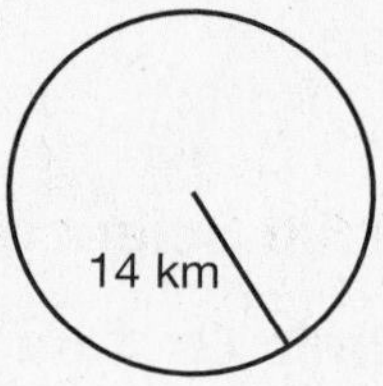

Given the radius, diameter, or circumference of a circle, find the other two measurements. Use $\pi \approx 3.14$, and round answers to the nearest tenth.

10. $r =$ ________
$d = 44$ cm
$C \approx$ ________

11. $r \approx$ ________
$d \approx$ ________
$C = 15$ ft

12. $r = 9$ mm
$d =$ ________
$C \approx$ ________

13. $r =$ ________
$d = 6.8$ mi
$C \approx$ ________

14. $r =$ ________
$d =$ ________
$C = 4\pi$ cm

15. $r = 12\frac{1}{2}$ ft
$d =$ ________
$C \approx$ ________

16. $r =$ ________
$d = 5.8$ m
$C \approx$ ________

17. $r =$ ________
$d =$ ________
$C = 7\pi$ in.

18. Science The radius of Pluto is about 1145 km. Find the length of Pluto's equator. ____________

Name ____________________

Practice 11-7

Area of a Circle

Find the area of each circle given its diameter or radius. Use $\pi \approx 3.14$, and round answers to the nearest tenth.

1. ____________________

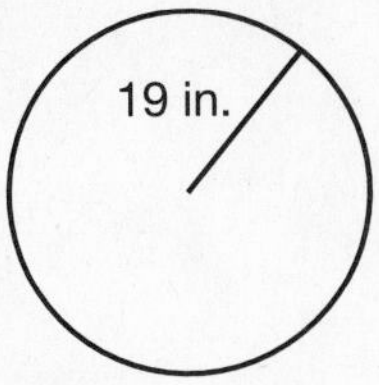

2. ____________________

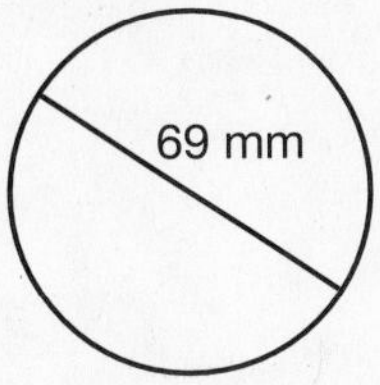

3. ____________________

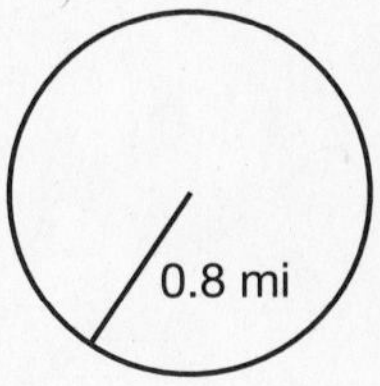

4. ____________________

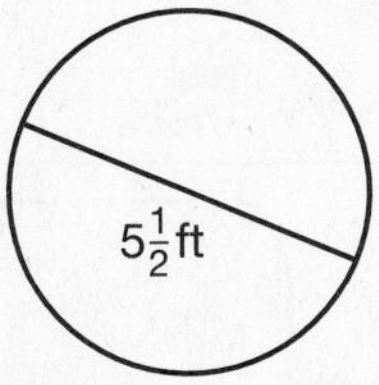

5. ____________________

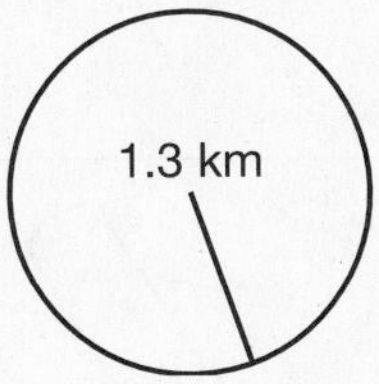

6. ____________________

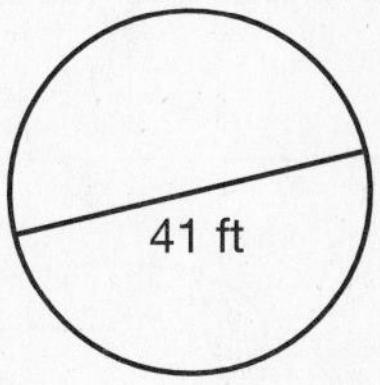

Find the area of each circle given its diameter or radius. Use $\pi \approx \frac{22}{7}$, and express answers in lowest terms.

7. ____________________

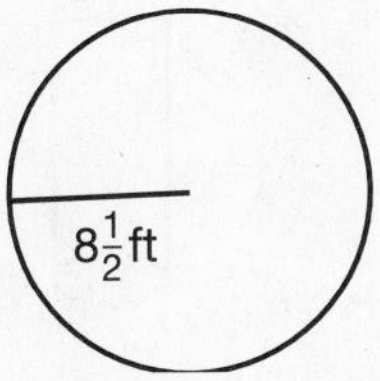

8. ____________________

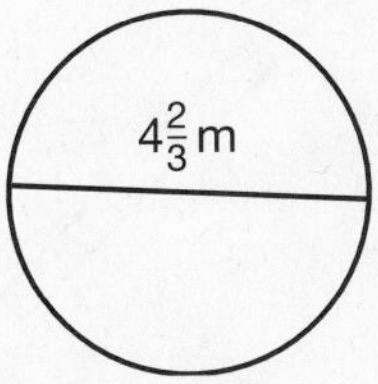

9. ____________________

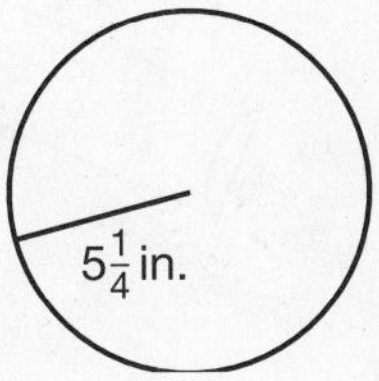

Given the radius or diameter of a circle, find its area. Use $\pi \approx 3.14$, and round answers to the nearest tenth.

10. $r = 18\frac{1}{4}$ in.

$A \approx$ ____________________

11. $d = 27$ cm

$A \approx$ ____________________

12. $r = 38$ mi

$A \approx$ ____________________

13. $d = 5$ ft

$A \approx$ ____________________

14. $r = 9.1$ cm

$A \approx$ ____________________

15. $d = \frac{5}{8}$ in.

$A \approx$ ____________________

16. Find the area of a pizza if the diameter is 15 in. ____________________

17. The radius of a U.S. quarter is about 12 mm. Find the area of a quarter. ____________________

Name ____________________

Practice
11-8

Surface Area of Cylinders

Make a perspective drawing of each object.

1. A sphere

2. A cone

3. A cylinder

Find the surface area of each cylinder. Use $\pi \approx 3.14$, and round answers to the nearest tenth.

4. ____________

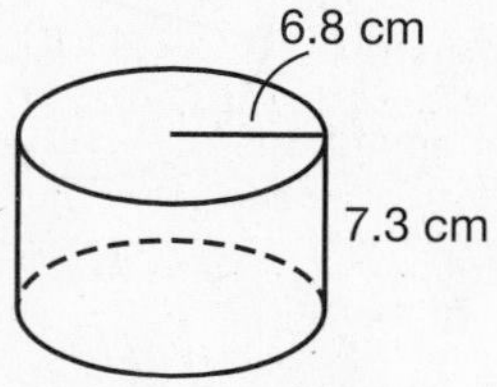

5. ____________

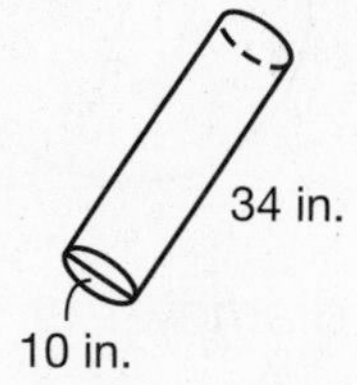

6. ____________

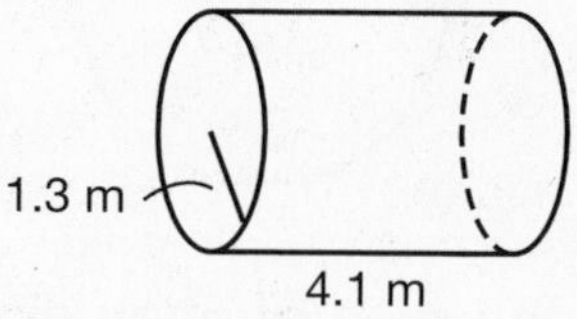

7. ____________

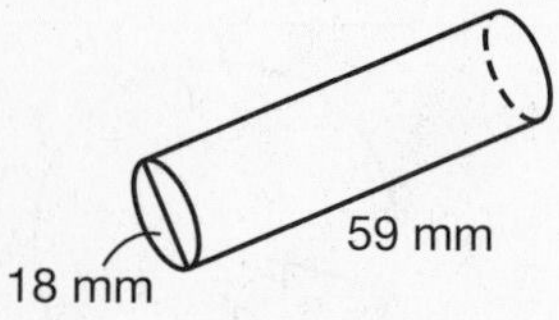

8. ____________

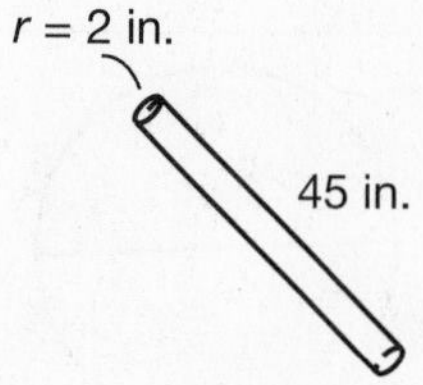

9. ____________

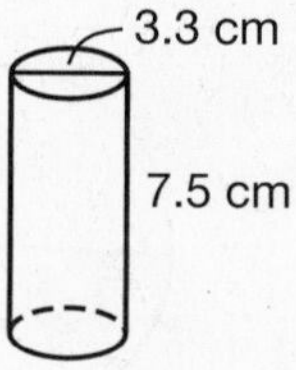

10. ____________

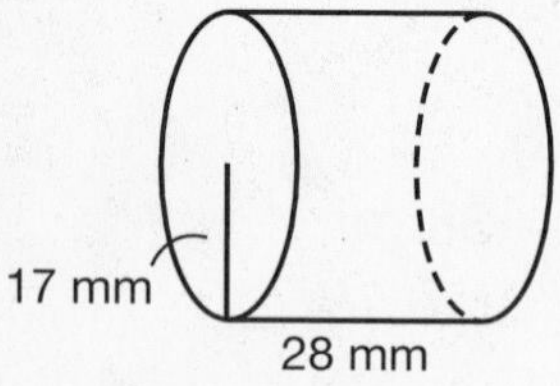

11. ____________

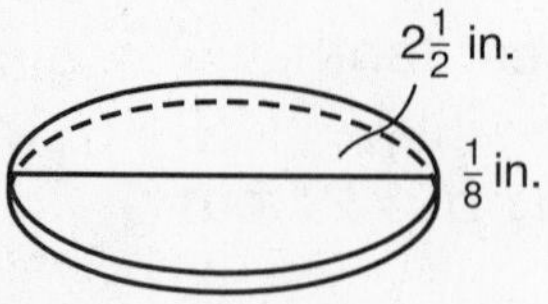

12. ____________

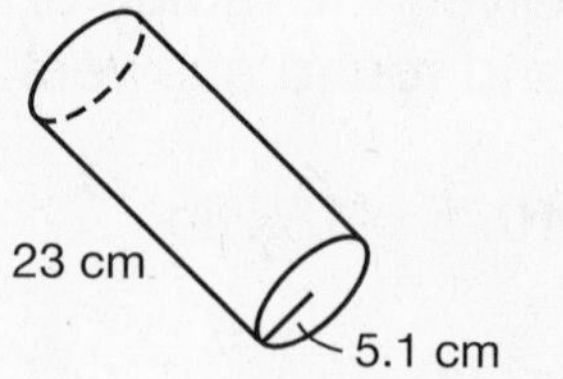

13. A can of dog food has diameter 7.4 cm and height 10.3 cm. How many square centimeters of metal were used to make this can? ____________

14. A lighthouse has the shape of a cylinder with radius 13 ft and height 60 ft. If you paint the outside of the lighthouse (not including the roof), how much surface area will you cover? ____________

Name ______________________________

Practice
11-9

Volume of Cylinders

Find the volume of each cylinder. Use $\pi \approx 3.14$, and round answers to the nearest tenth.

1. ____________

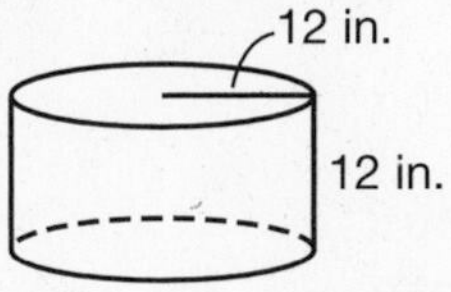

2. ____________

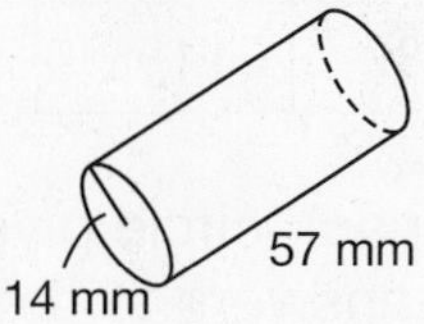

3. ____________

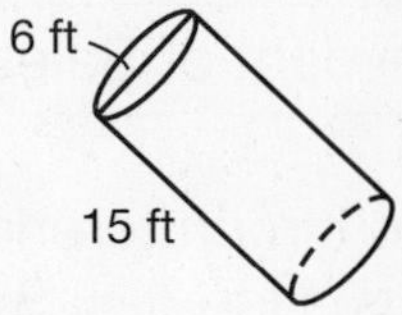

4. ____________

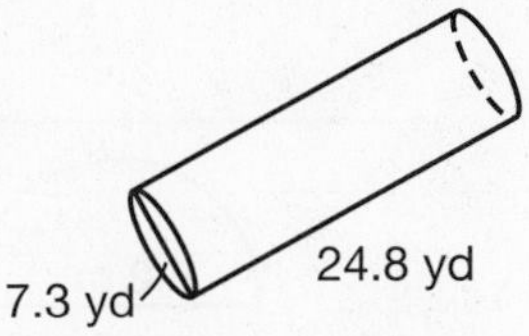

5. ____________

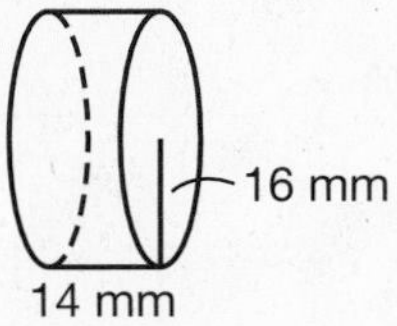

6. ____________

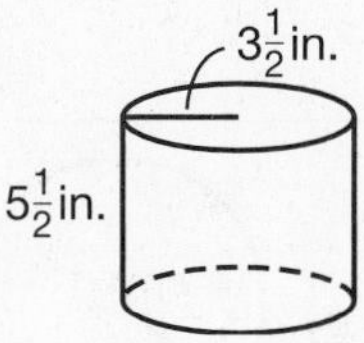

7. ____________

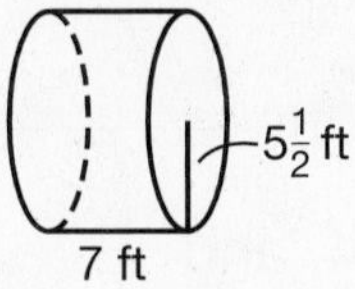

8. ____________

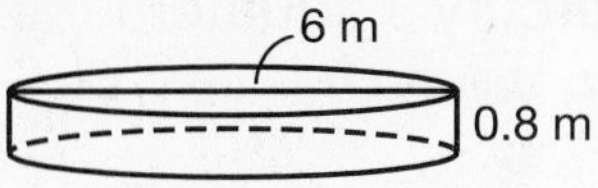

9. ____________

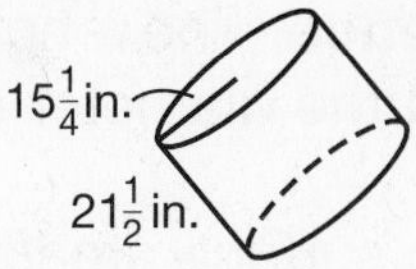

10. ____________

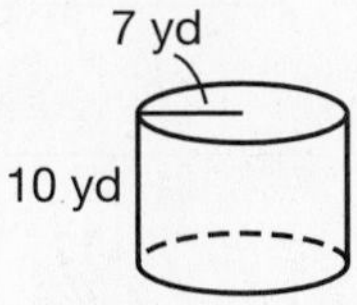

11. ____________

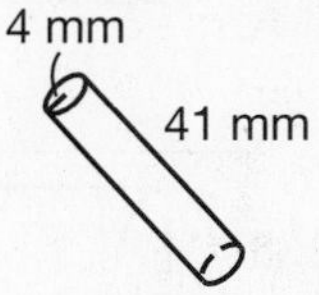

12. ____________

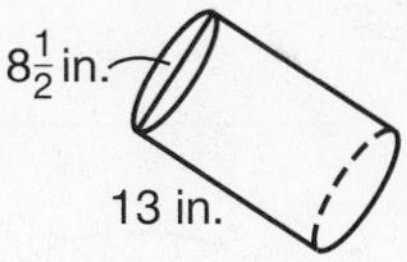

Given the height and radius, find the capacity of each cylindrical can to the nearest tenth of a milliliter. Use $\pi \approx 3.14$.

13. $h = 13$ cm
$r = 4$ cm

$V \approx$ ____________

14. $h = 22$ cm
$r = 9.3$ cm

$V \approx$ ____________

15. $h = 9.3$ cm
$r = 3.6$ cm

$V \approx$ ____________

16. History The largest single-cylinder steam engine ever built was used in 1849 for land draining in the Netherlands. Its cylinder was 12 ft in diameter and it had a stroke of about 19 ft. How much water was lifted by each stroke? ____________

Name ______________________________

Practice

Section 11B Review

1. The table gives data about 1993 retail car sales in the U.S. Draw a circle graph to show the data.

Category	Small	Midsize	Large	Luxury
Percent of Sales	33%	43%	11%	13%

Find the circumference and area of each circle given its diameter or radius. Use $\pi \approx 3.14$, and round answers to the nearest tenth.

2. $C \approx$ ______________ $A \approx$ ______________

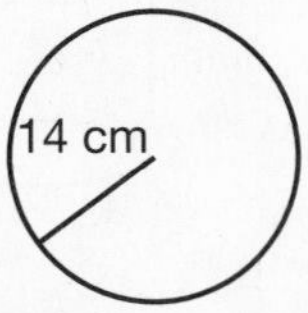

3. $C \approx$ ______________ $A \approx$ ______________

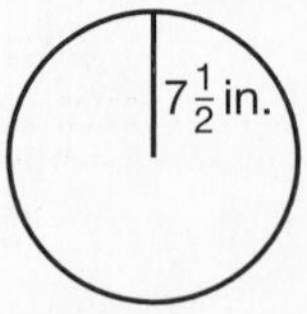

4. $C \approx$ ______________ $A \approx$ ______________

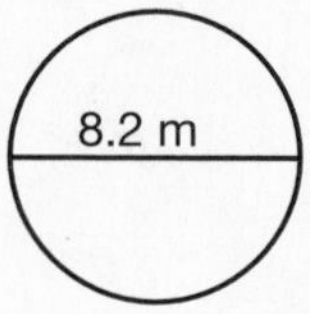

5. Science The length of Mercury's equator is about 9522 mi. Find the diameter of Mercury. ______________

Find the surface area and volume of each cylinder. Use $\pi \approx 3.14$, and round answers to the nearest tenth.

6. $SA \approx$ ______________ $V \approx$ ______________

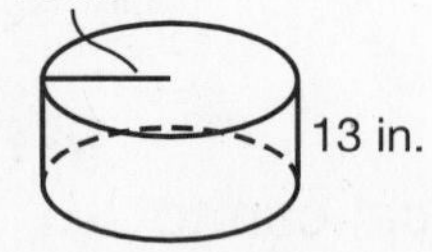

7. $SA \approx$ ______________ $V \approx$ ______________

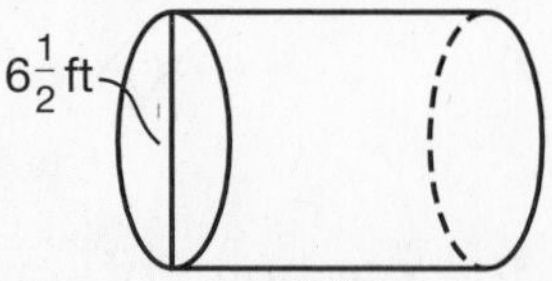

8. $SA \approx$ ______________ $V \approx$ ______________

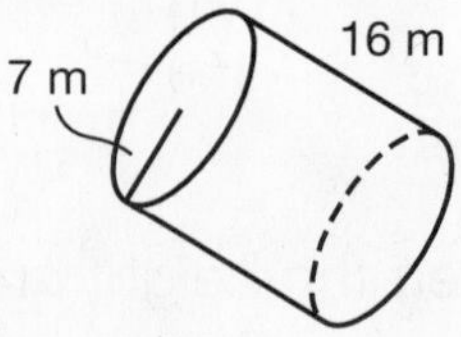

9. A skydiver jumps out of an airplane flying at an elevation of 940 ft above sea level. She lands in Death Valley, California, (elevation −282 ft). How far did she fall? *[Lesson 9-5]* ______________

10. Science The saltopus was a small dinosaur that lived in Scotland and weighed 2 lb. An equation to represent the weight of several of these creatures is $w = 2s$, where w represents the weight in pounds and s represents the number of saltopuses. Graph this equation on a coordinate plane. *[Lesson 10-5]*

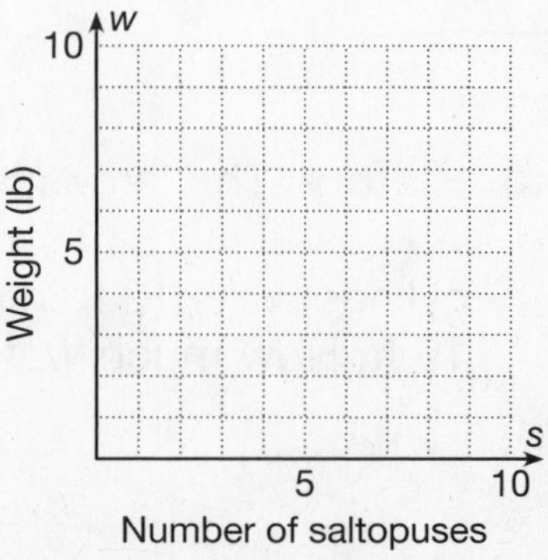

Name ______________________________

Practice
11-10

Translations

For each group of figures, identify all lettered polygons that are translations of the shaded polygon.

1. ______________

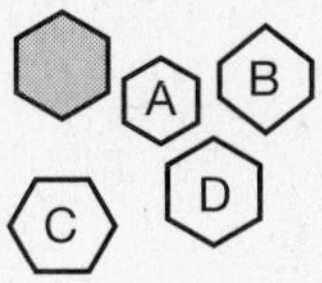

2. ______________

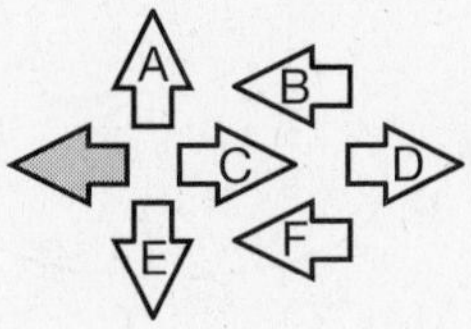

3. ______________

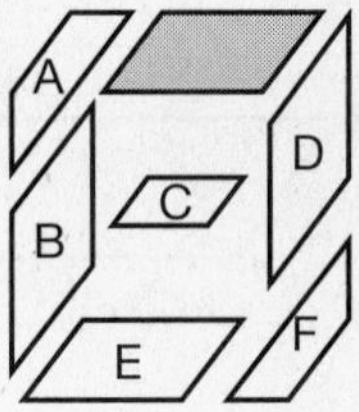

Write a rule for each translation.

4. Left 8

____

5. Right 2, down 3

____

Point P is located at (4, −1). Use each rule to find the coordinates of P'.

6. $(x, y) \rightsquigarrow (x - 4, y + 3)$ __________

7. $(x, y) \rightsquigarrow (x + 10, y + 2)$ __________

8. $(x, y) \rightsquigarrow (x + 3, y)$ __________

9. $(x, y) \rightsquigarrow (x - 7, y + 1)$ __________

Using each rule, draw a translation of figure *QRST* on a coordinate plane. Give the coordinates of the vertices of the translation.

10. Left 4, up 2

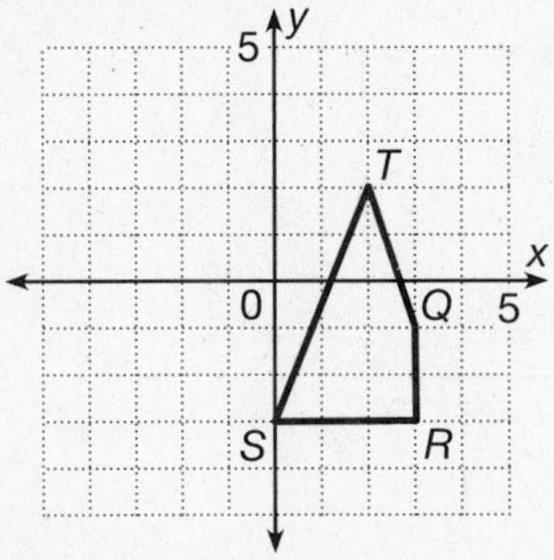

Q' __________ R' __________

S' __________ T' __________

11. $(x, y) \rightsquigarrow (x + 5, y + 3)$

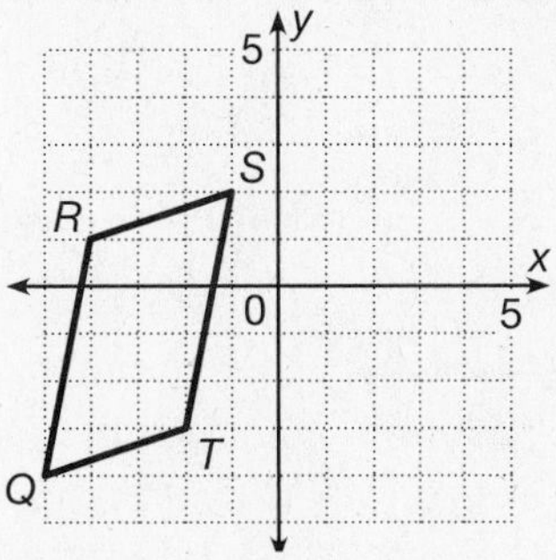

Q' __________ R' __________

S' __________ T' __________

12. Language Arts The Japanese word shown at the right means "extensive forest." Circle the portions of this word that are translations of each other.

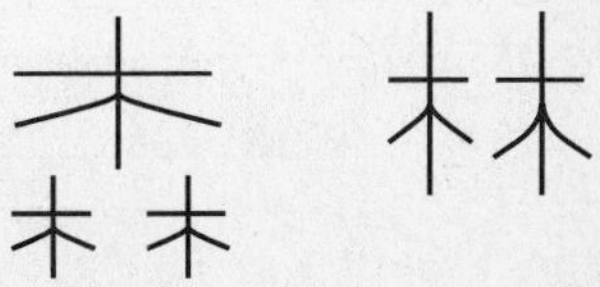

Name ____________________

Practice 11-11

Reflections and Line Symmetry

Decide whether each figure has line symmetry. If it does, draw and number the lines of symmetry.

1. Parallelogram ______ **2.** Ellipse ______ **3.** Isosceles Trapezoid ______

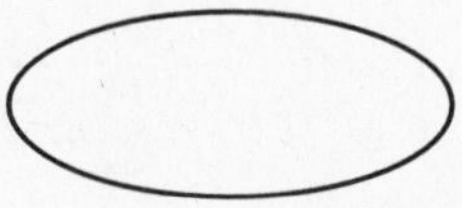

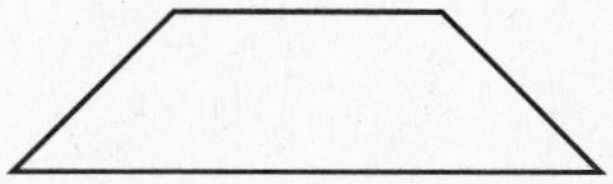

Decide whether each pattern or object has line symmetry. If it does, draw and number the lines of symmetry.

4. ______ **5.** ______ **6.** ______

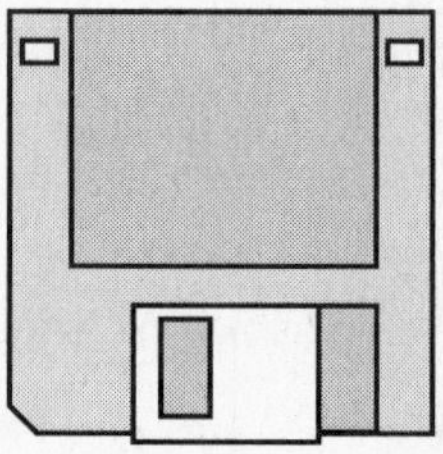

Draw each figure and its reflection on a coordinate plane.

7. $\triangle ABC$ with $A(-3, 4)$, $B(-1, 2)$ and $C(-5, 1)$ reflected across the x-axis.

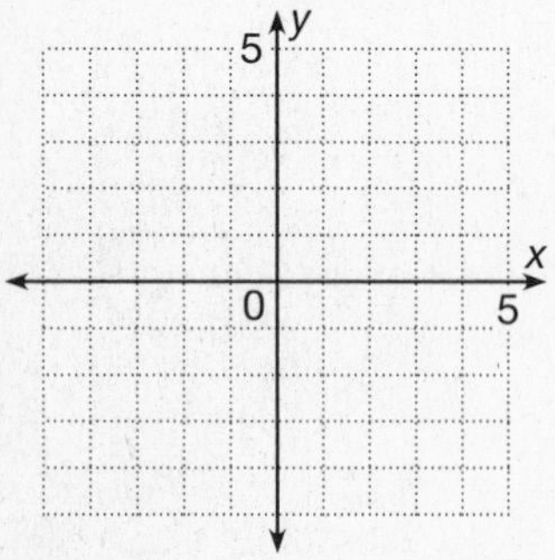

8. $DEFG$ with $D(-4, 0)$, $E(-5, -4)$, $F(-2, -3)$ and $G(-1, -1)$, reflected across the y-axis

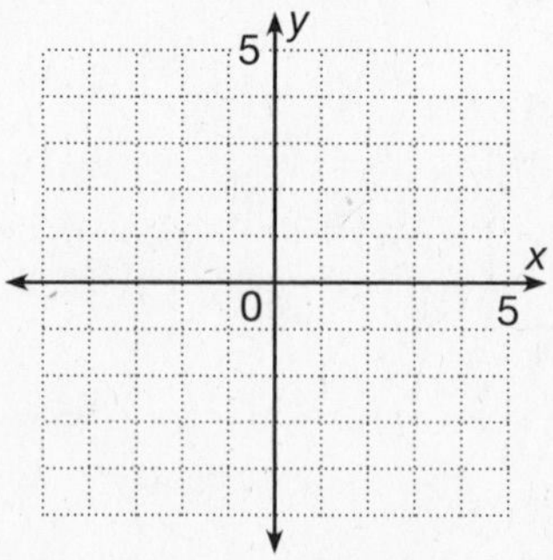

Geography Tell how many lines of symmetry are in each flag.

9. Sweden ______ **10.** Japan ______ **11.** Trinidad and Tobago ______

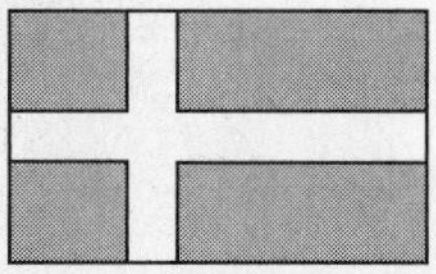

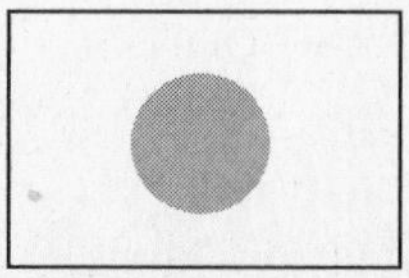

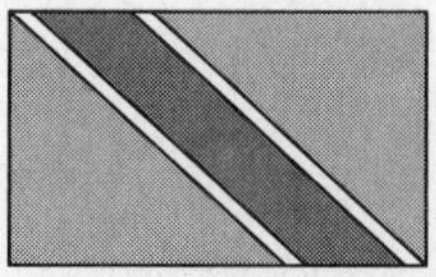

Name ______________________________

Practice 11-12

Rotations and Rotational Symmetry

Decide whether each figure has rotational symmetry. If it does, name the fractional turns that rotate the figure onto itself.

1. Rhombus __________

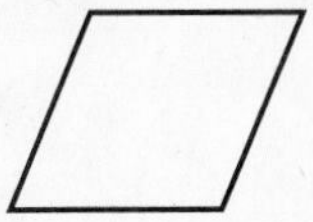

2. Rectangle __________

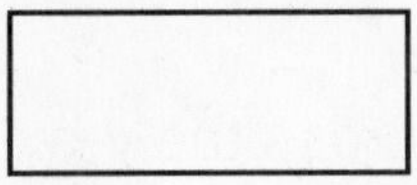

3. Scalene triangle __________

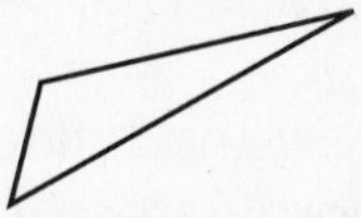

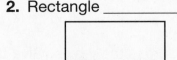

4. List all of the images in Exercises **1–3** that have point symmetry. __________

Give the smallest fractional turn that each figure has been rotated clockwise. Express your answer in degrees.

5. Clock face __________

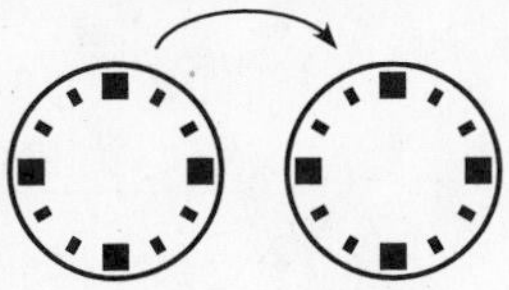

6. Dumb bell __________

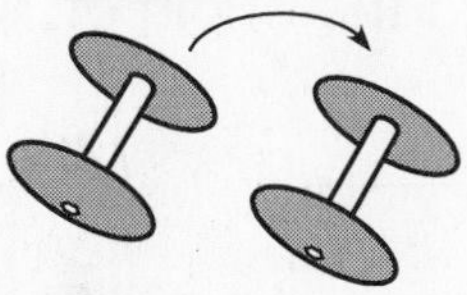

7. Puerto Rican flag __________

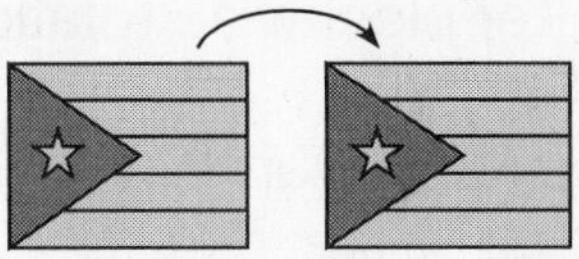

8. Give the coordinates of $\triangle PQR$ after clockwise rotations around the origin of:

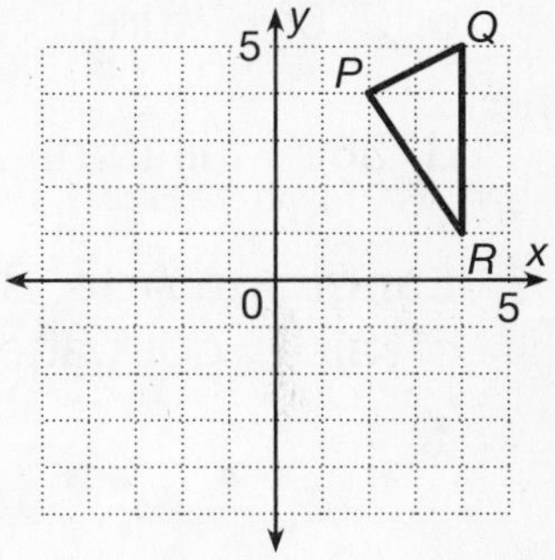

a. $90° \left(\frac{1}{4} \text{ turn}\right)$ P' ________ Q' ________ R' ________

b. $180° \left(\frac{1}{2} \text{ turn}\right)$ P'' ________ Q'' ________ R'' ________

c. $270° \left(\frac{3}{4} \text{ turn}\right)$ P''' ________ Q''' ________ R''' ________

d. 360° (full turn) P'''' ________ Q'''' ________ R'''' ________

9. Draw rectangle *STUV* with $S(0, 3)$, $T(1, 4)$, $U(3, 2)$ and $V(2, 1)$.
Give the coordinates of rotations of *STUV* after clockwise rotations of:

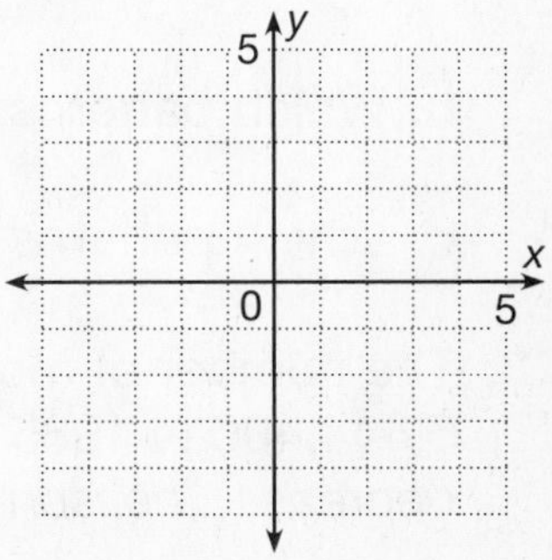

a. $90° \left(\frac{1}{4} \text{ turn}\right)$ S' ________ T' ________

U' ________ V' ________

b. $180° \left(\frac{1}{2} \text{ turn}\right)$ S'' ________ T'' ________

U'' ________ V'' ________

c. $270° \left(\frac{3}{4} \text{ turn}\right)$ S''' ________ T''' ________

U''' ________ V''' ________

d. 360° (full turn) S'''' ________ T'''' ________

U'''' ________ V'''' ________

Name ____________________

Practice

Section 11C Review

Point K is at (5, −3). Use each translation rule to find the coordinates of K'.

1. $(x, y) \rightsquigarrow (x, y - 7)$ ____________

2. $(x, y) \rightsquigarrow (x + 3, y + 3)$ ____________

3. $(x, y) \rightsquigarrow (x - 5, y + 6)$ ____________

4. $(x, y) \rightsquigarrow (x - 12, y)$ ____________

5. Draw the reflection of $\triangle LMN$ across the y-axis. Give the coordinates of the vertices of the reflection.

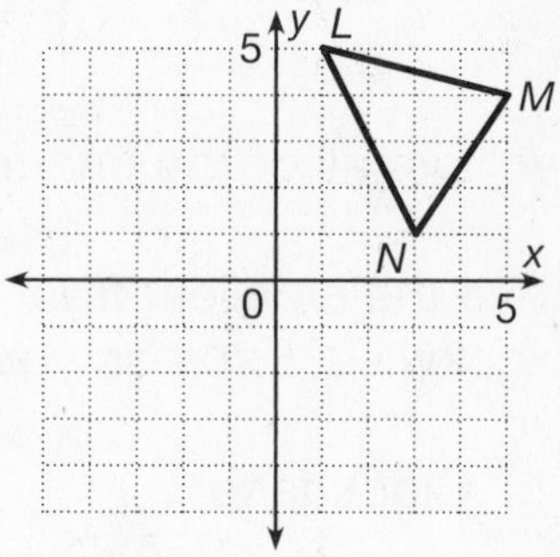

L' ____________ M' ____________ N' ____________

6. Give the coordinates of the vertices of rotations of $\triangle LMN$ after clockwise rotations around the origin of:

a. 90° $\left(\frac{1}{4}\text{ turn}\right)$ L' ________ M' ________ N' ________

b. 180° $\left(\frac{1}{2}\text{ turn}\right)$ L'' ________ M'' ________ N'' ________

c. 270° $\left(\frac{3}{4}\text{ turn}\right)$ L''' ________ M''' ________ N''' ________

d. 360° (full turn) L'''' ________ M'''' ________ N'''' ________

7. Language Arts Blind people can read using the Braille alphabet of raised dot patterns. Eleven of these patterns are shown below.

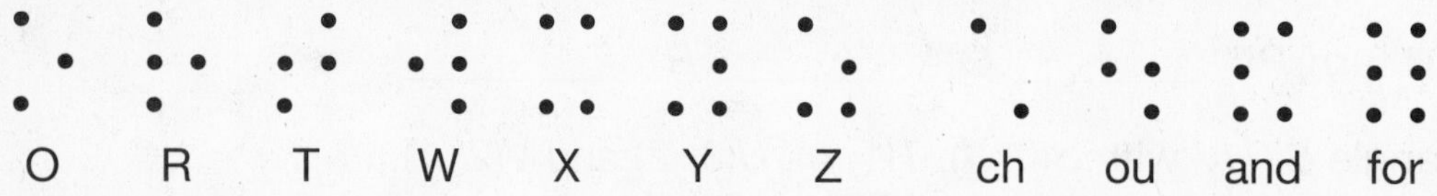

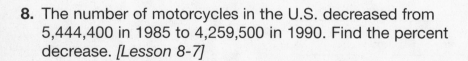

a. Which patterns have a horizontal line of symmetry? ____________

b. Which patterns have a vertical line of symmetry? ____________

c. Which patterns have rotational symmetry? ____________

8. The number of motorcycles in the U.S. decreased from 5,444,400 in 1985 to 4,259,500 in 1990. Find the percent decrease. *[Lesson 8-7]* ____________

9. The Fujiyama roller coaster in Japan is designed to travel at speeds up to 118.8 feet per second. Convert this speed to miles per hour *[Lesson 7-7]* ____________

Name ______________________

Practice

Cumulative Review Chapters 1–11

Find the area of each figure. *[Lesson 5-10]*

1. ______________

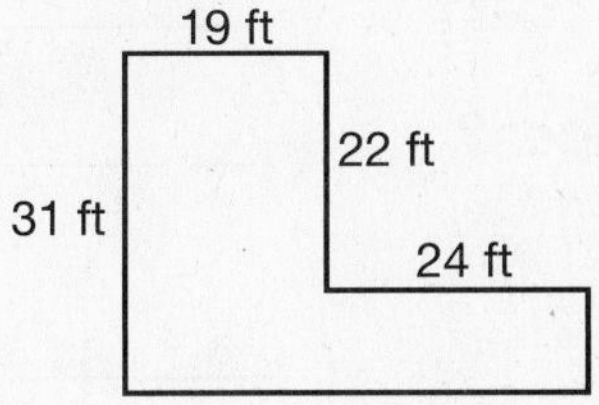

2. ______________

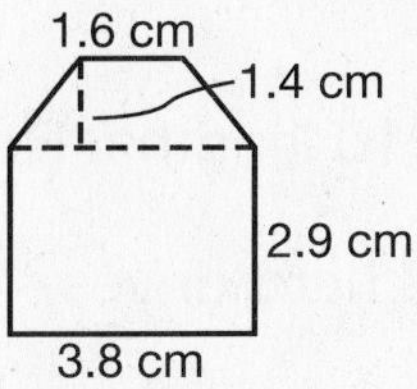

3. ______________

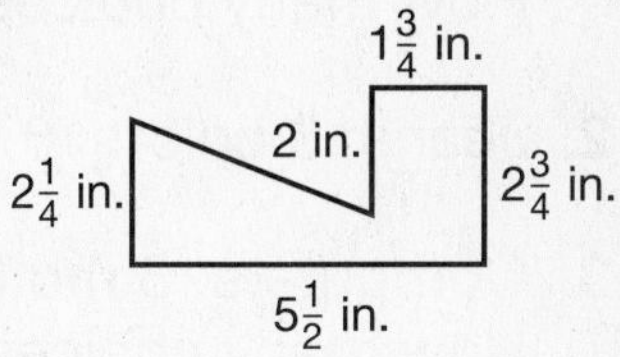

Find the missing side lengths in each pair of similar figures. *[Lesson 7-9]*

4. $t =$ _____ $u =$ _____

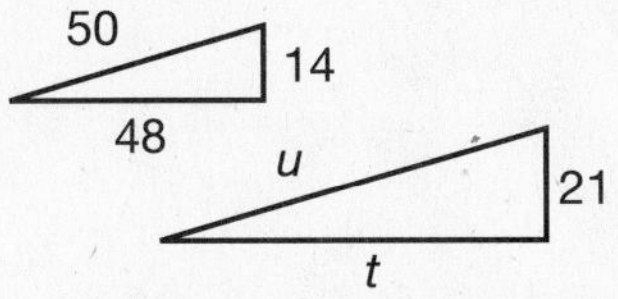

5. $v =$ _____ $w =$ _____

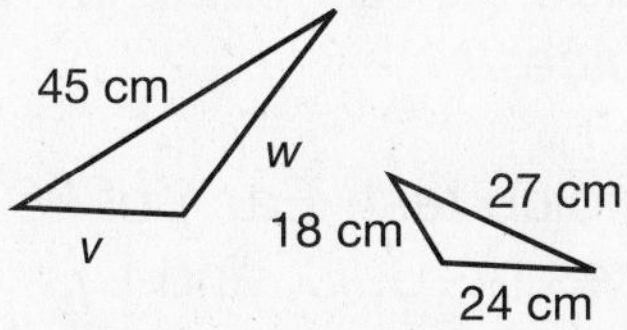

6. $x =$ ___ $y =$ ___ $z =$ ___

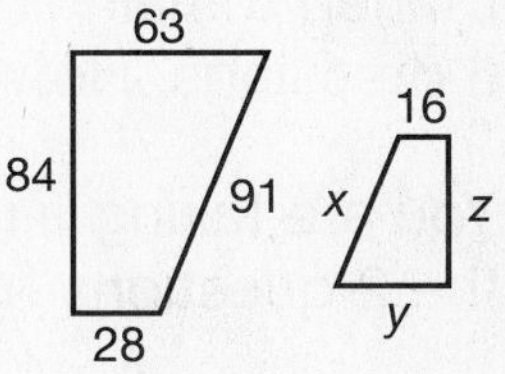

Write each fraction or decimal as a percent. Where necessary, use a repeating decimal to help express your percent. *[Lesson 8-2]*

7. 0.67 ________ **8.** 0.045 ________ **9.** $\frac{3}{20}$ ________ **10.** $\frac{17}{25}$ ________

11. $\frac{5}{6}$ ________ **12.** $\frac{3}{50}$ ________ **13.** $\frac{5}{8}$ ________ **14.** $\frac{2}{5}$ ________

Find the area of the circle, given its diameter or radius. Use $\pi \approx 3.14$, and round answers to the nearest tenth. *[Lesson 11-7]*

15. ______________

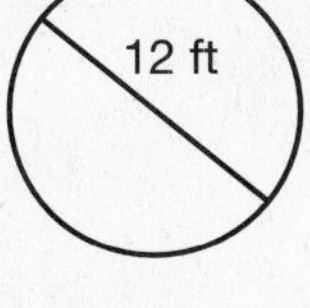

16. ______________

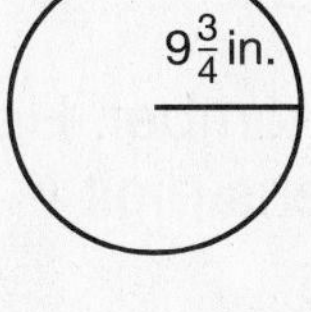

17. ______________

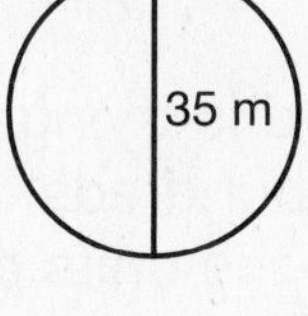

For each group of figures, identify all lettered polygons that are translations of the shaded polygon. *[Lesson 11-10]*

18. ______________

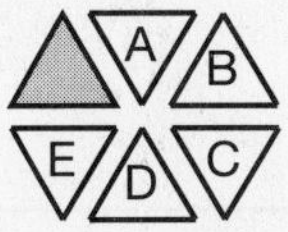

19. ______________

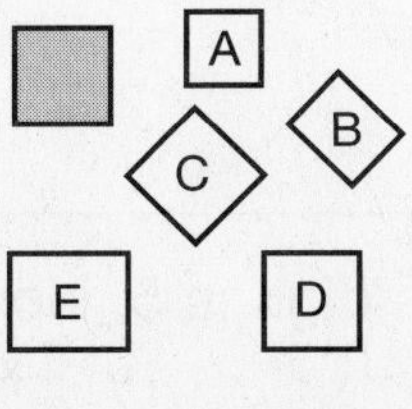

20. ______________

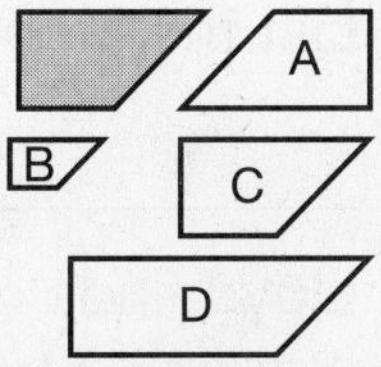

Name ______________________

Practice 12-1

Counting Methods

Use the Counting Principle to find the number of outcomes in each situation.

1. Magazine subscriptions: 4 magazines, 3 subscription lengths. How many choices? ________

2. Jeans: 3 colors, 6 waist sizes, 10 lengths. How many choices? ________

3. Computers: 3 motherboards, 3 hard drives, 4 monitors. How many choices? ________

4. Stereos: 5 receivers, 3 CD players, 4 types of speakers. How many systems? ________

5. Dinner: 4 main courses, 3 side dishes, salad with one of 6 dressings. How many choices? ________

6. You are taking a multiple-choice test. Each of the 2 questions has 4 choices (A, B, C, and D).

   a. Make a tree diagram to show the possible outcomes for the answers for this test. How many outcomes are there?

   ____

   What are the outcomes?

   ____

   b. Suppose the correct answers are CB. How many of the outcomes in **a** provide a correct response for both questions? ________

   For only one question? ________ For neither question? ________

7. Lloyd is trying to guess a 3-digit number. He knows that the hundreds digit is 4 or 7, the tens digit is 3, 6, or 9, and the units digit is 0 or 5.

   a. Make a tree diagram to show the possible outcomes for the number. How many outcomes are possible?

   ____

   List the outcomes.

   ____

   b. Lloyd finds out that the units digit is 5. Now how many outcomes are possible? ________

Name ______________________________

Practice
12-2

Arrangements

Give each factorial product.

1. 6! ________ **2.** 2! ________ **3.** 4! ________ **4.** 5! ________

5. 1! ________ **6.** 9! ________ **7.** 8! ________ **8.** 12! ________

9. Every morning Harold feeds his dog, takes a shower, eats breakfast, and reads the newspaper. In how many different orders can he do these tasks? ______

10. Matt, Nat, and Pat are having a swimming race. List all the possible orders in which they can finish the race.

____

____

11. Sandra displays her collection of compact discs on a shelf. Use factorial notation to give the number of ways she can arrange her discs if she has:

a. 5 discs ____ **b.** 15 discs ____ **c.** 34 discs ____ **d.** 182 discs ____

12. List all of the possible ways to order the letters in the word MATH (without repeating letters).

____

____

____

13. Keith must choose a 3-letter password for a computer account. He can use any of the 26 upper-case letters of the alphabet, but he cannot repeat letters. How many passwords are possible? ________

14. Jarita is making a simple jigsaw puzzle for her very young cousin. She plans to arrange the shapes shown in a row. How many ways can she arrange the shapes? (The shapes are not to be rotated.) ________

15. The president, vice president, secretary, and treasurer of a school club are lining up for a photograph. In how many different orders can they line up? ________

Name ______________________

Practice 12-3

Choosing a Group

Decide whether or not order matters in each situation. Write *Yes* or *No.*

1. Choosing the digits in a lock combination ________

2. Choosing 5 books to check out from the library ________

3. Electing the president, vice president, and secretary of a club ________

4. Choosing 5 club members to serve on a committee ________

You plan to paint a clay pot. The hobby store offers appropriate paints in 6 colors. How many different ways can you choose the colors for your design if you plan to use:

5. Two colors? ________ **6.** Three colors? ________ **7.** Five colors? ________

8. At the video store, you've selected 4 videos you want to watch, but you only have time to watch 2 of them. How many ways can you select 2 of the 4 videos? ________

9. Abe, Bo, Cal, Duc, and Eve are student council members. Two of them need to meet with the school principal today.

a. How many different ways are there to choose two of these students? ________

b. List the possibilities.

____

____

10. A bakery makes 3 kinds of bread: white, whole what, and nine-grain. You want to buy 2 different loaves. How many ways can you make your selection? ________

11. You have 3 extra tickets for a concert. How many ways can you choose 3 of your 5 best friends to go with you? ________

12. History In 1849, President Zachary Taylor chose 7 men as cabinet members. How many ways could Taylor choose 2 cabinet members with whom to consult about a particular issue? ________

Name ______________________________

Practice

Section 12A Review

Use the Counting Principle to find the number of outcomes in each situation.

1. Books: 5 authors, 4 books by each author. How many choices? __________

2. Shirts: 6 styles, 3 sizes, 5 colors in each style. How many choices? __________

3. Bookcases: 3 widths, 2 heights, 4 kinds of wood. How many choices? __________

4. The employee cafeteria at a certain company offers a choice of a sandwich, casserole, or quiche for lunch. Each lunch includes soup or salad. Make a tree diagram to show the possible meals.

How many possibilities are there?

____

Give each factorial product.

5. 3! __________ **6.** 7! __________ **7.** 9! __________ **8.** 5! __________

9. You and some friends are at a Chinese restaurant that offers 6 dishes. How many ways can you select 3 of the dishes to share? __________

10. You are taking a test and the instructions say, "Answer 2 of the next 5 questions." How many different ways can you select 2 questions to answer? __________

11. How many different four-number license plates can be made from the digits 1–5 if:

a. digits can be repeated __________ **b.** digits cannot be repeated __________

12. At a grooming parlor, 6 dogs need to be put into 6 cages. How many different ways can this be done with only one dog per cage? __________

13. One sunny day in Houston, Texas, the First Interstate Bank Plaza building cast an 81-ft shadow and the Transco Tower cast a 75-ft shadow. The Transco Tower is 900 ft tall. How tall is the First Interstate Bank Plaza? *[Lesson 7-9]* __________

14. The largest sundial in the world is located in Orlando Florida. It has the shape of a circle with diameter 37.2 m. Find the area of the sundial. *[Lesson 11-7]* __________

Name ____________________

Practice 12-4

Odds and Fairness

Name the possible outcomes for each experiment.

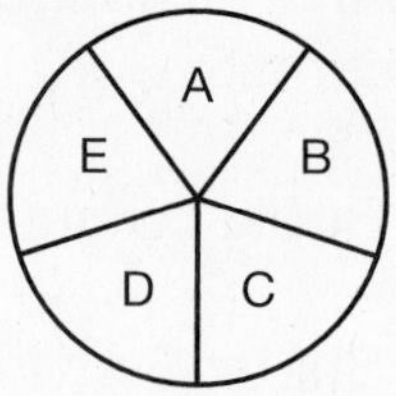

1. Spinning the spinner shown

____

2. Selecting a coin from a bag of quarters, dimes, and nickels

____

3. Rolling a number cube and flipping a coin at the same time

____

____

Give the odds of each event.

4. Getting a 3 or a 6 on a roll of a number cube ____________

5. Getting a vowel on a spin of the spinner in Exercise **1** ____________

6. Choosing a yellow M&M® from a bag containing 5 yellow M&M's and 8 red M&M's ____________

The game of Rummikub® contains 13 red tiles, 13 blue tiles, 13 black tiles, 13 orange tiles, and 2 jokers. The red, blue, black, and orange tiles are numbered 1–13. If you choose one Rummikub tile, what are the odds that it is:

7. Orange? ____________ **8.** A prime number? ____________

For each game described, give each player's odds of winning. Then tell whether the game is fair.

9. Spin the spinner in Exercise **1**. Tad gets a point for an A, B, or C. Jill gets a point for a D or E.

Tad's odds: ________ Jill's odds: ________ Fair? ____________

10. Roll a number cube. Ed gets a point for a 1 or 2. Fred gets a point for a 3 or 6. Gwen gets a point for a 4 or 5.

Ed's odds: _____ Fred's odds: _____ Gwen's odds: _____ Fair? ________

Name ______________________________

Practice 12-5

Probability

Give the probability of each event as a fraction, a percent, and a decimal.

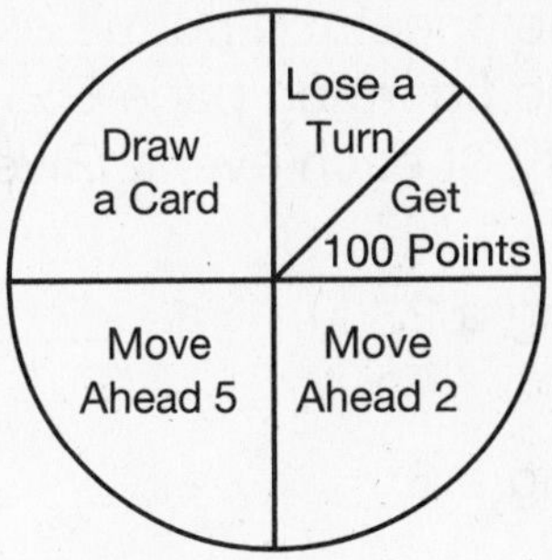

1. Spinning "Draw a Card" on the spinner shown

   ____

2. Spinning "Get 100 Points" on the spinner shown

   ____

3. Drawing a green marble from a bag containing the following marbles:

   a. 21 green ________ **b.** 5 black and 7 white ________ **c.** 3 green, 7 yellow ________

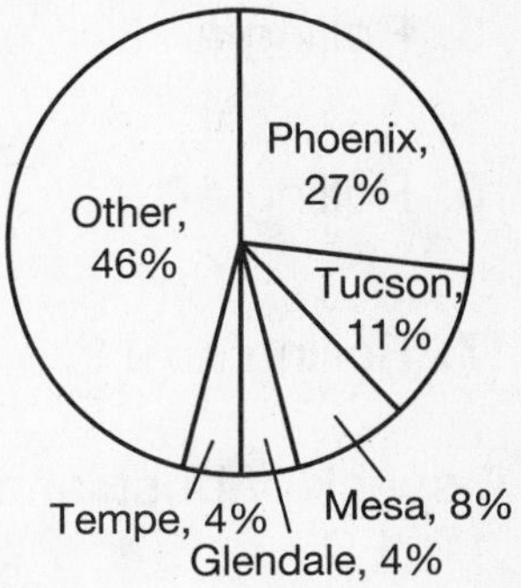

4. **Social Studies** The circle graph shows the percent of the population of Arizona that lived in its five largest cities in 1990. What is the probability that a randomly selected resident:

   a. Lives in Phoenix? ________ **b.** Does *not* live in Phoenix? ________

   c. Lives in Tempe, Mesa, or Glendale? ________

5. Complete the table.

Probability of event	$\frac{1}{3}$			$\frac{3}{8}$		
Probability that event does not happen		$\frac{1}{5}$			$\frac{3}{10}$	
Odds of event			2 : 10			12 : 4

Give the probability that corresponds to each of the odds. Express each answer as a fraction in lowest terms.

6. 5 : 7 ______ **7.** 8 : 2 ______ **8.** 21 : 21 ______ **9.** 16 : 20 ______

10. 24 : 1 ______ **11.** 44 : 56 ______ **12.** 35 : 15 ______ **13.** 27 : 81 ______

Assume you are drawing the first tile in a Scrabble® game. Use the table on page 653 of your textbook to find each probability. Express each as a percent.

14. *P*(W) ________ **15.** *P*(Not an A) ________ **16.** *P*(E, F, or G) ________

Name ______________________________

Practice 12-6

Experimental Probability

The tally shows the results for several rolls of two number cubes.
a. Use the sheet to find the experimental probability of each event.
b. Use the figure on page 655 of your textbook to find the theoretical probability of each event. Give your answers as fractions in lowest terms.

Roll	Frequency
2	1
3	3
4	4
5	6
6	8
7	7
8	9
9	5
10	3
11	2
12	2

1. Rolling a 2 **a.** __________ **b.** __________

2. Rolling a 3 **a.** __________ **b.** __________

3. Rolling a 5 **a.** __________ **b.** __________

4. Rolling a 7 **a.** __________ **b.** __________

5. Rolling an 8 **a.** __________ **b.** __________

6. Rolling a 10 **a.** __________ **b.** __________

7. Rolling an 11 **a.** __________ **b.** __________

A speck of dust lands on the grid shown. What is the probability that it:

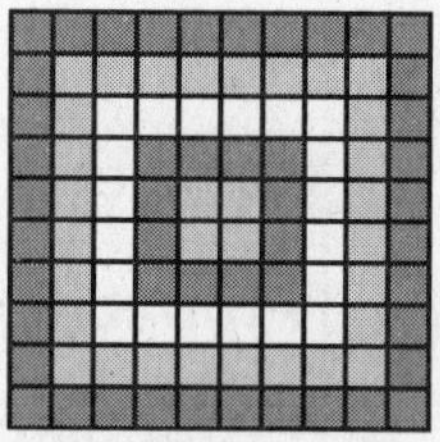

8. Lands on the dark shaded area? __________

9. Lands on the light shaded area? __________

10. Lands on the unshaded area? __________

In a coin toss game, you earn points for landing on the shaded figures. Assume coins land randomly in the large square. What is the probability that a coin:

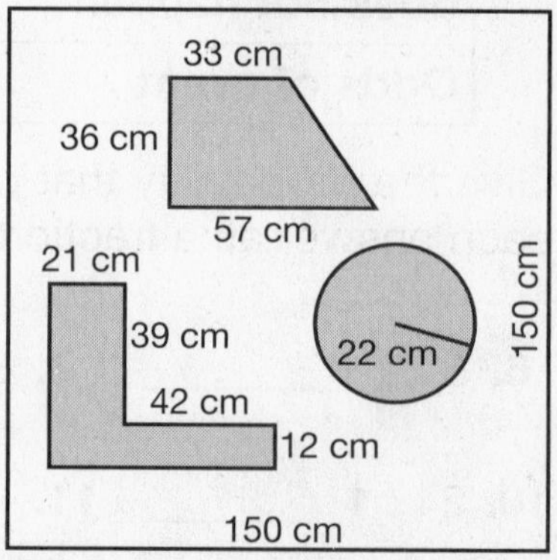

11. Lands on the trapezoid? __________

12. Lands on the circle? __________

13. Lands on the "L" shape? __________

14. During the 1994–1995 basketball season, the Charlotte Hornets won 50 out of 82 games. Based on these results, what is the experimental probability that the Hornets will win a game? Express your answer as a percent. __________

Name ____________________

Practice
12-7

Independent and Dependent Events

Tell whether the events are dependent or independent.

1. A coin toss landing tails and a number cube coming up 5 ____________

2. Sunshine in Boston, Massachusetts, and sunshine in Hartford, Connecticut ____________

3. Drawing a blue Rummikub® tile, then drawing a red tile (after replacing the first tile) ____________

Exercises 4–6 refer to tossing a coin, then spinning the spinner shown. Find each probability.

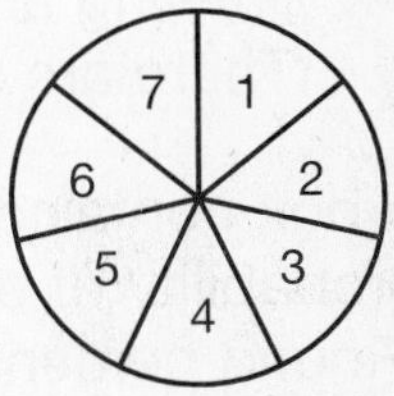

4. *P*(coin landing heads and spinning a 5) ______

5. *P*(coin landing heads and spinning a prime number) ______

6. *P*(coin landing tails and spinning a 3, 4, 5, 6, or 7) ______

Exercises 7–9 refer to rolling a green number cube, then rolling a red number cube. Find each probability.

7. *P*(rolling a green 3 and a red 2) ______

8. *P*(rolling a green 4 and a red prime number) ______

9. *P*(rolling a green number less than 6 and a red number greater than 3) ______

10. A set of Scrabble® tiles includes 12 E's and 9 I's out of 100 tiles. Suppose you draw a tile, and then draw another tile without replacing the first.

a. Are the two tile draws dependent or independent events? ____________

b. What is the probability that the first tile is an E and the second tile is an I? ____________

11. Some role-playing games use dice with different numbers of sides. You roll a four-sided die (numbered 1 to 4) and then a ten-sided die (numbered 1 to 10). What is the probability that the first number is greater than 1 and the second number is less than 7 ? ____________

Name ____________________

Practice

Section 12B Review

Name the possible outcomes for each experiment.

1. Spinning a spinner whose 7 sectors are labeled with the days of the week

____

2. Tossing a coin twice ____________________

Give the odds of each event.

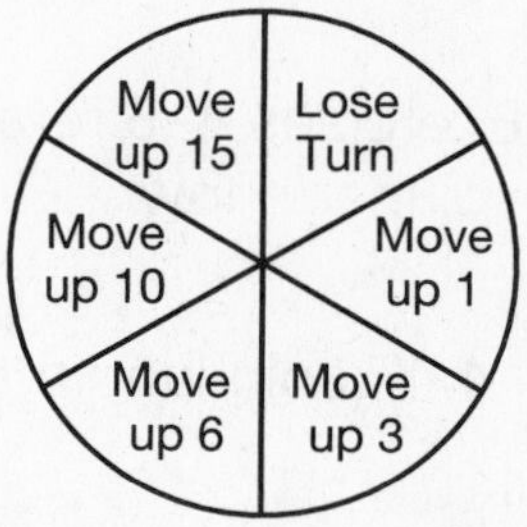

3. Spinning "Move Up 3" on the spinner at the right ________

4. Drawing an A, B, or C from a set of Scrabble® tiles (There are 9 A's, 2 B's, and 2 C's out of 100 tiles.) ________

A box contains 7 yellow, 3 green, and 4 blue pencils. Give the probability of each event as a fraction, a percent, and a decimal. (Round percent and decimal answers to two digits if necessary.)

5. *P*(blue) ____________

6. *P*(yellow) ____________

7. *P*(not blue) ____________

8. *P*(not yellow) ____________

9. If you select two pencils from the box, what is *P*(green, then yellow)? Assume you do not put the first pencil back. ____________

Tell whether the events are dependent or independent.

10. Getting an even number on the first roll of a number cube, then getting an even number on the second roll ____________

11. Getting a face card on the first draw from a deck of playing cards, then getting a face card on the second draw (The first card is not replaced. A deck of 52 cards has 12 face cards.) ____________

12. Refer to the spinner in Exercise **3.** If you spin the spinner twice, what is the probability that you move up 6 or more on the first spin, and then lose a turn? ____________

13. Geography Bulgaria has 220 miles of coastline. This is 200 miles less than three times Romania's coastline. How much coastline does Romania have? *[Lesson 10-11]* ____________

14. A shelf is $\frac{1}{2}$ in. thick, 10 in. wide, and 48 in. long. Find the volume of the shelf. *[Lesson 11-4]* ____________

Name ______________________________

Practice

Cumulative Review Chapters 1–12

Find the area of each figure. *[Lessons 5-8, 5-9]*

1. __________

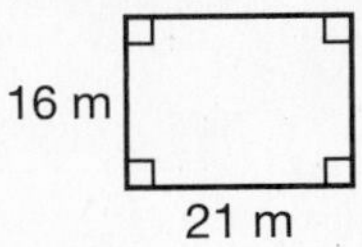

2. __________

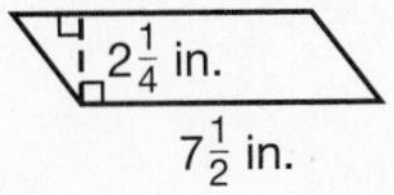

3. __________

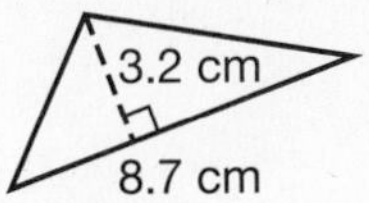

4. __________

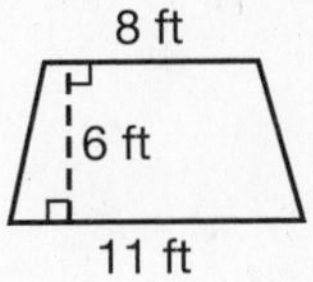

Solve each problem. If necessary, round answers to the nearest tenth. *[Lessons 8-5, 8-6]*

5. 84% of 365 is what number? ______

6. 23% of what number is 17? __________

7. 65 is what percent of 127? _______

8. 863 is 128% of what number? ________

Solve each equation. Check your solution. *[Lesson 10-11]*

9. $\frac{m}{16} + (-5) = 4$ $\quad m =$ __________

10. $6g - 43 = 35$ $\quad g =$ __________

11. $\frac{t}{-4} + 31 = -8$ $\quad t =$ __________

12. $5y + 123 = 68$ $\quad y =$ __________

Find the surface area and volume of each polyhedron or cylinder. Where necessary, use $\pi \approx 3.14$ and round answers to the nearest tenth. *[Lessons 11-3, 11-4, 11-8, and 11-9]*

13. $SA =$ ________________ $V =$ ________________

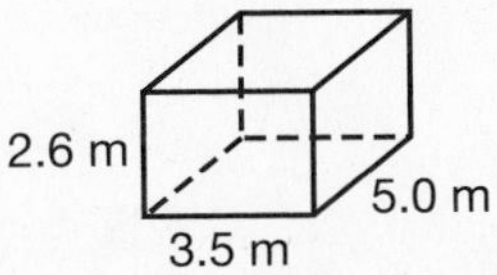

14. $SA \approx$ ________________ $V \approx$ ________________

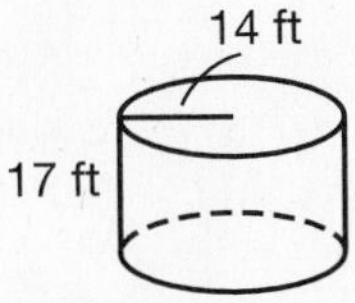

15. $SA \approx$ ________________ $V \approx$ ________________

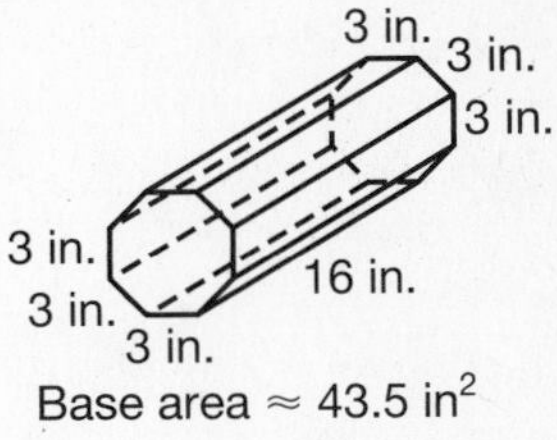

Give the probability of each event as a fraction, a percent, and a decimal. *[Lesson 12-5]*

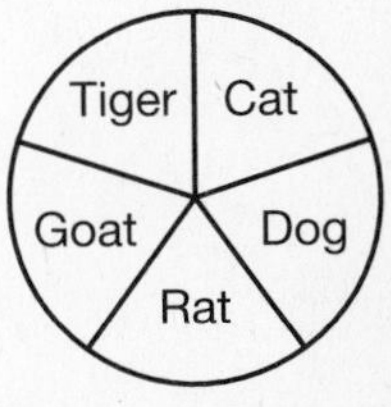

16. Spinning "Dog" on the spinner shown ________________

17. Rolling a number less than 5 on a number cube ________________

18. Drawing a yellow marble from a bag containing the following marbles:

a. 9 red ________________

b. 6 red and 4 yellow ________________

c. 12 yellow ________________

Name ______________________

Practice 1-1

Interpreting Graphs

Use the graph showing the three largest rice exporters for Exercises 1–3.

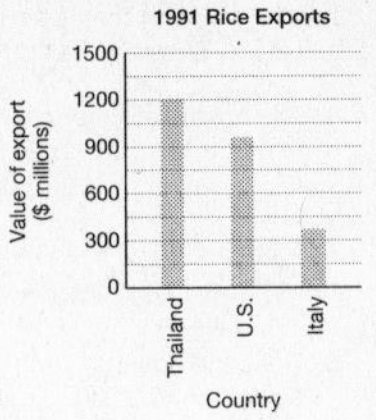

1. Use the graph to estimate the value of U.S. rice exports in 1991.

   $950,000,000

2. List the countries in order from the most exported rice to the least exported rice.

   Thailand, U.S., Italy

3. Thailand exports about how many times as much rice as Italy?

   About 3.3

Career Use the graph showing reasons for unemployment in America for Exercises 4–6.

4. Which reason describes about $\frac{1}{4}$ of unemployed Americans?

   Took a break from working

5. What was the most common reason for unemployment?

   Lost job

6. About what percent of unemployed Americans were looking for a job for the first time?

   About 10%

Use the graph showing U.S. recycling habits for Exercises 7–8.

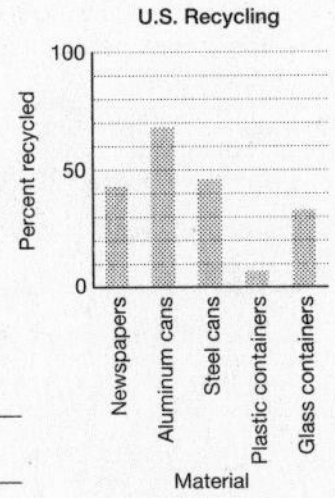

7. About what percent of steel cans are recycled?

   About 46%

8. List the five recyclables shown in order from the most likely to be recycled to the least likely to be recycled.

   Aluminum cans, steel cans, newspapers, glass containers, plastic containers

Name ______________________

Practice 1-2

Making Bar Graphs

Choose a convenient scale and interval to use for graphing each set of data.

1. 85, 32, 91, 15, 24 scale 100 interval 10 or 20
2. 324, 430, 125, 63, 260 scale 500 interval 50 or 100

3. **Social Science** Make a bar graph to show the percentages of foreign-born people in the United States from 1960 to 1993.

Year	1960	1970	1980	1990	1993
Percentage	5.4%	4.7%	6.2%	7.9%	8.6%

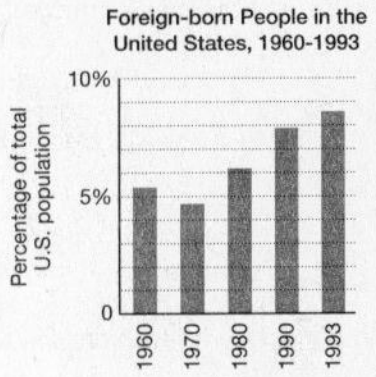

4. In 1991 U.S. residents traveled for many reasons–226 million visited friends and relatives, 240 million had other pleasure reasons, 153 million traveled for business or convention, and 46 million traveled for other reasons. Make a bar graph to show the purpose of travel by U.S. residents.

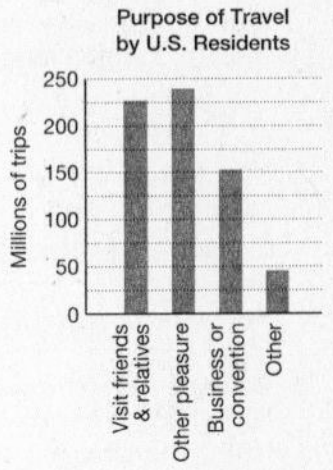

5. **Health** Make a double-bar graph showing how Americans improved their diets in 1991 and 1993.

Percentage of surveyed adults who improved their diet by:	1991	1993
Adding vegetables	40%	52%
Adding fruits	27%	36%
Avoiding fats	21%	29%

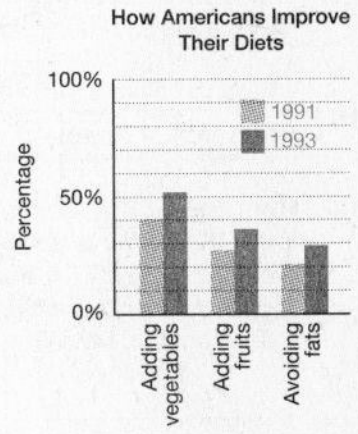

Name ______________________

Practice 1-3

Line Plots and Stem-and-Leaf Diagrams

Make a line plot for each set of data and name any outliers.

1. 6, 9, 7, 9, 2, 8, 7, 9

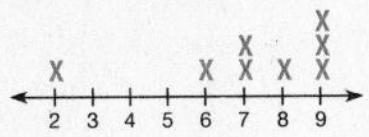

   Outliers: 2

2. 31, 29, 32, 30, 33, 32, 30, 32

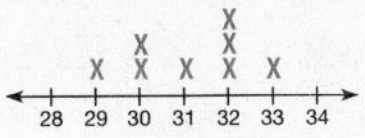

   Outliers: None

Make a stem-and-leaf diagram for each set of data.

3. Number of musicians in local orchestras:
   63, 41, 49, 34, 47, 62, 60, 38

   What is the smallest number of musicians? 34

   What is the largest number of musicians? 63

stem	leaf
3	48
4	179
5	
6	023

4. Salaries (in thousands of dollars) at a local company:
   36, 61, 42, 55, 39, 31, 47, 52, 33, 40, 39

stem	leaf
3	13699
4	027
5	25
6	1

5. The stem-and-leaf plot shows the number of customers during different hours of the day at a local fast-food restaurant. How many customers arrived during the busiest hour?

stem	leaf
1	1 7 9
2	1 1 4 7 7
3	1 6 7 8
4	2 3 5 8 9

   49

6. **Social Studies** The number of state senators in each of the southern states is given below. Make a stem-and-leaf diagram for the data.

stem	leaf
2	1
3	1345589
4	00678
5	026

State	AL	AR	DE	FL	GA	KY	LA	MD	MS	NC	OK	SC	TN	TX	VA	WV
Senators	35	35	21	40	56	38	39	47	52	50	48	46	33	31	40	34

Name ______________________

Practice 1-4

Mean, Median, Mode, and Range

Find the mean, median, mode(s), and range for each set of data.

1. 14, 16, 23, 18, 16, 16, 18, 21

   mean 17.75
   median 17
   mode(s) 16
   range 9

2. 3, 6, 12, 7, 9, 14, 8, 10

   mean 8.625
   median 8.5
   mode(s) None
   range 11

3. 13, 12, 11, 12, 13, 11, 12, 11, 13, 12

   mean 12
   median 12
   mode(s) 12
   range 2

4. 3, 0, 15, 11, 7, 6, 14, 7, 9

   mean 8
   median 7
   mode(s) 7
   range 15

5. **Social Science** The table shows the number of congressional representatives for each of the 50 states.

Number of reps.	1	2	3	4	5	6	7	8	9	10	11	12	13	16	19	20	21	23	30	31	52
Number of states	7	6	4	2	3	6	2	2	4	2	2	1	1	1	1	1	1	1	1	1	1

   a. Find the mean, median, and mode(s) for the number of representatives in a state.

   mean 8.7 median 6 mode(s) 1

   b. Which of these measures best summarizes the data set? Explain.

   Mean or median; Explanations will vary

   c. After the next census, the number of representatives in most states will change, but the total number will stay the same. Assuming that there are 50 states, do you expect the mean number of representatives per state to change? Explain.

   No, the mean will still be $\frac{435}{50} = 8.7$.

Name ______________________________

Practice

Section 1A Review

The line plot shows the number of students in classes at Pike Elementary School. Use it for Exercises 1–3.

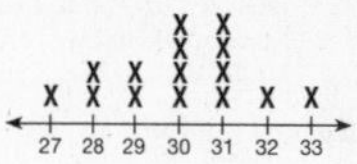

1. Name the outliers, if any. None
2. Find the mean, median, and mode(s) for the data.

   mean 30   median 30   mode(s) 30, 31
3. Make a stem-and-leaf diagram of the data.

stem	leaf
2	78899
3	0000111123

The double bar graph shows the distribution of American hog farm sizes, as a percent of all hog farms. Use it for Exercises 4–5.

Size of Hog Farms

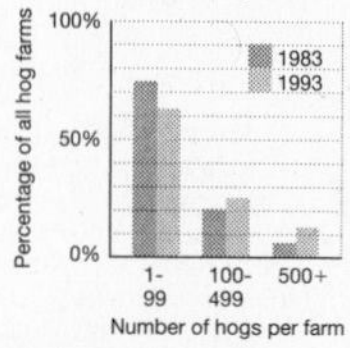

4. Would you say the average hog farm in 1993 was larger, smaller, or about the same size as the average hog farm in 1983?

   Larger
5. How could circle graphs be used to display this information?

   Make one circle graph for 1983, and another circle graph for 1993.
6. **Science** As more pesticides are used, they become less effective because insects become resistant to them. The table shows the number of insect species that were resistant to pesticides from 1956 to 1989. Make a vertical bar graph to show the data.

Year	1956	1970	1976	1984	1989
Number of species	69	224	364	447	504

Insect Resistance to Pesticides

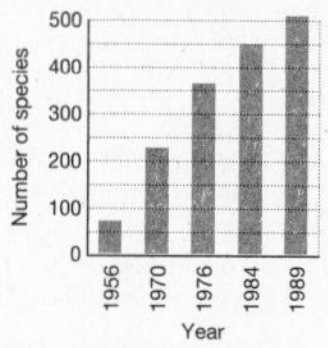

7. **Geography** The summit of Mt. Whitney in California is 14,494 ft above sea level. A mountain climber is at a height of 11,677 ft above sea level. How much higher does the climber need to go in order to reach the summit of Mt. Whitney? *[Previous Course]*

   2,817 ft

Name ______________________________

Practice 1-5

Line Graphs

Use the graph of the number of pieces of mail sent in the United States for Exercises 1–3.

Mailings in the U.S.

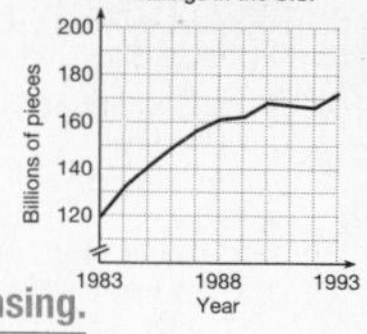

1. Predict the number of pieces of mail in 1997.

   About 180 billion
2. Describe any trend you see in the graph.

   The number of mailings has been increasing.
3. Describe how this graph would appear different if a scale from 0 to 200 billion pieces of mail were used.

   The trend would not look as steep.

History The Voting Rights Act was passed into law in 1965. The table shows the number of African-American elected officials since this time. Use this information in Exercises 4–5.

Year	1965	1970	1975	1980	1985	1990
Elected officials	280	1469	3503	4890	6016	7355

African-American Elected Officials

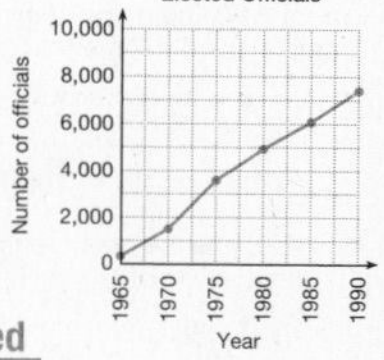

4. Make a line graph to display this information.
5. Describe any trend you see in the graph.

   The number of African-American elected officials has been increasing.

Use the table showing the number of accident-related deaths (in thousands) in the United States for Exercises 6–7.

Year	'30	'40	'50	'60	'70	'80	'90
Deaths at home	29	30	28	28	27	22	20
Deaths at work	19	18	16	14	13	12	9

Accidental Deaths

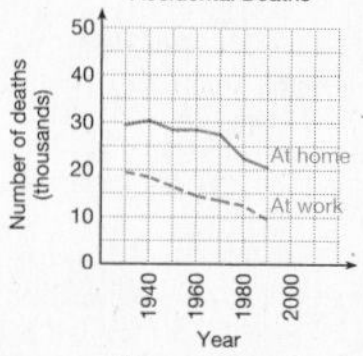

6. Use the data to make a double-line graph.
7. Describe any trend you see in the graph.

   The number of accidents has been falling steadily, both at home and at work.

Name ______________________________

Practice 1-6

Scatterplots and Relationships

Use the scatterplot showing weights and maximum speeds of animals for Exercises 1–3.

Weights and Speeds of Animals

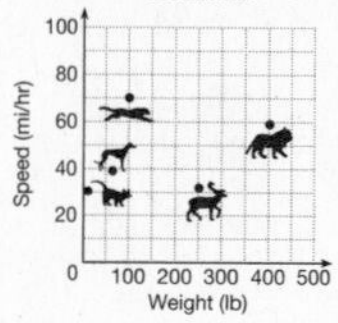

1. Which is the heaviest of these animals? Lion

   the lightest? Cat
2. Which is the fastest of these animals? Cheetah

   the slowest? Cat
3. What is the weight of a reindeer? 250 lb

   the maximum speed of a cheetah? 70 mi/hr

The table shows the number of passengers (millions) and the number of paid passenger-miles (billions) flown for the top 9 U.S. airlines in 1993. Use this information for Exercises 4–5.

Airline	Delta	American	US Air	United	Northwest
Passengers	84	83	70	54	44
Paid miles	82.9	99.0	101	35.3	58

Airline	Southwest	Continental	TWA	America West
Passengers	38	37	19	15
Paid miles	16.7	39.9	22.7	11.2

Top Nine U.S. Airlines

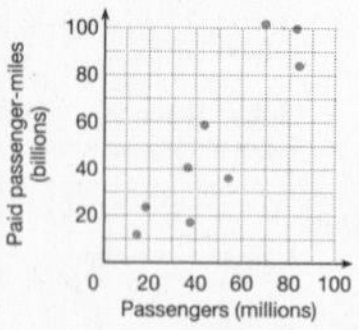

4. Make a scatterplot of the data.
5. What kind of relationship is shown? Positive

Describe whether the sets would show a positive relationship, a negative relationship, or no relationship.

6. The distance an airplane has to travel and the time it takes to make the flight. Positive
7. The number of a family's street address and their annual income. None
8. The number of songs on a compact disc and the average length of the songs. Negative
9. The number of bedrooms in a house and the price of the house. Positive

Name ______________________________

Practice 1-7

Trend Lines

1. **Consumer** The table shows prices of packages containing 100-megabyte computer disks. Make a scatterplot of the data. Draw the trend line.

Number of disks	1	2	3	6	10
Price ($)	20	37	50	100	150

100 MB Computer Disks

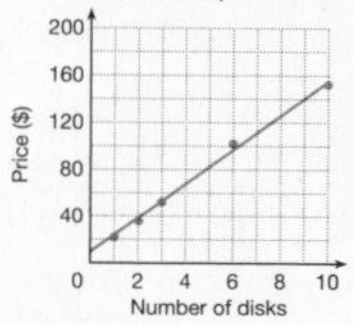

Careers The scatterplot shows the 1989 median income of male year-round workers and the number of years of school. The trend line is shown. Use this scatterplot for Exercises 2–3.

Median Income

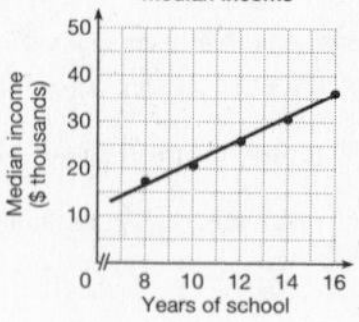

2. Predict the median income for men who have spent 20 years in school.

   About $46,000
3. Do you think you can use this scatterplot to predict the median salary for women who have spent 20 years in school? Explain.

   Answers will vary.

The table shows average monthly temperatures in degrees Fahrenheit for American cities in January and July. Use this information for Exercises 4–6.

City	Seattle	Baltimore	Boise	Chicago	Dallas	Miami	LA
Jan.	39.1	32.7	29.9	21.4	44.0	67.1	56.0
Jul.	64.8	76.8	74.6	73.0	86.3	82.5	69.0

City	Anchorage	Honolulu	New York	Portland	New Orleans
Jan.	13.0	72.6	31.8	21.5	52.4
Jul.	58.1	80.1	76.4	68.1	82.1

Average Monthly Temperatures

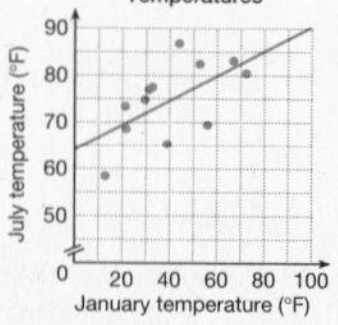

4. Make a scatterplot and draw a trend line.
5. Use your trend line to predict the July temperature of a city whose average January temperature is 10°F.

   About 66°F
6. Use your trend line to predict the January temperature of a city whose average July temperature is 75°F.

   About 43°F

Name ______________________

Practice

Section 1B Review

Use the data in the table for Exercises 1–2.

Year	1994	1995	1996	July 1996
Unemployment rate	6.5%	5.3%	5.3%	5.1%

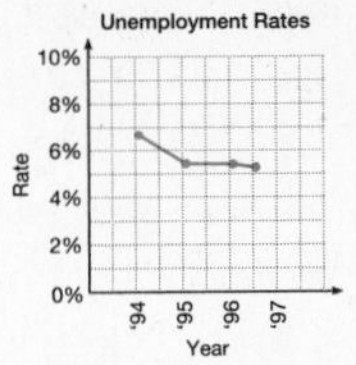

1. Make a line graph of the data in the table.
2. Use your line graph to predict the unemployment rate in 1997.
   About 5%

Ron's Bookstore is having a sale. The table shows the regular and sale prices for several books. Use the data for Exercises 3–5.

Regular price ($)	5.00	7.50	10.00	15.00	25.00	35.00
Sale price ($)	4.00	6.00	7.50	12.00	19.00	25.00

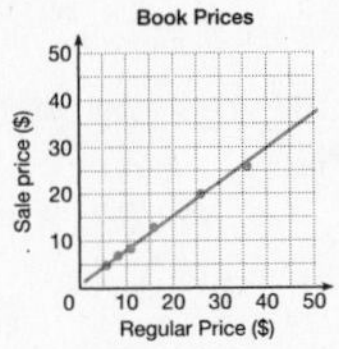

3. Make a scatterplot of the data.
4. Draw a trend line on your scatterplot.
5. Use your trend line to predict the sale price of a book whose regular price is $50.00.
   About $36

The graph shows the top five largest-grossing movies from 1990–1995. Use this information for Exercises 6–7. *[Lesson 1-1]*

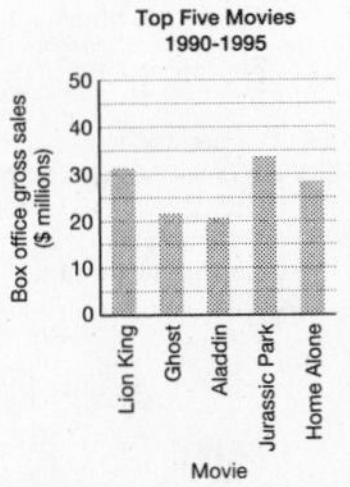

6. List these movies in order from the most sales to the least sales.
   Jurassic Park, Lion King, Home Alone,
   Ghost, Aladdin
7. Give the dollar amount of ticket sales for *Home Alone*.
   About $285,000,000

Name ______________________

Practice

Cumulative Review Chapter 1

Add, subtract, multiply, or divide. *[Previous Course]*

1. 385 + 649 = 1034
2. 964 − 129 = 835
3. 643 × 81 = 52,083
4. 839 × 27 = 22,653
5. 638 + 416 = 1054
6. 429 − 57 = 372
7. 14)2282 → 163
8. 37)26,418 → 714
9. 61)34,587 → 567

The graph shows the top five largest-grossing concert tours in 1993. Use this information for Exercises 10–11. *[Lesson 1-1]*

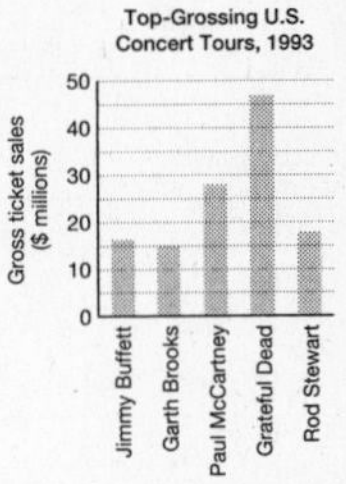

10. List the performers in order from the most sales to the least sales.
    Grateful Dead, Paul McCartney, Rod
    Stewart, Jimmy Buffett, Garth Brooks
11. The sales from the Grateful Dead tour were about how many times as great as the sales from the Jimmy Buffett tour?
    About 3 times
12. Find the mean, median, and mode(s) for the following data set. *[Lesson 1-4]*
    37, 30, 39, 45, 39, 38, 47, 35
    mean 38.75 median 38.5 mode(s) 39

Tell whether each scatterplot shows a positive relationship, a negative relationship, or no relationship. *[Lesson 1-5]*

13. Negative
14. None
15. Positive

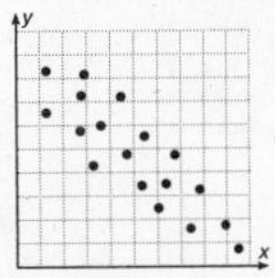

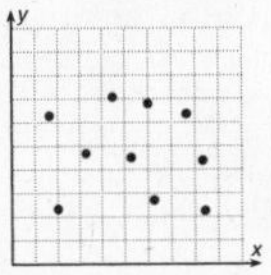

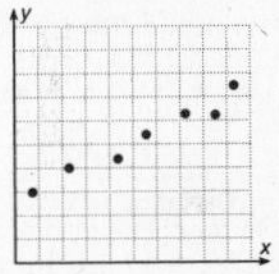

Name ______________________

Practice 2-1

Formulas and Variables

Geometry You can use the formula $A = \frac{1}{2}bh$ to find the area of a triangle. Substitute the given values into the formula. Then use the formula to find *A*.

1. $b = 8$ in., $h = 5$ in., $A =$ 20 in^2
2. $b = 18$ cm, $h = 10$ cm, $A =$ 90 cm^2
3. $b = 4$ m, $h = 3$ m, $A =$ 6 m^2
4. $b = 3$ ft, $h = 8$ ft, $A =$ 12 ft^2
5. $b = 3$ mi, $h = 8$ mi, $A =$ 12 mi^2
6. $b = 12$ km, $h = 3$ km, $A =$ 18 km^2

Science The formula $t = \frac{d}{v}$ is used to find *t* (time) when you know *d* (distance) and *v* (rate or average speed). Substitute the values for *d* and *v* into the formula. Then use the formula to find *t*.

7. $d = 465$ km, $v = 93$ km/hr
   $t =$ 5 hr
8. $d = 180$ mi, $v = 45$ mi/hr
   $t =$ 4 hr
9. $d = 200$ ft, $v = 25$ ft/sec
   $t =$ 8 sec
10. $d = 85$ km, $v = 85$ km/hr
    $t =$ 1 hr

Use the table for Exercises 11–12.

Street	Main St	Harbor Blvd	Oak Hwy	River Fwy
Speed Limit (mi/hr)	25	35	50	65

11. How far can you travel in 3 hours on Harbor Blvd? 105 mi
    On Oak Hwy? 150 mi On River Fwy? 195 mi
12. How much farther can you travel in 5 hours on Harbor Blvd than on Main St? 50 mi
13. **Geometry** You can use the formula $A = \frac{h}{2}(b_1 + b_2)$ to find the area of a trapezoid with bases b_1 and b_2 and height *h*. Find the area of a trapezoid with bases 9 cm and 13 cm, and height 7 cm. 77 cm^2
14. **Health** Sheri's pulse rate is 150 beats per minute when she exercises. The formula $b = 150t$ relates the number of beats (*b*) to the time (*t*) in minutes. Find the number of beats in 8 minutes of exercise. 1200 beats

Name ______________________

Practice 2-2

Order of Operations

Does the expression contain grouping symbols? What are they?

1. $\frac{10 + 6}{7 + 1}$ Yes, fraction bar
2. $8 \cdot 4 - 2 \cdot 3$ No
3. $8 - 3 + 7$ No
4. $17(3 + 5)$ Yes, parentheses
5. $(5 + 3) \div 4$ Yes, parentheses
6. $4 \div 2 - 5$ No

Find the value of each expression.

7. $6 + 8 \times 9$ 78
8. $10(8 - 3)$ 50
9. $\frac{2 \cdot 3 + 8}{5 + 2}$ 2
10. $\frac{25}{5} + \frac{18}{3}$ 11
11. $4 + \frac{8 + 10}{2}$ 13
12. $\frac{15}{8 - 7} + 6$ 21
13. $5 \times \frac{4}{4 - 2}$ 10
14. $\frac{5 \cdot 10}{25} + 4 \div 2$ 4

Operation Sense Insert parentheses to make each sentence true.

15. (3 + 7) × (4 − 2) = 20
16. 10 − (3 + 7) + 4 = 4
17. 300 ÷ 50 ÷ (2 × 3) = 1
18. 24 ÷ (2 + 30 ÷ 3) = 2
19. 6 + (4 ÷ 2) ÷ 2 = 7
20. (4 − 2) × (9 − 4) = 10

Which property is being shown?

21. 11 · (12 · 13) = (11 · 12) · 13 Associative property of multiplication
22. 8(3 + 7) = (8 · 3) + (8 · 7) Distributive property
23. 13 + 18 = 18 + 13 Commutative property of addition
24. (3 + 5) + 8 = 3 + (5 + 8) Associative property of addition
25. 11 · (12 + 13) = (11 · 12) + (11 · 13) Distributive property
26. To calculate a distance, Herb used the formula $d = rt$. Sal used the formula $d = tr$. What property assures that Herb and Sal should get the same answer?
    Commutative property of multiplication

Name ______________________

Practice 2-3

Formulas and Tables

1. The formula $P = 4s$ gives the perimeter (P) of a square, where s is the length of a side. Use this formula to make a table of the perimeters of squares with sides of length 1, 2, 4, 6, 9, 12, and 18 cm.

Side (s)	1	2	4	6	9	12	18
Perimeter (P)	4	8	16	24	36	48	72

Find a formula relating the variables.

2. Formula: $y = 4x$

x	2	3	4	5
y	8	12	16	20

3. Formula: $t = s + 8$

s	4	5	6	7
t	12	13	14	15

4. Formula: $r = h - 4$

h	11	12	13	14
r	7	8	9	10

5. Formula: $v = u + 10$

u	5	6	7	8
v	15	16	17	18

6. Formula: $z = 7x$

x	2	3	4	5
z	14	21	28	35

7. Formula: $b = a - 5$

a	8	9	10	11
b	3	4	5	6

8. For a given distance, the formula $i = 12f$ relates the number of inches (i) to the number of feet (f). Make a table that shows the number of inches equal to 1, 2, 5, 8, 10, 12, and 20 feet.

Number of feet (f)	1	2	5	8	10	12	20
Number of inches (i)	12	24	60	96	120	144	240

9. **Science** The formula $d = 16 \cdot t \cdot t$ gives the distance (d) in feet that a ball has fallen t seconds after it has been dropped. Make a table to show the distance the ball has fallen after 0, 1, 2, 3, 4, 5, and 6 seconds.

Time (t), sec	0	1	2	3	4	5	6
Distance (d), ft	0	16	64	144	256	400	576

Name ______________________

Practice

Section 2A Review

Evaluate each expression.

1. $6 + 8 \div 2 - 4$ 6
2. $2 \times 3 + 4 \times 5$ 26
3. $7 + 3 \cdot 8 \div 6$ 11
4. $\frac{7 + 8}{5 - 2}$ 5
5. $3 + \frac{10 - 2}{4}$ 5
6. $2 \times 5 - \frac{3 + 9}{5 - 1}$ 7

Place parentheses to make each sentence true.

7. $(4 + 6) \div (2 - 1) = 10$
8. $(7 \times 7 - 7) \div 7 = 6$
9. $40 + 20 \div (10 - 5) = 44$
10. $7 \times (10 - 8) \div 2 = 7$

Evaluate each formula for the given values.

11. $A = \ell w$, $\ell = 3$, $w = 7$; $A =$ 21
12. $d = rt$, $r = 30$, $t = 2$; $d =$ 60
13. $P = 2\ell + 2w$, $\ell = 6$, $w = 5$; $P =$ 22
14. $r = \frac{d}{t}$, $d = 150$, $t = 3$; $r =$ 50

Find a formula relating the variables.

15. $y = 3x$

x	2	3	4	5
y	6	9	12	15

16. $v = u - 8$

u	11	12	13	14
v	3	4	5	6

17. The formula $r = \frac{d}{t}$ gives the average speed of travel for a distance d and time t. New Orleans, Louisiana, is a 400-mile drive from Memphis, Tennessee. Complete the table to find the average speed if the trip from Memphis to New Orleans is made in different times.

Time (t) in hours	2	4	8	10	20
Speed (r) in mi/hr	200	100	50	40	20

18. The per capita public debt (in thousands of dollars) of the United States for the years 1940 to 1990 appears below. Create a scatterplot and determine a trend line. Based on your scatterplot, what do you expect the per capita public debt to be in 2020? *[Lesson 1-7]*

Year	1940	1950	1960	1970	1980	1990
Amount ($)	325	1688	1572	1807	3970	12,823

About 14,600

United States Public Debt

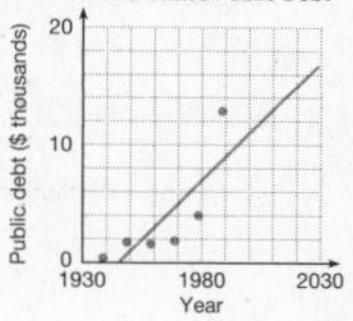

Name ______________________

Practice 2-4

Inverse Operations

The machines below are inverse operation machines. What will be the result when the given number is entered into each machine? Record each step.

1. 10: (10) → Add 7 → (17) → Multiply by 5 → (85) → Divide by 5 → (17) → Subtract 7 → (10)
2. 16: (16) → Divide by 4 → (4) → Add 10 → (14) → Subtract 10 → (4) → Multiply by 4 → (16)
3. 23: (23) → Subtract 3 → (20) → Divide by 5 → (4) → Multiply by 5 → (20) → Add 3 → (23)
4. 5: (5) → Multiply by 8 → (40) → Subtract 13 → (27) → Add 13 → (40) → Divide by 8 → (5)

Add labels to each machine below so that the output will be the same as the input.

5. ( ) → Subtract 4 → ( ) → Multiply by 7 → ( ) → Divide by 7 → ( ) → Add 4 → ( )
6. ( ) → Divide by 3 → ( ) → Add 15 → ( ) → Subtract 15 → ( ) → Multiply by 3 → ( )

7. Maxine locked the door when she left her apartment. What will she need to do to get back inside?

Unlock the door

8. At the mall, Tony went from his car to the shoe store, then the music store, then the card shop, and finally the video arcade. Suddenly he realized that he had lost his wallet, so he decided to retrace his steps back to his car. What route did he take going back?

From the video arcade, he went to the card shop, then the music store, then the shoe store, and finally back to his car.

Name ______________________

Practice 2-5

Translating Words to Expressions

Write an algebraic expression for each phrase.

1. the product of a number (x) and 3 $x \cdot 3$ or $3x$
2. 13 less than a number (m) $m - 13$
3. the quotient of a number (s) and 7 $s \div 7$
4. 7 less than twice a number (d) $2d - 7$
5. the difference between three times a number (k) and 4 $3k - 4$
6. 15 more than one-third of a number (m) $\frac{m}{3} + 15$

Write a phrase for each algebraic expression.

7. $r + 12$ a number (r) increased by 12
8. $3(x + 4)$ the product of 3 and the sum of a number (x) and 4
9. $c - 18$ a number (c) decreased by 18
10. $\frac{12}{u}$ the quotient of 12 and a number (u)
11. $7z - 5$ 5 less than the product of 7 and a number (z)
12. $\frac{m}{n}$ the quotient of a number (m), and a number (n)

13. **Career** Miguel earns $8.00 per hour at his job. Write an expression for the number of dollars he earns for working n hours. $8n$

14. Thomas likes to paint bird houses in his garage on Saturday. He spends a total of one hour setting up and cleaning up, and during the rest of the day he can paint 3 bird houses every hour.

   a. If Thomas spends n hours in his garage, how many hours can he spend actually painting? $n - 1$

   b. Write an expression for the number of bird houses Thomas can paint if he is in his garage for n hours. $3(n - 1)$

Name ______________________

Practice 2-6

Solving Addition and Subtraction Equations

Tell if the given number is a solution to the equation.

1. $x + 18 = 99$; 80 No
2. $u - 3 = 56$; 53 No
3. $17 + t = 74$; 57 Yes
4. $k - 12 = 84$; 96 Yes
5. $r - 5 = 10$; 15 Yes
6. $w + 15 = 40$; 20 No

Solve each equation. Check your answer.

7. $y + 15 = 23$ $y =$ 8
8. $27 + s = 51$ $s =$ 24
9. $w - 31 = 25$ $w =$ 56
10. $64 + q = 123$ $q =$ 59
11. $41 = d - 28$ $d =$ 69
12. $37 = 11 + g$ $g =$ 26

Write an equation for each statement.

13. The number of students (x) decreased by 15 equals 81. $x - 15 = 81$
14. The revenue (r) increased by \$3,200 is \$38,500. $r + 3{,}200 = 38{,}500$
15. The number of hours (h) decreased by 12 equals 64. $h - 12 = 64$

Estimate a solution to each equation.

16. $m - 483 = 1703$ $m \approx$ 2200
17. $6309 = 4120 + p$ $p \approx$ 2200
18. $3240 + y = 7735$ $y \approx$ 4500
19. $v - 847 = 1256$ $v \approx$ 2100

20. **Career** Xochitl is a real estate agent. This month she earned commissions of \$6240, which is \$3460 more than she earned last month. Write and solve an equation to find last month's commissions.
$x + 3460 = 6240$; $x = 2780$; she earned \$2780 last month
21. **History** Thomas Edison invented the phonograph in 1887, 98 years before the introduction of the compact disc (CD). Write and solve an equation to find the year (y) that CDs were introduced.
$1887 = y - 98$; $y = 1985$; CDs were introduced in 1985

Name ______________________

Practice 2-7

Solving Multiplication and Division Equations

Tell if the given number is a solution to the equation.

1. $5x = 20$; 100 No
2. $t \div 3 = 7$; 21 Yes
3. $\frac{u}{9} = 36$; 4 No
4. $8m = 88$; 11 Yes
5. $\frac{b}{5} = 5$; 30 No
6. $r \div 4 = 10$; 40 Yes
7. $3x = 81$; 9 No
8. $6c = 42$; 7 Yes
9. $\frac{d}{11} = 1$; 11 Yes

Solve each equation. Check your answer.

10. $12 = s \div 4$ $s =$ 48
11. $17x = 85$ $x =$ 5
12. $63 = p \cdot 3$ $p =$ 21
13. $6u = 222$ $u =$ 37
14. $\frac{w}{11} = 22$ $w =$ 242
15. $13 = \frac{z}{5}$ $z =$ 65
16. $38 = 19t$ $t =$ 2
17. $9q = 108$ $q =$ 12
18. $\frac{c}{5} = 35$ $c =$ 175
19. $\frac{k}{18} = 72$ $k =$ 1296
20. $21j = 294$ $j =$ 14
21. $y \cdot 4 = 168$ $y =$ 42

Estimate a reasonable solution to each equation.

22. $210x = 4119$ $x \approx$ 20
23. $64{,}382 = 39y$ $y \approx$ 1600
24. $\frac{m}{98} = 43$ $m \approx$ 4000
25. $295 = \frac{r}{51}$ $r \approx$ 15,000

26. A 7-inch phonograph record turns at a rate of 45 revolutions per minute. Write and solve an equation to find the number of minutes to complete 315 revolutions.
$45x = 315$; $x = 7$; it takes 7 minutes
27. **Geometry** A rectangle has area 50 in^2 and base 10 in. Write and solve an equation to find the height of the rectangle.
$10h = 50$; $h = 5$; height is 5 in.

Name ______________________

Practice 2-8

Problem Solving with Two-Step Equations

Solve each equation. Check your answer.

1. $3x + 7 = 37$ $x =$ 10
2. $31 = 7x - 11$ $x =$ 6
3. $11k - 84 = 92$ $k =$ 16
4. $4r + 13 = 57$ $r =$ 11
5. $\frac{z}{4} + 16 = 21$ $z =$ 20
6. $7 = \frac{t}{6} - 3$ $t =$ 60
7. $6q - 18 = 30$ $q =$ 8
8. $\frac{w}{15} + 26 = 42$ $w =$ 240
9. $15u + 18 = 18$ $u =$ 0
10. $9 = 7b - 12$ $b =$ 3
11. $\frac{x}{11} + 21 = 35$ $x =$ 154
12. $\frac{s}{7} - 11 = 17$ $s =$ 196

Explain what was done to the first equation to get the second equation.

13. $\frac{x}{5} - 3 = 12 \rightarrow x = 75$
Add 3 to both sides, then multiply both sides by 5.
14. $6x + 7 = 31 \rightarrow x = 4$
Subtract 7 from both sides, then divide both sides by 6.
15. $\frac{x}{3} + 2 = 4 \rightarrow x = 6$
Subtract 2 from both sides, then multiply both sides by 3.
16. Hideki baked 41 cookies. He gave the same number of cookies to each of 5 friends, saving 11 cookies for himself. How many cookies did each friend receive? 6 cookies
17. **Consumer** Estelle is buying dresses by mail. She pays \$65 for each dress, plus a shipping and handling charge of \$8 for the entire order. If her order costs \$268, how many dresses did she buy? 4 dresses
18. Ms. Juarez planted a 7-ft-tall tree. The height (h) of the tree, in feet, after n years is given by the equation $h = 4n + 7$. In how many years will the height be 39 feet? 8 years

Name ______________________

Practice

Section 2B Review

1. Before gym class, Scott takes off his boots, takes off his jeans, puts on his shorts, and puts on his shoes. Describe the inverse operations he would use after class.
take off shoes, take off shorts, put on jeans, put on boots

Write an algebraic expression for each phrase.

2. Fourteen less than a number (g) $g - 14$
3. Eight more than the product of a number (k) and ten $10k + 8$

Write a phrase for each algebraic expression.

4. $15x$ the product of fifteen and a number (x)
5. $d + 17$ the sum of a number (d) and 17

Find the value of each expression.

6. $3 + 6 \times 4 =$ 27
7. $\frac{23 - 5}{4 + 2} =$ 3
8. $3 \times 4 - \frac{35}{5} =$ 5

Solve each equation.

9. $5s = 45$ $s =$ 9
10. $y - 12 = 31$ $y =$ 43
11. $2x + 8 = 46$ $x =$ 19
12. $\frac{w}{7} - 3 = 10$ $w =$ 91

13. An online service charges \$10.00 for the first 5 hours in a month, and \$2.50 for each additional hour. If Seth's bill is \$22.50, how many hours did he use the service?
10 hours
14. Draw a bar graph to show the number of registered motorcycles (in thousands) in several states in 1990. *[Lesson 1-2]*

State	CA	FL	NY	TX	WA
Reg. motorcycles	627	206	196	175	216

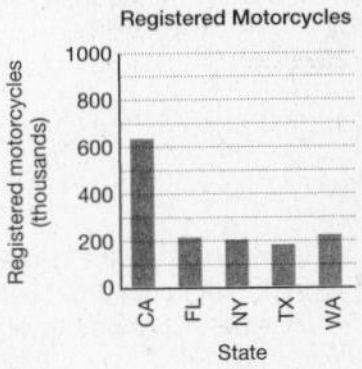

15. The formula $A = b \cdot h$ is used to find the area of a parallelogram with base b and height h. Find the area of a parallelogram with base 7 cm and height 5 cm. *[Lesson 2-1]*
35 cm^2

Name ______________________

Practice

Cumulative Review Chapters 1–2

Use the circle graph to answer each question. *[Lesson 1-1]*

Kids Ages 14 and Under by Race and Ethnic Group 1994

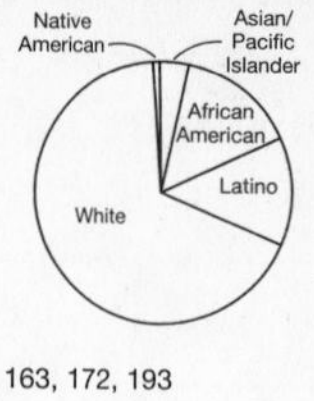

1. About what percent of American kids are white? 67%
2. List the ethnic groups in order from the largest to the smallest. White, African American, Latino Asian/Pacific Islander, Native American

Find the mean, median, and mode(s) for each set of data. *[Lesson 1-4]*

3. 35, 26, 28, 26, 31, 35, 29
   Mean 30
   Median 29
   Mode(s) 26, 35
4. 161, 163, 186, 163, 172, 193
   Mean 173
   Median 167.5
   Mode(s) 163

Find the value of each expression. *[Lesson 2-2]*

5. $7 \times 4 - 6 \times 3$ 10
6. $7(6 - 5) + 2$ 9
7. $(8 - 3) \div (4 + 1)$ 1
8. $\frac{12}{3} - \frac{18}{9}$ 2
9. $\frac{20 + 10}{10 - 5}$ 6
10. $25 - 3 \cdot \frac{33}{11}$ 16

Write a phrase for each algebraic expression. *[Lesson 2-5]*

11. $2 + 7t$ the sum of 2 and the product of 7 and a number (t)
12. $\frac{4}{5 + x}$ the quotient of 4 and the sum of 5 and a number (x)
13. $3(8 + r)$ the product of 3 and the sum of 8 and a number (r)

Solve each equation. Check your answer. *[Lesson 2-8]*

14. $3x - 10 = 35$ $x =$ 15
15. $12 = 7c - 9$ $c =$ 3
16. $62 = 6g + 14$ $g =$ 8
17. $10k - 18 = 32$ $k =$ 5
18. $\frac{m}{6} + 5 = 21$ $m =$ 96
19. $11 = \frac{z}{4} - 10$ $z =$ 84

Name ______________________

Practice 3-1

Place Value: Comparing and Ordering Decimals

Give the value of each 1.

1. 316.24 10
2. 587.13 0.1
3. 201.473 1
4. 17,364.9 10,000
5. 8,447.301 0.001
6. 8,139.64 100
7. 9.4321 0.0001
8. 3,142,864.3 100,000

Give the value of each 8.

9. 384.29 80
10. 506.83 0.8
11. 84,163.2 80,000
12. 1841.67 800

Give the value of each 3.

13. 1,203.7 3
14. 382.87 300
15. 610.731 0.03
16. 53,042.75 3,000

Use the symbols $<$ or $>$ to show which number is larger.

17. 387.65 $>$ 387.56
18. 72.83 $<$ 73.73
19. 0.005 $>$ 0.0005
20. 58.006 $<$ 58.060
21. 17.341 $>$ 17.3409
22. 312.745 $<$ 312.746
23. **Health** One cup of canned orange juice has 1.1 mg of iron. A 10-oz package of frozen peaches has 1.05 mg of iron. Which has more iron? Orange juice
24. The table shows the top 5 earned-run averages in the history of major league baseball. Who had the highest of these averages? Rube Waddel
    Who had the lowest of these averages? Ed Walsh

Player	Mordecai Brown	Addie Joss	Christy Mathewson	Rube Waddel	Ed Walsh
Earned-run average	2.06	1.88	2.13	2.16	1.82

Name ______________________

Practice 3-2

Estimating by Rounding

Round each number to the nearest whole number.

1. 3.874 4
2. 5.132 5
3. 21.635 22
4. 17.5 18
5. 36.498 36
6. 163.094 163
7. 843.17 843
8. 562.63 563

Round each number to the nearest whole number and multiply.

9. 8.37×12.13 96
10. 9.76×4.173 40
11. 16.53×2.75 51
12. 15.84×3.14 48
13. 18.5×6.19 114
14. 8.137×2.071 16
15. 5.384×3.481 15
16. 7.36×30.08 210

Estimate.

17. 3.76×28.4 ≈ 120
18. $238.4 - 88.3$ ≈ 150
19. $19.47 + 3.21$ ≈ 22
20. $\frac{81.37}{8.65}$ ≈ 9
21. 6.83×98.6 ≈ 700
22. $361.238 - 23.7$ ≈ 340
23. $835.4 + 173.2$ ≈ 1000
24. $157.3 \div 42.4$ ≈ 4

Round to (a) the nearest hundredth (b) the nearest tenth (c) the nearest thousandth

25. 81.3074 (a) 81.31 (b) 81.3 (c) 81.307
26. 123.6855 (a) 123.69 (b) 123.7 (c) 123.686
27. 3.41987 (a) 3.42 (b) 3.4 (c) 3.420
28. During the 1968 Olympic Games, Mamo Wolde of Ethiopia ran 26.21875 miles in 2.341 hours. Estimate the number of miles he ran each hour. About 13 mi
29. At the farmer's market, Saul bought 1.83 lb of broccoli, 0.84 lb of carrots, and 1.23 lb of onions. Estimate the total weight of his purchases. About 4 lb

Name ______________________

Practice 3-3

Problem-Solving: Sums and Differences of Decimals

Estimate each sum or difference.

1. $63.7 + 24.3$ ≈ 80
2. $841.63 - 124.8$ ≈ 700
3. $364.78 - 37.2$ ≈ 320
4. $53.87 + 81.3$ ≈ 130
5. $738.2 - 18.37$ ≈ 720
6. $98.76 - 21.3$ ≈ 80
7. $8.7388 + 9.01$ ≈ 18
8. $31.49 + 63.9$ ≈ 90
9. $38.754 - 21.4$ ≈ 20
10. $3.7 + 8.4 + 9.2$ ≈ 21
11. $9.3 + 1.4 + 8.9$ ≈ 19
12. $2.8 + 1.3 + 0.6$ ≈ 5
13. $87.43 + 9.06$ ≈ 96
14. $53.21 - 8.7$ ≈ 44
15. $321.846 + 0.049$ ≈ 322
16. $68.037 - 5.9$ ≈ 62

Solve each equation.

17. $x + 0.37 = 9.42$ $x =$ 9.05
18. $x - 6.43 = 8.7$ $x =$ 15.13
19. $3.841 = x + 1.2$ $x =$ 2.641
20. $8.93 = x - 0.41$ $x =$ 9.34
21. $x + 2.75 = 11.3$ $x =$ 8.55
22. $x - 5.2 = 10.17$ $x =$ 15.37
23. $3.6 = x - 8.471$ $x =$ 12.071
24. $5.2 = x + 2.13$ $x =$ 3.07
25. $88.43 = x + 1.8$ $x =$ 86.63
26. $x - 12.87 = 3.6$ $x =$ 16.47
27. $x + 37.4 = 91.6$ $x =$ 54.2
28. $63.24 = x - 9.3$ $x =$ 72.54
29. **Career** A designer needs 4.83 yards of a certain fabric to make curtains. If the designer already has 1.9 yards of the fabric, how much additional fabric must be purchased? 2.93 yd
30. The Lucky Seven Discount Store calculates the retail price (R) of every item using the formula $R = W + 7.77$, where W is the wholesale price. If a chair retails for \$61.23, what is the wholesale price? \$53.46

Name ______________________

Practice 3-4

Problem-Solving: Products and Quotients of Decimals

Estimate each product or quotient.

1. 0.05×0.86 — ≈ 0.045
2. 0.809×1.2 — ≈ 0.8
3. 3.54×0.07 — ≈ 0.28
4. $\frac{21.44}{13.4}$ — ≈ 2
5. $\frac{0.1944}{0.9}$ — ≈ 0.2
6. $\frac{4.716}{3.6}$ — ≈ 1.25
7. 13.9×0.35 — ≈ 5.6
8. 7.5×0.41 — ≈ 3.2
9. 0.348×0.3 — ≈ 0.09
10. $\frac{64.32}{13.4}$ — ≈ 5
11. $\frac{9.4325}{0.686}$ — ≈ 13
12. $\frac{161.56}{8.8}$ — ≈ 18
13. 0.009×80 — ≈ 0.72
14. 2.9×0.1 — ≈ 0.3
15. 14.58×0.2 — ≈ 3
16. $\frac{0.1572}{0.4}$ — ≈ 0.4

Solve each equation.

17. $8.5d = 112.2$ — $d = 13.2$
18. $\frac{a}{0.29} = 8.9$ — $a = 2.581$
19. $0.1n = 0.313$ — $n = 3.13$
20. $\frac{b}{0.7} = 8.953$ — $b = 6.2671$
21. $\frac{s}{11.39} = 0.48$ — $s = 5.4672$
22. $1.13f = 0.2712$ — $f = 0.24$
23. $\frac{k}{4.1} = 15$ — $k = 61.5$
24. $9.2d = 30.222$ — $d = 3.285$
25. $\frac{x}{8.5} = 9.378$ — $x = 79.713$
26. $2.1d = 6.3$ — $d = 3$
27. $\frac{m}{4.33} = 1.5$ — $m = 6.495$
28. $\frac{u}{15.5} = 4.79$ — $u = 74.245$
29. $4.7z = 19.458$ — $z = 4.14$
30. $\frac{u}{3.155} = 6.4$ — $u = 20.192$
31. $2.08m = 5.3456$ — $m = 2.57$
32. $\frac{v}{4.4} = 8.37$ — $v = 36.828$

33. **Measurement** The formula $p = 2.2k$ relates the mass (k) in kilograms and the weight (p) in pounds. Find the mass, in kilograms, of a casserole weighing 1.474 pounds. — 0.67 kg

34. Find the price of 1.83 lb of cauliflower costing \$0.63 per pound. Round your answer to the nearest cent. — \$1.15

Name ______________________

Practice 3-5

Powers of 10 and Scientific Notation

Evaluate.

1. 4^2 — 16
2. 5^4 — 625
3. 3^3 — 27
4. 9^2 — 81

Write each number in scientific notation.

5. 30 — 3×10^1
6. 84,000 — 8.4×10^4
7. 400 — 4×10^2
8. 390 — 3.9×10^2
9. 3,820 — 3.82×10^3
10. 470 — 4.7×10^2
11. 976,000 — 9.76×10^5
12. 3,740,000 — 3.74×10^6

Write each number in standard form.

13. 3.5×10^3 — 3500
14. 7.8×10^6 — 7,800,000
15. 6.38×10^4 — 63,800
16. 1.87×10^7 — 18,700,000
17. 3.41×10^2 — 341
18. 3.841×10^3 — 3,841
19. 8.4×10^4 — 84,000
20. 9.3×10^6 — 9,300,000
21. 5.1×10^{11} — 510,000,000,000
22. 9×10^{13} — 90,000,000,000,000

23. **Social Science** The table shows estimated 1995 populations of some eastern Asian nations. List the populations, in standard form, in order from least to greatest.

Nation	China	Hong Kong	Japan	North Korea	South Korea	Mongolia
Population	1.22×10^9	5.9×10^6	1.25×10^8	2.39×10^7	4.5×10^7	2.4×10^6

2,400,000, 5,900,000, 23,900,000, 45,000,000,
125,000,000, 1,220,000,000

24. The average person has about 1×10^4 taste buds. Use your calculator and the information in Exercise 23 to estimate the number of human taste buds in China. Give your answer in scientific notation. — 1.22×10^{13}

Name ______________________

Practice

Section 3A Review

Put the correct symbol (<, >, or =) to make a true statement.

1. $17.651 > 17.65$
2. $2.940 > 2.904$
3. $37.84 < 38.74$

Estimate.

4. $143.74 - 31.2$ — ≈ 110
5. 4.631×9.31 — ≈ 45
6. $87.4 \div 10.9$ — ≈ 8

Solve each equation. Estimate the solution first.

7. $2.83x = 13.301$ — $x = 4.7$
8. $x + 5.3 = 8.241$ — $x = 2.941$
9. $x - 8.972 = 7.6$ — $x = 16.572$
10. $\frac{x}{12.3} = 4.89$ — $x = 60.147$

Write in scientific notation.

11. 16,430 — 1.643×10^4
12. 370,000 — 3.7×10^5
13. 94,300,000 — 9.43×10^7

Write in standard form.

14. 4.91×10^3 — 4910
15. 3×10^6 — 3,000,000
16. 1.8×10^8 — 180,000,000

17. Shagufta is going on a backpacking trip. She wants to carry no more than 30 lb. If her backpack weighs 4.87 lb, her food weighs 8.6 lb, and her clothing weighs 7.3 lb, find the maximum weight of other items she can bring. — 9.23 lb

18. Monte has \$18.60. Can he buy 2 lb of shiitake mushrooms priced at \$0.59 per ounce? Explain. (Hint: 1 lb = 16 oz)
No, 2 lb = 32 oz and $32 \times \$0.59 = \$18.88$

The line graph shows the number of American newspapers being published from 1920 to 1990. Use the graph for Exercises 19–20.

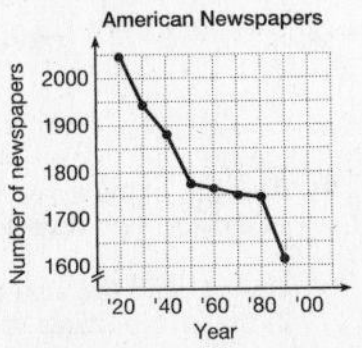

19. Estimate the number of newspapers that were being published in 1940. — About 1880

20. Predict the number of newspapers in 2010. — About 1400–1500

Name ______________________

Practice 3-6

Divisibility and Prime Factorization

Test each number for divisibility by 2, 3, 4, 5, 6, 8, 9, and 10.

1. 7040 — 2, 4, 5, 8, 10
2. 4532 — 2, 4
3. 250 — 2, 5
4. 554 — 2
5. 2168 — 2, 4, 8
6. 1992 — 2, 3, 4, 6, 8
7. 3215 — 5
8. 2291 — None
9. 2180 — 2, 4, 5, 10
10. 2604 — 2, 3, 4, 6
11. 1197 — 3, 9
12. 873 — 3, 9

Determine whether each of these numbers is composite or prime.

13. 181 — Prime
14. 674 — Composite
15. 373 — Prime
16. 64 — Composite
17. 377 — Composite
18. 345 — Composite
19. 569 — Prime
20. 205 — Composite

Use factor trees to find the prime factorization of the following numbers.

21. $144 = 2^4 \times 3^2$

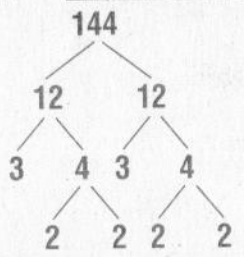

22. $385 = 5 \times 7 \times 11$

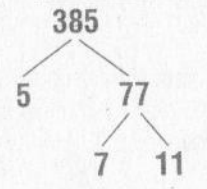

23. $90 = 2 \times 3^2 \times 5$

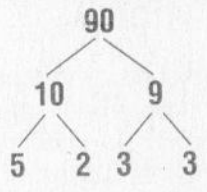

24. Zelda wants to divide a 96-inch-long plank into equal sections. If the length of each section is to be a whole number of inches, what lengths can she use?
1 in., 2 in., 3 in., 4 in., 6 in., 8 in., 12 in., 16 in., 24 in., 32 in., 48 in., 96 in.

25. Give the ways 30 students can be divided into groups of the same size.
Groups of 1, 2, 3, 5, 6, 10, 15, or 30

Name ______________________

Practice 3-7

GCF and LCM

Find the GCF by listing all the factors of each number.

1. 145, 100

   Factors of 145 **1, 5, 29, 145**

   Factors of 100 **1, 2, 4, 5, 10, 20, 25, 50, 100**

   GCF: **5**

Find the GCF by writing the prime factorization of each number.

2. 243, 54

   243 = **$3 \times 3 \times 3 \times 3 \times 3$**

   54 = **$2 \times 3 \times 3 \times 3$**

   GCF = **27**

3. 150, 155

   150 = **$2 \times 3 \times 5 \times 5$**

   155 = **5×31**

   GCF = **5**

4. 96, 84

   96 = **$2 \times 2 \times 2 \times 2 \times 2 \times 3$**

   84 = **$2 \times 2 \times 3 \times 7$**

   GCF = **12**

5. 57, 285

   57 = **3×19**

   285 = **$3 \times 5 \times 19$**

   GCF = **57**

Find the LCM of each pair of numbers.

6. 11, 5 **55**
7. 5, 12 **60**
8. 12, 7 **84**
9. 5, 9 **45**
10. 5, 18 **90**
11. 5, 20 **20**
12. 7, 10 **70**
13. 17, 13 **221**
14. 14, 8 **56**
15. 11, 23 **253**
16. 14, 5 **70**
17. 16, 9 **144**

18. Cameron is making bead necklaces. He has 90 green beads and 108 blue beads. What is the greatest number of identical necklaces he can make if he wants to use all of the beads? **18**

19. A radio station broadcasts a weather forecast every 18 minutes and a commercial every 15 minutes. If the station broadcasts both a weather forecast and a commercial at noon, when is the next time that both will be broadcast at the same time? **At 1:30 P.M.**

Name ______________________

Practice 3-8

Equivalent Fractions and Lowest Terms

Find an equivalent fraction with (a) a smaller and (b) a larger denominator.

1. $\frac{4}{28}$ (a) $\frac{1}{7}$ (b) $\frac{8}{56}$
2. $\frac{9}{69}$ (a) $\frac{3}{23}$ (b) $\frac{18}{138}$
3. $\frac{7}{35}$ (a) $\frac{1}{5}$ (b) $\frac{14}{70}$
4. $\frac{6}{30}$ (a) $\frac{1}{5}$ (b) $\frac{12}{60}$
5. $\frac{52}{86}$ (a) $\frac{26}{43}$ (b) $\frac{104}{172}$
6. $\frac{45}{75}$ (a) $\frac{3}{5}$ (b) $\frac{90}{150}$
7. $\frac{34}{56}$ (a) $\frac{17}{28}$ (b) $\frac{68}{112}$
8. $\frac{42}{52}$ (a) $\frac{21}{26}$ (b) $\frac{84}{104}$
9. $\frac{30}{38}$ (a) $\frac{15}{19}$ (b) $\frac{60}{76}$
10. $\frac{10}{18}$ (a) $\frac{5}{9}$ (b) $\frac{20}{36}$
11. $\frac{72}{81}$ (a) $\frac{8}{9}$ (b) $\frac{144}{162}$
12. $\frac{12}{22}$ (a) $\frac{6}{11}$ (b) $\frac{24}{44}$

Express each fraction in lowest terms.

13. $\frac{46}{62}$ $\frac{23}{31}$
14. $\frac{5}{60}$ $\frac{1}{12}$
15. $\frac{15}{24}$ $\frac{5}{8}$
16. $\frac{20}{58}$ $\frac{10}{29}$
17. $\frac{12}{14}$ $\frac{6}{7}$
18. $\frac{26}{64}$ $\frac{13}{32}$
19. $\frac{8}{342}$ $\frac{4}{171}$
20. $\frac{30}{46}$ $\frac{15}{23}$
21. $\frac{30}{64}$ $\frac{15}{32}$
22. $\frac{6}{14}$ $\frac{3}{7}$
23. $\frac{18}{98}$ $\frac{9}{49}$
24. $\frac{24}{46}$ $\frac{12}{23}$
25. $\frac{30}{45}$ $\frac{2}{3}$
26. $\frac{14}{24}$ $\frac{7}{12}$
27. $\frac{48}{80}$ $\frac{3}{5}$
28. $\frac{49}{77}$ $\frac{7}{11}$
29. $\frac{123}{171}$ $\frac{41}{57}$
30. $\frac{38}{72}$ $\frac{19}{36}$
31. $\frac{22}{60}$ $\frac{11}{30}$
32. $\frac{8}{10}$ $\frac{4}{5}$
33. $\frac{210}{304}$ $\frac{105}{152}$
34. $\frac{18}{39}$ $\frac{6}{13}$
35. $\frac{42}{104}$ $\frac{21}{52}$
36. $\frac{40}{116}$ $\frac{10}{29}$

37. The city of Austin, Texas, typically has 115 clear days out of the 365 days in a year. What fraction of Austin's days are clear? Write your answer in lowest terms. $\frac{23}{73}$

38. In 1985, American education expenditures totaled \$247.7 billion, of which \$137 billion was spent on public elementary and secondary schools. About what fraction of education expenditures were spent on public elementary and secondary schools? **About $\frac{11}{20}$**

Name ______________________

Practice 3-9

Comparing and Ordering Fractions

Compare.

1. $\frac{16}{21} > \frac{28}{38}$
2. $\frac{12}{40} > \frac{13}{44}$
3. $\frac{5}{22} < \frac{8}{32}$
4. $\frac{12}{26} > \frac{16}{36}$
5. $\frac{12}{35} < \frac{7}{18}$
6. $\frac{7}{16} < \frac{16}{35}$
7. $\frac{10}{20} > \frac{20}{41}$
8. $\frac{4}{6} < \frac{9}{12}$
9. $\frac{4}{9} > \frac{19}{44}$
10. $\frac{4}{6} = \frac{10}{15}$
11. $\frac{21}{25} > \frac{18}{22}$
12. $\frac{20}{24} > \frac{16}{20}$
13. $\frac{20}{25} > \frac{10}{13}$
14. $\frac{4}{13} < \frac{8}{25}$
15. $\frac{26}{45} > \frac{3}{6}$
16. $\frac{23}{27} < \frac{16}{18}$
17. $\frac{4}{12} > \frac{13}{41}$
18. $\frac{4}{11} > \frac{7}{21}$
19. $\frac{4}{8} = \frac{25}{50}$
20. $\frac{6}{24} < \frac{8}{31}$
21. $\frac{4}{6} < \frac{12}{17}$
22. $\frac{22}{25} > \frac{22}{26}$
23. $\frac{11}{26} < \frac{14}{32}$
24. $\frac{7}{12} < \frac{30}{50}$
25. $\frac{11}{20} > \frac{25}{46}$
26. $\frac{13}{47} < \frac{3}{9}$
27. $\frac{19}{21} < \frac{32}{35}$
28. $\frac{16}{22} > \frac{25}{35}$
29. $\frac{4}{6} = \frac{22}{33}$
30. $\frac{4}{42} < \frac{2}{19}$
31. $\frac{8}{38} > \frac{8}{39}$
32. $\frac{4}{7} < \frac{27}{47}$
33. $\frac{6}{32} < \frac{4}{18}$
34. $\frac{22}{33} < \frac{34}{50}$
35. $\frac{39}{48} > \frac{38}{47}$
36. $\frac{4}{15} < \frac{3}{11}$
37. $\frac{4}{6} > \frac{9}{14}$
38. $\frac{38}{46} < \frac{38}{45}$
39. $\frac{20}{48} > \frac{16}{39}$
40. $\frac{9}{21} < \frac{22}{50}$
41. $\frac{4}{18} > \frac{4}{19}$
42. $\frac{15}{19} > \frac{15}{20}$
43. $\frac{6}{18} < \frac{13}{37}$
44. $\frac{15}{42} < \frac{8}{21}$

45. Kenny estimates that the distance from his home to the library is between $\frac{1}{3}$ and $\frac{1}{2}$ mile. Find four fractions in that range and list them in order from least to greatest. Express the fractions in lowest terms.

    Possible answer: $\frac{11}{30}, \frac{2}{5}, \frac{13}{30}, \frac{7}{15}$

46. The table shows the approximate fraction of new books and editions published in 1993 in each of several subjects. Order these fractions from least to greatest.

Art	Biography	Fiction	History	Technology
$\frac{3}{100}$	$\frac{21}{500}$	$\frac{1}{9}$	$\frac{2}{43}$	$\frac{7}{155}$

$\frac{3}{100}, \frac{21}{500}, \frac{7}{155}, \frac{2}{43}, \frac{1}{9}$

Name ______________________

Practice 3-10

Converting Between Fractions and Decimals

Convert to a fraction in lowest terms.

1. 0.405 $\frac{81}{200}$
2. 0.874 $\frac{437}{500}$
3. 0.26 $\frac{13}{50}$
4. 0.497 $\frac{497}{1000}$
5. 0.216 $\frac{27}{125}$
6. 0.684 $\frac{171}{250}$
7. 0.465 $\frac{93}{200}$
8. 0.865 $\frac{173}{200}$
9. 0.38 $\frac{19}{50}$
10. 0.72 $\frac{18}{25}$
11. 0.79 $\frac{79}{100}$
12. 0.464 $\frac{58}{125}$
13. 0.204 $\frac{51}{250}$
14. 0.392 $\frac{49}{125}$
15. 0.108 $\frac{27}{250}$
16. 0.042 $\frac{21}{500}$

Convert to a decimal. Tell if the decimal terminates or repeats.

17. $\frac{3}{5}$ **0.6; terminates**
18. $\frac{8}{9}$ **$0.\overline{8}$; repeats**
19. $\frac{7}{8}$ **0.875; terminates**
20. $\frac{5}{11}$ **$0.\overline{45}$; repeats**
21. $\frac{37}{50}$ **0.74; terminates**
22. $\frac{3}{16}$ **0.1875; terminates**
23. $\frac{22}{55}$ **0.4; terminates**
24. $\frac{4}{12}$ **$0.\overline{3}$; repeats**
25. $\frac{17}{34}$ **0.5; terminates**

Use a calculator to convert each repeating decimal to a fraction.

26. $0.\overline{6}$ $\frac{2}{3}$
27. $0.\overline{7}$ $\frac{7}{9}$
28. $0.\overline{27}$ $\frac{3}{11}$
29. $0.0\overline{227}$ $\frac{1}{44}$
30. $0.1\overline{6}$ $\frac{1}{6}$
31. $0.\overline{15}$ $\frac{5}{33}$
32. $0.\overline{47}$ $\frac{47}{99}$
33. $0.\overline{90}$ $\frac{10}{11}$

34. About $\frac{7}{25}$ of the residents of Seattle, Washington, have attended 16 or more years of school. Convert $\frac{7}{25}$ to a decimal. **0.28**

35. **Geography** The area of Brazil is about 0.908 of the area of the United States. Convert 0.908 to a fraction in lowest terms. $\frac{227}{250}$

Name ______________________

Practice

Section 3B Review

Compare.

1. $\frac{11}{28} < \frac{18}{44}$ 2. $\frac{6}{8} > \frac{7}{10}$ 3. $\frac{4}{6} = \frac{14}{21}$ 4. $\frac{7}{12} > \frac{14}{25}$

5. $\frac{4}{7} > \frac{28}{50}$ 6. $\frac{9}{22} > \frac{13}{33}$ 7. $\frac{4}{7} < \frac{29}{49}$ 8. $\frac{5}{7} < \frac{36}{50}$

Find the prime factorization of each number.

9. 36 $2^2 \times 3^2$ 10. 945 $3^3 \times 5 \times 7$ 11. 693 $3^2 \times 7 \times 11$

12. 100 $2^2 \times 5^2$ 13. 539 $7^2 \times 11$ 14. 117 $3^2 \times 13$

Find the GCF and LCM.

15. 45, 36 GCF: 9 LCM: 180

16. 140, 28 GCF: 28 LCM: 140

17. 44, 55 GCF: 11 LCM: 220

18. 25, 30 GCF: 5 LCM: 150

19. A bottle contains 0.296 L of teriyaki sauce. Write 0.296 as a fraction in lowest terms. $\frac{37}{125}$

Convert each fraction to a decimal.

20. $\frac{3}{4}$ 0.75 21. $\frac{18}{25}$ 0.72 22. $\frac{5}{9}$ $0.\overline{5}$ 23. $\frac{8}{24}$ $0.\overline{3}$

24. $\frac{6}{11}$ $0.\overline{54}$ 25. $\frac{21}{80}$ 0.2625 26. $\frac{4}{7}$ $0.\overline{571428}$ 27. $\frac{13}{250}$ 0.052

28. Life expectancies for people in eastern and southeastern Asian and African nations are 71, 78, 79, 71, 71, 64, 51, 63, 51, 71, 58, 65, 64, 69, and 64 years. Make a stem-and-leaf diagram to display the data. *[Lesson 1-3]*

stem	leaf
5	1 1 8
6	3 4 4 4 5 9
7	1 1 1 1 8 9

29. The table relates the number *m* of miles to the number *k* of kilometers. Write a formula relating these values. *[Lesson 2-3]* $k = 1.61m$

m	1	2	3	4	5
k	1.61	3.22	4.83	6.44	8.05

Name ______________________

Practice

Cumulative Review Chapters 1–3

The bar graph shows how many American homes had access to electronic media in 1990. Use the graph for Exercises 1–2. *[Lesson 1-1]*

Electronic Media in U.S. Homes, 1990

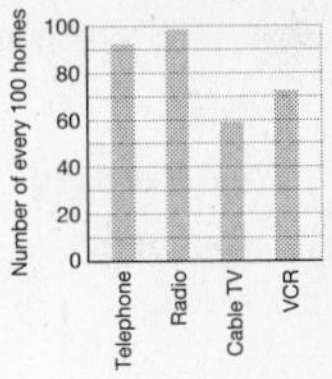

1. About how many of every 100 homes had a videocassette recorder (VCR)? 72

2. Which item was in the most homes? Radio

The fewest homes? Cable TV

Find the value of each expression. *[Lesson 2-2]*

3. $18 + 21 \div 3$ 25 4. $7 \times 2 + 5 \times 3$ 29 5. $3(8 - 2) + 4$ 22

6. $2 + \frac{10 - 2}{1 + 3}$ 4 7. $\frac{12}{3} - \frac{24}{6 + 2}$ 1 8. $30 - (10 - 7) \times 2$ 24

Use the given formula to complete each table. *[Lesson 2-3]*

9. $y = 2x - 5$

x	5	6	7	8
y	5	7	9	11

10. $D = 25t$

t	3	4	5	6
D	75	100	125	150

11. $t = 45 - 6s$

s	2	3	4	5
t	33	27	21	15

12. $p = \frac{100}{n + 6}$

n	4	14	19	44
p	10	5	4	2

Use the symbols > or < to show which number is larger. *[Lesson 3-1]*

13. 8.631 > 8.63 14. 4.354 < 4.356 15. 18.73 > 17.83

16. 2.070 > 2.007 17. 5.386 > 5.376 18. 12.39 > 12.3899

Solve each equation. *[Lessons 3-3, 3-4]*

19. $x + 1.7 = 8.63$ $x =$ 6.93 20. $y - 5.83 = 12.3$ $y =$ 18.13 21. $6.54 = j + 2.87$ $j =$ 3.67 22. $8.273 = q - 4.13$ $q =$ 12.403

23. $2.3x = 20.93$ $x =$ 9.1 24. $\frac{u}{1.49} = 3.65$ $u =$ 5.4385 25. $18 = 4.8k$ $k =$ 3.75 26. $9.03 = \frac{c}{17.8}$ $c =$ 160.734

Name ______________________

Practice 4-1

Estimating: Fractions and Mixed Numbers

Estimate each sum or difference.

1. $\frac{3}{8} + \frac{2}{3}$ 1 2. $\frac{7}{8} - \frac{1}{2}$ $\frac{1}{2}$ 3. $\frac{3}{16} + \frac{11}{12}$ 1 4. $\frac{9}{10} - \frac{3}{8}$ $\frac{1}{2}$

5. $\frac{2}{3} - \frac{3}{8}$ 0 6. $\frac{5}{6} + \frac{1}{3}$ $1\frac{1}{2}$ 7. $\frac{4}{5} - \frac{1}{7}$ 1 8. $\frac{1}{5} + \frac{7}{15}$ $\frac{1}{2}$

Round each mixed number to the nearest whole number, then estimate each sum or difference.

9. $2\frac{7}{8} + 3\frac{1}{4}$ 6 10. $12\frac{5}{8} - 3\frac{4}{5}$ 9 11. $7\frac{5}{6} + 4\frac{1}{3}$ 12 12. $12\frac{2}{5} - 8\frac{3}{7}$ 4

13. $15\frac{2}{3} - 7\frac{1}{6}$ 9 14. $11\frac{1}{2} + 9\frac{3}{5}$ 22 15. $10\frac{1}{4} - 5\frac{1}{2}$ 4 16. $8\frac{1}{5} + 6\frac{5}{7}$ 15

17. $12\frac{7}{8} + 6\frac{4}{5}$ 20 18. $14\frac{1}{8} - 2\frac{3}{4}$ 11 19. $13\frac{3}{8} + 2\frac{1}{3}$ 15 20. $14\frac{2}{9} - 9\frac{9}{10}$ 4

Use compatible numbers to estimate each product or quotient.

21. $8\frac{1}{3} \times \frac{1}{2}$ 4 22. $23\frac{1}{6} \div 7\frac{1}{2}$ 3 23. $\frac{1}{6} \times 40\frac{2}{3}$ 7 24. $35\frac{2}{3} \div 4\frac{7}{8}$ 7

25. $43\frac{1}{2} \div 4\frac{1}{2}$ 11 26. $\frac{1}{3} \times 32\frac{1}{4}$ 11 27. $73\frac{4}{11} \div 6\frac{1}{4}$ 12 28. $62\frac{1}{2} \times \frac{1}{8}$ 8

29. $\frac{1}{4} \times 35\frac{1}{7}$ 9 30. $28\frac{6}{7} \div 5\frac{2}{3}$ 5 31. $41\frac{1}{7} \times \frac{1}{5}$ 8 32. $83\frac{3}{8} \div 11\frac{9}{16}$ 7

33. The hypsilophodon was about $2\frac{1}{3}$ m long, and the geranosaurus was about $1\frac{1}{5}$ m long. Use rounding to estimate the difference between the length of these dinosaurs. About 1 m

34. Tim's bucket can hold up to $12\frac{1}{3}$ quarts of liquid. If it is $\frac{1}{3}$ full of water, estimate the number of quarts of water in the bucket. 4 quarts

Name ______________________

Practice 4-2

Adding and Subtracting Fractions

Find the least common denominator for each pair of fractions.

1. $\frac{2}{5}, \frac{3}{8}$ 40 2. $\frac{3}{4}, \frac{5}{8}$ 8 3. $\frac{2}{3}, \frac{1}{7}$ 21 4. $\frac{3}{5}, \frac{7}{10}$ 10

5. $\frac{5}{6}, \frac{1}{14}$ 42 6. $\frac{3}{8}, \frac{3}{10}$ 40 7. $\frac{5}{7}, \frac{1}{4}$ 28 8. $\frac{7}{8}, \frac{5}{12}$ 24

Find each sum or difference. Rewrite in lowest terms.

9. $\frac{9}{11} - \frac{5}{11}$ $\frac{4}{11}$ 10. $\frac{3}{4} + \frac{1}{14}$ $\frac{23}{28}$ 11. $\frac{19}{60} - \frac{1}{4}$ $\frac{1}{15}$ 12. $\frac{1}{2} + \frac{1}{3}$ $\frac{5}{6}$

13. $\frac{7}{15} - \frac{1}{5}$ $\frac{4}{15}$ 14. $\frac{1}{3} + \frac{1}{25}$ $\frac{28}{75}$ 15. $\frac{7}{9} - \frac{1}{9}$ $\frac{2}{3}$ 16. $\frac{11}{25} - \frac{1}{5}$ $\frac{6}{25}$

Solve each equation.

17. $m - \frac{4}{15} = \frac{3}{5}$ $m =$ $\frac{13}{15}$ 18. $q - \frac{1}{2} = \frac{1}{8}$ $q =$ $\frac{5}{8}$ 19. $h - \frac{1}{9} = \frac{1}{2}$ $h =$ $\frac{11}{18}$ 20. $z + \frac{3}{11} = \frac{10}{11}$ $z =$ $\frac{7}{11}$

21. $s - \frac{2}{25} = \frac{2}{3}$ $s =$ $\frac{56}{75}$ 22. $s - \frac{1}{4} = \frac{4}{7}$ $s =$ $\frac{23}{28}$ 23. $g + \frac{1}{3} = \frac{8}{9}$ $g =$ $\frac{5}{9}$ 24. $s + \frac{2}{5} = \frac{9}{10}$ $s =$ $\frac{1}{2}$

25. $a - \frac{14}{25} = \frac{1}{5}$ $a =$ $\frac{19}{25}$ 26. $j + \frac{1}{9} = \frac{34}{63}$ $j =$ $\frac{3}{7}$ 27. $q - \frac{5}{11} = \frac{1}{4}$ $q =$ $\frac{31}{44}$ 28. $y + \frac{11}{15} = \frac{14}{15}$ $y =$ $\frac{1}{5}$

29. The price of Rolando's stock went up $\frac{7}{8}$ the day he bought it, but the next day it went down $\frac{3}{16}$. What was the total increase over the two days? $\frac{11}{16}$

30. In 1994, about $\frac{3}{5}$ of the federal budget was spent on human resources, and $\frac{1}{20}$ of the federal budget was spent on physical resources. About what fraction of the federal budget was spent on human and physical resources combined? $\frac{13}{20}$

Name ______

Practice 4-3

Adding and Subtracting Mixed Numbers

Rewrite each mixed number as an improper fraction.

1. $4\frac{3}{8}$ $\frac{35}{8}$ 2. $7\frac{1}{9}$ $\frac{64}{9}$ 3. $2\frac{3}{5}$ $\frac{13}{5}$ 4. $3\frac{5}{6}$ $\frac{23}{6}$

Find each sum or difference.

5. $27\frac{7}{10} - 15\frac{7}{10}$ 12
6. $29\frac{8}{15} - 20\frac{1}{3}$ $9\frac{1}{5}$
7. $7\frac{3}{10} + 23\frac{8}{25}$ $30\frac{31}{50}$
8. $3\frac{1}{6} + 8\frac{5}{8}$ $11\frac{19}{24}$
9. $8\frac{13}{18} + 11\frac{11}{18}$ $20\frac{1}{3}$
10. $24\frac{5}{7} + 23\frac{1}{8}$ $47\frac{47}{56}$
11. $3\frac{4}{25} + 3\frac{4}{5}$ $6\frac{24}{25}$
12. $32\frac{24}{25} - 14\frac{19}{25}$ $18\frac{1}{5}$

Solve each equation.

13. $k - 7\frac{1}{10} = 4\frac{5}{18}$ $k =$ $11\frac{17}{45}$
14. $q + 1\frac{1}{2} = 23\frac{2}{3}$ $q =$ $22\frac{1}{6}$
15. $f + 13\frac{1}{6} = 20\frac{17}{30}$ $f =$ $7\frac{2}{5}$
16. $r - \frac{1}{5} = 7\frac{3}{7}$ $r =$ $7\frac{22}{35}$
17. $z - 17\frac{17}{20} = 11\frac{2}{15}$ $z =$ $28\frac{59}{60}$
18. $m - 19\frac{5}{9} = 4\frac{4}{7}$ $m =$ $24\frac{8}{63}$

Geometry Find the perimeter of each figure.

19. $12\frac{1}{5}$ cm

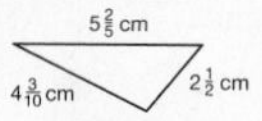

20. $5\frac{5}{8}$ in.

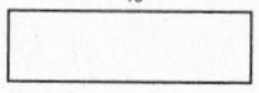

21. On May 21, 1996, Iomega stock was priced at $43\frac{3}{8}$. On May 22, it was priced at 54.

a. How much did the price go up on May 22? $10\frac{5}{8}$

b. On May 23, the price went down $2\frac{3}{4}$. What was the closing price on May 23? $51\frac{1}{4}$

Name ______

Practice

Section 4A Review

Round each addend to 0, $\frac{1}{2}$, or 1, then estimate each sum or difference.

1. $\frac{4}{5} - \frac{3}{8}$ $\frac{1}{2}$
2. $\frac{1}{3} + \frac{9}{16}$ 1
3. $\frac{1}{7} + \frac{4}{9}$ $\frac{1}{2}$
4. $\frac{8}{9} - \frac{3}{7}$ $\frac{1}{2}$

Round each mixed number to the nearest whole number, then estimate each sum or difference.

5. $4\frac{1}{5} + 9\frac{7}{8}$ 14
6. $8\frac{3}{8} - 2\frac{3}{4}$ 5
7. $11\frac{4}{5} + 7\frac{2}{7}$ 19
8. $12\frac{4}{9} - 5\frac{1}{3}$ 7

Find each sum or difference.

9. $\frac{37}{40} - \frac{3}{10}$ $\frac{5}{8}$
10. $\frac{23}{65} - \frac{1}{5}$ $\frac{2}{13}$
11. $\frac{1}{24} + \frac{1}{16}$ $\frac{5}{48}$
12. $\frac{13}{25} + \frac{1}{5}$ $\frac{18}{25}$

Solve each equation.

13. $j + \frac{5}{8} = \frac{65}{72}$ $j =$ $\frac{5}{18}$
14. $n - \frac{1}{10} = \frac{3}{8}$ $n =$ $\frac{19}{40}$
15. $h + \frac{3}{4} = \frac{11}{12}$ $h =$ $\frac{1}{6}$
16. $q - \frac{3}{16} = \frac{1}{3}$ $q =$ $\frac{25}{48}$
17. $k + 2\frac{7}{20} = 8\frac{2}{5}$ $k =$ $6\frac{1}{20}$
18. $d - 9\frac{1}{12} = 10\frac{1}{4}$ $d =$ $19\frac{1}{3}$
19. $c - 17\frac{5}{7} = 5\frac{4}{21}$ $c =$ $22\frac{19}{21}$
20. $p + 11\frac{1}{2} = 20\frac{7}{10}$ $p =$ $9\frac{1}{5}$

21. A cake recipe calls for $\frac{3}{4}$ cup cocoa plus enough flour to make a total of $3\frac{1}{3}$ cups. How much flour is in the recipe? $2\frac{7}{12}$ cups

22. A computer printer can print 8 pages per minute. *[Lesson 2-5]*

a. Write an expression for the number of pages that can be printed in t minutes. $8t$

b. How many pages can be printed in 9 minutes? 72

23. **Science** A male American toad can reach a length of 13.97 cm, which is 5.08 cm longer than the length of a female American toad. Write and solve an equation to find the length of a female American toad.

$13.97 = x + 5.08$; 8.89 cm

Name ______

Practice 4-4

Multiplying Fractions

Find each product. Rewrite in lowest terms.

1. $\frac{1}{8} \cdot \frac{2}{3}$ $\frac{1}{12}$
2. $\frac{5}{9} \cdot \frac{3}{5}$ $\frac{1}{3}$
3. $\frac{1}{2} \cdot \frac{4}{5}$ $\frac{2}{5}$
4. $\frac{8}{9} \cdot \frac{5}{6}$ $\frac{20}{27}$
5. $\frac{2}{9} \cdot \frac{3}{5}$ $\frac{2}{15}$
6. $\frac{7}{9} \cdot \frac{9}{10}$ $\frac{7}{10}$
7. $\frac{5}{6} \cdot \frac{4}{9}$ $\frac{10}{27}$
8. $\frac{5}{8} \cdot \frac{4}{9}$ $\frac{5}{18}$
9. $\frac{1}{8} \cdot \frac{6}{7}$ $\frac{3}{28}$
10. $\frac{1}{2} \cdot \frac{4}{5}$ $\frac{2}{5}$
11. $\frac{3}{4} \cdot \frac{5}{6}$ $\frac{5}{8}$
12. $\frac{2}{5} \cdot \frac{3}{10}$ $\frac{3}{25}$
13. $\frac{2}{7} \cdot \frac{3}{4}$ $\frac{3}{14}$
14. $\frac{3}{10} \cdot \frac{1}{9}$ $\frac{1}{30}$
15. $\frac{8}{9} \cdot \frac{3}{7}$ $\frac{8}{21}$

Divide the numerator and the denominator of the following fractions by common factors *before* you multiply. Then multiply the fractions that remain.

16. $\frac{10}{17} \cdot \frac{7}{16}$ $\frac{35}{136}$
17. $\frac{3}{40} \cdot \frac{5}{21}$ $\frac{1}{56}$
18. $\frac{12}{35} \cdot \frac{10}{21}$ $\frac{8}{49}$
19. $\frac{19}{36} \cdot \frac{9}{13}$ $\frac{19}{52}$
20. $\frac{11}{32} \cdot \frac{9}{11}$ $\frac{9}{32}$
21. $\frac{35}{72} \cdot \frac{36}{43}$ $\frac{35}{86}$
22. $\frac{9}{28} \cdot \frac{8}{15}$ $\frac{6}{35}$
23. $\frac{9}{11} \cdot \frac{25}{27}$ $\frac{25}{33}$
24. $\frac{6}{19} \cdot \frac{19}{50}$ $\frac{3}{25}$
25. $\frac{5}{36} \cdot \frac{16}{45}$ $\frac{4}{81}$
26. $\frac{45}{91} \cdot \frac{13}{33}$ $\frac{15}{77}$
27. $\frac{16}{51} \cdot \frac{63}{80}$ $\frac{21}{85}$

Measurement Find the area of each rectangle.

28. $\frac{9}{25}$ cm^2

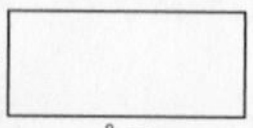

29. $\frac{7}{24}$ in^2

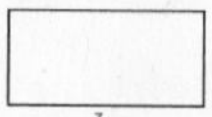

30. A sheet of plywood is $\frac{5}{8}$ in. thick. How tall is a stack of 21 sheets of plywood? $13\frac{1}{8}$ in.

31. A poster measures 38 cm across. If a photocopy machine is used to make a copy that is $\frac{3}{5}$ of the original size, what is the width of the copy? $22\frac{4}{5}$ cm

Name ______

Practice 4-5

Multiplying Mixed Numbers

Use the distributive property to find each product mentally.

1. $6 \cdot 7\frac{3}{5}$ $45\frac{3}{5}$
2. $7 \cdot 2\frac{9}{10}$ $20\frac{3}{10}$
3. $3 \cdot 6\frac{3}{5}$ $19\frac{4}{5}$
4. $4\frac{1}{8} \cdot 7$ $28\frac{7}{8}$
5. $1\frac{2}{7} \cdot 7$ 9
6. $5 \cdot 5\frac{1}{6}$ $25\frac{5}{6}$
7. $6 \cdot 2\frac{4}{9}$ $14\frac{2}{3}$
8. $8 \cdot 3\frac{3}{4}$ 30
9. $6\frac{3}{5} \cdot 4$ $26\frac{2}{5}$
10. $4\frac{7}{9} \cdot 4$ $19\frac{1}{9}$
11. $4\frac{1}{6} \cdot 9$ $37\frac{1}{2}$
12. $2 \cdot 5\frac{6}{7}$ $11\frac{5}{7}$

Find each product.

13. $9\frac{1}{2} \cdot 1\frac{1}{2}$ $14\frac{1}{4}$
14. $8\frac{5}{8} \cdot 3\frac{3}{5}$ $31\frac{1}{20}$
15. $1\frac{5}{7} \cdot 4\frac{2}{3}$ 8
16. $7\frac{6}{7} \cdot 8\frac{1}{3}$ $65\frac{10}{21}$
17. $6\frac{1}{2} \cdot 5\frac{3}{4}$ $37\frac{3}{8}$
18. $9\frac{1}{3} \cdot 4\frac{3}{7}$ $41\frac{1}{3}$
19. $4\frac{9}{10} \cdot \frac{1}{2}$ $2\frac{9}{20}$
20. $4\frac{3}{5} \cdot 6\frac{1}{9}$ $28\frac{1}{9}$
21. $2\frac{1}{2} \cdot 6\frac{1}{3}$ $15\frac{5}{6}$
22. $6\frac{3}{4} \cdot 1\frac{2}{3}$ $11\frac{1}{4}$
23. $8\frac{1}{2} \cdot 3\frac{3}{4}$ $31\frac{7}{8}$
24. $6\frac{2}{3} \cdot 3\frac{2}{3}$ $24\frac{4}{9}$
25. $5\frac{5}{6} \cdot 3\frac{7}{10}$ $21\frac{7}{12}$
26. $8\frac{6}{7} \cdot 3\frac{1}{4}$ $28\frac{11}{14}$
27. $8\frac{2}{3} \cdot 7\frac{1}{3}$ $63\frac{5}{9}$
28. $2\frac{1}{7} \cdot 5\frac{5}{8}$ $12\frac{3}{56}$
29. $7\frac{2}{7} \cdot 2\frac{1}{7}$ $15\frac{30}{49}$
30. $7\frac{3}{4} \cdot 5\frac{2}{3}$ $43\frac{11}{12}$
31. $3\frac{1}{3} \cdot 2\frac{1}{10}$ 7
32. $5\frac{1}{2} \cdot 1\frac{3}{4}$ $9\frac{5}{8}$
33. $6\frac{5}{8} \cdot 4\frac{3}{5}$ $30\frac{19}{40}$
34. $2\frac{1}{2} \cdot 4\frac{2}{5}$ 11
35. $8\frac{1}{3} \cdot 5\frac{8}{9}$ $49\frac{2}{27}$
36. $7\frac{1}{8} \cdot 7\frac{1}{3}$ $52\frac{1}{4}$

37. **Measurement** A one-kilogram object weighs about $2\frac{1}{5}$ pounds. Find the weight, in pounds, of a computer monitor with mass $7\frac{3}{8}$ kilograms. $16\frac{9}{40}$ lb

38. **Social Science** The population of Sweden is about $1\frac{11}{16}$ times as great as the population of Denmark. Find the population of Sweden if the population of Denmark is about 5,190,000. About 8,760,000

Name ______________________

Practice 4-6

Dividing Fractions and Mixed Numbers

Change each mixed number to an improper fraction and write its reciprocal.

1. $1\frac{1}{5}$ $\frac{6}{5}; \frac{5}{6}$
2. $4\frac{5}{6}$ $\frac{29}{6}; \frac{6}{29}$
3. $3\frac{1}{4}$ $\frac{13}{4}; \frac{4}{13}$
4. $5\frac{7}{9}$ $\frac{52}{9}; \frac{9}{52}$
5. $7\frac{3}{5}$ $\frac{38}{5}; \frac{5}{38}$
6. $2\frac{5}{7}$ $\frac{19}{7}; \frac{7}{19}$
7. $6\frac{7}{8}$ $\frac{55}{8}; \frac{8}{55}$
8. $9\frac{3}{10}$ $\frac{93}{10}; \frac{10}{93}$
9. $3\frac{6}{7}$ $\frac{27}{7}; \frac{7}{27}$

Rewrite each division expression as a multiplication expression to find the quotient.

10. $\frac{1}{9} \div \frac{5}{6}$ $\frac{1}{9} \cdot \frac{6}{5} = \frac{2}{15}$
11. $\frac{1}{2} \div \frac{4}{5}$ $\frac{1}{2} \cdot \frac{5}{4} = \frac{5}{8}$
12. $\frac{1}{2} \div \frac{2}{3}$ $\frac{1}{2} \cdot \frac{3}{2} = \frac{3}{4}$
13. $\frac{3}{5} \div \frac{4}{9}$ $\frac{3}{5} \cdot \frac{9}{4} = 1\frac{7}{20}$
14. $\frac{2}{3} \div \frac{5}{6}$ $\frac{2}{3} \cdot \frac{6}{5} = \frac{4}{5}$
15. $\frac{1}{2} \div 3\frac{1}{4}$ $\frac{1}{2} \cdot \frac{4}{13} = \frac{2}{13}$
16. $4\frac{2}{5} \div \frac{4}{5}$ $\frac{22}{5} \cdot \frac{5}{4} = 5\frac{1}{2}$
17. $6\frac{2}{3} \div \frac{3}{4}$ $\frac{20}{3} \cdot \frac{4}{3} = 8\frac{8}{9}$
18. $1\frac{3}{8} \div \frac{2}{3}$ $\frac{11}{8} \cdot \frac{3}{2} = 2\frac{1}{16}$
19. $3\frac{2}{9} \div 2\frac{1}{3}$ $\frac{29}{9} \cdot \frac{3}{7} = 1\frac{8}{21}$
20. $5\frac{1}{2} \div 1\frac{1}{2}$ $\frac{11}{2} \cdot \frac{2}{3} = 3\frac{2}{3}$
21. $11\frac{1}{2} \div 3\frac{1}{2}$ $\frac{23}{2} \cdot \frac{2}{7} = 3\frac{2}{7}$

Find each quotient. Rewrite in lowest terms.

22. $\frac{1}{2} \div \frac{6}{7}$ $\frac{7}{12}$
23. $\frac{1}{10} \div \frac{8}{9}$ $\frac{9}{80}$
24. $\frac{2}{7} \div \frac{3}{4}$ $\frac{8}{21}$
25. $\frac{3}{4} \div \frac{3}{5}$ $1\frac{1}{4}$
26. $5\frac{1}{3} \div \frac{5}{7}$ $7\frac{7}{15}$
27. $2\frac{4}{5} \div \frac{1}{3}$ $8\frac{2}{5}$
28. $2\frac{1}{2} \div \frac{1}{10}$ 25
29. $\frac{4}{5} \div 4\frac{2}{3}$ $\frac{6}{35}$
30. $1\frac{1}{8} \div 1\frac{4}{5}$ $\frac{5}{8}$
31. $2\frac{1}{3} \div 1\frac{3}{4}$ $1\frac{1}{3}$
32. $3\frac{3}{4} \div 4\frac{1}{2}$ $\frac{5}{6}$
33. $2\frac{5}{8} \div 2\frac{4}{5}$ $\frac{15}{16}$

34. **Measurement** A mile is about $1\frac{3}{5}$ km. How many miles are in $6\frac{4}{5}$ km? $4\frac{1}{4}$ mi

35. **Measurement** A 10-oz drinking glass holds $1\frac{1}{4}$ cups of liquid. How many drinking glasses are needed for 5 gallons (80 cups) of lemonade? 64 glasses

Name ______________________

Practice

Section 4B Review

Find each product. Rewrite in lowest terms.

1. $\frac{1}{3} \cdot \frac{1}{5}$ $\frac{1}{15}$
2. $\frac{6}{7} \cdot \frac{1}{5}$ $\frac{6}{35}$
3. $\frac{7}{10} \cdot \frac{2}{5}$ $\frac{7}{25}$
4. $\frac{1}{8} \cdot \frac{3}{5}$ $\frac{3}{40}$
5. $\frac{11}{14} \cdot \frac{7}{22}$ $\frac{1}{4}$
6. $\frac{2}{45} \cdot \frac{9}{10}$ $\frac{1}{25}$
7. $\frac{11}{26} \cdot \frac{8}{11}$ $\frac{4}{13}$
8. $\frac{20}{21} \cdot \frac{15}{22}$ $\frac{50}{77}$
9. $\frac{3}{4} \cdot 2\frac{6}{7}$ $2\frac{1}{7}$
10. $\frac{1}{2} \cdot 3\frac{5}{7}$ $1\frac{6}{7}$
11. $\frac{8}{9} \cdot 6\frac{1}{5}$ $5\frac{23}{45}$
12. $\frac{2}{5} \cdot 6\frac{2}{7}$ $2\frac{18}{35}$
13. $1\frac{1}{3} \cdot 3\frac{1}{2}$ $4\frac{2}{3}$
14. $6\frac{2}{3} \cdot 2\frac{3}{7}$ $16\frac{4}{21}$
15. $7\frac{2}{3} \cdot 9\frac{3}{4}$ $74\frac{3}{4}$
16. $4\frac{1}{5} \cdot 3\frac{2}{3}$ $15\frac{2}{5}$
17. $2\frac{2}{7} \cdot 1\frac{1}{5}$ $2\frac{26}{35}$
18. $\frac{7}{11} \cdot \frac{5}{13}$ $\frac{35}{143}$

Find each quotient. Rewrite in lowest terms.

19. $\frac{1}{5} \div \frac{1}{3}$ $\frac{3}{5}$
20. $\frac{7}{10} \div \frac{3}{4}$ $\frac{14}{15}$
21. $\frac{1}{2} \div \frac{8}{9}$ $\frac{9}{16}$
22. $\frac{1}{2} \div \frac{8}{9}$ $\frac{9}{16}$
23. $2\frac{2}{3} \div 3$ $\frac{8}{9}$
24. $11\frac{1}{2} \div \frac{1}{5}$ $57\frac{1}{2}$
25. $2 \div 3\frac{1}{3}$ $\frac{3}{5}$
26. $1\frac{7}{9} \div 2\frac{2}{5}$ $\frac{20}{27}$
27. $2\frac{4}{5} \div 1\frac{1}{2}$ $1\frac{13}{15}$
28. $5\frac{1}{3} \div 2\frac{4}{5}$ $1\frac{19}{21}$
29. $\frac{1}{4} \div \frac{9}{10}$ $\frac{5}{18}$
30. $2\frac{1}{5} \div 5\frac{4}{5}$ $\frac{11}{29}$

31. A recipe calls for $1\frac{2}{3}$ cups of flour. If Ron is making $1\frac{1}{2}$ times the recipe, how much flour should he use? $2\frac{1}{2}$ cups

32. **Geometry** The table shows the relationship between the side length *x*, and the perimeter *P*, of a square. Find a formula relating the variables. *[Lesson 2-3]* $P = 4x$

x	2	4	6	8
P	8	16	24	32

33. **Science** The spider *tegenaria atrica* can travel at speeds up to 1.17 mi/hr. How long will this spider take to travel 1.638 miles at that speed? *[Lesson 3-4]* 1.4 hr

Name ______________________

Practice

Cumulative Review Chapters 1–4

The circle graph shows sources of funding for American public elementary and secondary schools. Use the graph to answer Exercises 1–3. *[Lesson 1-1]*

Public School Funding, 1992

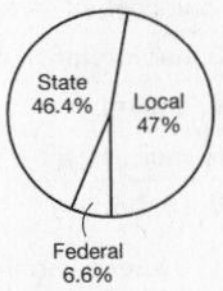

1. List the sources of funding in order of size from largest to smallest. Local, State, Federal
2. Which two sources provide about the same amount of funding? Local, State
3. Which source provides about 6.6% of public school funding? Federal

Write an algebraic expression for each phrase. *[Lesson 2-5]*

4. one-fifth of a number (*w*) $\frac{w}{5}$
5. seven more than a number (*k*) $k + 7$
6. three times the difference of a number (*g*) and 8 $3(g - 8)$

Solve each equation. *[Lessons 3-3, 3-4]*

7. $3.16 = x - 5.23$ $x = 8.39$
8. $n + 8.3 = 12.147$ $n = 3.847$
9. $7.1 = j + 1.85$ $j = 5.25$
10. $p - 2.1 = 8.99$ $p = 11.09$
11. $3.21s = 17.013$ $s = 5.3$
12. $0.9s = 13.86$ $s = 15.4$
13. $\frac{m}{2.36} = 5.9$ $m = 13.924$
14. $\frac{z}{3.72} = 1.54$ $z = 5.7288$

Find each sum or difference. *[Lesson 4-3]*

15. $15\frac{10}{11} + 14\frac{2}{3}$ $30\frac{19}{33}$
16. $15\frac{20}{21} - 2\frac{2}{7}$ $13\frac{2}{3}$
17. $37\frac{68}{75} - 22\frac{21}{25}$ $15\frac{1}{15}$
18. $13\frac{3}{35} - \frac{4}{5}$ $12\frac{2}{7}$
19. $19\frac{1}{3} + 11\frac{9}{20}$ $30\frac{47}{60}$
20. $28\frac{9}{10} - 16\frac{2}{5}$ $12\frac{1}{2}$

Find each product. *[Lesson 4-5]*

21. $3\frac{1}{2} \cdot 7\frac{7}{8}$ $27\frac{9}{16}$
22. $3\frac{7}{10} \cdot 5\frac{3}{4}$ $21\frac{11}{40}$
23. $7\frac{2}{5} \cdot 4\frac{1}{2}$ $33\frac{3}{10}$
24. $7\frac{1}{6} \cdot 6\frac{4}{5}$ $48\frac{11}{15}$
25. $4\frac{4}{9} \cdot 7\frac{5}{8}$ $33\frac{8}{9}$
26. $5\frac{1}{2} \cdot 2\frac{4}{9}$ $13\frac{4}{9}$

Name ______________________

Practice 5-1

Angles

Name each angle and give its measure.

1. ∠ABC; 65°
2. ∠TUV; 125°
3. ∠PQR; 40°

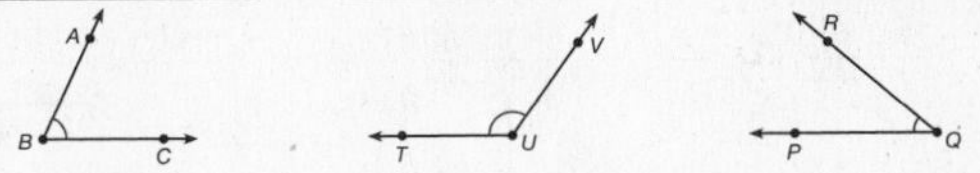

Find the complement and the supplement of ∠P.

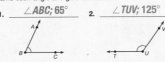

4. complement: 37° supplement: 127°
5. complement: 12° supplement: 102°
6. complement: None supplement: 62°

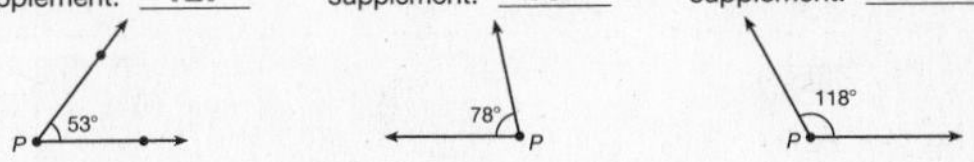

Measure each angle using a protractor.

7. 95°
8. 125°
9. 165°

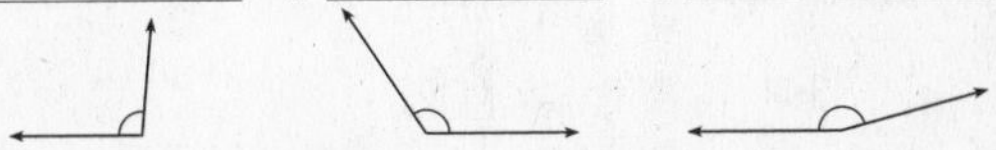

Classify each angle.

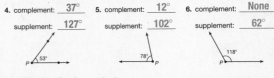

10. Obtuse
11. Acute
12. Right
13. Straight

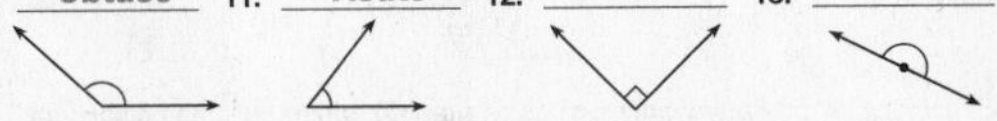

14. **Science** When a beam of light strikes a flat mirror, the light reflects at the same angle at which it hits the mirror's surface.

a. If light strikes a mirror at 63°, at what angle will the light reflect? 63°

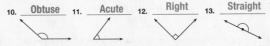

b. What is the measure of the angle between the angle at which the light strikes the mirror (63°), and the angle at which the light reflects? 54°

Name ______________________

Practice 5-2

Parallel and Perpendicular Lines

Write the word that describes the lines or segments.

1. the strings on a guitar Parallel
2. the marks left by a skidding car Parallel
3. sidewalks on opposite sides a street Parallel
4. the segments that make up a + sign Perpendicular
5. the wires suspended between telephone poles Parallel
6. the hands of a clock at 9:00 P.M. Perpendicular
7. two palm trees in Los Angeles Parallel

Use the figure to name each pair of angles or lines.

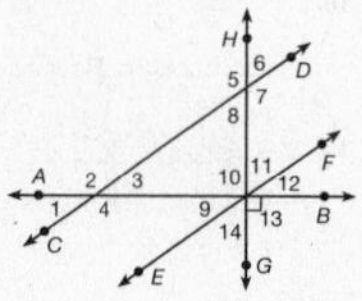

8. a pair of parallel lines $\overleftrightarrow{CD}$ and $\overleftrightarrow{EF}$
9. a pair of perpendicular lines $\overleftrightarrow{AB}$ and $\overleftrightarrow{GH}$
10. a pair of supplementary angles ∠5 and ∠6
11. a pair of corresponding angles ∠3 and ∠12
12. a pair of alternate interior angles ∠8 and ∠11
13. a pair of complementary angles ∠11 and ∠12
14. a pair of vertical angles ∠9 and ∠12

Possible answers: Exercises 10–14

15. In the figure above, name three angles that are congruent to ∠6.

∠8, ∠11, and ∠14

16. Use a ruler to draw a segment bisector of $\overline{UV}$.

17. Use a ruler and a protractor to draw a perpendicular bisector of $\overline{XY}$.

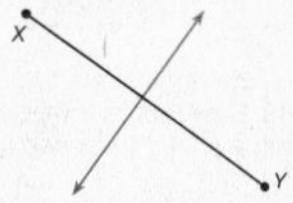

Name ______________________

Practice 5-3

Triangles and Quadrilaterals

Classify each triangle by its sides and by its angles.

1. Isosceles, acute

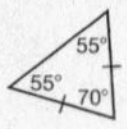

2. Scalene, obtuse

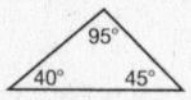

3. Scalene, right

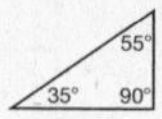

Classify each quadrilateral in as many ways as you can.

4. Quadrilateral, parallelogram, rectangle

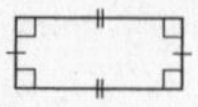

5. Quadrilateral, trapezoid

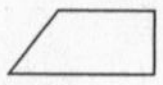

6. Quadrilateral, parallelogram, rhombus

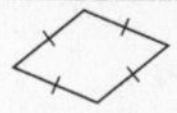

Find the missing angle in each triangle or quadrilateral.

7. $x =$ 75°

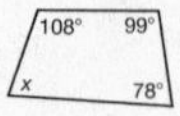

8. $n =$ 97°

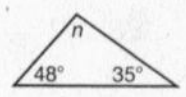

9. $u =$ 95°

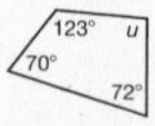

Fill in each blank with *always, sometimes,* or *never.*

10. A trapezoid is never a parallelogram.
11. A rectangle is sometimes a rhombus.
12. **Social Science** The flag of the Congo is shown at the right.

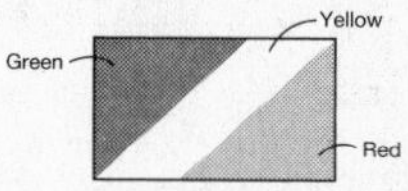

a. Classify the red and green portions of the flag in as many ways as you can. (Hint: The top edge of the green region is slightly longer than the height of the flag.)

Right triangles, scalene triangles

b. Classify the yellow portion of the flag in as many ways as you can. Quadrilateral, parallelogram

Name ______________________

Practice 5-4

Polygons

Tell why each polygon is not a regular polygon.

1. Angles are not all congruent.
2. Sides are not all congruent.
3. Angles are not all congruent.

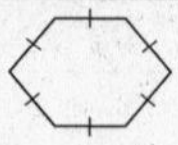

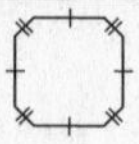

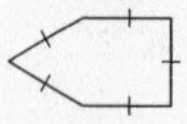

In each design, identify as many polygons as you can. Possible answers:

4. Trapezoids, rectangles
5. Regular hexagons
6. Right triangles, squares

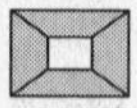

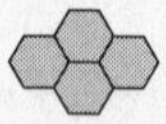

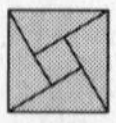

7. Equilateral triangle, trapezoid, hexagons
8. Triangles, pentagons, square
9. Trapezoids, regular pentagons

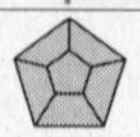

Find the sum of the measures of the angles of each polygon.

10. pentagon 540°
11. 10-sided polygon 1440°
12. 32-sided polygon 5400°

13. Recall that an equilateral polygon has all sides congruent, and an equiangular polygon has all angles congruent. Draw each of the following, if possible.

a. equiangular hexagon that is not regular — Possible answer:

b. equilateral quadrilateral that is not regular — Possible answer:

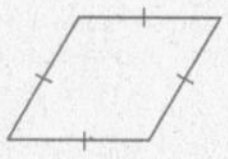

c. equiangular triangle that is not equilateral — Not possible

Name ______________________

Practice 5-5

Perimeter and Area

Find the perimeter and area of each playing area.

Game	Base (length)	Height (width)	Perimeter	Area
1. tennis, singles	26 yd	9 yd	70 yd	234 yd^2
2. volleyball	60 ft	30 ft	180 ft	1,800 ft^2
3. badminton, singles	44 ft	17 ft	122 ft	748 ft^2
4. cricket	170 m	160 m	660 m	27,200 m^2
5. racquetball	40 ft	20 ft	120 ft	800 ft^2
6. ice hockey	61 m	30 m	182 m	1,830 m^2

Find the area and the perimeter of each bridge or canal. Assume that each has the shape of a rectangle.

7. Busiest bridge: Howrah Bridge, Calcutta, India—1500 ft by 72 ft

area: 108,000 ft^2 perimeter: 3144 ft

8. Widest bridge: Sydney Harbor Bridge, Australia—49 m by 503 m

area: 24,647 m^2 perimeter: 1,104 m

9. Longest canal: Erie Barge Canal, New York—0.028 mi by 365 mi

area: 10.22 mi^2 perimeter: 730.056 mi

10. Largest lock: Berendrecht lock, Antwerp, Belgium—1640 ft by 223 ft

area: 365,720 ft^2 perimeter: 3726 ft

11. Largest cut: Corinth Canal, Greece—6917 yd by 27 yd

area: 186,759 yd^2 perimeter: 13,888 yd

12. **Geography** The state of Wyoming is shaped like a rectangle, with a base measuring about 350 miles and a height of about 280 miles. Find the approximate area and perimeter of Wyoming.

area: 98,000 mi^2 perimeter: 1,260 mi

13. Orlando painted a mural measuring 3.7 m by 4.6 m. Find the area and perimeter of the mural.

area: 17.02 m^2 perimeter: 16.6 m

Name ______________________

Practice

Section 5A Review

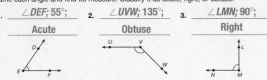

Name each angle and find its measure. Classify it as acute, right, or obtuse.

1. $\angle DEF$; 55°; Acute
2. $\angle UVW$; 135°; Obtuse
3. $\angle LMN$; 90°; Right

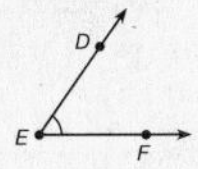

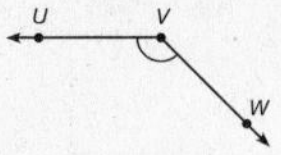

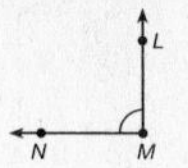

Find the missing angle in each quadrilateral.

4. $k =$ 142°
5. $x =$ 57°
6. $c =$ 95°

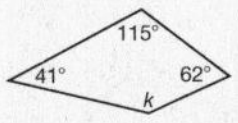

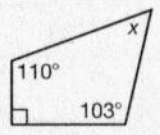

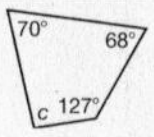

Classify each figure in as many ways as you can.

7. Trapezoid, quadrilateral
8. Rhombus, parallelogram, quadrilateral

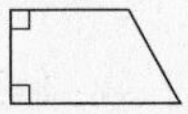
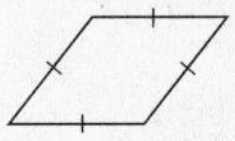

Find the sum of the measures of the angles of each polygon.

9. octagon 1080°
10. 14-sided polygon 2160°

11. A door measures 30 in. by 96 in. Find the perimeter and the area of the door.
perimeter: 252 in. area: 2880 in^2

12. Heather and Denise are running laps. They start together at the same starting point. Heather completes a lap every 120 sec, and Denise completes a lap every 96 sec. In how many seconds will they again meet at the starting point? *[Lesson 3-7]* After 480 sec

13. On October 15, 1996, shares of Chips and Technologies stock increased $\$4\frac{7}{8}$ to $\$19\frac{3}{4}$. What was the original price? *[Lesson 4-3]* $\$14\frac{7}{8}$

Name ______________________

Practice 5-6

Squares and Square Roots

Determine if each number is a perfect square.

1. 90 No
2. 225 Yes
3. 49 Yes
4. 28 No
5. 289 Yes
6. 144 Yes
7. 240 No
8. 1000 No

Find each square root.

9. $\sqrt{196}$ 14
10. $\sqrt{4}$ 2
11. $\sqrt{289}$ 17
12. $\sqrt{16}$ 4
13. $\sqrt{361}$ 19
14. $\sqrt{64}$ 8
15. $\sqrt{1}$ 1
16. $\sqrt{25}$ 5
17. $\sqrt{9}$ 3
18. $\sqrt{484}$ 22
19. $\sqrt{256}$ 16
20. $\sqrt{400}$ 20
21. $\sqrt{324}$ 18
22. $\sqrt{729}$ 27
23. $\sqrt{36}$ 6
24. $\sqrt{1296}$ 36
25. $\sqrt{1600}$ 40
26. $\sqrt{49}$ 7
27. $\sqrt{22,500}$ 150
28. $\sqrt{3025}$ 55

Use a calculator to find each square root. Round the answer to two decimal places.

29. $\sqrt{10}$ 3.16
30. $\sqrt{48}$ 6.93
31. $\sqrt{28}$ 5.29
32. $\sqrt{55}$ 7.42
33. $\sqrt{72}$ 8.49
34. $\sqrt{37}$ 6.08
35. $\sqrt{86}$ 9.27
36. $\sqrt{98}$ 9.90
37. $\sqrt{946}$ 30.76
38. $\sqrt{14}$ 3.74
39. $\sqrt{62}$ 7.87
40. $\sqrt{316}$ 17.78
41. $\sqrt{68}$ 8.25
42. $\sqrt{146}$ 12.08
43. $\sqrt{76}$ 8.72
44. $\sqrt{521}$ 22.83
45. $\sqrt{813}$ 28.51
46. $\sqrt{83}$ 9.11
47. $\sqrt{23}$ 4.80
48. $\sqrt{617}$ 24.84
49. $\sqrt{35}$ 5.92
50. $\sqrt{123}$ 11.09
51. $\sqrt{51}$ 7.14
52. $\sqrt{463}$ 21.52
53. $\sqrt{583}$ 24.15
54. $\sqrt{96}$ 9.80
55. $\sqrt{203}$ 14.25
56. $\sqrt{1200}$ 34.64
57. $\sqrt{278}$ 16.67
58. $\sqrt{43}$ 6.56
59. $\sqrt{401}$ 20.02
60. $\sqrt{328}$ 18.11
61. $\sqrt{1365}$ 36.95
62. $\sqrt{785}$ 28.02
63. $\sqrt{635}$ 25.20
64. $\sqrt{2424}$ 49.23

65. The largest pyramid in Egypt, built almost 5000 years ago, covers an area of about 63,300 yd^2. Find the length of each side of the square base. About 252 yd

66. Square floor tiles frequently have an area of 929 cm^2. Find the length of a side of one of these tiles. About 30 cm

Name ______________________

Practice 5-7

The Pythagorean Theorem

Use the Pythagorean Theorem to write an equation expressing the relationship between the legs and the hypotenuse for each triangle.

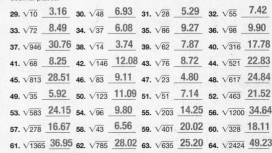

1. $g^2 + h^2 = f^2$
2. $x^2 + z^2 = y^2$
3. $u^2 + v^2 = w^2$

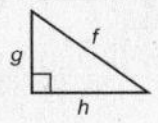

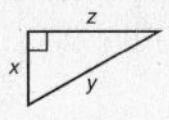

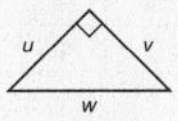

Determine if each triangle is a right triangle.

4. Yes
5. No
6. Yes

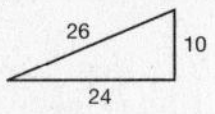

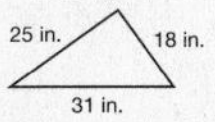

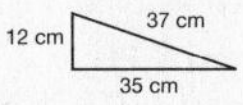

Find the missing length in each right triangle.

7. $t =$ 8
8. $d =$ 53 m
9. $m =$ 56 in.

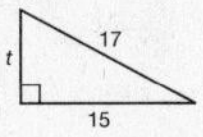

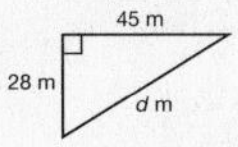

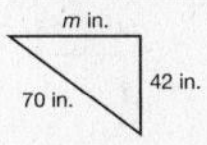

10. $x =$ 21 yd
11. $u =$ 41 cm
12. $r =$ 55 ft

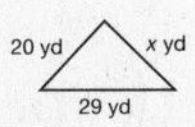

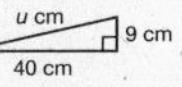

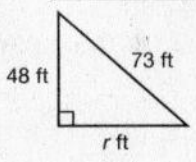

13. **Geography** The state of Colorado is shaped like a rectangle, with a base measuring about 385 mi and a height of about 275 mi. About how far is it from the northwest corner to the southeast corner of Colorado? About 473 mi

14. A drawing tool is shaped like a right triangle. One leg measures about 14.48 cm, and the hypotenuse measures 20.48 cm. What is the length of the other leg? Round your answer to the nearest hundredth of a centimeter. 14.48 cm

15. An 8-foot ladder is leaned against a high wall from 4 feet away. How high up the wall does the ladder reach? Round your answer to the nearest tenth of a foot. 6.9 ft

Name ______________________

Practice 5-8

Area of Triangles

Find the area of each triangle.

1. $b = 3$ m, $h = 8$ m, $A =$ 12 m^2
2. $b = 12$ mi, $h = 5$ mi, $A =$ 30 mi^2
3. $b = 7$ in., $h = 14$ in., $A =$ 49 in^2
4. $b = 21$ cm, $h = 16$ cm, $A =$ 168 cm^2
5. $b = 6.8$ km, $h = 11.0$ km, $A =$ 37.4 km^2
6. $b = 3\frac{1}{4}$ yd, $h = 8\frac{1}{2}$ yd, $A =$ $13\frac{13}{16}$ yd^2
7. $b = 5.7$ m, $h = 2.4$ m, $A =$ 6.84 m^2
8. $b = \frac{1}{4}$ ft, $h = \frac{3}{5}$ ft, $A =$ $\frac{3}{40}$ ft^2

9. $A =$ 76.5 km^2
10. $A =$ 3.905 yd^2
11. $A =$ $6\frac{7}{8}$ in^2

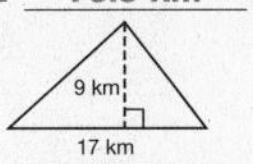

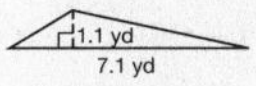

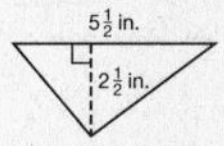

12. $A =$ 11.1 cm^2
13. $A =$ 27 ft^2
14. $A =$ 8.64 m^2

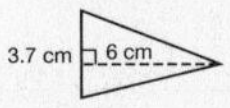

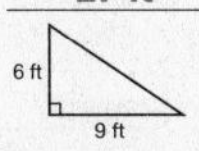

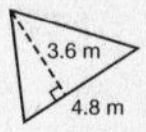

Find the missing measurements of the following triangles.

15. $b =$ 64 mi, $h = 81$ mi, $A = 2592$ mi^2
16. $b = 46$ cm, $h =$ 16 cm, $A = 368$ cm^2
17. $b =$ 40 in., $h = 35$ in., $A = 700$ in^2
18. $b = 63$ m, $h =$ 34 m, $A = 1071$ m^2
19. $b =$ 39 km, $h = 24$ km, $A = 468$ km^2
20. $b = 10$ yd, $h =$ 83 yd, $A = 415$ yd^2
21. $b = 68$ cm, $h =$ 22 cm, $A = 748$ cm^2
22. $b =$ 74 ft, $h = 25$ ft, $A = 925$ ft^2

23. **Social Studies** The flag of Puerto Rico features three red stripes and a blue triangle with a white star inside. Find the area of the triangle (including the star). 270 in^2

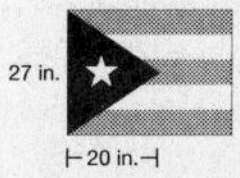

Name ______________________

Practice 5-9

Area of Parallelograms and Trapezoids

Which formula would you use to find the area of each figure, $A = bh$ or $A = \frac{1}{2}h(b_1 + b_2)$?

1. $A = \frac{1}{2}h(b_1 + b_2)$

2. $A = bh$

3. $A = \frac{1}{2}h(b_1 + b_2)$

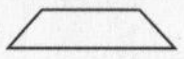

Find the area of each parallelogram.

4. $288\ m^2$

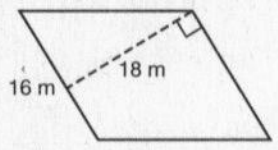

5. $67.41\ cm^2$

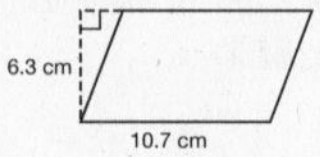

6. $1\frac{11}{16}\ in^2$

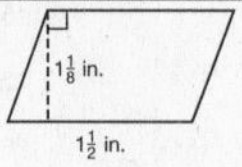

Find the area of each trapezoid.

7. $7.36\ cm^2$

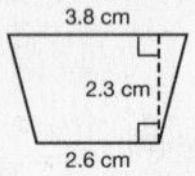

8. $76\ ft^2$

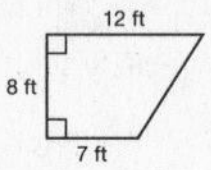

9. $47\frac{1}{4}\ in^2$

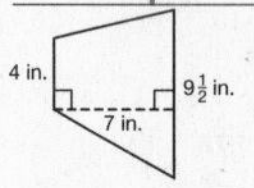

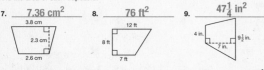

10. A 2-ft wide swing is suspended from a horizontal branch by 8-ft long ropes. Find the area that is formed when the swing is pushed sideways so that it is only $7\frac{1}{2}$ ft below the branch, as shown.

$15\ ft^2$

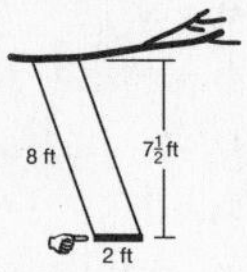

11. **Social Science** The flag of Kuwait is shown at the right. Find each area.

a. Black region $2{,}560\ cm^2$

b. Green region (top stripe) $5{,}504\ cm^2$

c. White region $4{,}864\ cm^2$

d. Red region (bottom stripe) $5{,}504\ cm^2$

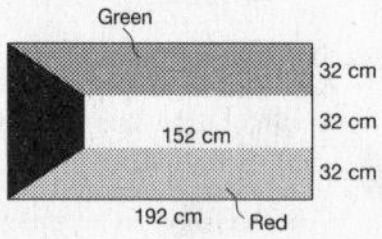

Name ______________________

Practice 5-10

Problem-Solving: Areas of Irregular Figures

Find the area of each figure.

1. $1001\ ft^2$

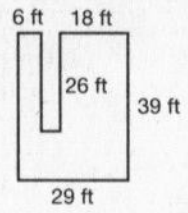

2. $249\ km^2$

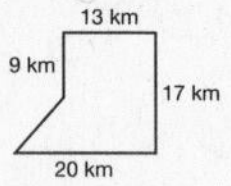

3. $984\ yd^2$

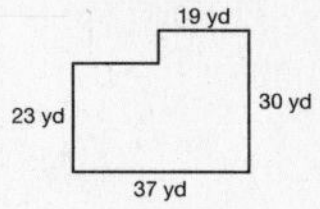

4. $86\ cm^2$

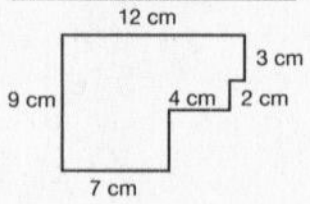

5. $289\ in^2$

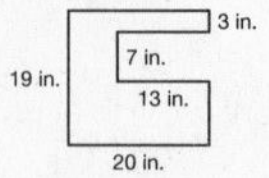

6. $2848\ m^2$

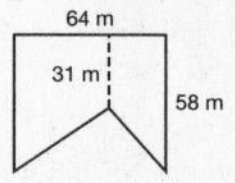

7. $5.46\ cm^2$

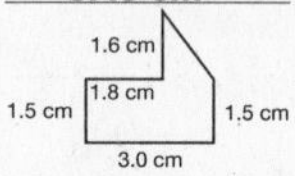

8. $785\ mi^2$

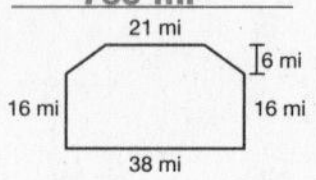

9. $51.5\ ft^2$

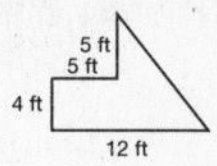

10. $7800\ m^2$

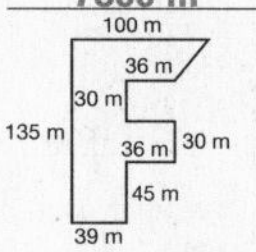

11. $5\frac{1}{4}\ in^2$

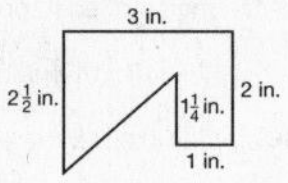

12. $33\ cm^2$

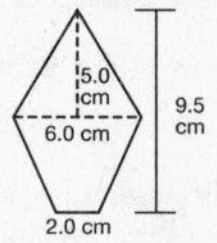

13. The flag of Switzerland features a white cross on a red background.

a. Each of the 12 sides of the cross has length 15 cm. Find the area of the white cross. $1125\ cm^2$

b. The flag has dimensions 60 cm by 60 cm. Find the area of the red region. $2475\ cm^2$

Name ______________________

Practice

Section 5B Review

Find the value of each expression.

1. $\sqrt{81}$ 9
2. 7^2 49
3. $\sqrt{625}$ 25
4. 14^2 196
5. 3.8^2 14.44
6. $\sqrt{144}$ 12
7. $\left(\frac{8}{11}\right)^2$ $\frac{64}{121}$
8. $\sqrt{225}$ 15

Find the missing length in each right triangle.

9. 80 cm

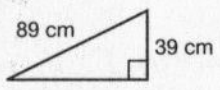

10. 44 ft

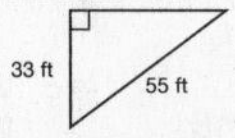

11. 65 m

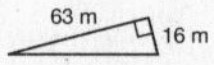

Find the area of each figure.

12. $7.59\ cm^2$

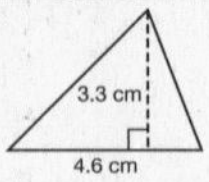

13. $748\ ft^2$

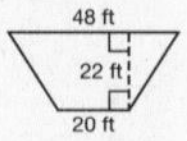

14. $33\frac{1}{4}\ in^2$

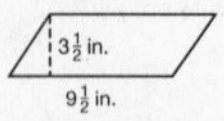

15. $98\ m^2$

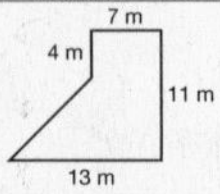

16. $838\ km^2$

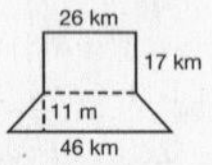

17. $2586\ yd^2$

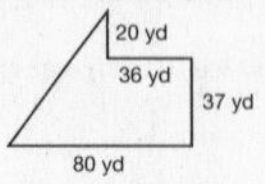

18. **Measurement** The Johnsons' living room measures 14 ft by 23 ft, and their kitchen measures 9 ft by 13 ft. How much greater is the living room area than the kitchen area? $205\ ft^2$

19. The element carbon makes up $\frac{9}{50}$ of the matter in your body. Convert $\frac{9}{50}$ to a decimal. *[Lesson 3-10]* 0.18

20. The population of Asia is about $7\frac{8}{13}$ times as great as the population of North America. If the population of North America was 436,000,000 in 1992, what was the population of Asia? About 3,320,000,000

Name ______________________

Practice

Cumulative Review Chapters 1–5

Use the given formula to complete each table. *[Lesson 2-3]*

1. $y = 5x + 8$

x	4	5	6	7
y	28	33	38	43

2. $D = 60t$

D	3	4	5	6
t	180	240	300	360

Find the GCF and LCM of each pair of numbers. *[Lesson 3-7]*

3. 14, 49 GCF: 7 LCM: 98
4. 65, 26 GCF: 13 LCM: 130
5. 24, 60 GCF: 12 LCM: 120
6. 32, 45 GCF: 1 LCM: 1440

Solve each equation. *[Lesson 4-3]*

7. $5\frac{7}{8} + x = 10\frac{1}{4}$ $x = 4\frac{3}{8}$
8. $p - 12\frac{1}{3} = 6\frac{5}{6}$ $p = 19\frac{1}{6}$
9. $z + 3\frac{1}{4} = 10$ $z = 6\frac{3}{4}$
10. $c - 12\frac{1}{2} = 2\frac{1}{3}$ $c = 14\frac{5}{6}$
11. $k + 5\frac{3}{11} = 8\frac{1}{2}$ $k = 3\frac{5}{22}$
12. $d - 7\frac{3}{10} = 4\frac{1}{5}$ $d = 11\frac{1}{2}$
13. $4\frac{2}{3} + u = 6\frac{4}{15}$ $u = 1\frac{3}{5}$
14. $t - 9\frac{1}{8} = 7\frac{5}{12}$ $t = 16\frac{13}{24}$

Find the sum of the measures of the angles of each polygon. *[Lesson 5-4]*

15. octagon 1080°
16. 14-sided polygon 2160°
17. 18-sided polygon 2880°
18. 29-sided polygon 4860°
19. 36-sided polygon 6120°
20. 57-sided polygon 9900°

Find the missing length in each right triangle. *[Lesson 5-7]*

21. $n =$ 53

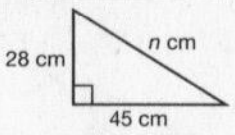

22. $u =$ 11

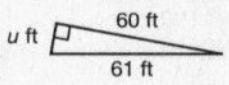

23. $p =$ 77

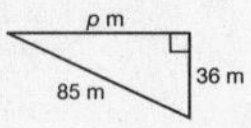

Name ______________________

Practice 6-1

Exploring and Estimating Ratios

Write each ratio in three ways. Write in lowest terms if possible.

1. 8 jazz CDs to 14 rock CDs — $\frac{4}{7}$, 4 : 7, 4 to 7
2. 25 oranges to 45 apples — $\frac{5}{9}$, 5 : 9, 5 to 9
3. $12 for 8 sandwiches — $\frac{3}{2}$, 3 : 2, 3 to 2
4. 8 dentists out of 10 dentists — $\frac{4}{5}$, 4 : 5, 4 to 5
5. 32 points in 18 games — $\frac{16}{9}$, 16 : 9, 16 to 9
6. 21 boys to 24 girls — $\frac{7}{8}$, 7 : 8, 7 to 8

A bag contains 5 red, 6 yellow, 8 green, 10 blue, and 15 clear marbles. Write each of the following ratios in lowest terms.

7. yellow to blue $\frac{3}{5}$
8. green to yellow $\frac{4}{3}$
9. blue to clear $\frac{2}{3}$
10. blue to red $\frac{2}{1}$
11. yellow to clear $\frac{2}{5}$
12. red to clear $\frac{1}{3}$

The table shows several popular TV programs and the number of years that each was produced. Write each of the following ratios in lowest terms.

Program	Number of Years
Walt Disney	33
Ed Sullivan	24
Gunsmoke	20
Meet the Press	18
Lassie	17

13. *Lassie* to *Gunsmoke* — $\frac{17}{20}$
14. *Walt Disney* to *Meet the Press* — $\frac{11}{6}$
15. *Ed Sullivan* to *Walt Disney* — $\frac{8}{11}$
16. A vase of flowers is shown. Estimate the ratio of the width of the vase to the total height of the vase and flowers. — About $\frac{2}{5}$

Name ______________________

Practice 6-2

Exploring and Estimating Rates

Find each rate. Remember to include units in your rates.

1. 60 students for 3 teachers — $\frac{60 \text{ students}}{3 \text{ teachers}}$
2. $8 for 4 books — $\frac{\$8}{4 \text{ books}}$
3. 200 sit-ups in 5 minutes — $\frac{200 \text{ sit-ups}}{5 \text{ minutes}}$
4. $36.00 paid for 6 hours work — $\frac{\$36}{6 \text{ hours}}$

Express each rate as a unit rate.

5. 48 inches in 4 feet — $\frac{12 \text{ inches}}{1 \text{ foot}}$
6. $15 for 5 keychains — $\frac{\$3}{1 \text{ keychain}}$
7. 80 pages in 5 hours — $\frac{16 \text{ pages}}{1 \text{ hour}}$

Consumer Use unit prices to find the better buy. Underline the correct choice.

8. Peaches: 87¢ for 3 peaches or $1.12 for 4 peaches
9. Video game tokens: $1.00 for 5 tokens or $5.00 for 30 tokens
10. Facial tissue: $3.50 for 2 boxes or $9.00 for 5 boxes

Determine whether each ratio is a rate. Explain. **Possible answers:**

11. $\frac{\$5}{20 \text{ oranges}}$ This is a rate because it is a ratio of quantities with different units of measure.
12. $\frac{14}{21}$ This is not a rate because there are no units.
13. $\frac{32 \text{ ounces}}{1 \text{ pint}}$ This is a rate because it is a ratio of quantities with different units of measure.
14. **Science** A black-billed cuckoo bird can eat 48 caterpillars in 6 minutes. Find the unit rate. — $\frac{8 \text{ caterpillars}}{1 \text{ minute}}$
15. The population of Stockton, California increased by 62,660 people during the 10 years from 1980 to 1990. Find the unit rate. — $\frac{6{,}266 \text{ people}}{1 \text{ year}}$

Name ______________________

Practice 6-3

Equivalent Ratios and Rates

Multiply and divide to find two ratios equivalent to each ratio. **Possible answers:**

1. $\frac{12}{15}$: $\frac{24}{30}, \frac{4}{5}$ 2. $\frac{6}{9}$: $\frac{24}{36}, \frac{2}{3}$ 3. $\frac{8}{14}$: $\frac{24}{42}, \frac{4}{7}$ 4. $\frac{6}{12}$: $\frac{30}{60}, \frac{1}{2}$
5. $\frac{10}{12}$: $\frac{20}{24}, \frac{5}{6}$ 6. $\frac{6}{8}$: $\frac{18}{24}, \frac{3}{4}$ 7. $\frac{5}{10}$: $\frac{15}{30}, \frac{1}{2}$ 8. $\frac{16}{22}$: $\frac{64}{88}, \frac{8}{11}$
9. $\frac{6}{12}$: $\frac{12}{24}, \frac{1}{2}$ 10. $\frac{8}{30}$: $\frac{40}{150}, \frac{4}{15}$ 11. $\frac{20}{34}$: $\frac{60}{102}, \frac{10}{17}$ 12. $\frac{15}{18}$: $\frac{30}{36}, \frac{5}{6}$
13. $\frac{16}{36}$: $\frac{32}{72}, \frac{4}{9}$ 14. $\frac{9}{12}$: $\frac{27}{36}, \frac{3}{4}$ 15. $\frac{24}{27}$: $\frac{48}{54}, \frac{8}{9}$ 16. $\frac{6}{10}$: $\frac{24}{40}, \frac{3}{5}$
17. $\frac{6}{33}$: $\frac{30}{165}, \frac{2}{11}$ 18. $\frac{30}{42}$: $\frac{90}{126}, \frac{5}{7}$ 19. $\frac{10}{16}$: $\frac{20}{32}, \frac{5}{8}$ 20. $\frac{24}{28}$: $\frac{72}{84}, \frac{6}{7}$
21. $\frac{16}{18}$: $\frac{64}{72}, \frac{8}{9}$ 22. $\frac{6}{15}$: $\frac{30}{75}, \frac{2}{5}$ 23. $\frac{14}{16}$: $\frac{56}{64}, \frac{7}{8}$ 24. $\frac{8}{10}$: $\frac{24}{30}, \frac{4}{5}$
25. $\frac{20}{50}$: $\frac{40}{100}, \frac{2}{5}$ 26. $\frac{15}{30}$: $\frac{75}{150}, \frac{1}{2}$ 27. $\frac{19}{38}$: $\frac{57}{114}, \frac{1}{2}$ 28. $\frac{28}{30}$: $\frac{140}{150}, \frac{14}{15}$
29. $\frac{10}{18}$: $\frac{30}{54}, \frac{5}{9}$ 30. $\frac{8}{12}$: $\frac{16}{24}, \frac{2}{3}$ 31. $\frac{12}{57}$: $\frac{24}{114}, \frac{4}{19}$ 32. $\frac{16}{20}$: $\frac{48}{60}, \frac{4}{5}$
33. $\frac{26}{44}$: $\frac{78}{132}, \frac{13}{22}$ 34. $\frac{14}{24}$: $\frac{70}{120}, \frac{7}{12}$ 35. $\frac{35}{42}$: $\frac{70}{84}, \frac{5}{6}$ 36. $\frac{28}{34}$: $\frac{84}{102}, \frac{14}{17}$
37. $\frac{13}{65}$: $\frac{65}{325}, \frac{1}{5}$ 38. $\frac{52}{78}$: $\frac{260}{390}, \frac{2}{3}$ 39. $\frac{10}{52}$: $\frac{20}{104}, \frac{5}{26}$ 40. $\frac{12}{18}$: $\frac{48}{72}, \frac{2}{3}$
41. $\frac{6}{82}$: $\frac{24}{328}, \frac{3}{41}$ 42. $\frac{24}{48}$: $\frac{96}{192}, \frac{1}{2}$ 43. $\frac{25}{45}$: $\frac{100}{180}, \frac{5}{9}$ 44. $\frac{12}{68}$: $\frac{60}{340}, \frac{3}{17}$
45. $\frac{20}{30}$: $\frac{40}{60}, \frac{2}{3}$ 46. $\frac{24}{39}$: $\frac{48}{78}, \frac{8}{13}$ 47. $\frac{12}{36}$: $\frac{48}{144}, \frac{1}{3}$ 48. $\frac{33}{44}$: $\frac{66}{88}, \frac{3}{4}$
49. $\frac{46}{72}$: $\frac{92}{144}, \frac{23}{36}$ 50. $\frac{14}{54}$: $\frac{42}{162}, \frac{7}{27}$ 51. $\frac{18}{27}$: $\frac{90}{135}, \frac{2}{3}$ 52. $\frac{10}{15}$: $\frac{50}{75}, \frac{2}{3}$
53. $\frac{6}{38}$: $\frac{30}{190}, \frac{3}{19}$ 54. $\frac{24}{26}$: $\frac{72}{78}, \frac{12}{13}$ 55. $\frac{18}{28}$: $\frac{36}{56}, \frac{9}{14}$ 56. $\frac{8}{56}$: $\frac{40}{280}, \frac{1}{7}$
57. $\frac{6}{14}$: $\frac{12}{28}, \frac{3}{7}$ 58. $\frac{26}{32}$: $\frac{52}{64}, \frac{13}{16}$ 59. $\frac{35}{40}$: $\frac{70}{80}, \frac{7}{8}$ 60. $\frac{30}{96}$: $\frac{120}{384}, \frac{5}{16}$

61. **Science** Neptune rotates 12 times in 18 Earth days. How many times will Neptune rotate in 6 Earth days? — 4 times
62. **Measurement** There are 8 pints in a gallon. How many pints are in 7 gallons? — 56 pints

---

Name ______________________

Practice 6-4

Using Tables to Explore Ratios and Rates

1. Using multiplication, complete the table to find 5 ratios equivalent to $\frac{3}{11}$.

3	6	9	12	15	18
11	22	33	44	55	66

Ratios: $\frac{6}{22}, \frac{9}{33}, \frac{12}{44}, \frac{15}{55}, \frac{18}{66}$

2. Using division, complete the table to find 5 ratios equivalent to $\frac{90}{225}$.

90	30	18	10	6	2
225	75	45	25	15	5

Ratios: $\frac{30}{75}, \frac{18}{45}, \frac{10}{25}, \frac{6}{15}, \frac{2}{5}$

Fill in each table to find four ratios equal to the ratio in the first column.

3.

5	10	15	30	40
8	16	24	48	64

Ratios: $\frac{10}{16}, \frac{15}{24}, \frac{30}{48}, \frac{40}{64}$

4.

21	7	42	63	84
36	12	72	108	144

Ratios: $\frac{7}{12}, \frac{42}{72}, \frac{63}{108}, \frac{84}{144}$

5. In 1946, Stella Pajunas set a record by typing 216 words in a minute on an electric typewriter. Use the table to estimate how long it took her to type 100 words. — About 28 seconds

Number of words	36	72	108	144	180	216
Number of seconds	10	20	30	40	50	60

Use a table to find two rates equivalent to each rate. **Possible answers:**

6. $15 per CD

Price ($1)	15	30	45
CDs	1	2	3

Rates: $\frac{\$30}{2 \text{ CDs}}, \frac{\$45}{3 \text{ CDs}}$

7. 16 pages typed in 4 hours

Pages	16	8	4
Hours	4	2	1

Rates: $\frac{8 \text{ pages}}{2 \text{ hours}}, \frac{4 \text{ pages}}{1 \text{ hour}}$

8. A walrus can swim at a rate of 24 kilometers per hour. Make a table to find five rates equivalent to this unit rate. **Possible answer:**

Distance (km)	24	48	72	96	120	144
Time (hr)	1	2	3	4	5	6

Rates: $\frac{48 \text{ km}}{2 \text{ hr}}, \frac{72 \text{ km}}{3 \text{ hr}}, \frac{96 \text{ km}}{4 \text{ hr}}, \frac{120 \text{ km}}{5 \text{ hr}}, \frac{144 \text{ km}}{6 \text{ hr}}$

Name ______________________

Practice

Section 6A Review

Write each ratio in lowest terms.

1. $\frac{8}{10}$ $\frac{4}{5}$ 2. 36 to 48 3 to 4 3. 16 : 20 4 : 5

Express each rate as a unit rate.

4. baked 72 cookies in 3 hours $\frac{24 \text{ cookies}}{1 \text{ hour}}$
5. played 6 games in 2 hours $\frac{3 \text{ games}}{1 \text{ hour}}$
6. \$45 to 5 hours work $\frac{\$9}{1 \text{ hour}}$
7. 60 students for 12 computers $\frac{5 \text{ students}}{1 \text{ computer}}$
8. Which price is better, \$4.32 for 2 pounds of granola or \$6.51 for 3 pounds? \$4.32 for 2 pounds

Multiply and divide to find two ratios equivalent to each ratio. Possible answers:

9. $\frac{18}{24}$ $\frac{90}{120}, \frac{3}{4}$ 10. $\frac{22}{36}$ $\frac{66}{108}, \frac{11}{18}$ 11. $\frac{12}{15}$ $\frac{24}{30}, \frac{4}{5}$

12. **Consumer** When buying a car, it is important to consider fuel efficiency. A more efficient car will travel a greater distance per gallon of gas. Make a table for each car to find five rates equivalent to each unit rate. Possible answers:

a. Yachtomobile: 13 miles per gallon

Mi	13	26	39	52	65	78
Gal	1	2	3	4	5	6

Rates: $\frac{26 \text{ mi}}{2 \text{ gal}}, \frac{39 \text{ mi}}{3 \text{ gal}}, \frac{52 \text{ mi}}{4 \text{ gal}}, \frac{65 \text{ mi}}{5 \text{ gal}}, \frac{78 \text{ mi}}{6 \text{ gal}}$

b. Pepster: 45 miles per gallon

Mi	45	90	135	180	225	270
Gal	1	2	3	4	5	6

Rates: $\frac{90 \text{ mi}}{2 \text{ gal}}, \frac{135 \text{ mi}}{3 \text{ gal}}, \frac{180 \text{ mi}}{4 \text{ gal}}, \frac{225 \text{ mi}}{5 \text{ gal}}, \frac{270 \text{ mi}}{6 \text{ gal}}$

13. The Tremendous T-shirt Co. sells T-shirts by mail for \$7.00 each. Since there is a \$5.00 shipping charge, the price for n T-shirts is given by the formula $P = 7n + 5$. If Maria paid \$47, how many T-shirts did she order? *[Lesson 2-8]* 6 T-shirts

14. **Science** A typical male elk weighs about $\frac{7}{20}$ of a ton. How many elk would weigh 21 tons altogether? *[Lesson 4-6]* 60 male elk

Name ______________________

Practice 6-5

Creating Proportions

Complete each table. Then write four proportions involving ratios in the table.

1.

3	6	9	12
5	10	15	20

Possible answer: $\frac{3}{5} = \frac{6}{10}$, $\frac{9}{15} = \frac{12}{20}$, $\frac{9}{15} = \frac{3}{5}$, $\frac{6}{10} = \frac{12}{20}$

2.

4	8	20	32
11	22	55	88

Possible answer: $\frac{4}{11} = \frac{8}{22}$, $\frac{20}{55} = \frac{8}{22}$, $\frac{4}{11} = \frac{32}{88}$, $\frac{32}{88} = \frac{20}{55}$

For each ratio, make a table and create three equal ratios. Then use your ratios to write three proportions. Possible answers:

3. $\frac{5}{7}$

5	10	15	20
7	14	21	28

$\frac{5}{7} = \frac{10}{14}$, $\frac{15}{21} = \frac{20}{28}$, $\frac{15}{21} = \frac{5}{7}$

4. $\frac{11}{15}$

11	22	33	44
15	30	45	60

$\frac{11}{15} = \frac{22}{30}$, $\frac{33}{45} = \frac{44}{60}$, $\frac{22}{30} = \frac{33}{45}$

5. $\frac{16}{20}$

16	32	48	64
20	40	60	80

$\frac{16}{20} = \frac{32}{40}$, $\frac{16}{20} = \frac{48}{60}$, $\frac{16}{20} = \frac{64}{80}$

6. $\frac{8}{6}$

8	16	24	32
6	12	18	24

$\frac{8}{6} = \frac{16}{12}$, $\frac{24}{18} = \frac{8}{6}$, $\frac{16}{12} = \frac{32}{24}$

Use each proportion to write two other proportions. Possible answers:

7. $\frac{5}{8} = \frac{15}{24}$ $\frac{8}{5} = \frac{24}{15}$, $\frac{5}{15} = \frac{8}{24}$

8. $\frac{4}{18} = \frac{6}{27}$ $\frac{27}{6} = \frac{18}{4}$, $\frac{4}{6} = \frac{18}{27}$

9. $\frac{\$2}{7 \text{ apples}} = \frac{\$6}{21 \text{ apples}}$ $\frac{\$6}{\$2} = \frac{21 \text{ apples}}{7 \text{ apples}}$, $\frac{21 \text{ apples}}{\$6} = \frac{7 \text{ apples}}{\$2}$

10. $\frac{80 \text{ miles}}{15 \text{ hours}} = \frac{32 \text{ miles}}{6 \text{ hours}}$ $\frac{15 \text{ hours}}{80 \text{ miles}} = \frac{6 \text{ hours}}{32 \text{ miles}}$, $\frac{6 \text{ hours}}{15 \text{ hours}} = \frac{32 \text{ miles}}{80 \text{ miles}}$

11. An electronics kit contains 7 resistors, 3 capacitors, and 2 transistors. Tell how many of each part would be in 2, 3, and 4 kits.

2 kits: 14 resistors, 6 capacitors, 4 transistors

3 kits: 21 resistors, 9 capacitors, 6 transistors

4 kits: 28 resistors, 12 capacitors, 8 transistors

Name ______________________

Practice 6-6

Testing for Proportionality

Decide if each pair of ratios is proportional.

1. $\frac{14}{10} \stackrel{?}{=} \frac{9}{7}$ Not proportional
2. $\frac{18}{8} \stackrel{?}{=} \frac{36}{16}$ Proportional
3. $\frac{6}{10} \stackrel{?}{=} \frac{15}{25}$ Proportional
4. $\frac{7}{16} \stackrel{?}{=} \frac{4}{9}$ Not proportional
5. $\frac{6}{4} \stackrel{?}{=} \frac{12}{8}$ Proportional
6. $\frac{19}{3} \stackrel{?}{=} \frac{114}{18}$ Proportional
7. $\frac{5}{14} \stackrel{?}{=} \frac{6}{15}$ Not proportional
8. $\frac{6}{27} \stackrel{?}{=} \frac{8}{36}$ Proportional
9. $\frac{27}{15} \stackrel{?}{=} \frac{45}{25}$ Proportional
10. $\frac{3}{18} \stackrel{?}{=} \frac{4}{20}$ Not proportional
11. $\frac{5}{2} \stackrel{?}{=} \frac{15}{6}$ Proportional
12. $\frac{20}{15} \stackrel{?}{=} \frac{4}{3}$ Proportional

Make a scatterplot to see if each relationship is proportional.

13.

Oranges	2	4	6	8
Price (\$)	0.50	1.00	1.50	2.00

Proportional

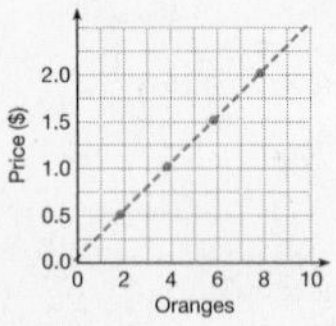

14.

Oats (cups)	0.50	1	2	3
Water (cups)	1	1.75	3.5	5

Not proportional

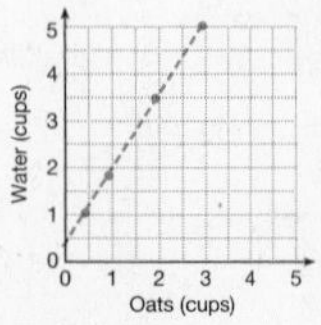

15. During the breaststroke competitions of the 1992 Olympics, Nelson Diebel swam 100 meters in 62 seconds, and Mike Bowerman swam 200 meters in 130 seconds. Are the rates proportional? No

16. During a vacation, the Vasquez family traveled 174 miles in 3 hours on Monday, and 290 miles in 5 hours on Tuesday. Are the rates proportional? Yes

Name ______________________

Practice 6-7

Solving Proportions Using Unit Rates

1. Bananas are on sale at 8 for \$0.96.
   a. Find the cost of 1 banana. \$0.12
   b. Find the cost of 7 bananas. \$0.84
2. Sylvia earned \$199.20 for 24 hours of work.
   a. Find her hourly rate. \$8.30 per hour
   b. Find her earnings for 15 hours of work. \$124.50
3. **History** In 1927, Charles Lindbergh flew 3600 miles from New York to Paris in $33\frac{2}{3}$ hours.
   a. Find Lindbergh's rate in miles per hour. Round to the nearest tenth. 106.9 mi/hr
   b. At this rate, how far did Lindbergh fly in 24 hours? 2565.6 mi
   c. Find Lindbergh's rate in hours per mile. About 0.00935 hr/mi
   d. How long did it take Lindbergh to travel 1600 miles? About 15.0 hours
4. **Health** A 4.3-ounce raw tomato has about 24 calories.
   a. Find the unit rate in calories per ounce. About 5.6 calories per oz
   b. How many calories are in a pound (16 oz) of tomatoes? About 90 calories
5. The hair in a typical man's beard grows about 3.5 mm per week.
   a. Find the unit rate in mm per day. 0.5 mm per day
   b. October has 31 days. How long will the hair grow in October? 15.5 mm
6. In 1993, President Clinton received an average of 25,000 letters per day. How many letters did he receive during the entire year? 9,125,000

Name ______________________

Practice 6-8

Cross Multiplication

Find the cross products for each proportion.

1. $\frac{6}{16} = \frac{9}{24}$ $6 \cdot 24 = 144$; $16 \cdot 9 = 144$
2. $\frac{21}{49} = \frac{3}{7}$ $21 \cdot 7 = 147$; $49 \cdot 3 = 147$
3. $\frac{4}{3} = \frac{16}{12}$ $4 \cdot 12 = 48$; $3 \cdot 16 = 48$

Decide whether each pair of ratios forms a proportion.

4. $\frac{2}{10} \overset{?}{=} \frac{4}{16}$ Not a proportion
5. $\frac{12}{7} \overset{?}{=} \frac{34}{20}$ Not a proportion
6. $\frac{20}{18} \overset{?}{=} \frac{30}{27}$ Proportion
7. $\frac{40}{45} \overset{?}{=} \frac{8}{9}$ Proportion
8. $\frac{7}{14} \overset{?}{=} \frac{3}{7}$ Not a proportion
9. $\frac{2}{6} \overset{?}{=} \frac{3}{9}$ Proportion
10. $\frac{10}{11} \overset{?}{=} \frac{18}{20}$ Not a proportion
11. $\frac{5}{13} \overset{?}{=} \frac{2}{6}$ Not a proportion
12. $\frac{4}{28} \overset{?}{=} \frac{2}{14}$ Proportion
13. $\frac{12}{9} \overset{?}{=} \frac{4}{3}$ Proportion
14. $\frac{18}{16} \overset{?}{=} \frac{45}{40}$ Proportion
15. $\frac{19}{18} \overset{?}{=} \frac{9}{8}$ Not a proportion

Solve each proportion.

16. $\frac{k}{8} = \frac{14}{4}$ $k =$ 28
17. $\frac{u}{3} = \frac{10}{5}$ $u =$ 6
18. $\frac{14}{6} = \frac{d}{15}$ $d =$ 35
19. $\frac{5}{1} = \frac{m}{4}$ $m =$ 20
20. $\frac{36}{32} = \frac{n}{8}$ $n =$ 9
21. $\frac{5}{30} = \frac{1}{x}$ $x =$ 6
22. $\frac{t}{4} = \frac{5}{10}$ $t =$ 2
23. $\frac{9}{2} = \frac{v}{4}$ $v =$ 18
24. $\frac{x}{10} = \frac{6}{4}$ $x =$ 15
25. $\frac{8}{12} = \frac{2}{b}$ $b =$ 3
26. $\frac{v}{15} = \frac{4}{6}$ $v =$ 10
27. $\frac{3}{18} = \frac{2}{s}$ $s =$ 12
28. The 1991 income for a typical 8-acre cotton farm was $3040. Estimate the income for a 13-acre cotton farm. $4940
29. A 150-pound person contains about 97.5 pounds of the element oxygen. Estimate the amount of oxygen in a 216-pound person. 140.4 lb

Name ______________________

Practice

Section 6B Review

1. Complete the table with equivalent ratios. Then write four proportions using ratios in the table.

Possible answer: $\frac{8}{11} = \frac{16}{22}$, $\frac{24}{33} = \frac{40}{55}$, $\frac{32}{44} = \frac{48}{66}$, $\frac{40}{55} = \frac{16}{22}$

8	16	24	32	40	48
11	22	33	44	55	66

Decide whether each pair of ratios forms a proportion.

2. $\frac{14}{2} \overset{?}{=} \frac{35}{5}$ Proportion
3. $\frac{2}{6} \overset{?}{=} \frac{7}{18}$ Not a proportion

Solve each proportion.

4. $\frac{35}{30} = \frac{28}{j}$ $j =$ 24
5. $\frac{8}{20} = \frac{d}{5}$ $d =$ 2
6. $\frac{1}{x} = \frac{5}{10}$ $x =$ 2
7. $\frac{16}{n} = \frac{40}{15}$ $n =$ 6
8. Make a scatterplot to see if the relationship is proportional.

Boys	5	9	13	17
Girls	4	7	10	13

Not proportional

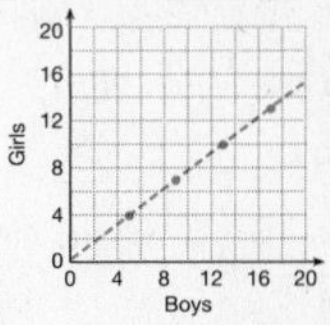

9. A certain brand of pen is priced at 5 for $2.90. Find the unit price. Then tell how many pens you can buy for $10.44. $0.58; 18 pens
10. In 1991, the average household received 10 mail-order catalogs every 26 days. How many catalogs did the average household receive in 91 days? 35 catalogs

For Exercises 11–12, use the picture showing the approximate shape of Samuel Crawford Memorial Park in Dallas, Texas.

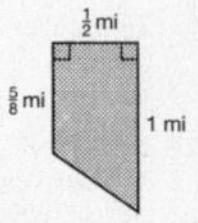

11. The perimeter of the polygon is $2\frac{3}{4}$ mi. Write and solve an equation to find the length of the unknown side. *[Lesson 4-3]*
Possible equation: $x + \frac{5}{8} + \frac{1}{2} + 1 = 2\frac{3}{4}$; $x = \frac{5}{8}$ mi
12. Classify the polygon in as many ways as you can. *[Lesson 5-3]*
Quadrilateral, trapezoid

Name ______________________

Practice

Cumulative Review Chapters 1–6

Express each fraction in lowest terms. *[Lesson 3-8]*

1. $\frac{27}{72}$ $\frac{3}{8}$
2. $\frac{12}{18}$ $\frac{2}{3}$
3. $\frac{20}{28}$ $\frac{5}{7}$
4. $\frac{21}{70}$ $\frac{3}{10}$
5. $\frac{24}{52}$ $\frac{6}{13}$
6. $\frac{32}{88}$ $\frac{4}{11}$
7. $\frac{45}{90}$ $\frac{1}{2}$
8. $\frac{48}{120}$ $\frac{2}{5}$

Find each sum or difference. *[Lesson 4-3]*

9. $2\frac{1}{2} + 7\frac{3}{4}$ $10\frac{1}{4}$
10. $8\frac{2}{3} - 5\frac{1}{9}$ $3\frac{5}{9}$
11. $7\frac{1}{6} + 4\frac{1}{2}$ $11\frac{2}{3}$
12. $7\frac{3}{8} - 1\frac{3}{4}$ $5\frac{5}{8}$
13. $6\frac{4}{7} + 9\frac{5}{7}$ $16\frac{2}{7}$
14. $4\frac{2}{5} - 2\frac{7}{10}$ $1\frac{7}{10}$
15. $\frac{15}{16} + 3\frac{5}{8}$ $4\frac{9}{16}$
16. $14\frac{5}{7} - 8\frac{1}{2}$ $6\frac{3}{14}$
17. $6\frac{5}{9} + 3\frac{7}{11}$ $10\frac{19}{99}$

Use the figure to name each pair of angles or lines if it is possible. *[Lesson 5-2]*

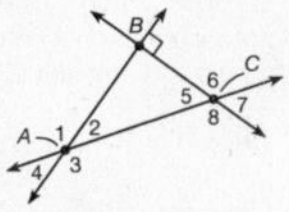

18. a pair of parallel lines None
19. a pair of perpendicular lines $\overleftrightarrow{AB}$ and $\overleftrightarrow{BC}$
20. a pair of vertical angles Possible answer: ∠2 and ∠4
21. a pair of supplementary angles Possible answer: ∠6 and ∠7

Consumer Use unit prices to find the better buy. Underline the correct choice. *[Lesson 6-2]*

22. Used books: <u>$1.00 for 5 books</u> or $1.47 for 7 books
23. Candied apples: <u>$9.60 for 8 apples</u> or $7.32 for 6 apples
24. Ribbon: $2.82 for 60 ft or <u>$3.68 for 80 ft</u>
25. Baseball cards: <u>$8.19 for 7 cards</u> or $12.98 for 11 cards

Solve each proportion. *[Lesson 6-8]*

26. $\frac{3}{7} = \frac{x}{21}$ $x =$ 9
27. $\frac{n}{16} = \frac{15}{24}$ $n =$ 10
28. $\frac{6}{u} = \frac{14}{35}$ $u =$ 15
29. $\frac{42}{24} = \frac{28}{r}$ $r =$ 16

Name ______________________

Practice 7-1

Measurement: Estimating Actual and Scale Distances

Write each scale in two other ways.

1. 1 in. : 25 mi $\frac{1 \text{ in.}}{25 \text{ mi}}$, 1 in. = 25 mi
2. 3 cm = 100 km $\frac{3 \text{ cm}}{100 \text{ km}}$, 3 cm : 100 km
3. $\frac{2 \text{ in.}}{17 \text{ mi}}$ 2 in. : 17 mi, 2 in. = 17 mi
4. 5 cm : 8 km $\frac{5 \text{ cm}}{8 \text{ km}}$, 5 cm = 8 km
5. 4 in. = 21 mi $\frac{4 \text{ in.}}{21 \text{ mi}}$, 4 in. : 21 mi
6. $\frac{1 \text{ cm}}{85 \text{ km}}$ 1 cm : 85 km, 1 cm = 85 km

Use the following measurements to find the scale of each map.

7. A 540-mile river is 10 inches long. $\frac{1 \text{ in.}}{54 \text{ mi}}$
8. A 15-km street is 3 cm long. 1 cm : 5 km
9. A 2-mile-wide park is 5 inches wide. 5 in. = 2 mi
10. A 390-km freeway is 13 cm long. $\frac{1 \text{ cm}}{30 \text{ km}}$
11. A 375-km railroad route is 15 cm long. 1 cm = 25 km

Geography Estimate each map distance.

12. Dallas, Texas, is 803 miles from Chicago, Illinois. About how far apart will these cities appear on a map with scale 1 in. = 40 mi? About 20 in.
13. Shanghai, China, is 1229 km from Hong Kong. About how far apart will these cities appear on a map with scale 1 cm : 500 km? About 2.5 cm
14. **Science** The largest scale model of our solar system features a "Sun" at the Lakeview Museum in Peoria, Illinois. "Jupiter" is located about 20,600 feet away from the museum. The actual distance between the Sun and Jupiter is about 480,000,000 miles. Estimate the scale of the model solar system. About 1 ft : 23,000 mi

Name ______________________

Practice 7-2

Calculating with Scales

Measure the scale drawing and find the length of the locomotive for each scale.

1. 1 cm = 1 m **8 m**
2. 1 cm = 0.7 m **5.6 m**
3. 2 cm = 1 m **4 m**
4. 4 cm = 5 m **10 m**
5. 5 cm = 4 m **6.4 m**

A scale drawing of a house is 5 in. long. Use each scale to find the actual length of the house.

6. 1 in. = 8 ft **40 ft**
7. 1 in. = $9\frac{1}{2}$ ft **$47\frac{1}{2}$ ft**
8. 1 in. = 18 ft **90 ft**
9. 1 in. = 15 ft **75 ft**
10. 1 in. = $6\frac{1}{4}$ ft **$31\frac{1}{4}$ ft**
11. 1 in. = 14.3 ft **71.5 ft**
12. 2 in. = 17 ft **$42\frac{1}{2}$ ft**
13. 1 in. = $12\frac{3}{4}$ ft **$63\frac{3}{4}$ ft**
14. 4 in. = 35 ft **$43\frac{3}{4}$ ft**

Solve for *x* in each proportion.

15. $\frac{3\text{ in.}}{5\text{ft}} = \frac{x}{10\text{ ft}}$ $x =$ **6 in.**
16. $\frac{8\text{ cm}}{20\text{ m}} = \frac{2\text{ cm}}{x}$ $x =$ **5 m**
17. $\frac{9\text{ in.}}{6\text{ mi}} = \frac{x}{2\text{ mi}}$ $x =$ **3 in.**
18. $\frac{15\text{ cm}}{3\text{ km}} = \frac{20\text{ cm}}{x}$ $x =$ **4 km**
19. $\frac{3\text{ cm}}{9\text{ m}} = \frac{4\text{ cm}}{x}$ $x =$ **12 m**
20. $\frac{9\text{ in.}}{10\text{ ft}} = \frac{27\text{ in.}}{x}$ $x =$ **30 ft**
21. $\frac{30\text{ cm}}{9\text{ km}} = \frac{x}{12\text{ km}}$ $x =$ **40 cm**
22. $\frac{8\text{ in.}}{x} = \frac{12\text{ in.}}{3\text{ mi}}$ $x =$ **2 mi**
23. $\frac{x}{40\text{ ft}} = \frac{20\text{ in.}}{32\text{ ft}}$ $x =$ **25 in.**
24. $\frac{9\text{ cm}}{12\text{ km}} = \frac{15\text{ cm}}{x}$ $x =$ **20 km**
25. $\frac{x}{21\text{ mi}} = \frac{81\text{ in.}}{7\text{ mi}}$ $x =$ **243 in.**
26. $\frac{45\text{ cm}}{x} = \frac{27\text{ cm}}{30\text{ m}}$ $x =$ **50 m**

27. **Science** For a science project, Lucinda built a model of Hawaii's Hualalai volcano using a scale of 3 in. : 1000 ft. If the model was $24\frac{3}{4}$ in. high, how high is the actual volcano? **8250 ft**

28. **Geography** Thomas has a map of Europe that uses a scale of 1 cm = 50 km. He has found that London, England, and Berlin, Germany, are 18.6 cm apart on this map. What is the actual distance between these cities? **930 km**

Name ______________________

Practice 7-3

Problem Solving Using Maps

Margaret left home at 8:00 A.M. and traveled 120 miles. Find her arrival time for each of the following speeds.

1. 30 mi/hr **12:00 noon**
2. 45 mi/hr **10:40 A.M.**
3. 72 mi/hr **9:40 A.M.**
4. 40 mi/hr **11:00 A.M.**
5. 60 mi/hr **10:00 A.M.**
6. 50 mi/hr **10:24 A.M.**

7. After a camping trip, Anh drove 75 miles home at a rate of 60 mi/hr. If he arrived home at 8:30 P.M., what time did he begin his drive? **7:15 P.M.**

8. Scott drove 115 miles from Cleveland, Ohio to Pittsburgh, Pennsylvania, at a rate of 69 mi/hr. If he arrived in Pittsburgh at 11:30 A.M., what time did he leave Cleveland? **9:50 A.M.**

9. Carol and Mike have decided to go see a movie that is playing tonight at 9:00 P.M. at both Cinema Six and Acme Theater. Cinema Six is 20 miles away on the freeway, where the speed limit is 60 mi/hr. Acme Theater is only 10 miles away, but the speed limit on the road to Acme Theater is 25 mi/hr.
   a. Which theater should they choose if they want to get there in the shortest time? Explain how you decided.
   Cinema Six; Possible answer: It takes 20 min to drive to Cinema Six and 24 min to drive to Acme Theater.
   b. What time do they need to leave to get to the theater you chose in part a? **By 8:40 P.M.**

10. The Yamada family plans to go to a ball game at 7:30 P.M. They drive 45 mi/hr on Atlantic Parkway.

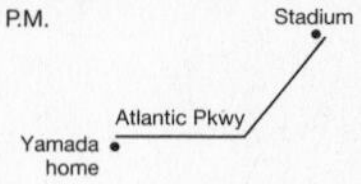

Scale: 1 in. = 16 mi

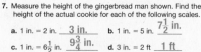

   a. What is the distance from home to the stadium? **24 mi**
   b. How long will it take them to get from home to the stadium? **32 min**
   c. When do they need to leave to get to the stadium at 7:30 P.M.? **6:58 P.M.**

11. Howard plans to drive from Seattle, Washington, to Portland, Oregon, a road distance of 172 miles. He needs to be in Portland by 11:45 A.M. If he drives at a rate of 60 mi/hr, what is the latest time he can leave Seattle? **8:53 A.M.**

Name ______________________

Practice 7-4

Creating Scale Drawings and Scale Models

The Statue of Liberty is 152 ft tall. Find the maximum scale you can use for a model of the Statue of Liberty if the model must fit in a:

1. room with an 8-foot ceiling **1 : 19**
2. 4-inch tall toy box **1 in. : 38 ft**
3. 12-foot-tall crate **3 : 38**
4. hotel lobby with a 38-ft ceiling **1 : 4**

5. Determine an appropriate scale to make a scale drawing of this figure on an $8\frac{1}{2}$-in. × 11-in. sheet of paper. Then make the scale drawing on a separate sheet of paper.

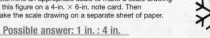

Possible answer: 1 in. : 6 in.

6. **Geography** Utah is approximately 275 miles from east to west and 350 miles from north to south. What is the largest scale that can be used to fit a map of Utah on an $8\frac{1}{2}$-in. × 11-in. sheet of paper, if:
   a. the 11-in. side runs north-south
   17 in. : 550 mi or about 1 in. : 32.4 mi
   b. the $8\frac{1}{2}$-in. side runs north-south
   17 in. : 700 mi or about 1 in. : 41.2 mi

7. A $3\frac{1}{2}$-in. × 5-in. photograph is enlarged to a 28-in. × 40 in. poster. What is the scale of the poster? **8 : 1**

8. A painting measures 45 cm × 55 cm. What is the largest scale that can be used to create a print of this painting if the print must fit in a 20-cm × 25-cm frame? **4 : 9**

9. Estimate the scale of the map whose scale of miles is shown. **3 in. : 80 mi**

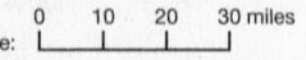

10. A postage stamp measures $\frac{7}{8}$ in. × 1 in. Find the largest scale that can be used to make an enlargement of the stamp on a 3-in. × 5-in. note card. **24 : 7**

11. Determine an appropriate scale to make a scale drawing of this figure on a 4-in. × 6-in. note card. Then make the scale drawing on a separate sheet of paper.

Possible answer: 1 in. : 4 in.

Name ______________________

Practice

Section 7A Review

Give two other ways to write each scale. **Possible answers:**

1. 2 cm : 5 km
   $\frac{2\text{ cm}}{5\text{ km}}$, 2 cm = 5 km
2. 3 in. = 40 mi
   $\frac{3\text{ in.}}{40\text{ mi}}$, 3 in. : 40 mi
3. $\frac{1\text{ cm}}{250\text{ km}}$
   1 cm : 250 km, 1 cm = 250 km
4. 4 in. : 50 mi
   $\frac{4\text{ in.}}{50\text{ mi}}$, 4 in. = 50 mi

Use the following measurements to find the scale of each map.

5. A 15-mi road is 4 in. long. **4 in. = 15 mi**
6. A 120-km river is 6 cm long. **$\frac{1\text{ cm}}{20\text{ km}}$**

7. Measure the height of the gingerbread man shown. Find the height of the actual cookie for each of the following scales.

   a. 1 in. = 2 in. **3 in.**
   b. 1 in. = 5 in. **$7\frac{1}{2}$ in.**
   c. 1 in. = $6\frac{1}{2}$ in. **$9\frac{3}{4}$ in.**
   d. 3 in. = 2 ft **1 ft**

8. The Transamerica Pyramid in San Francisco, California, is 260 m tall. If a model of this building uses a scale of 5 cm = 13 m, how tall is the model? **100 cm or 1 m**

9. Peter has both an LP and a CD copy of his favorite album. The LP cover art measures $12\frac{3}{8}$ in. on each side. The CD insert measures $4\frac{3}{4}$ in. on each side.
   a. Estimate the scale if the LP cover is viewed as an enlarged copy of the CD insert. **99 : 38 or about 2.6 : 1**
   b. Estimate the scale if the CD insert is viewed as a reduced copy of the LP cover. **38 : 99 or about 1 : 2.6**

10. A tree trunk makes an angle of 72° with the ground. A pole making an angle of 55° with the ground is used to support the tree. What angle does the pole make with the tree? *[Lesson 5-3]*

53°

11. **Health** The average secretary burns 88 calories every 60 minutes while working. How many calories are burned in 21 minutes? *[Lesson 6-3]* **30.8 calories**

Name ______________________

Practice 7-5

Choosing Appropriate Rates and Units

Suggest appropriate units for each rate.
You may use the same units more than once. Possible answers:

1. The speed of a roller coaster — miles per hour
2. The rate at which water comes out of a hose — gallons per hour
3. The rate at which a child grows — inches per year
4. The amount of music a radio station plays — songs per hour

Give a unit rate that describes each situation.

5. 200 miles in 4 hours — $\frac{50\text{ mi}}{\text{hr}}$
6. 80 students for 16 computers — $\frac{5\text{ students}}{\text{computer}}$
7. \$96.00 for 12 hours of work — $\frac{\$8.00}{\text{hr}}$
8. 42 books shared by 14 people — $\frac{3\text{ books}}{\text{person}}$

Do the rates in each pair have the same meaning? Write *yes* or *no*.

9. $\frac{15\text{ mi}}{\text{hr}}, \frac{15\text{ hr}}{\text{mi}}$ — No
10. $\frac{\$5.00}{\text{hr}}, \frac{0.2\text{ hr}}{\text{dollar}}$ — Yes
11. $\frac{3\text{ cats}}{\text{dog}}, \frac{\frac{1}{3}\text{ dog}}{\text{cat}}$ — Yes
12. $\frac{12\text{ in.}}{\text{ft}}, \frac{\frac{1}{12}\text{ ft}}{\text{in.}}$ — Yes
13. $\frac{2\text{ oz}}{\text{cookie}}, \frac{\frac{1}{2}\text{ oz}}{\text{cookie}}$ — No
14. $\frac{1\text{ ft}}{\text{sec}}, \frac{1\text{ sec}}{\text{ft}}$ — Yes

For each rate, give a reciprocal unit rate that has the same meaning.

15. $\frac{4\text{ tomatoes}}{\text{lb}}$ — $\frac{0.25\text{ lb}}{\text{tomato}}$
16. $\frac{100\text{ beats}}{\text{min}}$ — $\frac{0.01\text{ min}}{\text{beat}}$
17. $\frac{20\text{ mi}}{\text{hr}}$ — $\frac{0.05\text{ hr}}{\text{mi}}$
18. $\frac{0.08\text{ hr}}{\text{dollar}}$ — $\frac{\$12.50}{\text{hr}}$
19. $\frac{\frac{1}{8}\text{ teacher}}{\text{student}}$ — $\frac{8\text{ students}}{\text{teacher}}$
20. $\frac{40\text{ gal}}{\text{min}}$ — $\frac{0.025\text{ min}}{\text{gal}}$

21. The average American worker needs to work about $\frac{1}{2}$ hour to earn enough money to buy a Barbie doll. Is this rate equivalent to 2 Barbie dolls per hour? — Yes
22. In 1990, there were, on the average, about 2.5 persons per American household. Find the number of households per person. — $\frac{0.4\text{ households}}{\text{person}}$

Name ______________________

Practice 7-6

Converting Units

Write two conversion factors involving each pair of units. (Use the chart on page 346 of your textbook if you do not remember how some of these units compare.)

1. feet, yards — $\frac{3\text{ ft}}{1\text{ yd}}, \frac{1\text{ yd}}{3\text{ ft}}$
2. minutes, seconds — $\frac{1\text{ min}}{60\text{ sec}}, \frac{60\text{ sec}}{1\text{ min}}$
3. meters, kilometers — $\frac{1000\text{ m}}{1\text{ km}}, \frac{1\text{ km}}{1000\text{ m}}$
4. fluid ounces, cups — $\frac{8\text{ fl oz}}{1\text{ cup}}, \frac{1\text{ cup}}{8\text{ fl oz}}$
5. weeks, days — $\frac{1\text{ week}}{7\text{ days}}, \frac{7\text{ days}}{1\text{ week}}$
6. tons, pounds — $\frac{1\text{ ton}}{2000\text{ lb}}, \frac{2000\text{ lb}}{1\text{ ton}}$
7. ounces, pounds — $\frac{16\text{ oz}}{1\text{ lb}}, \frac{1\text{ lb}}{16\text{ oz}}$
8. minutes, hours — $\frac{60\text{ min}}{1\text{ hr}}, \frac{1\text{ hr}}{60\text{ min}}$
9. gallons, quarts — $\frac{1\text{ gal}}{4\text{ qt}}, \frac{4\text{ qt}}{1\text{ gal}}$
10. miles, feet — $\frac{1\text{ mi}}{5280\text{ ft}}, \frac{5280\text{ ft}}{1\text{ mi}}$

Convert each quantity to the given units. (Use the chart on page 346 of your textbook if you do not remember how some of these units compare.)

11. 5.8 meters to centimeters — 580 cm
12. 21 days to hours — 504 hr
13. 63 feet to inches — 756 in.
14. 45 kilometers to meters — 45,000 m
15. 150 hours to minutes — 9000 min
16. 487 grams to kilograms — 0.487 kg
17. 93 yards to feet — 279 ft
18. 360 hours to days — 15 days
19. 24 fluid ounces to cups — 3 cups
20. 21 gallons to quarts — 84 qt
21. 1500 pounds to tons — 0.75 ton
22. 78 inches to feet — 6.5 ft
23. 2.5 kilograms to grams — 2500 g
24. 165 centimeters to meters — 1.65 m
25. 49 days to weeks — 7 weeks
26. 64 gallons to fluid ounces — 8192 fl oz
27. United States farms produced 2,460,000,000 bushels of soybeans in 1994. How many quarts is this? (A bushel is 32 quarts.) — 78,720,000,000 quarts
28. In 1994, Brian Berg set a record by building an 81-story "house" using standard playing cards. The house was $15\frac{2}{3}$ ft tall. How many inches is this? — 188 in.

Name ______________________

Practice 7-7

Problem Solving: Converting Rates

Convert each rate to an equivalent rate.

1. 35 pounds per minute to pounds per hour — 2100 pounds per hour
2. \$72.00 per hour to dollars per minute — \$1.20 per minute
3. 75 feet per second to feet per minute — 4500 feet per minute
4. 2.54 centimeters per inch to meters per inch — 0.0254 meters per inch
5. 90 quarts per hour to quarts per minute — 1.5 quarts per minute
6. 28.35 grams per ounce to grams per pound — 453.6 grams per pound
7. 7.2 inches per second to feet per second — 0.6 feet per second
8. \$1.44 per gallon to cents per quart — 36¢ per quart
9. \$8.00 per pound to dollars per ounce — \$0.50 per ounce

Science Use conversion factors to complete the table.

	Name of Animal	Maximum Speed (mi/hr)	Maximum Speed (ft/sec)
10.	Elk	45	66
11.	Grizzly bear	30	44
12.	Spider	1.17	1.716
13.	Three-toed sloth	0.15	0.22
14.	Squirrel	12	17.6

15. The average North American consumes about 26 barrels of petroleum per year, and the average African consumes about one barrel of petroleum per year. Convert these rates to gallons per day. (One barrel is 42 gallons.)

    North America: About 2.99 gal per day

    Africa: About 0.115 gal per day

16. In 1994, American farmers produced 133.8 bushels of corn per acre of corn crops. Convert this rate to pecks per square foot. (A bushel is equal to 4 pecks, and an acre is equal to 43,560 square feet.)

    About 0.0123 pecks per square foot

Name ______________________

Practice

Section 7B Review

Suggest appropriate units for each rate. Possible answers:

1. The rate at which someone mows a lawn — square feet per minute
2. The rate of pay for a secretary — dollars per hour
3. A craftsman made 18 flower pots in 6 days. Write two unit rates that describe this situation. Is one of your rates more useful?

   $\frac{3\text{ pots}}{\text{day}}, \frac{\frac{1}{3}\text{ day}}{\text{pot}}$; Possible answer: Both rates can be useful

Do the rates in each pair have the same meaning? Write *yes* or *no*.

4. $\frac{25\text{ gal}}{\text{min}}, \frac{25\text{ min}}{\text{gal}}$ — No
5. $\frac{\$1.60}{\text{hr}}, \frac{0.625\text{ hr}}{\text{dollar}}$ — Yes
6. $\frac{100\text{ L}}{\text{day}}, \frac{0.01\text{ day}}{\text{L}}$ — Yes
7. $\frac{40\text{ mi}}{\text{hr}}, \frac{0.025\text{ hr}}{\text{mi}}$ — Yes
8. $\frac{5\text{ tons}}{\text{week}}, \frac{\frac{1}{5}\text{ ton}}{\text{week}}$ — No
9. $\frac{\$4.00}{\text{ft}}, \frac{\frac{1}{4}\text{ ft}}{\text{dollar}}$ — Yes

Convert each quantity to the given units.

10. 6.42 kilograms to grams — 6420 g
11. 12 centimeters to meters — 0.12 m
12. 64 fluid ounces to quarts — 2 qt
13. 45 hours to seconds — 162,000 sec

Convert each rate to an equivalent rate.

14. 24 ounces per minute to pounds per minute — 1.5 pounds per minute
15. \$2.50 per minute to dollars per hour — \$150.00 per hour
16. 21 pounds per foot to pounds per inch — 1.75 pounds per inch
17. The average American eats 150 pounds of canned food per year. Convert this rate to ounces per day. — ≈ 6.58 ounces per day
18. A steel shelving unit uses a diagonal brace to prevent wobbling. Find the length of the brace. *[Lesson 5-7]* — 53 in.

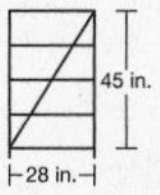

19. **Fine Arts** Pablo Picasso produced about 13,500 paintings during his 78-year career. Assuming that he painted at a consistent rate for his entire career, estimate the number of paintings he produced during the last 12 years. *[Lesson 6-7]* — About 2400 paintings

Name ______________________________

Practice 7-8

Creating and Exploring Similar Figures

Tell if the figures are similar. If they are, write a similarity statement using ~ and give the scale factor. If they're not, explain why not.

1. Similar; *RSUT* ~ *WXYV*; 2

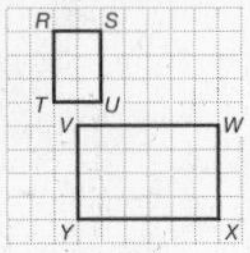

2. Not similar; Different angles

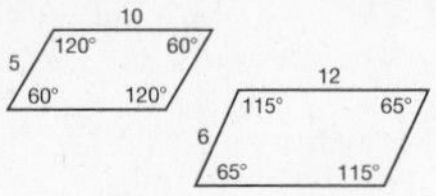

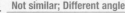

3. Similar; $\triangle ABC \sim \triangle FDE$; $\frac{3}{4}$

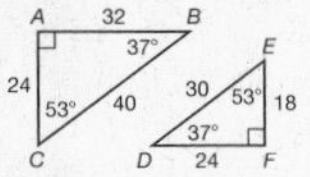

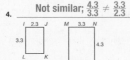

4. Not similar; $\frac{4.3}{3.3} \neq \frac{3.3}{2.3}$

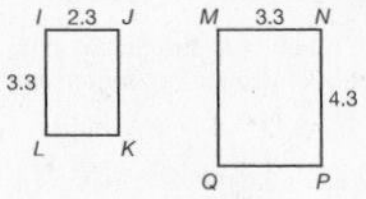

5. Draw two rhombuses that are similar and two that are not similar.

Similar:

Not Similar:

6. Suppose *ABCD* ~ *FEHG*. If $m\angle A = 86°$, $m\angle B = 113°$, $m\angle C = 90°$, and $m\angle D = 71°$, find the measures of $\angle E$, $\angle F$, $\angle G$, and $\angle H$.

$m\angle E =$ 113° $m\angle F =$ 86° $m\angle G =$ 71° $m\angle H =$ 90°

7. The One Liberty Place building in Philadelphia, Pennsylvania, is 945 feet tall. A model of this building used in a movie set is 18 inches tall. Find the scale factor of the model to the real building.

1 : 630 or 1 in. : 52.5 ft

8. **Fine Arts** Leonardo da Vinci's famous painting, the *Mona Lisa*, measures 53 cm × 77.5 cm. Suppose a postcard reproduction of the painting measures 12 cm × 17 cm. Is the postcard similar to the original? Explain.

No. Possible explanation: $\frac{12}{53} \neq \frac{17}{77.5}$

Name ______________________________

Practice 7-9

Finding Measures of Similar Figures

Find *x* in each pair of similar figures.

1. $\triangle UVW \sim \triangle XYZ$ $x =$ 22.5

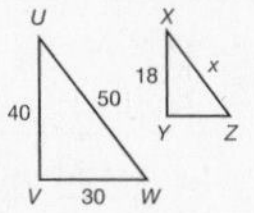

2. *JKLM* ~ *QRST* $x =$ 14

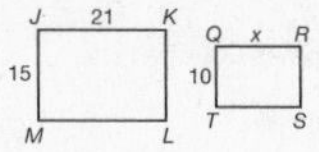

3. $\triangle DEF \sim \triangle GHI$ $x =$ 20

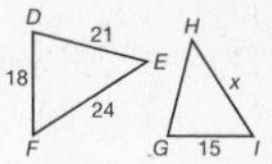

Find the missing side lengths in each pair of similar figures.

4. $\triangle PQR \sim \triangle STU$ $a =$ 3.75 $b =$ 9

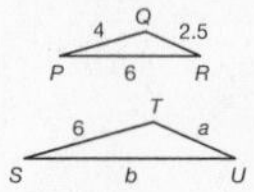

5. *EFGH* ~ *QRST* $c =$ 24 $d =$ 40 $e =$ 12

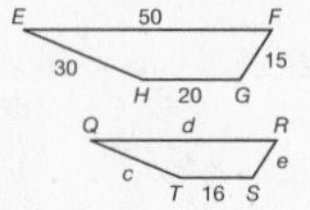

6. $\triangle ABC \sim \triangle DEF$ $m =$ 21 $n =$ 75

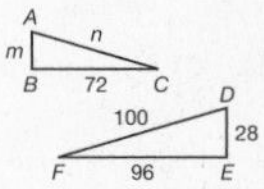

7. *ABCD* ~ *WXYZ* $k =$ 20

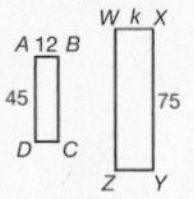

8. *GHIJ* ~ *KLMN* $r =$ 98 $s =$ 42 $t =$ 63

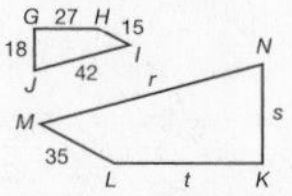

9. $\triangle JKL \sim \triangle UVW$ $x =$ 46.75 $y =$ 27.5

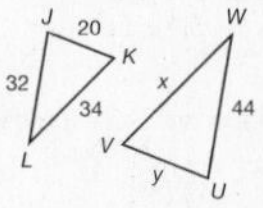

10. On a sunny day, if a 36-inch yardstick casts a 21-inch shadow, how tall is a building whose shadow is 168 ft? 288 ft

11. **Geography** Oregon is about 400 miles from west to east, and 300 miles from north to south. If a map of Oregon is 15 inches tall (from north to south), about how wide is the map? 20 in.

12. The Grand Coulee Dam on the Columbia River, Washington, is 4173 ft long and 550 ft high. If a scale model of the dam used in a movie is 16 ft high, how long is the model? About 121.4 ft

Name ______________________________

Practice 7-10

Perimeters and Areas of Similar Figures

Predict the ratio of the areas of each pair of similar figures. Check your predictions by calculating the perimeters and the areas.

1. scale factor 3

area ratio = 9

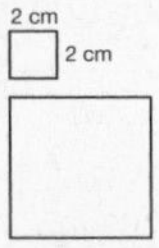

2. scale factor $\frac{1}{2}$

area ratio = $\frac{1}{4}$

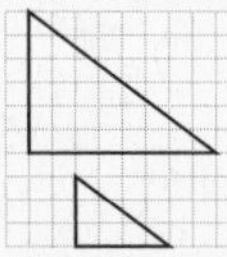

3. scale factor $\frac{4}{3}$

area ratio = $\frac{16}{9}$

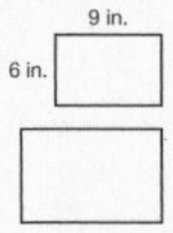

Suppose two figures are similar.

4. scale factor = 4, perimeter of smaller = 30 in.; area of smaller = 22 in^2
Find the perimeter and area of the larger figure.

perimeter = 120 in. area = 352 in^2

5. scale factor = $\frac{5}{3}$, perimeter of larger = 24 m; area of larger = 20 m^2
Find the perimeter and area of the smaller figure.

perimeter = 14.4 m area = 7.2 m^2

Perimeter and area ratios of similar figures are given. Find each scale factor.

6. perimeter ratio = 81 scale factor = 81
7. area ratio = 16 scale factor = 4
8. perimeter ratio = 100 scale factor = 100

9. A common postage stamp has perimeter $3\frac{3}{4}$ in. and area $\frac{7}{8}$ in. Find the perimeter and area of a scale drawing of this stamp if the scale factor is 8.

perimeter = 30 in. area = 56 in^2

10. All circles are similar. The diameter of a long-playing record is about $\frac{5}{2}$ times the diameter of a compact disc. If the area of a compact disc is about 115 cm^2, estimate the area of a record.

About 690 cm^2

Name ______________________________

Practice

Section 7C Review

Tell if the figures are similar. If they are, write a similarity statement using ~ and give the scale factor. If they're not, explain why not.

Possible answers:

1. Similar; $\triangle ABC \sim \triangle FED$; $\frac{3}{2}$

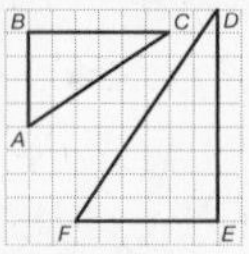

2. Not similar; $\frac{18}{21} \neq \frac{30}{36}$

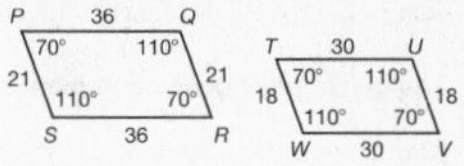

Find *x* in each pair of similar figures.

3. *DEFG* ~ *HIJK*; $x =$ 67.5

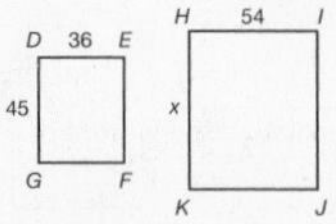

4. *PQRS* ~ *TUVW*; $x =$ 21

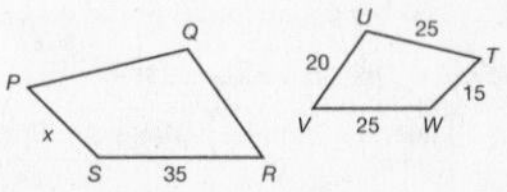

5. Two triangles are similar, and the scale factor is $\frac{3}{7}$. The perimeter of the larger triangle is 210 m, and its area is 2940 m^2. Find the perimeter and area of the smaller triangle.

perimeter = 90 m area = 540 m^2

6. **Health** An ounce of garbanzo beans contains about 0.835 mg of iron. Write and solve an equation to find the number of ounces of garbanzo beans you would need to eat to obtain the recommended daily allowance of 18 mg. *[Lesson 3-4]*

Possible answer: $0.835x = 18$; About 21.6 oz

7. The figure at the right shows the approximate shape of Nebraska. Use the figure to find the approximate area of Nebraska. *[Lesson 5-10]*

77,000 mi^2

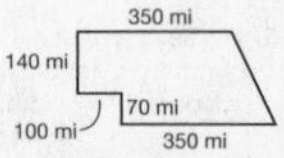

Name ______________________

Practice

Cumulative Review Chapters 1–7

Find the GCF and LCM. *[Lesson 3-7]*

1. 57, 76 GCF: 19 LCM: 228 **2.** 60, 100 GCF: 20 LCM: 300

3. 84,144 GCF: 12 LCM: 1008 **4.** 25, 35 GCF: 5 LCM: 175

5. 64, 112 GCF: 16 LCM: 448 **6.** 126, 56 GCF: 14 LCM: 504

Solve each equation. *[Lesson 4-3]*

7. $t - 4\frac{6}{7} = 3\frac{2}{7}$ $t =$ $8\frac{1}{7}$ **8.** $c - 2\frac{1}{2} = 5\frac{3}{7}$ $c =$ $7\frac{13}{14}$ **9.** $p - 3\frac{2}{9} = 21\frac{4}{9}$ $p =$ $24\frac{2}{3}$ **10.** $u + 12\frac{1}{6} = 21\frac{19}{24}$ $u =$ $9\frac{5}{8}$

Classify each figure in as many ways as you can. *[Lesson 5-3]*

11. Quadrilateral, trapezoid **12.** Obtuse isosceles triangle **13.** Right scalene triangle

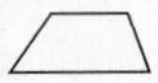

A model train is 30 in. long. Use each scale to find the length of the actual train. *[Lesson 7-2]*

14. scale: 1 in. = 8 ft actual length: 240 ft **15.** scale: 1 in. = 12 ft actual length: 360 ft **16.** scale: 2 in. = 15 ft actual length: 225 ft

Find the missing side lengths in each pair of similar figures. *[Lesson 7-9]*

17. $ABCD \sim EFGH$ $x =$ 64 **18.** $\triangle IJK \sim \triangle LMN$ $p =$ 36 $q =$ 45 **19.** $PQRS \sim TUVW$ $a =$ 20 $b =$ 50 $c =$ 30

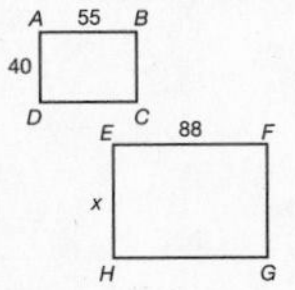

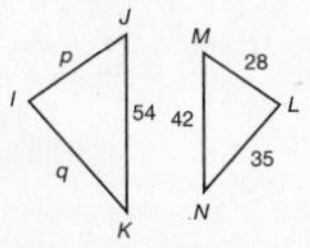

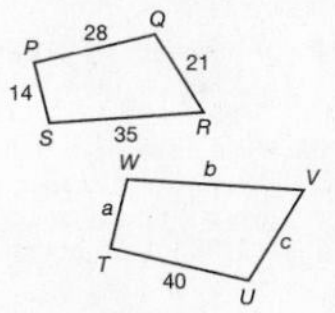

Name ______________________

Practice 8-1

Understanding Percents

Express each fraction as a percent.

1. $\frac{21}{100}$ 21% **2.** $\frac{38}{100}$ 38% **3.** $\frac{7}{10}$ 70% **4.** $\frac{11}{20}$ 55%

5. $\frac{9}{25}$ 36% **6.** $\frac{21}{50}$ 42% **7.** $\frac{3.7}{25}$ 14.8% **8.** $\frac{18.2}{25}$ 72.8%

Use percents to compare.

9. $\frac{1}{4}$ and $\frac{1}{5}$ 25 % $>$ 20 % **10.** $\frac{17}{20}$ and $\frac{22}{25}$ 85 % $<$ 88 % **11.** $\frac{3}{10}$ and $\frac{17}{50}$ 30 % $<$ 34 %

12. $\frac{7}{25}$ and $\frac{13}{50}$ 28 % $>$ 26 % **13.** $\frac{3}{4}$ and $\frac{19}{25}$ 75 % $<$ 76 % **14.** $\frac{13}{20}$ and $\frac{6}{10}$ 65 % $>$ 60 %

Use percents to compare the shaded areas on each grid.

15. 28 % $<$ 30 % **16.** 16 % $>$ 12 % **17.** 32 % $<$ 36 %

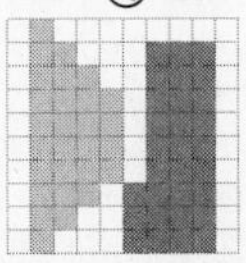
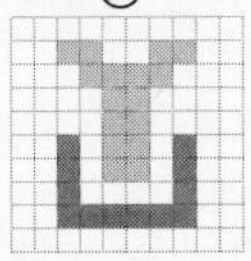
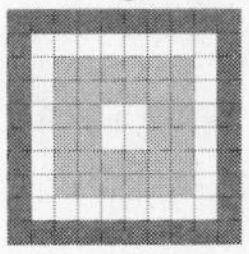

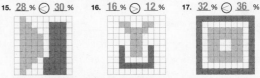

Measurement There are 100 cm in a meter. Express each length as a percent of a meter.

18. 5 cm 5% **19.** 70 cm 70% **20.** 48.5 cm 48.5% **21.** 2.8 cm 2.8%

Consumer Express each amount of money as a percent of a dollar.

22. 8 pennies 8% **23.** 4 dimes and a nickel 45%

24. 3 quarters and 4 pennies 79% **25.** 2 quarters and 3 nickels 65%

26. Science In the wild, only 1 out of 5 cottontail rabbits lives to be six months old. What percent is this? 20%

Name ______________________

Practice 8-2

Linking Fractions, Decimals, and Percents

Write each percent as a decimal.

1. 83% 0.83 **2.** 65% 0.65 **3.** 24% 0.24 **4.** 7% 0.07

5. 12.7% 0.127 **6.** 8.75% 0.0875 **7.** $62\frac{1}{2}$% 0.625 **8.** $33\frac{1}{3}$% $0.\overline{3}$

9. 2.9% 0.029 **10.** 18.3% 0.183 **11.** 99% 0.99 **12.** $23\frac{1}{4}$% 0.2325

Write each percent as a fraction in lowest terms.

13. 93% $\frac{93}{100}$ **14.** 45% $\frac{9}{20}$ **15.** 62% $\frac{31}{50}$ **16.** 44% $\frac{11}{25}$

17. 10% $\frac{1}{10}$ **18.** 62.5% $\frac{5}{8}$ **19.** 94% $\frac{47}{50}$ **20.** 40% $\frac{2}{5}$

21. 32% $\frac{8}{25}$ **22.** 25% $\frac{1}{4}$ **23.** 70% $\frac{7}{10}$ **24.** 87.5% $\frac{7}{8}$

Write each decimal as a percent.

25. 0.47 47% **26.** 0.41 41% **27.** 0.34 34% **28.** 0.215 21.5%

29. 0.3 30% **30.** 0.07 7% **31.** 0.999 99.9% **32.** 0.085 8.5%

Write each fraction as a percent. Where necessary, use a repeating decimal to help express your percent.

33. $\frac{2}{5}$ 40% **34.** $\frac{14}{25}$ 56% **35.** $\frac{11}{20}$ 55% **36.** $\frac{19}{50}$ 38%

37. $\frac{17}{100}$ 17% **38.** $\frac{2}{3}$ $66.\overline{6}$% **39.** $\frac{7}{10}$ 70% **40.** $\frac{3}{5}$ 60%

41. In 1994, there were 10,057 commercial radio stations in the United States. Of these, 926 stations were devoted to talk (including news, business, or sports). What percent of commercial radio stations were devoted to talk? About 9.2%

42. Geography The table lists the percent of the world's land in each continent. Express each percent as a fraction and a decimal.

Continent	Africa	Antarctica	Asia	Australia	Europe	N. America	S. America
Percent of total	20	9	30	5	7	16	9
Fraction	$\frac{1}{5}$	$\frac{9}{100}$	$\frac{3}{10}$	$\frac{1}{20}$	$\frac{7}{100}$	$\frac{4}{25}$	$\frac{9}{100}$
Decimal	0.2	0.09	0.3	0.05	0.07	0.16	0.09

Name ______________________

Practice 8-3

Percents Greater Than 100 or Less Than 1

Classify each of the following as: (A) less than 1%, (B) greater than 100%, or (C) between 1% and 100%.

1. $\frac{1}{2}$ (C) **2.** $\frac{4}{3}$ (B) **3.** $\frac{2}{300}$ (A) **4.** $\frac{3}{10}$ (C)

5. 10.8 (B) **6.** 0.7 (C) **7.** 1.4 (B) **8.** 0.06 (C)

9. 1.03 (B) **10.** 0.009 (A) **11.** 0.635 (C) **12.** 0.0053 (A)

Use >, <, or = to compare the numbers in each pair.

13. $\frac{1}{4} > 20\%$ **14.** $\frac{1}{2}\% < 50$ **15.** $0.008 < 8\%$ **16.** $35\% < \frac{3}{8}$

17. $150\% > \frac{5}{4}$ **18.** $3 = 300\%$ **19.** $\frac{7}{250} > 0.3\%$ **20.** $650\% < 7$

Write each fraction as a percent.

21. $\frac{7}{5}$ 140% **22.** $\frac{137}{100}$ 137% **23.** $\frac{0.8}{100}$ 0.8%

24. $\frac{21}{4}$ 525% **25.** $\frac{17}{10}$ 170% **26.** $\frac{65}{40}$ 162.5%

27. $\frac{37}{20}$ 185% **28.** $\frac{7}{500}$ 1.4% **29.** $\frac{9}{8}$ 112.5%

Write each decimal as a percent.

30. 0.003 0.3% **31.** 1.8 180% **32.** 0.0025 0.25%

33. 5.3 530% **34.** 0.0041 0.41% **35.** 0.083 8.3%

36. 0.0009 0.09% **37.** 0.83 83% **38.** 20 2000%

Write each percent as a decimal.

39. 175% 1.75 **40.** 120% 1.2 **41.** $\frac{2}{5}$% 0.004

42. $\frac{5}{8}$% 0.00625 **43.** 750% 7.5 **44.** $8\frac{1}{4}$% 0.0825

45. Social Science In 1990, the population of Kansas was 2,477,574, which included 21,965 Native Americans. What percent of the people living in Kansas were Native Americans? About 0.89%

46. Science The mass of Earth is $\frac{1}{318}$ of the mass of Jupiter. What percent is this? About 0.31%

Name ______________________

Practice 8-4

Finding a Percent of a Number

Find 50%, 10%, and 1% of each number.

1. 2,400 — 1,200; 240; 24
2. 36 — 18; 3.6; 0.36
3. 580 — 290; 58; 5.8
4. 60 — 30; 6; 0.6
5. 14,000 — 7,000; 1,400; 140
6. 620 — 310; 62; 6.2
7. 21 — 10.5; 2.1; 0.21
8. 122 — 61; 12.2; 1.22

Use mental math to find each percent of 4800.

9. 10% — 480
10. 40% — 1920
11. 25% — 1200
12. 20% — 960
13. 5% — 240
14. 75% — 3600
15. 15% — 720
16. 90% — 4320

Use mental math to find each percent.

17. 5% of 300 — 15
18. 75% of 6000 — 4500
19. 20% of 800 — 160
20. 60% of 700 — 420
21. 40% of $90 — $36
22. 10% of 450 — 45
23. 50% of 28 — 14
24. 30% of 200 — 60

Estimate each answer.

25. 30% of 808 — About 240
26. 11% of 128 — About 14
27. 44% of 764 — About 340
28. 10% of 382 — About 380
29. 49% of 1737 — About 850
30. 62% of 923 — About 570
31. 71% of 416 — About 300
32. 15% of 620 — About 90

33. **Social Science** In 1993, 904,292 people immigrated to the United States. 7.3% of the immigrants came from mainland China. How many people immigrated to the U.S. from mainland China in 1993? — About 66,000

34. **Science** It is estimated that there are about 20,000 native plant species in the United States. About 21% of these species are threatened with extinction. How many native plant species are threatened with extinction? — About 4,200

Name ______________________

Practice

Section 8A Review

Write each fraction or decimal as a percent.

1. 0.38 — 38%
2. $\frac{2}{5}$ — 40%
3. $\frac{36}{40}$ — 90%
4. $\frac{3}{20}$ — 15%
5. $\frac{13}{250}$ — 5.2%
6. $\frac{63}{50}$ — 126%
7. 0.423 — 42.3%
8. 5.5 — 550%

9. Carolyn correctly answered 43 out of 50 problems on a multiple choice test.

   What percent of the problems did she answer correctly? — 86%

   What percent did she answer incorrectly? — 14%

Write each percent as a decimal.

10. 42% — 0.42
11. 25% — 0.25
12. 160% — 1.6
13. 0.05% — 0.0005
14. 0.12% — 0.0012
15. 9.5% — 0.095
16. 850% — 8.5
17. 0.4% — 0.004

Write each percent as a fraction in lowest terms.

18. 67% — $\frac{67}{100}$
19. 125% — $\frac{5}{4}$
20. 0.2% — $\frac{1}{500}$
21. 28% — $\frac{7}{25}$
22. 65% — $\frac{13}{20}$
23. 70% — $\frac{7}{10}$
24. 0.68% — $\frac{17}{2500}$
25. 230% — $\frac{23}{10}$

Use mental math to find each percent.

26. 20% of 65 — 13
27. 40% of 120 — 48
28. 65% of 700 — 455
29. 90% of 400 — 360

30. A drug manufacturer claims that 512 out of 633 doctors who were surveyed recommend using the manufacturer's product. Estimate the percent of surveyed doctors who recommend using this product. — About 80%

31. The average American ate 12.3 pounds of cookies and crackers in 1993. How many ounces is this? *[Lesson 7-6]* — About 197 oz

32. Hans drove from Buffalo, New York, to Pittsburgh, Pennsylvania, a road distance of 219 miles. His average speed was 50 mi/hr, and he arrived in Pittsburgh at 6:30 P.M. What time did he leave Buffalo? *[Lesson 7-3]* — At about 2:07 P.M.

Name ______________________

Practice 8-5

Using Equations to Solve Percent Problems

Solve each problem. If necessary, round answers to the nearest tenth.

1. What percent of 64 is 48? — 75%
2. 16% of 130 is what number? — 20.8
3. 25% of what number is 24? — 96
4. What percent of 18 is 12? — 66.7%
5. 48% of 83 is what number? — 39.8
6. 40% of what number is 136? — 340
7. What percent of 530 is 107? — 20.2%
8. 74% of 643 is what number? — 475.8
9. 62% of what number is 84? — 135.5
10. What percent of 84 is 50? — 59.5%
11. 37% of 245 is what number? — 90.7
12. 12% of what number is 105? — 875
13. What percent of 42 is 7.5? — 17.9%
14. 98% of 880 is what number? — 862.4
15. 7% of what number is 63? — 900
16. What percent of 95 is 74? — 77.9%

17. Cafe Mediocre offers senior citizens a 15% discount off its regular price of $8.95 for the dinner buffet.

    a. What percent of the regular price is the price for senior citizens? — 85%

    b. What is the price for senior citizens? — $7.61

18. In 1990, 12.5% of the people in Oregon did not have health insurance. If the population of Oregon was 2,880,000, how many people were uninsured? — 360,000

Name ______________________

Practice 8-6

Solving Percent Problems with Proportions

Write a proportion and solve each problem. If necessary, round answers to the nearest tenth.

1. What number is 18% of 95? — $\frac{x}{95} = \frac{18}{100}$; 17.1
2. 37 is what percent of 50? — $\frac{37}{50} = \frac{x}{100}$; 74%
3. 12 is 20% of what number? — $\frac{12}{x} = \frac{20}{100}$; 60
4. What number is 54% of 82? — $\frac{x}{82} = \frac{54}{100}$; 44.3
5. 89 is what percent of 395? — $\frac{89}{395} = \frac{x}{100}$; 22.5%
6. 33 is 16% of what number? — $\frac{33}{x} = \frac{16}{100}$; 206.3
7. What number is 90% of 84? — $\frac{x}{84} = \frac{90}{100}$; 75.6
8. 108 is what percent of 647? — $\frac{108}{647} = \frac{x}{100}$; 16.7%
9. 64 is 178% of what number? — $\frac{64}{x} = \frac{178}{100}$; 36.0
10. What number is 46% of 835? — $\frac{x}{835} = \frac{46}{100}$; 384.1
11. 861 is what percent of 513? — $\frac{861}{513} = \frac{x}{100}$; 167.8%
12. 19 is 0.7% of what number? — $\frac{19}{x} = \frac{0.7}{100}$; 2714.3

13. A store that normally sells a compact stereo system for $128 is having a sale. Everything is discounted 35%. How much can you save by buying the stereo during the sale? — $44.80

14. In 1990, 17,339,000 Americans spoke Spanish at home. If 54.4% of non-English speakers spoke Spanish, find the number of non-English speakers. — About 31,873,000

15. **Measurement** An acre is 4,840 square yards. A hectare is 11,960 square yards. What percent of a hectare is an acre? — About 40.5%

Name ______________________

Practice 8-7

Problem Solving: Percent Increase and Decrease

Find each percent of increase or decrease. If necessary, round answers to the nearest tenth.

1. 12 is increased to 18. 50%
2. 36 is decreased to 24. 33.3%
3. 175 is increased to 208. 18.9%
4. 642 is decreased to 499. 22.3%

Find each amount of increase or decrease. If necessary, round answers to the nearest tenth.

5. 63 is increased by 40% 25.2
6. 93 is decreased by 17%. 15.8
7. 817 is increased by 62%. 506.5
8. 539 is decreased by 38%. 204.8

Find the new amount after each increase or decrease. If necessary, round answers to the nearest tenth.

9. 103 is increased by 28%. 131.8
10. $21 is decreased by 40%. $12.6
11. $65 is increased by 182%. $183.3
12. 417 is decreased by 8%. 383.6

Consumer Sales tax is an amount of increase. Find the amount of sales tax and the total price (including sales tax) for each of the following. If necessary, round answers to the nearest cent.

13. $17.50; 7% sales tax — tax: $1.23 total: $18.73
14. $21.95; 4.25% sales tax — tax: $0.93 total: $22.88

Geometry For each pair of similar figures, find the percent increase or decrease in area from figure A to figure B.

15. 44% increase A. 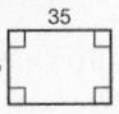

B. 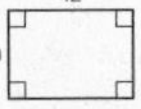

16. 51% decrease A. 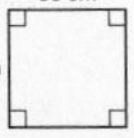

B. 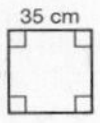

17. **Social Science** In 1990, there were 31,224,000 Americans of age 65-and-over. This population is expected to increase 71% by 2020. What is the expected 65-and-over population in 2020? About 53,393,000

Name ______________________

Practice

Section 8B Review

Solve each problem. If necessary, round answers to the nearest tenth.

1. What percent of 95 is 18? 18.9%
2. 68% of 68 is what number? 46.2
3. 43% of what number is 26? 60.5
4. What percent of 72 is 65? 90.3%
5. 27% of 582 is what number? 157.1
6. 59% of what number is 222? 376.3
7. What percent of 803 is 719? 89.5%
8. 215% of 78 is what number? 167.7
9. 77% of what number is 213? 276.6
10. What percent of 643 is 4.5? 0.7%
11. 85% of 468 is what number? 397.8
12. 93% of what number is 745? 801.1
13. What percent of 37 is 5? 13.5%
14. 4% of 890 is what number? 35.6
15. **Consumer** The Better Sweater Store sells a wool sweater for $37.95, plus 6.5% state sales tax. If you buy this sweater, how much will you pay? $40.42
16. A new top-selling compact disc is marked 25% off at Raspy Music, where the disc normally sells for $16.97. The same disc sells for $14.47 at Broken Records, where you have a coupon for 10% off anything in the store. Where would you buy the CD? Explain how you decided.
    Possible answer: Buy at Raspy Music, because $12.73 at Raspy Music is less than $13.02 at Broken Records.
17. The number of Americans who speak Yiddish at home decreased from 320,380 in 1980 to 213,064 in 1990. Find the percent decrease. About 33.5%
18. The slowest-moving crab in the world may be the *Neptune pelagines*. One of these crabs took 29 years to travel the 101.5 miles from the Red Sea to the Mediterranean Sea along the Suez Canal. If this crab maintained a constant rate, how long did it take to travel the first 40 miles? *[Lesson 6-3]* About 11.4 years
19. In 1935, Amelia Earhart made history by being the first woman to fly alone from Honolulu, Hawaii, to the U.S. mainland. Her average speed was about 133 miles per hour. Convert this rate to feet per second. *[Lesson 7-7]* About 195 ft/sec

Name ______________________

Practice

Cumulative Review Chapters 1–8

Express each fraction in lowest terms. *[Lesson 3-8]*

1. $\frac{8}{12}$ $\frac{2}{3}$
2. $\frac{24}{28}$ $\frac{6}{7}$
3. $\frac{55}{75}$ $\frac{11}{15}$
4. $\frac{21}{96}$ $\frac{7}{32}$
5. $\frac{30}{84}$ $\frac{5}{14}$
6. $\frac{32}{144}$ $\frac{2}{9}$
7. $\frac{15}{75}$ $\frac{1}{5}$
8. $\frac{42}{108}$ $\frac{7}{18}$

Find each product or quotient. Reduce to lowest terms. *[Lessons 4-5 and 4-6]*

9. $3\frac{1}{3} \cdot 1\frac{1}{2}$ 5
10. $13 \div 4\frac{2}{7}$ $3\frac{1}{30}$
11. $6\frac{3}{10} \cdot \frac{1}{3}$ $2\frac{1}{10}$
12. $2\frac{1}{3} \div 1\frac{8}{9}$ $1\frac{4}{17}$
13. $1\frac{5}{9} \div 3\frac{3}{5}$ $\frac{35}{81}$
14. $2\frac{3}{4} \cdot 3\frac{1}{2}$ $9\frac{5}{8}$
15. $19\frac{1}{6} \div 3\frac{5}{6}$ 5
16. $4 \cdot 6\frac{3}{8}$ $25\frac{1}{2}$

Find the sum of the measures of the angles in each polygon. *[Lesson 5-4]*

17. trapezoid 360°
18. hexagon 720°
19. 9-sided polygon 1260°
20. 17-sided polygon 2700°

Convert each rate to an equivalent rate. *[Lesson 7-7]*

21. 27 pounds per day to ounces per day 432 ounces per day
22. 45 kilograms per hour to grams per hour 45,000 grams per hour
23. 63 quarts per week to quarts per day 9 quarts per day
24. 154 feet per second to miles per hour 105 miles per hour

Write each percent as a fraction in lowest terms. *[Lesson 8-2]*

25. 12% $\frac{3}{25}$
26. 50% $\frac{1}{2}$
27. 38% $\frac{19}{50}$
28. 45% $\frac{9}{20}$
29. $66\frac{2}{3}\%$ $\frac{2}{3}$
30. 27% $\frac{27}{100}$
31. $12\frac{1}{2}\%$ $\frac{1}{8}$
32. 4% $\frac{1}{25}$

Solve each problem. If necessary, round answers to the nearest tenth. *[Lesson 8-6]*

33. What number is 26% of 83? 21.6
34. 4.3 is what percent of 738? 0.6%
35. 69 is 17% of what number? 405.9
36. What number is 135% of 216? 291.6
37. 57 is what percent of 188? 30.3%
38. 817 is 93% of what number? 878.5

Name ______________________

Practice 9-1

Using Integers to Represent Quantities

Tell whether each number is an integer. Write *Yes* or *No*.

1. 64 Yes
2. −9.31 No
3. $-2\frac{1}{2}$ No
4. 16.7 No
5. −37 Yes
6. $\frac{27}{3}$ Yes
7. 10.01 No
8. $\frac{3}{8}$ No

Use signs to write each number.

9. Spent $23 −$23
10. Gained 12 yards +12 yd
11. 14 degrees below zero −14°
12. Profit of $640 +$640
13. The distance from 0 to −4 on a number line +4
14. 7 units below the origin on a vertical number line −7

Write the opposite of each integer.

15. 42 −42
16. −163 163
17. −24 24
18. 69 −69
19. −39 39
20. 7 −7
21. −572 572
22. 18 −18

Find each absolute value.

23. |−12| 12
24. |23| 23
25. |−42| 42
26. |−58| 58
27. |937| 937
28. |−37| 37
29. |2640| 2640
30. |1329| 1329

31. **Science** The table gives the deepest recorded underwater dives of animals, as reported in the 1997 *Guinness Book of World Records*. Use an integer to represent the height of each animal during its dive. (The height at sea level is 0 ft.)

Animal	Depth (ft)	Height (ft)
Elephant Seal	5017	−5017
Leatherback Turtle	3973	−3973
Emperor Penguin	1584	−1584
Human (without equipment)	428	−428

32. **Science** The average surface temperature on Mercury is 332°F. On Pluto, it is −355°F.
    a. Find the absolute value of each temperature. 332°F; 355°F
    b. Which temperature is closer to 0°F? 332°F

Name ______________________

Practice 9-2

Comparing and Ordering Integers

Using the number line, write an inequality to tell which number is greater.

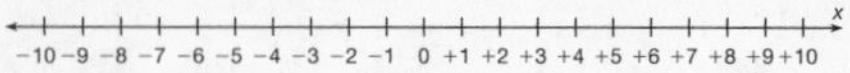

1. −3, 8 $-3 < 8$ 2. 7, 5 $7 > 5$ 3. −9, −1 $-9 < -1$

4. −3, 0 $-3 < 0$ 5. 9, −4 $9 > -4$ 6. 3, 4 $3 < 4$

7. −4, −2 $-4 < -2$ 8. −5, −6 $-5 > -6$ 9. −7, 7 $-7 < 7$

Use >, <, or = to compare each pair of numbers.

10. $-12 < 17$ 11. $-64 < -46$ 12. $367 > -376$ 13. $-23 > -32$

14. $-123 > -321$ 15. $14 > -15$ 16. $37 < 73$ 17. $265 > -265$

18. $412 < 421$ 19. $-98 < -89$ 20. $-21 < 21$ 21. $-482 < -284$

22. $|-65| > |64|$ 23. $|15| > |-14|$ 24. $|18| = |-18|$ 25. $|-84| < |-86|$

Order each set of numbers from greatest to least.

26. −42, 24, 58, −16, 44, −46 58, 44, 24, −16, −42, −46

27. −\$8, \$11, −\$12, \$7, −\$10, \$9 \$11, \$9, \$7, −\$8, −\$10, −\$12

28. 0°, 6°, −16°, −26°, −36°, 46° 46°, 6°, 0°, −16°, −26°, −36°

29. The chart shows the daily average minimum temperatures for fall and winter in McGrath, Alaska.

Month	Ave. Min. Temp. (°F)	Integer Temp. (°F)
October	18 above zero	18
November	4 below zero	−4
December	15 below zero	−15
January	18 below zero	−18
February	14 below zero	−14
March	3 below zero	−3

a. Complete the table by representing each temperature as an integer.

b. Order the integers in **a** from least to greatest.

−18, −15, −14, −4, −3, 18

Name ______________________

Practice 9-3

The Coordinate Plane

Find the coordinates of each point.

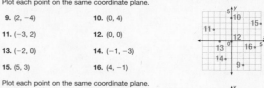

1. *S* (1, −5) 2. *T* (4, 0)

3. *U* (2, 3) 4. *V* (−3, 2)

5. *W* (0, −3) 6. *X* (5, −4)

7. *Y* (−4, −1) 8. *Z* (−4, 4)

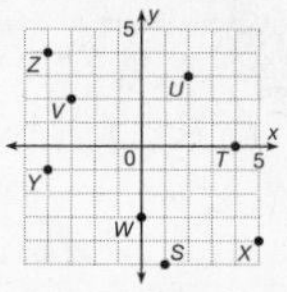

Plot each point on the same coordinate plane.

9. (2, −4) 10. (0, 4)

11. (−3, 2) 12. (0, 0)

13. (−2, 0) 14. (−1, −3)

15. (5, 3) 16. (4, −1)

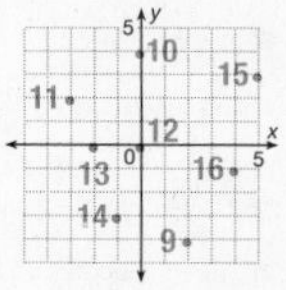

Plot each point on the same coordinate plane.

17. (8, 10) 18. (−14, 6)

19. (0, −12) 20. (2, −16)

21. (−5, 16) 22. (−12, −14)

23. (−18, −4) 24. (10, −13)

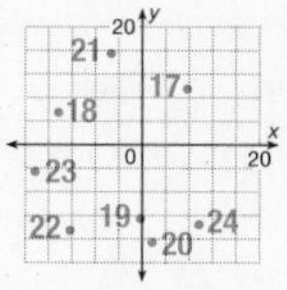

Name the quadrant or axis that contains each point.

25. (7, −12) IV 26. (16, 21) I 27. (−83, 12) II 28. (−61, −35) III

29. (−31, 24) II 30. (0, 3) *y*-axis 31. (−18, −25) III 32. (47, −38) IV

33. (16, −18) IV 34. (−7, 23) II 35. (−7, 0) *x*-axis 36. (17, 35) I

37. Plot the points (2, −2), (3, 4), (−1, 2), and (−2, −4) on the coordinate plane. Connect the points, in order, to form a polygon. What kind of polygon is formed? Be as specific as possible.

Parallelogram

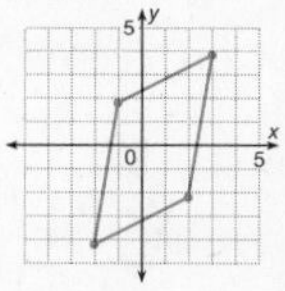

Name ______________________

Practice

Section 9A Review

Write the opposite of each integer.

1. 15 −15 2. −8 8 3. 27 −27 4. −58 58

5. −367 367 6. 222 −222 7. 638 −638 8. −412 412

Find each absolute value.

9. |37| 37 10. |−41| 41 11. |86| 86 12. |−101| 101

13. |−648| 648 14. |−3841| 3841 15. |2163| 2163 16. |−484| 484

Use >, <, or = to compare each pair of numbers.

17. $38 > -83$ 18. $-47 > -52$ 19. $-85 > -95$ 20. $637 < 763$

21. $-321 < -312$ 22. $418 > -481$ 23. $|18| < |-21|$ 24. $|-17| > |-15|$

Plot each point on the same coordinate plane.

25. (−4, −2) 26. (3, −3)

27. (3, 1) 28. (−1, 4)

29. (0, −2) 30. (2, 3)

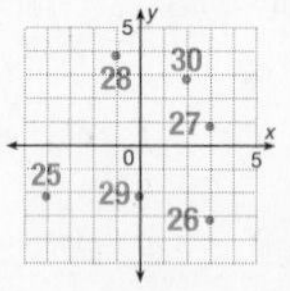

31. In 1968, John Gruener and R. Neal Watson used scuba equipment to dive to a depth of 437 ft below sea level. Use an integer to represent their height during the dive. −437 ft

32. During its first half-year, Anita's business earned monthly profits of −\$3285, −\$680, \$329, \$567, −\$240, and \$980. (A negative number represents a loss.) Order the dollar amounts from lowest to highest.

−\$3285, −\$680, −\$240, \$329, \$567, \$980

33. **Geography** The area of Peru is about $3\frac{4}{25}$ times the area of Paraguay. If Paraguay has an area of 157,000 mi², what is the area of Peru? *[Lesson 4-5]* About 496,000 mi²

34. In 1964, Steve's Cheese of Denmark, Wisconsin, made a cheddar cheese weighing $17\frac{1}{2}$ tons. The milk used to make the cheese equalled the daily production of 16,000 cows. How many tons of cheddar cheese could be made using the daily production of milk from 3,200 cows? *[Lesson 6-8]* $3\frac{1}{2}$ tons

Name ______________________

Practice 9-4

Adding Integers

Write the addition problem and the sum for each model. The lighter tiles represent positive numbers.

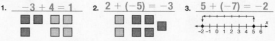

1. $-3 + 4 = 1$ 2. $2 + (-5) = -3$ 3. $5 + (-7) = -2$

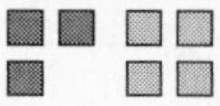

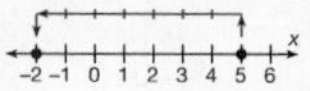

Find the additive inverse of each integer.

4. 7 −7 5. −9 9 6. 37 −37 7. 14 −14

8. −16 16 9. −23 23 10. 41 −41 11. −28 28

Use algebra tiles or a number line to find each sum.

12. 7 + (−4) 3 13. −1 + (−3) −4 14. 3 + 2 5 15. −7 + 8 1

16. −6 + (−1) −7 17. −1 + (−2) −3 18. −4 + 9 5 19. −8 + 6 −2

Find each sum.

20. 58 + 57 115 21. −110 + 19 −91 22. −49 + (−106) −155

23. 16 + (−47) −31 24. −40 + 16 −24 25. 35 + (−40) −5

26. −36 + (−58) −94 27. −17 + 13 −4 28. −146 + 16 −130

29. 10 + (−30) −20 30. −25 + (−21) −46 31. −66 + (−13) −79

Write the next integer in each pattern.

32. −12, −9, −6, −3 33. 6, −2, −10, −18 34. −20, −16, −12, −8

35. 10, 5, 0, −5 36. −11, −16, −21, −26 37. −11, −7, −3, 1

38. A diver is at a depth of 14 ft below sea level. If she is lifted to 10 ft above her present position, will she be above or below sea level? Write an addition problem and the sum to explain your answer. Below; $-14 + 10 = -4$

39. The average daily minimum temperature in International Falls, Minnesota, is 38°F warmer in March than in January. If the temperature in January is −10°F, what is the temperature in March? 28°F

Name ____________________

Practice 9-5

Subtracting Integers

Use algebra tiles to find each difference.

1. −7 − 2 **−9** 2. 7 − (−3) **10** 3. −4 − (−3) **−1** 4. 3 − (−4) **7**

5. −4 − (−1) **−3** 6. −4 − 5 **−9** 7. 3 − 7 **−4** 8. −3 − (−7) **4**

Use a number line to find each difference.

9. 1 − (−6) **7** 10. 2 − 4 **−2** 11. 8 − 3 **5** 12. −6 − 1 **−7**

13. −1 − (−1) **0** 14. 4 − 7 **−3** 15. 8 − (−1) **9** 16. 0 − 2 **−2**

Find each difference.

17. −38 − 50 **−88** 18. −110 − 118 **−228** 19. −16 − (−34) **18**

20. 10 − 73 **−63** 21. 10 − (−78) **88** 22. −12 − 15 **−27**

23. −24 − (−56) **32** 24. −56 − 42 **−98** 25. 13 − 100 **−87**

Write the next integer in each pattern.

26. 15, 3 −9, **−21** 27. −8, −11, −14, **−17** 28. 17, 12, 7, **2**

29. 12, 5, −2, **−9** 30. 4, −6, −16, **−26** 31. 18, 10, 2, **−6**

Find the unknown number in each difference.

32. $9 - y = 12$ **−3** 33. $-34 + x = -23$ **11** 34. $32 + z = -13$ **−45**

35. **Geography** The table shows the highest and lowest elevations of each continent. Find the range of elevations for each continent by subtracting the low elevation from the high elevation.

Continent	Africa	Antarctica	Asia	Europe	N. America	S. America	Australia
High el. (m)	5895	4897	8848	5642	6194	6960	2228
Low el. (m)	−156	−2538	−400	−28	−86	−40	−16
Range (m)	6051	7435	9248	5670	6280	7000	2244

Which continent has the widest range? **Asia**

Which continent has the narrowest range? **Australia**

Name ____________________

Practice 9-6

Multiplying Integers

Find each product.

1. −2 · (−16) **32** 2. −29 · 3 **−87** 3. −11 · 21 **−231**

4. 3 · 19 **57** 5. −2 · 16 **−32** 6. −10 · 12 **−120**

7. −2 · (−6) **12** 8. −8 · (−18) **144** 9. 13 · (−26) **−338**

10. −2 · 6 **−12** 11. −3 · 28 **−84** 12. −2 · (−2) **4**

13. −27 · 28 **−756** 14. 2 · (−3) **−6** 15. −2 · (−5) **10**

16. 2 · (−6) **−12** 17. 12 · (−14) **−168** 18. −14 · (−10) **140**

19. 46 · (−6) **−276** 20. −4 · 4 **−16** 21. −13 · 2 **−26**

22. −17 · (−4) **68** 23. 19 · 5 **95** 24. 16 · (−14) **−224**

25. −11 · (−34) **374** 26. 2 · (−34) **−68** 27. −17 · (−5) **85**

28. 9 · (−10) **−90** 29. 2 · (−13) **−26** 30. −16 · 3 **−48**

31. −17 · 19 **−323** 32. −17 · (−36) **612** 33. −22 · 4 **−88**

34. −9 · (−19) **171** 35. 4 · (−8) **−32** 36. −14 · (−2) **28**

37. −6 · (−23) **138** 38. −9 · 3 **−27** 39. −18 · 9 **−162**

40. −16 · 7 **−112** 41. −38 · 18 **−684** 42. −32 · (−6) **192**

43. −25 · (−10) **250** 44. −13 · 20 **−260** 45. 2 · (−9) **−18**

46. −9 · 11 **−99** 47. −4 · (−2) **8** 48. −11 · (−24) **264**

49. In 1995, Nigeria was losing its forest cover at the rate of 4000 km^2 per year.

a. Write the deforestation rate as a negative integer. **−4000 km^2 per yr**

b. Calculate the change in the amount of forest in a 5-year period. **−20,000 km^2**

50. Tabitha withdrew $85 a month from her savings account for seven months. What was the change in her balance? **−$595**

Name ____________________

Practice 9-7

Dividing Integers

Use the given product to find each quotient.

1. 11 · (−7) = −77; −77 ÷ (−7) = **11** 2. 7 · 14 = 98; 98 ÷ 7 = **14**

3. −5 · 10 = −50; −50 ÷ 10 = **−5** 4. 3 · (−6) = −18; −18 ÷ (−6) = **3**

Find each quotient.

5. 56 ÷ (−8) **−7** 6. −196 ÷ (−14) **14** 7. −10 ÷ (−10) **1**

8. −117 ÷ (−9) **13** 9. −49 ÷ (−7) **7** 10. −63 ÷ 7 **−9**

11. −40 ÷ 4 **−10** 12. −18 ÷ (−3) **6** 13. 7 ÷ (−7) **−1**

14. −120 ÷ (−8) **15** 15. −4 ÷ (−1) **4** 16. −50 ÷ (−10) **5**

17. −40 ÷ (−8) **5** 18. −99 ÷ 9 **−11** 19. −117 ÷ 9 **−13**

20. 44 ÷ (−4) **−11** 21. −24 ÷ 8 **−3** 22. −40 ÷ 10 **−4**

23. 18 ÷ (−6) **−3** 24. 180 ÷ 15 **12** 25. −48 ÷ (−8) **6**

26. −84 ÷ (−14) **6** 27. −84 ÷ 7 **−12** 28. −91 ÷ (−7) **13**

29. 9 ÷ (−3) **−3** 30. −144 ÷ 12 **−12** 31. 10 ÷ (−10) **−1**

32. −70 ÷ 10 **−7** 33. 117 ÷ (−13) **−9** 34. −36 ÷ 9 **−4**

35. −3 ÷ (−1) **3** 36. 120 ÷ (−10) **−12** 37. −24 ÷ (−4) **6**

38. 8 ÷ (−8) **−1** 39. −28 ÷ (−4) **7** 40. −112 ÷ (−8) **14**

41. −36 ÷ 6 **−6** 42. −126 ÷ (−14) **9** 43. −77 ÷ (−11) **7**

44. −143 ÷ 11 **−13** 45. −22 ÷ (−11) **2** 46. −48 ÷ 8 **−6**

47. −44 ÷ 4 **−11** 48. −117 ÷ (−13) **9** 49. −112 ÷ 8 **−14**

50. Some typical daily low temperatures for Alaska cities in February are: Anchorage, 12°F; Fairbanks, −14°F; Kotzebue, −12°F; Gulkana, −7°F; and Nome, −4°F. What is the average of these temperatures? **−5°F**

51. Over a 6-year period, a business reported annual profits of $8 million, −$5 million, −$9 million, $3 million, and −$7 million, and −$2 million. What was the mean annual profit? **−$2 million**

Name ____________________

Practice

Section 9B Review

Find each sum, difference, product, or quotient.

1. −135 ÷ 15 **−9** 2. −57 + 29 **−28** 3. 3 · (−5) **−15**

4. 21 − (−137) **158** 5. 64 ÷ (−8) **−8** 6. −76 + (−84) **−160**

7. −20 · (−16) **320** 8. −40 − 28 **−68** 9. −30 ÷ 3 **−10**

10. −26 + (−31) **−57** 11. −5 · 2 **−10** 12. 38 − 59 **−21**

13. 96 ÷ 8 **12** 14. 30 + (−60) **−30** 15. 8 · (−2) **−16**

Evaluate each expression.

16. 6 + (−4) − (−8) **10** 17. 3 · (−5) · 7 **−105** 18. −6 · 10 ÷ (−15) **4**

19. −3 + (−7) · (−4) **25** 20. 64 ÷ (−4) + 12 **−4** 21. −28 ÷ (−7) · (−4) **−16**

22. 4 · (−9) − (−25) **−11** 23. −2 + (−9) − (−15) **4** 24. 36 ÷ (−12) + (−6) **−9**

25. **Science** Temperatures on the moon can be as high as 273°F (134°C) and as low as −274°F (−170°C). Find the difference between these extreme temperatures in °F and °C. **547°F; 304°C**

26. Stephan is playing a card game. He started out with 100 points, and then he scored +20, −15, +30, −5, and −40 points. Then his score was tripled because he held all the aces. What was his final score? **270**

27. The population of Buffalo, New York, was about 580,000 in 1950 and 328,000 in 1990. Find the average rate of change of the population (in people per year) from 1950 to 1990. **−6300 people per year**

28. Rebecca is buying new carpet for the section of her home that is shown. How many square feet of carpet will she need? *[Lesson 5-10]* **348 ft^2**

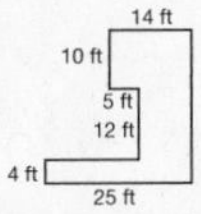

29. In 1980, independent presidential candidate John Anderson won 6.6% of the popular vote. He received about 5,720,000 votes. How many people voted in this election? *[Lesson 8-6]* **About 86,700,000 people**

Name ______________________

Practice

Cumulative Review Chapters 1–9

Convert to a fraction in lowest terms. *[Lesson 3-10]*

1. 0.63 $\frac{63}{100}$ 2. 0.75 $\frac{3}{4}$ 3. 0.56 $\frac{14}{25}$ 4. 0.45 $\frac{9}{20}$

5. 0.6 $\frac{3}{5}$ 6. 0.375 $\frac{3}{8}$ 7. 0.124 $\frac{31}{250}$ 8. 0.36 $\frac{9}{25}$

9. 0.888 $\frac{111}{125}$ 10. 0.98 $\frac{49}{50}$ 11. 0.413 $\frac{413}{1000}$ 12. 0.175 $\frac{7}{40}$

Find the missing length in each right triangle. *[Lesson 5-7]*

13. t = 45 m 14. x = 24 in. 15. m = 4.5 cm 16. q = 73 ft

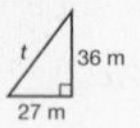

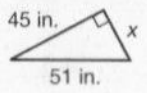

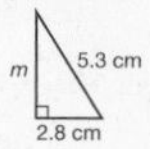

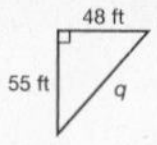

Consumer Use unit prices to find the better buy. Underline the correct choice. *[Lesson 6-2]*

17. Oranges: $1.44 for 3 lb or $2.50 for 5 lb

18. Granola cereal: $1.68 for 12 oz or $2.47 for 19 oz

19. Magazines: $21 for 12 issues or $44 for 24 issues

20. Blueberries: $2.98 for 2 baskets or $3.98 for 3 baskets

Perimeter and area ratios of similar figures are given. Find each scale factor. *[Lesson 7-10]*

21. Perimeter ratio = $\frac{49}{25}$ Scale factor = $\frac{49}{25}$

22. Area ratio = 16 Scale factor = 4

23. Perimeter ratio = 0.36 Scale factor = 0.36

24. Perimeter ratio = 81 Scale factor = 81

25. Area ratio = $\frac{9}{100}$ Scale factor = $\frac{3}{10}$

26. Area ratio = 2.25 Scale factor = 1.5

Find each sum, difference, product, or quotient. *[Lessons 9-4 to 9-7]*

27. $-21 + (-168)$ -189 28. $-41 - (-51)$ 10 29. $126 + (-146)$ -20

30. $30 \div (-6)$ -5 31. $53 + (-12)$ 41 32. $37 - (-44)$ 81

Name ______________________

Practice 10-1

Quantities, Constants, and Variables

Tell whether each quantity is a variable or a constant.

1. The number of ounces in a pound Constant
2. The population of Memphis, Tennessee Variable
3. The height of the Eiffel Tower Constant

For each quantity, define a variable and give a reasonable range of values. Possible answers:

4. The width of a desk Let w = width; 24 in. to 75 in.
5. The weight of a dog Let w = weight; 1 lb to 200 lb
6. The number of bathrooms in a house Let n = no. of bathrooms; 1 to 5
7. The number of staples in a stapler Let n = no. of staples; 0 to 210

Measurement Give an appropriate unit of measurement for each quantity. You may use metric or customary units. Possible answers:

8. The amount of time it takes to run a mile Minutes
9. The height of a tree Feet
10. The distance between two cities Kilometers

11. You are managing an apartment complex with 65 units. In a typical month, several people move in or out of the complex. Possible answers:
   a. Name two variable quantities related to the apartment complex.
   Number of residents, age of oldest resident
   b. Name two constant quantities related to the apartment complex.
   Number of units, size of smallest unit

12. The formula for the circumference of a circle is $C = 2\pi r$.
   a. Name all variable quantities in the formula. C, r
   b. Name all constant quantities in the formula. 2, π

Name ______________________

Practice 10-2

Relating Graphs to Stories

Name another quantity that each given quantity might depend on.
Possible answers:

1. The number of houses on a city block Length of the block
2. The volume of a cube Length of a side
3. The amount of a paycheck Number of hours worked
4. A student's score on a test Number of hours studied

In Exercises 5 and 6, choose the graph that best shows the story.

5. You catch the flu, so your temperature increases. As you regain your health, your temperature returns to normal.

a.
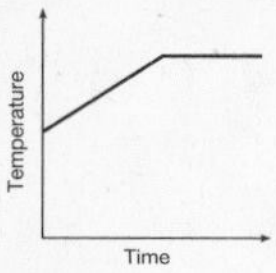

(b.)

c.
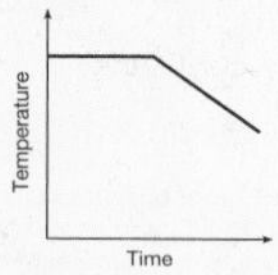

6. You leave for school in the morning. When you get halfway to school, you suddenly realize that you've left an important paper at home. You return home, and then go to school.

(a.)
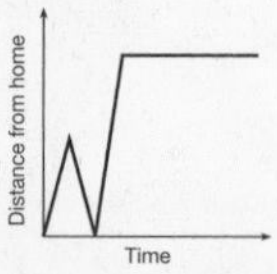

b.
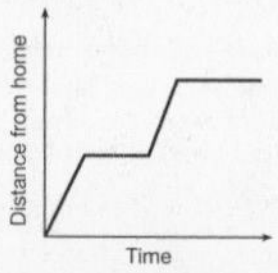

c.
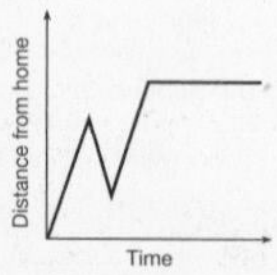

7. Tell a story that fits the graph. Possible answer:

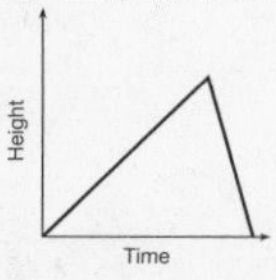

On a roller coaster, you rise slowly to the top of the tracks, and then descend rapidly.

Name ______________________

Practice 10-3

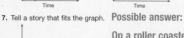

Tables and Expressions

Give the next term in each sequence or the next picture in each pattern.

1. 4, 8, 12, 16, 20, ...
2. −20, −18, −16, −14, −12, ...
3. 8, −8, 8, −8, 8, ...
4. 3, 6, 12, 24, 48, ...
5. 
6. 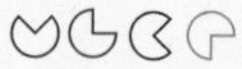

Write an expression describing the rule for each sequence. Then give the 100th term for the sequence.

7. 35, 36, 37, 38, ... Expression: $n + 34$ 100th term: 134
8. 8, 10, 12, 14, ... Expression: $2n + 6$ 100th term: 206
9. 1.5, 3, 4.5, 6, ... Expression: $1.5n$ 100th term: 150

Make a table showing the first 4 terms of the sequence for each rule.

10. $n + 20$

n	1	2	3	4
$n + 20$	21	22	23	24

11. $3n - 5$

n	1	2	3	4
$3n - 5$	−2	1	4	7

Tell whether each sequence is arithmetic, geometric, or neither. Then give the next term.

12. −5, 25, −125, 625, −3,125, ... Geometric

13. $\frac{1}{3}, \frac{1}{6}, \frac{1}{9}, \frac{1}{12}, \frac{1}{15}$, ... Neither

14. A pattern of squares is shown. 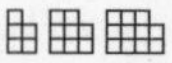
   a. Sketch the 4th and 5th figure in this pattern. 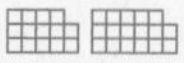
   b. Make a table comparing the figure number to the number of squares. Write an expression for the number of squares in the nth figure. $3n + 2$

Figure number	1	2	3	4	5
Number of Squares	5	8	11	14	17

   c. How many squares would there be in the 80th figure? 242

Name ______________________

Practice 10-4

Understanding and Writing Equations

For each table, write an equation to show the relationship between x and y. Use the equation to find y when $x = 7$.

1. $y = 8x$

x	1	2	3	4	7
y	8	16	24	32	56

2. $y = x - 4$

x	1	2	3	4	7
y	−3	−2	−1	0	3

Complete each table, and write an equation to show the relationship between the variables.

3. $t = s + 15$

s	3	5	7	15	50
t	18	20	22	30	65

4. $b = 7a$

a	10	20	30	80	100
b	70	140	210	560	700

5. $c = 3.14d$

d	1	2	3	7	12
c	3.14	6.28	9.42	21.98	37.68

6. $q = 12p$

p	0	2	4	9	20
q	0	24	48	108	240

Make a table of five pairs of values for each equation. **Possible answers:**

7. $y = x - 12$

x	1	2	3	4	5
y	−11	−10	−9	−8	−7

8. $y = 0.7x$

x	1	2	3	4	5
y	0.7	1.4	2.1	2.8	3.5

9. $p = 5m - 3$

m	1	2	3	4	5
p	2	7	12	17	22

10. $v = \frac{u}{5} + 7$

u	0	5	10	15	20
v	7	8	9	10	11

11. Science The relationship between the amount of time a zebra runs at maximum speed and the distance it covers is shown.

Time (min)	3	6	9	12	15
Distance (mi)	2	4	6	8	10

a. Write an equation to describe this relationship. **Possible answer: $d = \frac{2}{3}t$**

b. Use the equation to find the distance the zebra would travel in 48 minutes. **32 mi**

Name ______________________

Practice 10-5

Equations and Graphs

In Exercises 1–2, a table of points is given for each equation. Graph each equation on a coordinate plane.

1. $y = -2x$

x	−2	−1	0	1	2
y	4	2	0	−2	−4

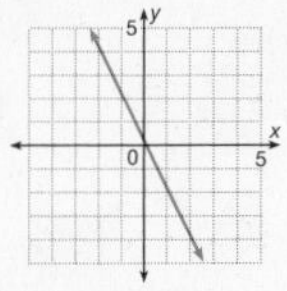

2. $y = x - 3$

x	−2	−1	0	2	4
y	−5	−4	−3	−1	1

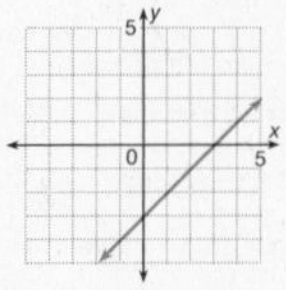

Graph each equation on a coordinate plane.

3. $y = x + 4$

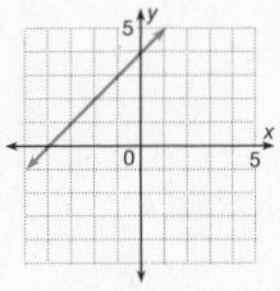

4. $y = 2x + 3$

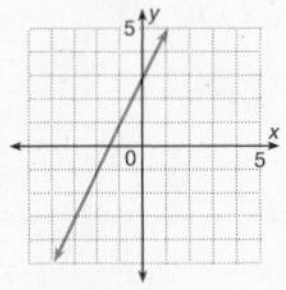

5. $y = x^2 - 2$

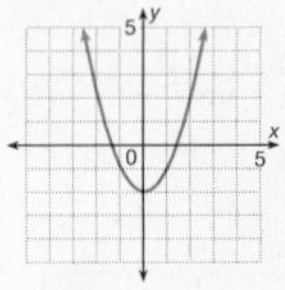

6. Health A typical slice of apple pie contains about 18 g of fat. An equation to represent the fat in several slices is $f = 18n$, where f represents the amount of fat in grams and n represents the number of slices. Graph this equation on a coordinate plane.

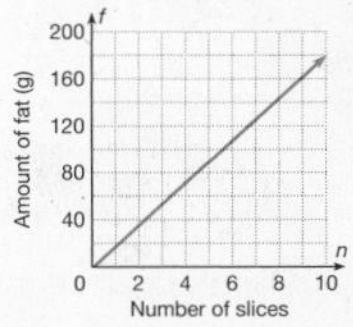

Name ______________________

Practice

Section 10A Review

1. Tell whether the depth of water in a bathtub is a variable or a constant. **Variable**

2. A person making deliveries rode an elevator from the lobby to the 17th floor to deliver a package. She then rode to the 9th floor to make another delivery, and then she returned to the lobby. Which graph could represent this story?

a.

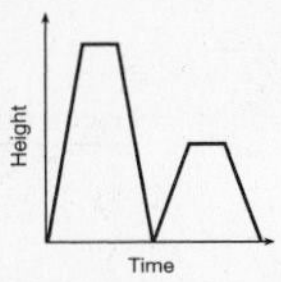

b.

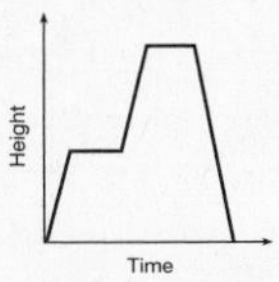

(c.)

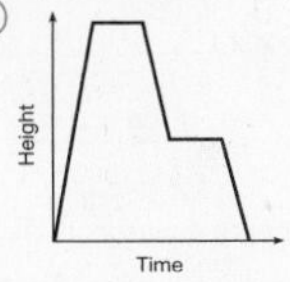

Write an expression describing the rule for each sequence. Then give the 100th term for the sequence.

3. −6, −12, −18, −24, ⋯

Expression: **$-6n$** 100th term: **−600**

4. −8, −7, −6, −5, ⋯

Expression: **$n - 9$** 100th term: **91**

5. Write an equation to show the relationship between x and y. Use the equation to find y when $x = 9$.

x	1	2	3	4	9
y	7	8	9	10	15

$y = x + 6$

Graph each equation on a coordinate plane.

6. $y = -4x$

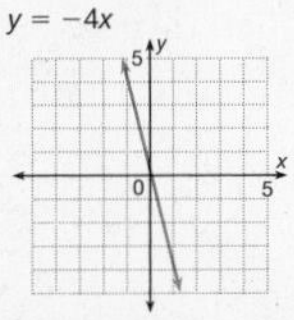

7. $y = x - 3$

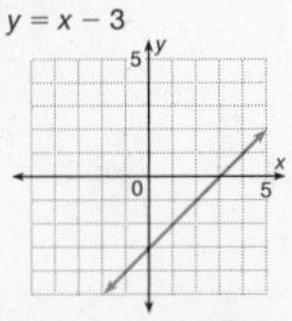

8. $y = -2x + 4$

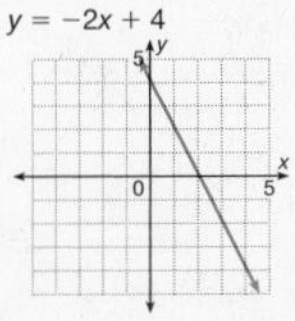

9. Dave traveled 271 mi from Philadelphia to Boston. He left at 10:00 A.M. and drove at 60 mi/hr. What time did he arrive? *[Lesson 7-3]* **2:31 P.M.**

10. Science Ice melts at 32°F. If the temperature of a block of ice increases 35°F from −10°F, does the ice melt? Explain your answer. *[Lesson 9-4]*

No. Possible answer: $-10 + 35 = 25$, and $25 < 32$.

Name ______________________

Practice 10-6

Solving Equations Using Tables

The table below represents the equation $y = 3x + 4$. Use it to solve the related equations below the table.

x	−4	−3	−2	−1	0	1	2	3	4
y	−8	−5	−2	1	4	7	10	13	16

1. $10 = 3x + 4$ $x =$ **2**

2. $-5 = 3x + 4$ $x =$ **−3**

3. $3x + 4 = 16$ $x =$ **4**

4. $-8 = 3x + 4$ $x =$ **−4**

5. Use the table above to estimate the solution to $8 = 3x + 4$. Explain how you found your answer.

$\approx 1\frac{1}{2}$; Possible answer: If y is between 7 and 10, then x is between 1 and 2.

Make and use a table to solve each equation.

6. $20 = 5x$ $x =$ **4**

7. $19 = x + 12$ $x =$ **7**

8. $-6 = -3x$ $x =$ **2**

9. $-5 = -2x + 5$ $x =$ **5**

10. $-54 = 7x - 12$ $x =$ **−6**

11. $8 = -8x$ $x =$ **−1**

12. $3 = x - 5$ $x =$ **8**

13. $2x - 3 = 9$ $x =$ **6**

Make and use a table to estimate the solution to each equation.

14. $30 = 7x$ $x \approx$ **$4\frac{1}{2}$**

15. $35 = 5x + 7$ $x \approx$ **$5\frac{1}{2}$**

16. $-4x = 10\frac{1}{2}$ $x \approx$ **$-2\frac{1}{2}$**

17. $-18 = 3x - 4$ $x \approx$ **$-4\frac{1}{2}$**

18. Suppose a trapezoid has height 10, and one of its bases has length 7. Then the area is given by $A = \frac{1}{2} \cdot 10(7 + x)$, or $A = 35 + 5x$, where x is the length of the other base.

a. Make a table of values for $A = 35 + 5x$. **Possible answer:**

x	2	4	6	8	10	12
A	45	55	65	75	85	95

b. Use your table to estimate the value of x for one of these trapezoids with area 78. **About $8\frac{1}{2}$**

Name ______________________

Practice 10-7

Solving Equations Using Graphs

1. Follow the steps to solve $1 = -2x + 3$ by graphing. **Possible answer:**
   a. Write the related equation for $1 = -2x + 3$ by replacing 1 with y. $y = -2x + 3$
   b. Make a table of values for the related equation.

x	4	3	2	1	0	−1
y	−5	−3	−1	1	3	5

   c. Plot the points in your table on a coordinate plane. Connect the points.
   d. Start at 1 on the y-axis of your coordinate plane. Go across until you reach the graph. Then, drop vertically to the x-axis, and read the solution. $x =$ 1

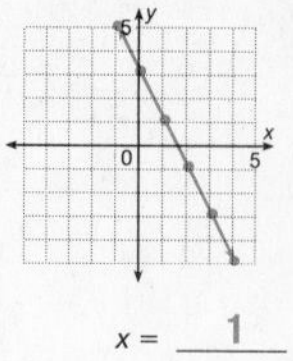

2. Use your graph above to estimate the solution to $-3\frac{1}{2} = -2x + 3$.
   $x \approx 3\frac{1}{4}$; Possible answer: When $y = -3\frac{1}{2}$, $x \approx 3\frac{1}{4}$.

Use a graph to solve each equation. **Possible answers:**

3. $-4x = 12$ $x =$ −3
4. $17 = -2x + 9$ $x =$ −4
5. $-15 = 3x - 6$ $x =$ −3
6. $11 = -5x - 4$ $x =$ −3
7. $10 = 2k - 4$ $k =$ 7
8. $p + 6 = 11$ $p =$ 5
9. $-13 = 5h - 3$ $h =$ −2
10. $-5 = -4m + 7$ $m =$ 3

Use a graph to estimate the solution to each equation.

11. $6 = 4x + 17$ $x \approx$ −3
12. $15 = -3u + 8$ $u \approx$ −2
13. $-10 = 7p - 5$ $p \approx$ −1
14. $15 = -5b + 8$ $b \approx$ −1

15. The MaxiTaxi Company charges $1.00 per mile, plus a base charge of $2.50 per trip. The cost, c, to travel d miles is given by $c = d + 2.5$.
   a. Graph this equation.
   b. Melinda paid $8.00 for her taxi ride. How far did she go? 5.5 mi

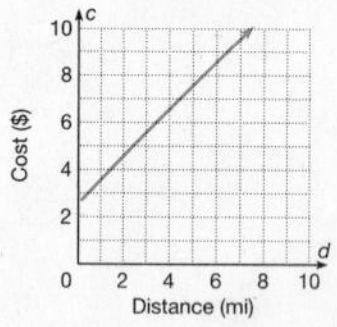

Name ______________________

Practice 10-8

Relating Equations and Inequalities

Graph each inequality on a number line.

1. $x \le 3$

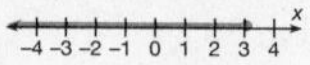

2. $t > 1$

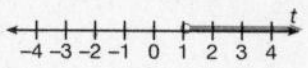

3. $q \ge -10$

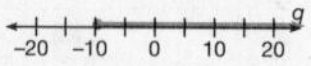

4. $m < 50$

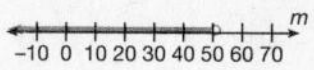

For each inequality, tell whether the number in bold is a solution.

5. $x < 7$; **7** No
6. $p > -3$; **3** Yes
7. $k \ge 5$; **0** No
8. $3z \le 12$; **4** Yes
9. $n - 5 > 3$; **6** No
10. $2g + 8 \ge 3$; **−1** Yes

Write an inequality for each graph.

11. $x > -2$

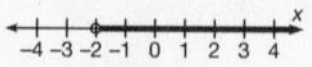

12. $z \le 30$

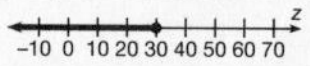

Write a real-world statement for each inequality. **Possible answers:**

13. $d \ge 60$ It is at least 60 mi away.
14. $p < 200$ The price is under $200.

Write and graph an inequality for each statement.

15. You can walk there in 20 minutes or less. $t \le 20$

16. Each prize is worth over $150. $v > 150$

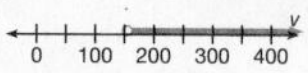

17. **Science** A species of catfish, *malapterurus electricus*, can generate up to 350 volts of electricity.
   a. Write an inequality to represent the amount of electricity generated by the catfish. $e \le 350$
   b. Draw a graph of the inequality you wrote in **a**.

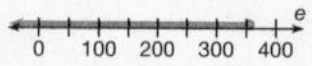

Name ______________________

Practice

Section 10B Review

The table represents the equation $y = 6x - 8$. Use it to solve the related equations beneath the table.

x	−3	−2	−1	0	1	2	3	4	5
y	−26	−20	−14	−8	−2	4	10	16	22

1. $-14 = 6x - 8$ $x =$ −1
2. $6x - 8 = -26$ $x =$ −3
3. $16 = 6x - 8$ $x =$ 4
4. $6x - 8 = -2$ $x =$ 1

The graph of $y = -2x - 2$ is shown at right. Use it to solve the related equations.

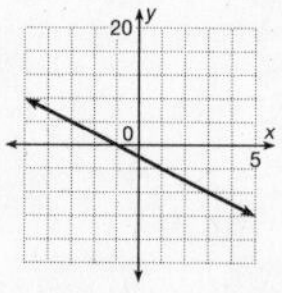

5. $-2x - 2 = 4$ $x =$ −3
6. $-4 = -2x - 2$ $x =$ 1
7. Use the graph to estimate the solution to $-9.5 = -2x - 2$. $x \approx$ 4
8. Dolphins can swim at rates up to 25 mi/hr. Write and graph an inequality for this statement. $r \le 25$

9. The Kitty Catalog offers T-shirts with kitten designs for $12.00 each. A shipping charge of $5.00 is added to the entire order.
   a. Write an equation for the amount of money, m, that you would pay if you bought t T-shirts. $m = 12t + 5$
   b. Make a table of values for your equation in **a**.

t	1	2	3	4
m	17	29	41	53

   c. Amy wants to buy as many shirts as she can. She has $50 to spend. How many shirts can she buy? 3 shirts
10. A typical credit card has an area of 7.17 in^2. A billboard artist draws a scale drawing of the credit card using a scale factor of 50. What is the area of the drawing? *[Lesson 7-10]* 17,925 in^2
11. **Social Science** The population of Americans who speak a language other than English at home increased 6.5% from 1980 to 1990. If this population was 216 million in 1980, what was it in 1990? *[Lesson 8-7]* About 230 million

Name ______________________

Practice 10-9

Integer Addition and Subtraction Equations

Write the equation represented by each equation box. Then solve the equation. The lighter tiles represent positive integers.

1. $x + (-3) = 2$ $x =$ 5

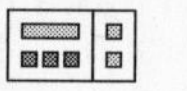

2. $x + 7 = 3$ $x =$ −4

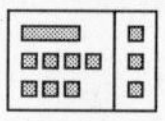

3. $x + (-4) = -5$ $x =$ −1

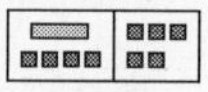

For each equation, tell whether the number in bold is a solution.

4. $x - 4 = 0$; **6** No
5. $h + (-3) = -13$; **16** No
6. $b - 1 = -4$; **−3** Yes
7. $m + (-6) = 8$; **2** No
8. $d - 7 = 6$; **13** Yes
9. $p + (-8) = -35$; **43** No

Solve each equation. Check your solutions.

10. $a - (-4) = -2$ $a =$ −6
11. $q + 2 = -47$ $q =$ −49
12. $s - (-5) = -7$ $s =$ −12
13. $t + 6 = 3$ $t =$ −3
14. $k + 8 = 2$ $k =$ −6
15. $f - (-7) = -24$ $f =$ −31
16. $c + (-2) = 51$ $c =$ 53
17. $y - 9 = 4$ $y =$ 13
18. $j + 15 = -9$ $j =$ −24
19. $u + (-21) = 18$ $u =$ 39
20. $g - 5 = 3$ $g =$ 8
21. $x - 31 = 74$ $x =$ 105
22. $w + (-45) = 11$ $w =$ 56
23. $r - 60 = -38$ $r =$ 22
24. $n + 3 = 26$ $n =$ 23
25. $z - (-72) = 62$ $z =$ −10

26. Yesterday's high temperature was 24°F. This was 33° higher than last night's low temperature. What was last night's low temperature? −9°F
27. The U.S. Postal Service handled 35.8 million pieces of library rate mail in 1994. This is 2.9 million pieces fewer than in 1993. How many library rate packages were mailed in 1993? 38.7 million

Name ______________________

Practice 10-10

Integer Multiplication and Division Equations

Write the equation represented by each equation box. Then solve the equation. The lighter tiles represent positive integers.

1. $-2x = 8$ $x =$ -4
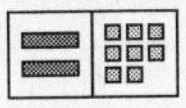

2. $-4x = -12$ $x =$ 3
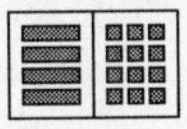

3. $3x = -6$ $x =$ -2
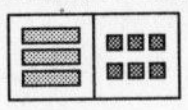

For each equation, tell whether the number in bold is a solution.

4. $\frac{x}{7} = 15$; **105** Yes
5. $3x = 21$; **63** No
6. $\frac{t}{-2} = 8$; **−4** No
7. $-5z = -34$; **7** No
8. $\frac{m}{4} = -9$; **−36** Yes
9. $-6t = -24$; **4** Yes

Solve each equation. Check your solutions.

10. $7n = 77$ $n =$ 11
11. $\frac{r}{-5} = 12$ $r =$ -60
12. $-2b = 34$ $b =$ -17
13. $\frac{g}{3} = 8$ $g =$ 24
14. $-8d = -64$ $d =$ 8
15. $-5k = 0$ $k =$ 0
16. $\frac{x}{10} = -6$ $x =$ -60
17. $\frac{u}{-8} = 15$ $u =$ -120
18. $-4a = 40$ $a =$ -10
19. $\frac{h}{-64} = 1$ $h =$ -64
20. $-7c = -56$ $c =$ 8
21. $\frac{f}{2} = -16$ $f =$ -32
22. $\frac{p}{-11} = -88$ $p =$ 968
23. $6t = -42$ $t =$ -7
24. $-12z = -96$ $z =$ 8
25. $\frac{y}{-18} = 3$ $y =$ -54

26. **Computer** Jerry recently bought a new modem for his computer. Yesterday, his new modem took 7 minutes to download a file. This is $\frac{1}{12}$ of the time it would have taken using his old modem. How long would it take to download the file using the old modem? 84 min

27. **Geography** In 1994, the population of Argentina was about 34,000,000 people This was about 170 times as great as the population of Belize. What was the population of Belize? About 200,000

Name ______________________

Practice 10-11

Solving Two-Step Equations

Write the equation represented by each equation box. Then solve the equation.

1. $-2x + 3 = -5$ $x =$ 4
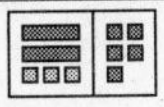

2. $10 = 4x + (-2)$ $x =$ 3
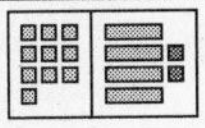

3. $3x + 4 = -2$ $x =$ -2
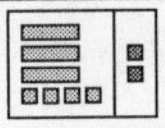

For each equation, tell whether the number in bold is a solution.

4. $\frac{p}{7} = -14$; **−98** Yes
5. $-2x + 3 = 5$; **2** No
6. $\frac{a}{-8} - 5 = -3$; **−16** Yes
7. $\frac{u}{-5} + 7 = 12$; **30** No
8. $4x + (-3) = 9$; **3** Yes
9. $\frac{q}{3} + (-4) = 11$; **−15** No

Solve each equation. Check your solutions.

10. $3b + (-7) = -25$ $b =$ -6
11. $\frac{n}{-4} + (-3) = 8$ $n =$ -44
12. $16 = 4h - 12$ $h =$ 7
13. $\frac{x}{6} - (-10) = 3$ $x =$ -42
14. $8w - 17 = -89$ $w =$ -9
15. $\frac{c}{7} - 12 = -4$ $c =$ 56
16. $\frac{p}{-5} + 12 = 20$ $p =$ -40
17. $5j + (-16) = -76$ $j =$ -12
18. $\frac{k}{-3} + (-8) = -8$ $k =$ 0
19. $-11z + 42 = 86$ $z =$ -4
20. $15 = \frac{d}{2} - (-12)$ $d =$ 6
21. $13r - (-12) = 103$ $r =$ 7
22. $\frac{g}{12} + (-8) = -5$ $g =$ 36
23. $24 = \frac{m}{-5} + 17$ $m =$ -35
24. $42 = 7t - 42$ $t =$ 12
25. $-18y + 14 = -166$ $y =$ 10

26. The area of a trapezoid is 32 cm^2. Its height is 8 cm and one base has length 3 cm. Write and solve an equation to find the length of the other base.
Possible answer: $\frac{1}{2} \cdot 8(3 + x) = 32$; 5 cm

27. **Science** Gorillas and chimpanzees can learn sign language to communicate with humans. By 1982, a gorilla named Koko had learned 700 words. This is 50 fewer than 5 times as many words as a chimp named Washoe knew a decade earlier. How many words did Washoe know? 150 words

Name ______________________

Practice 10-12

Problem-Solving with Integer Equations

1. Suppose the temperature increases 8° to −7°F. What was the starting temperature? −15°F

2. **Science** A typical giant squid is about 240 in. long, which is 16 times the diameter of one of its eyes. What is the diameter of the eye? About 15 in.

3. **Consumer** James went to the store to return a defective \$45 tape recorder for a refund. At the same time, he bought some batteries for \$3 per package. If he received \$33 of his refund, how many packages of batteries did he buy? 4 packages

4. The Rugyong Hotel in Pyongyang, North Korea, has 105 stories. This is 9 more than twice the number of stories of the Transamerica Pyramid in San Francisco, California. How many stories does the Transamerica Pyramid have? 48 stories

5. Rome, Italy, gets an average of 2 in. of rain in April. This is about $\frac{1}{4}$ the average April rainfall in Nairobi, Kenya. How much rain falls in Nairobi in April? About 8 in.

6. **Science** Neptune has 8 known moons. This is 2 more than $\frac{1}{3}$ of the number of known moons of Saturn. How many moons is Saturn known to have? 18 moons

7. **Science** Ohm's Law states that the electrical current, I, through a resistor is given by the formula $I = \frac{V}{R}$, where V is the voltage in volts and R is the resistance in ohms. If the current is 6 amperes and the resistance is 18 ohms, what is the voltage? 108 volts

8. During Super Bowl XX in 1986, the Chicago Bears scored 46 points against the New England Patriots. This was 24 less than 7 times the Patriots score. How many points did the Patriots score? 10 points

9. Fahrenheit and Celsius temperatures are related by the formula $F = \frac{9C}{5} + 32$. What is the Celsius temperature if
   a. the temperature is 77°F? 25°C
   b. the temperature is −22°F? −30°C

Name ______________________

Practice

Section 10C Review

Write the equation represented by each equation box. Then solve the equation.

1. $-3x = 9$ $x =$ -3
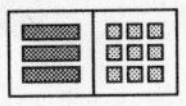

2. $x + (-6) = 2$ $x =$ 8
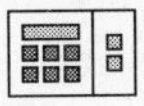

3. $7 = 3x + 4$ $x =$ 1
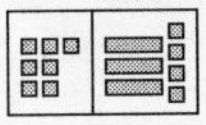

For each equation, tell whether the number in bold is a solution.

4. $k + (-16) = 4$; **20** Yes
5. $8z = -24$; **−3** Yes
6. $\frac{p}{-7} = 3$; **21** No
7. $\frac{w}{7} + (-4) = 10$; **2** No
8. $\frac{t}{5} - 12 = -2$; **50** Yes
9. $-4s + 16 = -12$; **7** Yes

Solve each equation. Check your solutions.

10. $b - 24 = -17$ $b =$ 7
11. $-7n = 49$ $n =$ -7
12. $\frac{h}{-3} + (-8) = -3$ $h =$ -15
13. $\frac{d}{5} = -8$ $d =$ -40
14. $8k + 4 = -20$ $k =$ -3
15. $c + 8 = -4$ $c =$ -12
16. $-6q = -78$ $q =$ 13
17. $\frac{s}{6} - 21 = -14$ $s =$ 42
18. $\frac{f}{-10} = 20$ $f =$ -200
19. $\frac{w}{7} = -17$ $w =$ -119
20. $y - (-12) = 43$ $y =$ 31
21. $4r + (-60) = -108$ $r =$ -12

22. A business lost \$38,000 in 1996. This is the same as a profit of −\$38,000, which is \$85,000 less than the 1995 profit. What was the profit in 1995? \$47,000

23. **Fine Arts** A mountain painting created by Kao K'o-kung in about 1300 is 32 in. wide and 48 in. tall. A reproduction of this painting in a book is 5 in. tall. How wide is the reproduction? *[Lesson 7-9]* $3\frac{1}{3}$ in.

24. **Geography** Temperatures in Siberia average about −35°F during the coldest months of the year. Temperatures in the arctic region of North America are about 10° warmer than this. Find the North American temperature. *[Lesson 9-4]* About −25°F

Name ______________________

Practice

Cumulative Review Chapters 1–10

Solve each proportion. *[Lesson 6-8]*

1. $\frac{y}{16} = \frac{7}{8}$ $y =$ 14
2. $\frac{8}{18} = \frac{20}{b}$ $b =$ 45
3. $\frac{3}{m} = \frac{15}{20}$ $m =$ 4
4. $\frac{25}{10} = \frac{j}{2}$ $j =$ 5
5. $\frac{6}{2} = \frac{9}{p}$ $p =$ 3
6. $\frac{8}{12} = \frac{r}{3}$ $r =$ 2
7. $\frac{7}{a} = \frac{28}{36}$ $a =$ 9
8. $\frac{n}{15} = \frac{30}{9}$ $n =$ 50

A model of a building is 8 in. tall. Use each scale to find the height of the actual building. *[Lesson 7-2]*

9. Scale: 1 in. = 3 ft — Actual height: 24 ft
10. Scale: 1 in. = 5 ft — Actual height: 40 ft
11. Scale: 1 in. = $1\frac{1}{2}$ ft — Actual height: 12 ft
12. Scale: 1 in. = $8\frac{1}{4}$ ft — Actual height: 66 ft
13. Scale: 2 in. = 11 ft — Actual height: 44 ft
14. Scale: 3 in. = 25 ft — Actual height: $66\frac{2}{3}$ ft

Find each sum, difference, product, or quotient. *[Lessons 9-4 to 9-7]*

15. $3 + (-16)$ -13
16. $7 \cdot (-5)$ -35
17. $-64 \div 4$ -16
18. $-8 - (-12)$ 4
19. $-14 \div (-7)$ 2
20. $-9 + (-32)$ -41

Graph each equation on a coordinate plane. *[Lesson 10-5]*

21. $y = -x + 4$

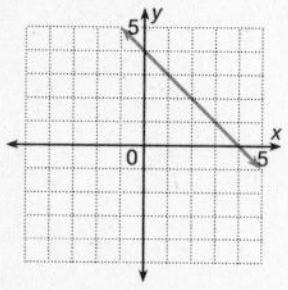

22. $y = 4x$

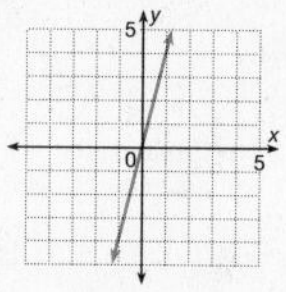

23. $y = 2x - 3$

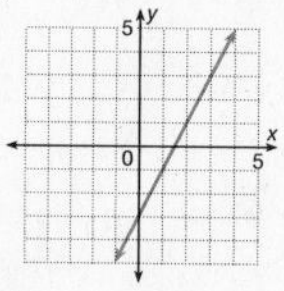

Solve each equation. Check your solutions. *[Lesson 10-12]*

24. $x + (-7) = 12$ $x =$ 19
25. $-4p = 28$ $p =$ -7
26. $\frac{t}{-5} + 8 = 13$ $t =$ -25
27. $-6n + 3 = 45$ $n =$ -7

Name ______________________

Practice 11-1

Exploring Polyhedrons

Use the sketch of the polyhedron to answer each question.

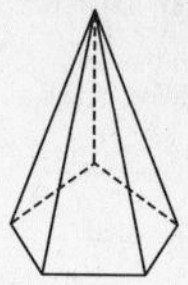

1. Name the polyhedron. Pentagonal pyramid
2. Name the polygons that are the faces of the polyhedron. How many of each type of polygon are there? 5 triangles, 1 pentagon
3. How many edges, faces, and vertices does the polyhedron have?

Edges: 10 Faces: 6 Vertices: 6

Name each polyhedron.

4. Hexagonal prism

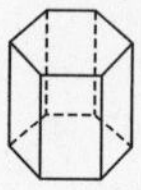

5. Triangular pyramid

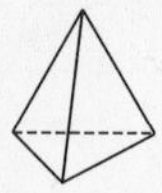

6. Rectangular prism

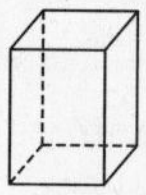

7. Octagonal pyramid

8. Square pyramid

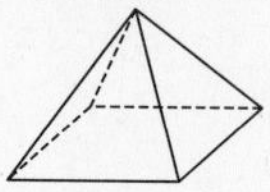

9. Octagonal prism

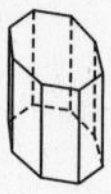

Sketch each polyhedron. Possible answers:

10. Triangular prism

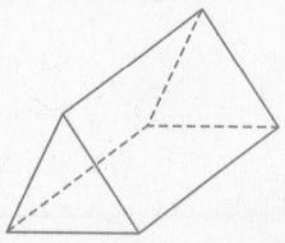

11. Hexagonal pyramid

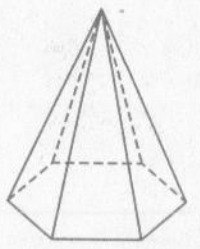

12. Pentagonal pyramid

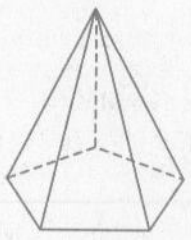

Name ______________________

Practice 11-2

Isometric and Orthographic Drawing

Find the number of cubes in each figure. Assume all cubes are visible.

1. 8

2. 7

3. 6

4. 7

Match each isometric drawing with a set of orthographic views.

5. D

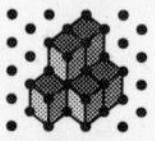

A.

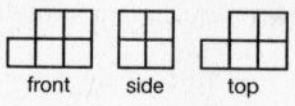

6. B

B.

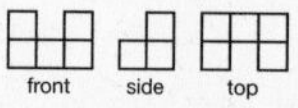

7. C

C.

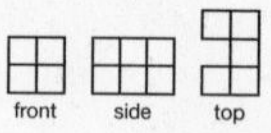

8. A

D.

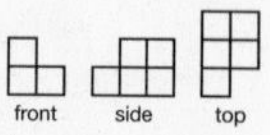

9. Sketch front, side, and top views of the object.

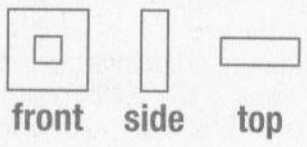

10. Make a perspective sketch of the object.

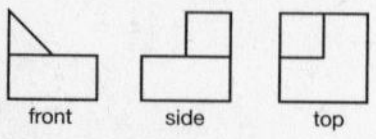

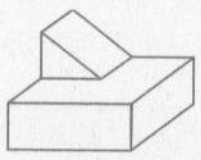

Name ______________________

Practice 11-3

Polyhedron Nets and Surface Areas

Sketch a net for each polyhedron. Possible answers:

1.

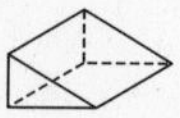

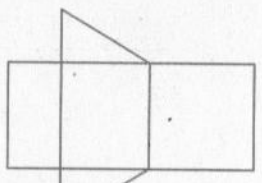

2.

3.

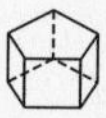

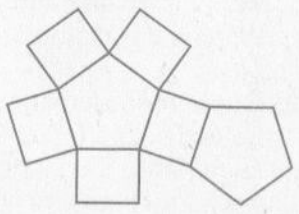

Sketch a net for each polyhedron, then find its surface area. Possible answers:

4. $186.52\ cm^2$

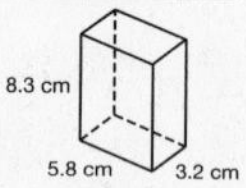

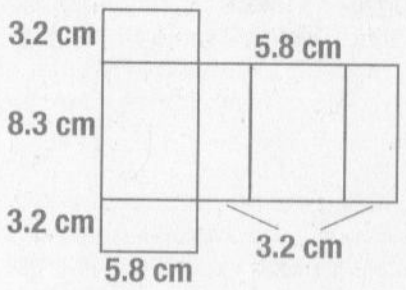

5. $3124\ in^2$

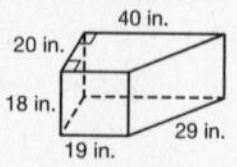

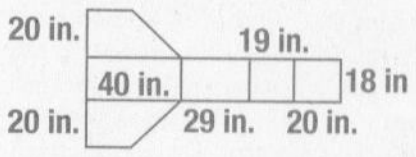

6. $63\frac{3}{8}\ ft^2$

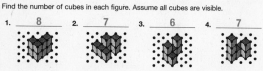

7. A box of facial tissue measures $9\frac{3}{8}$ in. by $4\frac{5}{8}$ in. by $3\frac{1}{4}$ in. Assuming no overlaps, how much cardboard was used to make the box? $177\frac{23}{32}\ in^2$

Name ______________________

Practice 11-4

Volumes of Prisms

Find the volume of each prism.

1. $1{,}008\ cm^3$

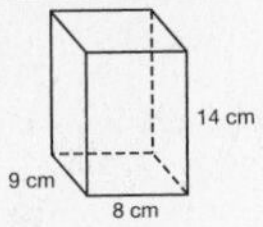

2. $20{,}790\ ft^3$

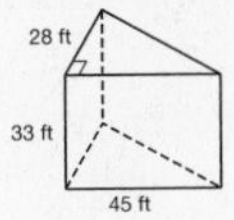

3. $1{,}467{,}235\ m^3$

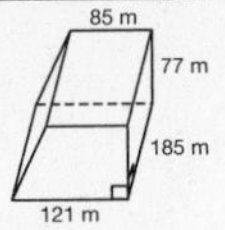

4. $1{,}441.5\ cm^3$

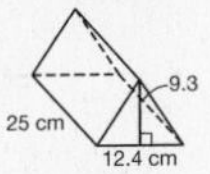

5. $546\ in^3$

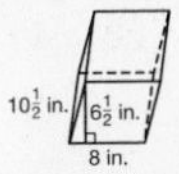

6. $228.2\ m^3$

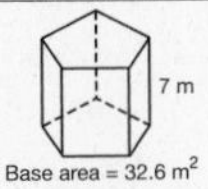

7. $9{,}568\ mm^3$

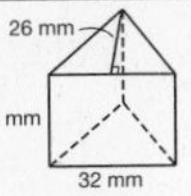

8. $2{,}592\frac{1}{2}\ in^3$

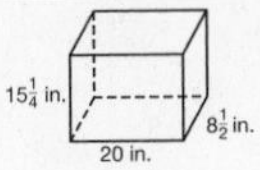

9. $273\ cm^3$

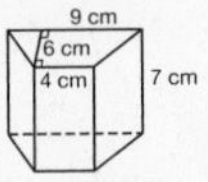

10. $2.016\ km^3$

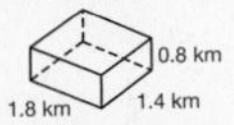

11. $110\frac{1}{4}\ ft^3$

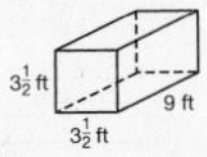

12. $104\ mm^3$

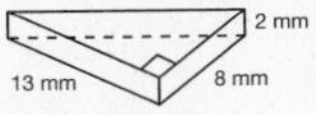

13. An asphalt speed bump has the shape of a trapezoidal prism. The prism is 450 cm long and each base has the dimensions shown. What is the volume of the speed bump?

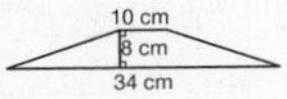

$79{,}200\ cm^3$

14. The tunnel on Yerba Buena Island near San Francisco, California, is about 78 ft wide, 56 ft tall, and 540 ft long. Estimate the amount of air in the tunnel by assuming that the tunnel has the shape of a rectangular prism.

About $2{,}400{,}000\ ft^3$

Name ______________________

Practice

Section 11A Review

Tell whether each statement is true or false.

1. A cube has 8 faces. False
2. All prisms are polyhedrons. True

3. Sketch a pentagonal pyramid and a hexagonal prism.

Possible answers:

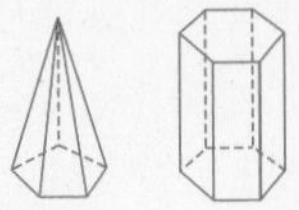

4. Sketch a net for the right triangular prism. Then find its surface area.

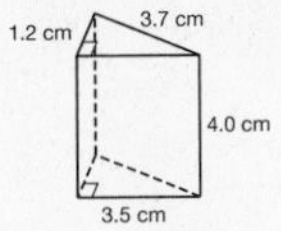

Possible answer: $37.8\ cm^2$

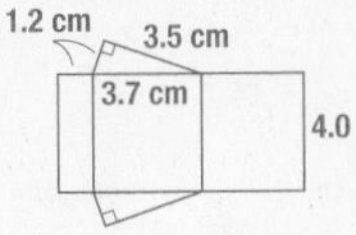

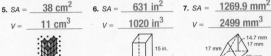

Find the surface area and volume of each figure.

5. $SA = 38\ cm^2$, $V = 11\ cm^3$

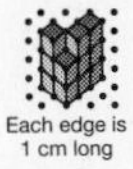

6. $SA = 631\ in^2$, $V = 1020\ in^3$

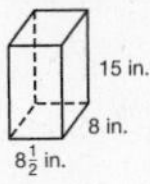

7. $SA = 1269.9\ mm^2$, $V = 2499\ mm^3$

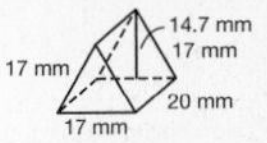

8. Sketch front, side, and top views of the hexagonal nut.

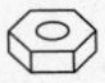

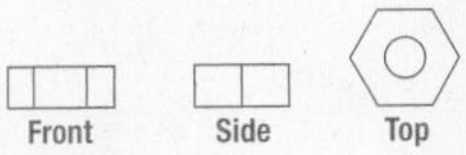

9. The floor plan of Andrea's home has the shape shown. What is the area of the floor? *[Lesson 5-10]*

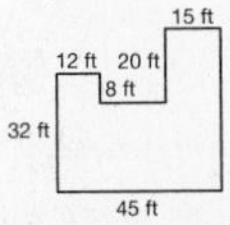

$1476\ ft^2$

10. A group of people pulled a 747 aircraft 328 ft in 61 seconds in London, England, in 1995. Use a unit rate to estimate how far they pulled the plane during the first 17 seconds.

About 91.4 ft

Name ______________________

Practice 11-5

Circles and Circle Graphs

Geography Use the circle graph to answer Exercises 1 and 2.

1. Estimate the percent of Cameroon's land in each category.

Arable land and crops	≈15%
Meadows and pastures	≈18%
Forest and woodland	≈54%
Other	≈13%

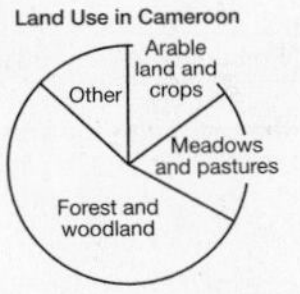

2. Identify any sectors that have central angles greater than 180°.

Forest and woodland

Sketch a circle graph to show the data. (Do *not* calculate or measure the central angles.)

3. **Social Science** About 50% of Djibouti's exports go to other African nations. About 40% go to the Middle East, and 10% go to other places.

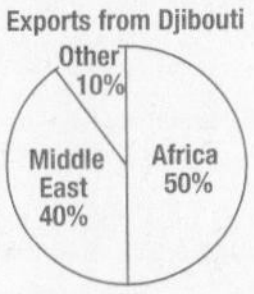

4. **Social Science**

Ethnic Groups in the Congo

Kongo	Sangha	Teke	M'Bochi	Other
48%	20%	17%	12%	3%

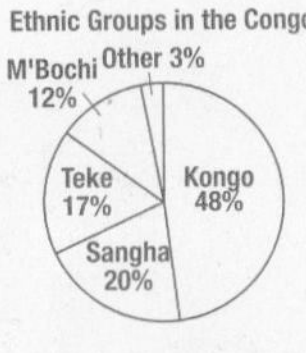

5. **Geography**

Areas of the Great Lakes (mi^2)

Ontario	Erie	Michigan	Huron	Superior
7,540	9,940	22,400	23,010	31,820

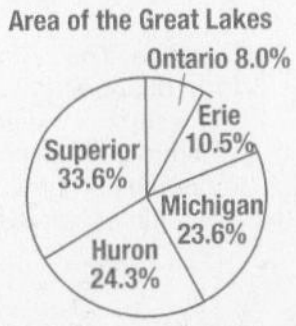

Name ______________________

Practice 11-6

Pi and Circumference

Find the circumference of each circle given its diameter or radius. Use $\pi \approx 3.14$, and round answers to the nearest tenth.

1. 37.7 in.

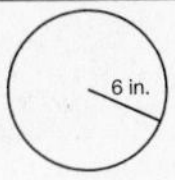

2. 113.0 cm

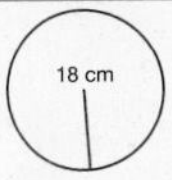

3. 65.9 ft

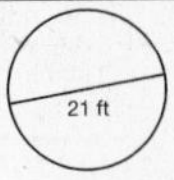

4. 6.3 mi

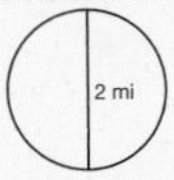

5. 30.8 mm

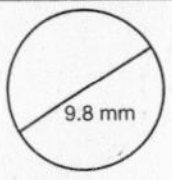

6. 69.1 in.

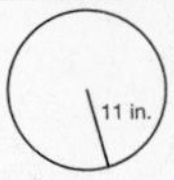

Find the circumference of each circle given its diameter or radius. Use $\pi \approx \frac{22}{7}$, and express answers in lowest terms.

7. 22 m

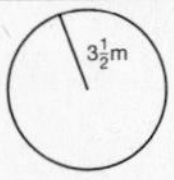

8. $51\frac{6}{7}$ ft

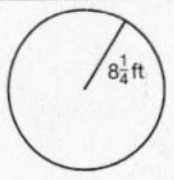

9. 88 km

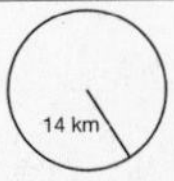

Given the radius, diameter, or circumference of a circle, find the other two measurements. Use $\pi \approx 3.14$, and round answers to the nearest tenth.

10. $r =$ 22 cm, $d = 44$ cm, $C \approx$ 138.2 cm
11. $r \approx$ 2.4 ft, $d \approx$ 4.8 ft, $C = 15$ ft
12. $r = 9$ mm, $d =$ 18 mm, $C \approx$ 56.5 mm
13. $r =$ 3.4 mi, $d = 6.8$ mi, $C \approx$ 21.4 mi
14. $r =$ 2 cm, $d =$ 4 cm, $C = 4\pi$ cm
15. $r = 12\frac{1}{2}$ ft, $d =$ 25 ft, $C \approx$ 78.5 ft
16. $r =$ 2.9 m, $d = 5.8$ m, $C \approx$ 18.2 m
17. $r =$ 3.5 in., $d =$ 7 in., $C = 7\pi$ in.

18. **Science** The radius of Pluto is about 1145 km. Find the length of Pluto's equator.

About 7191 km

Name ____________________

Practice 11-7

Area of a Circle

Find the area of each circle given its diameter or radius. Use $\pi \approx 3.14$, and round answers to the nearest tenth.

1. 1133.5 in^2 2. 3737.4 mm^2 3. 2.0 mi^2

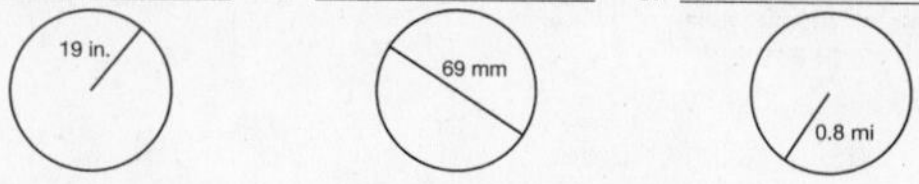

4. 23.7 ft^2 5. 5.3 km^2 6. 1319.6 ft^2

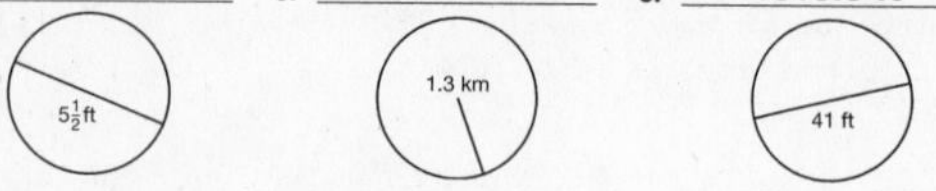

Find the area of each circle given its diameter or radius. Use $\pi \approx \frac{22}{7}$, and express answers in lowest terms.

7. $227\frac{1}{14}$ ft^2 8. $17\frac{1}{9}$ m^2 9. $86\frac{5}{8}$ in^2

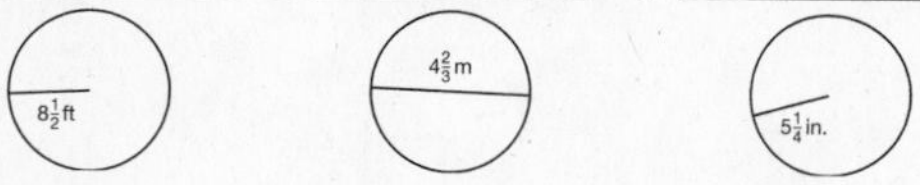

Given the radius or diameter of a circle, find its area. Use $\pi \approx 3.14$, and round answers to the nearest tenth.

10. $r = 18\frac{1}{4}$ in. $A \approx$ 1045.8 in^2
11. $d = 27$ cm $A \approx$ 572.3 cm^2
12. $r = 38$ mi $A \approx$ 4534.2 mi^2
13. $d = 5$ ft $A \approx$ 19.6 ft^2
14. $r = 9.1$ cm $A \approx$ 260.0 cm^2
15. $d = \frac{5}{8}$ in. $A \approx$ 0.3 in^2

16. Find the area of a pizza if the diameter is 15 in. About 176.6 in^2

17. The radius of a U.S. quarter is about 12 mm. Find the area of a quarter. About 452.2 mm^2

Name ____________________

Practice 11-8

Surface Area of Cylinders

Make a perspective drawing of each object. Possible answers:

1. A sphere 2. A cone 3. A cylinder

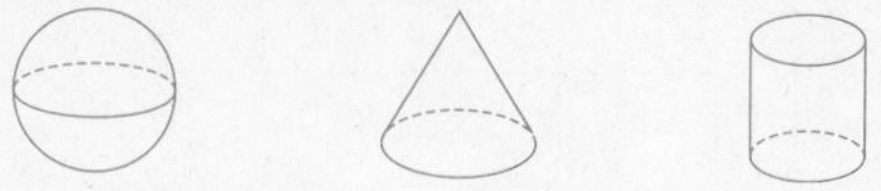

Find the surface area of each cylinder. Use $\pi \approx 3.14$, and round answers to the nearest tenth.

4. 602.1 cm^2 5. 1224.6 in^2 6. 44.1 m^2

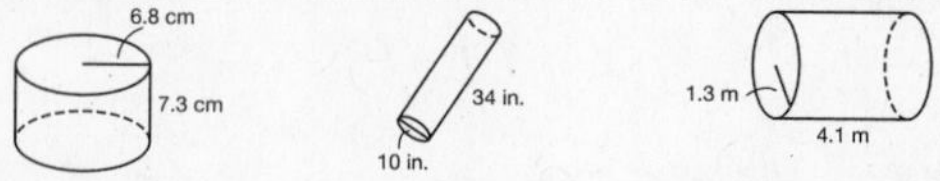

7. 3843.4 mm^2 8. 590.3 in^2 9. 94.8 cm^2

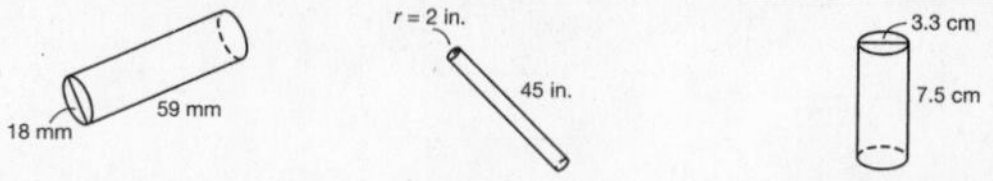

10. 4804.2 mm^2 11. 10.8 in^2 12. 900.0 cm^2

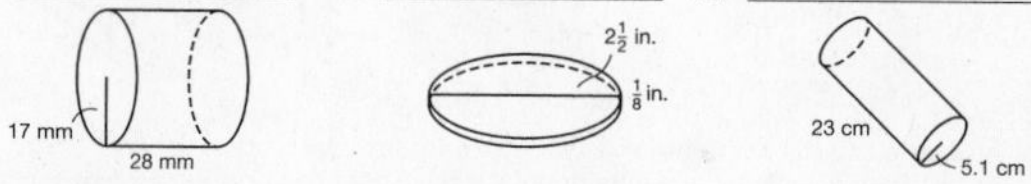

13. A can of dog food has diameter 7.4 cm and height 10.3 cm. How many square centimeters of metal were used to make this can? About 325.3 cm^2

14. A lighthouse has the shape of a cylinder with radius 13 ft and height 60 ft. If you paint the outside of the lighthouse (not including the roof), how much surface area will you cover? 4898.4 ft^2

Name ____________________

Practice 11-9

Volume of Cylinders

Find the volume of each cylinder. Use $\pi \approx 3.14$, and round answers to the nearest tenth.

1. 5,425.9 in^3 2. 35,080.1 mm^3 3. 423.9 ft^3

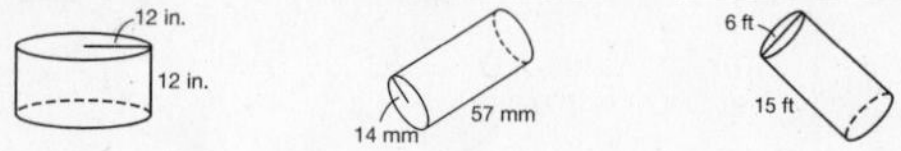

4. 1,037.4 yd^3 5. 11,253.8 mm^3 6. 211.6 in^3

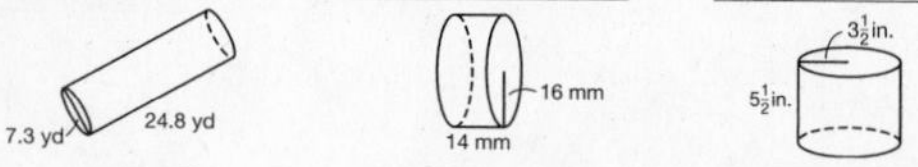

7. 664.9 ft^3 8. 22.6 m^3 9. 15,700.3 in^3

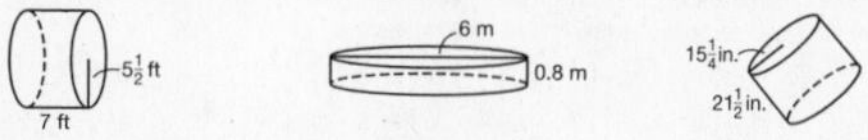

10. 1,538.6 yd^3 11. 2,059.8 mm^3 12. 737.3 in^3

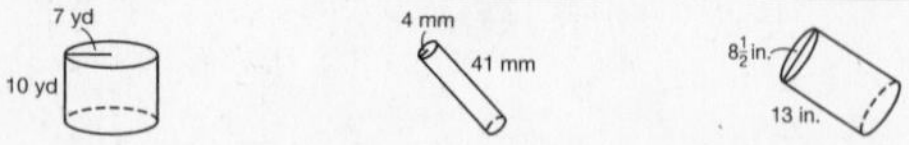

Given the height and radius, find the capacity of each cylindrical can to the nearest tenth of a milliliter. Use $\pi \approx 3.14$.

13. $h = 13$ cm, $r = 4$ cm, $V \approx$ 653.1 mL
14. $h = 22$ cm, $r = 9.3$ cm, $V \approx$ 5974.7 mL
15. $h = 9.3$ cm, $r = 3.6$ cm, $V \approx$ 378.5 mL

16. **History** The largest single-cylinder steam engine ever built was used in 1849 for land draining in the Netherlands. Its cylinder was 12 ft in diameter and it had a stroke of about 19 ft. How much water was lifted by each stroke? About 2150 ft^3

Name ____________________

Practice

Section 11B Review

1. The table gives data about 1993 retail car sales in the U.S. Draw a circle graph to show the data.

Category	Small	Midsize	Large	Luxury
Percent of Sales	33%	43%	11%	13%

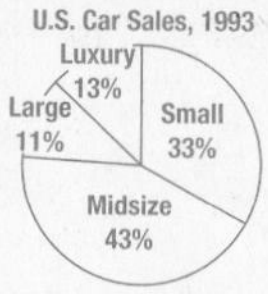

Find the circumference and area of each circle given its diameter or radius. Use $\pi \approx 3.14$, and round answers to the nearest tenth.

2. $C \approx$ 87.9 cm, $A \approx$ 615.4 cm^2
3. $C \approx$ 47.1 in., $A \approx$ 176.6 in^2
4. $C \approx$ 25.7 m, $A \approx$ 52.8 m^2

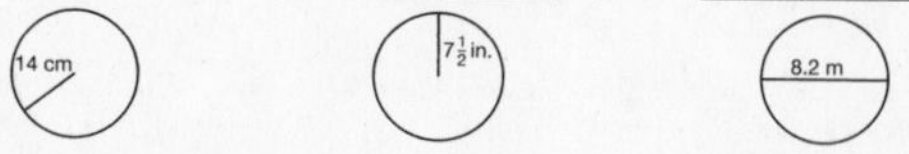

5. **Science** The length of Mercury's equator is about 9522 mi. Find the diameter of Mercury. About 3032 mi

Find the surface area and volume of each cylinder. Use $\pi \approx 3.14$, and round answers to the nearest tenth.

6. $SA \approx$ 3,504.2 in^2, $V \approx$ 13,225.7 in^3
7. $SA \approx$ 229.6 ft^2, $V \approx$ 265.3 ft^3
8. $SA \approx$ 1,011.1 m^2, $V \approx$ 2,461.8 m^3

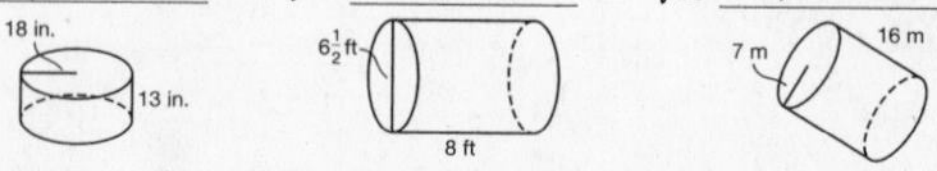

9. A skydiver jumps out of an airplane flying at an elevation of 940 ft above sea level. She lands in Death Valley, California, (elevation −282 ft). How far did she fall? *[Lesson 9-5]* 1222 ft

10. **Science** The saltopus was a small dinosaur that lived in Scotland and weighed 2 lb. An equation to represent the weight of several of these creatures is $w = 2s$, where w represents the weight in pounds and s represents the number of saltopuses. Graph this equation on a coordinate plane. *[Lesson 10-5]*

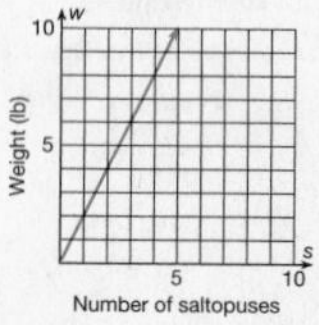

Name ______________________

Practice 11-10

Translations

For each group of figures, identify all lettered polygons that are translations of the shaded polygon.

1. D
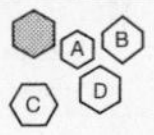

2. B, F
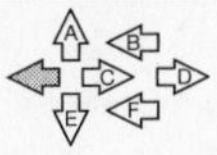

3. E
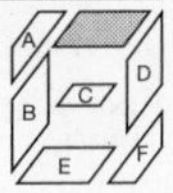

Write a rule for each translation.

4. Left 8 $(x, y) \rightarrow (x - 8, y)$

5. Right 2, down 3 $(x, y) \rightarrow (x + 2, y - 3)$

Point P is located at $(4, -1)$. Use each rule to find the coordinates of P'.

6. $(x, y) \rightarrow (x - 4, y + 3)$ $(0, 2)$

7. $(x, y) \rightarrow (x + 10, y + 2)$ $(14, 1)$

8. $(x, y) \rightarrow (x + 3, y)$ $(7, -1)$

9. $(x, y) \rightarrow (x - 7, y + 1)$ $(-3, 0)$

Using each rule, draw a translation of figure $QRST$ on a coordinate plane. Give the coordinates of the vertices of the translation.

10. Left 4, up 2
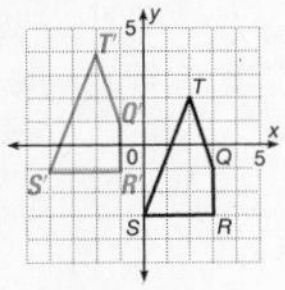

Q' $(-1, 1)$ R' $(-1, -1)$

S' $(-4, -1)$ T' $(-2, 4)$

11. $(x, y) \rightarrow (x + 5, y + 3)$
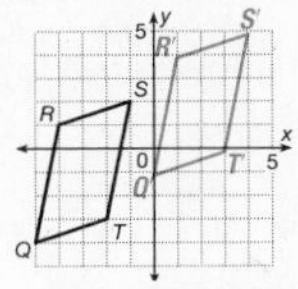

Q' $(0, -1)$ R' $(1, 4)$

S' $(4, 5)$ T' $(3, 0)$

12. **Language Arts** The Japanese word shown at the right means "extensive forest." Circle the portions of this word that are translations of each other.

Name ______________________

Practice 11-11

Reflections and Line Symmetry

Decide whether each figure has line symmetry. If it does, draw and number the lines of symmetry.

1. Parallelogram No
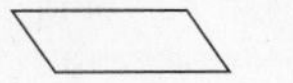

2. Ellipse Yes
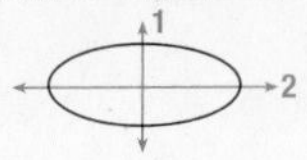

3. Isosceles Trapezoid Yes
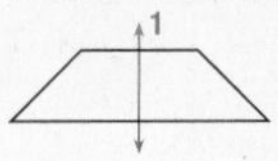

Decide whether each pattern or object has line symmetry. If it does, draw and number the lines of symmetry.

4. Yes

5. Yes
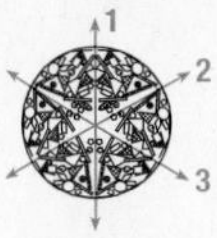

6. No
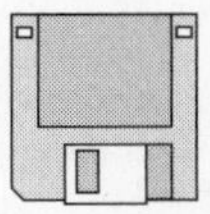

Draw each figure and its reflection on a coordinate plane.

7. $\triangle ABC$ with $A(-3, 4)$, $B(-1, 2)$ and $C(-5, 1)$ reflected across the x-axis.
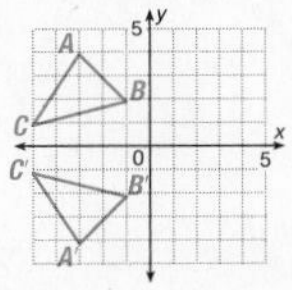

8. $DEFG$ with $D(-4, 0)$, $E(-5, -4)$, $F(-2, -3)$ and $G(-1, -1)$, reflected across the y-axis
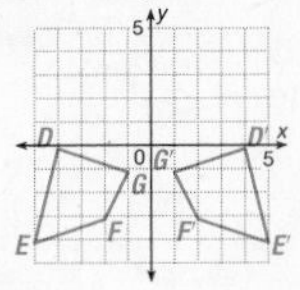

Geography Tell how many lines of symmetry are in each flag.

9. Sweden 1

10. Japan 2
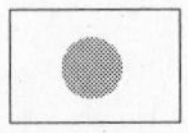

11. Trinidad and Tobago 0

Name ______________________

Practice 11-12

Rotations and Rotational Symmetry

Decide whether each figure has rotational symmetry. If it does, name the fractional turns that rotate the figure onto itself.

1. Rhombus Yes; $\frac{1}{2}$ turn
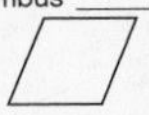

2. Rectangle Yes; $\frac{1}{2}$ turn

3. Scalene triangle No

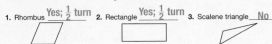

4. List all of the images in Exercises **1–3** that have point symmetry. 1, 2

Give the smallest fractional turn that each figure has been rotated clockwise. Express your answer in degrees.

5. Clock face 90°

6. Dumb bell 180°
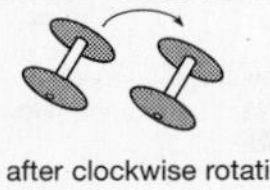

7. Puerto Rican flag 360°
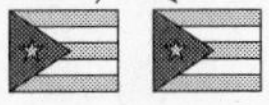

8. Give the coordinates of $\triangle PQR$ after clockwise rotations around the origin of:
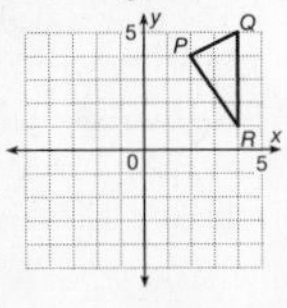

a. 90° $\left(\frac{1}{4}\text{ turn}\right)$ P' $(4, -2)$ Q' $(5, -4)$ R' $(1, -4)$

b. 180° $\left(\frac{1}{2}\text{ turn}\right)$ P'' $(-2, -4)$ Q'' $(-4, -5)$ R'' $(-4, -1)$

c. 270° $\left(\frac{3}{4}\text{ turn}\right)$ P''' $(-4, 2)$ Q''' $(-5, 4)$ R''' $(-1, 4)$

d. 360° (full turn) P'''' $(2, 4)$ Q'''' $(4, 5)$ R'''' $(4, 1)$

9. Draw rectangle $STUV$ with $S(0, 3)$, $T(1, 4)$, $U(3, 2)$ and $V(2, 1)$. Give the coordinates of rotations of $STUV$ after clockwise rotations around the origin of:
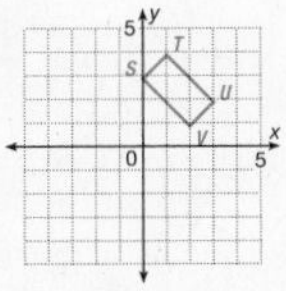

a. 90° $\left(\frac{1}{4}\text{ turn}\right)$ S' $(3, 0)$ T' $(4, -1)$ U' $(2, -3)$ V' $(1, -2)$

b. 180° $\left(\frac{1}{2}\text{ turn}\right)$ S'' $(0, -3)$ T'' $(-1, -4)$ U'' $(-3, -2)$ V'' $(-2, -1)$

c. 270° $\left(\frac{3}{4}\text{ turn}\right)$ S''' $(-3, 0)$ T''' $(-4, 1)$ U''' $(-2, 3)$ V''' $(-1, 2)$

d. 360° (full turn) S'''' $(0, 3)$ T'''' $(1, 4)$ U'''' $(3, 2)$ V'''' $(2, 1)$

Name ______________________

Practice

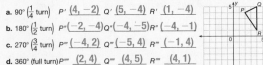

Section 11C Review

Point K is at $(5, -3)$. Use each translation rule to find the coordinates of K'.

1. $(x, y) \rightarrow (x, y - 7)$ $(5, -10)$

2. $(x, y) \rightarrow (x + 3, y + 3)$ $(8, 0)$

3. $(x, y) \rightarrow (x - 5, y + 6)$ $(0, 3)$

4. $(x, y) \rightarrow (x - 12, y)$ $(-7, -3)$

5. Draw the reflection of $\triangle LMN$ across the y-axis. Give the coordinates of the vertices of the reflection.

L' $(-1, 5)$ M' $(-5, 4)$ N' $(-3, 1)$
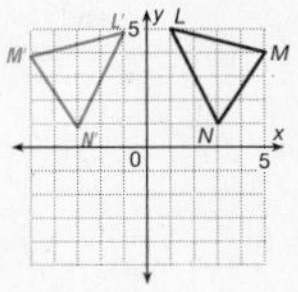

6. Give the coordinates of the vertices of rotations of $\triangle LMN$ after clockwise rotations around the origin of:

a. 90° $\left(\frac{1}{4}\text{ turn}\right)$ L' $(5, -1)$ M' $(4, -5)$ N' $(1, -3)$

b. 180° $\left(\frac{1}{2}\text{ turn}\right)$ L'' $(-1, -5)$ M'' $(-5, -4)$ N'' $(-3, -1)$

c. 270° $\left(\frac{3}{4}\text{ turn}\right)$ L''' $(-5, 1)$ M''' $(-4, 5)$ N''' $(-1, 3)$

d. 360° (full turn) L'''' $(1, 5)$ M'''' $(5, 4)$ N'''' $(3, 1)$

7. **Language Arts** Blind people can read using the Braille alphabet of raised dot patterns. Eleven of these patterns are shown below.

O R T W X Y Z ch ou and for

a. Which patterns have a horizontal line of symmetry? O, R, W, X, Y, and, for

b. Which patterns have a vertical line of symmetry? X, for

c. Which patterns have rotational symmetry? T, X, ch, ou, for

8. The number of motorcycles in the U.S. decreased from 5,444,400 in 1985 to 4,259,500 in 1990. Find the percent decrease. *[Lesson 8-7]* About 21.8%

9. The Fujiyama roller coaster in Japan is designed to travel at speeds up to 118.8 feet per second. Convert this speed to miles per hour *[Lesson 7-7]* 81 mi/hr

Name ______________________

Practice

Cumulative Review Chapters 1–11

Find the area of each figure. *[Lesson 5-10]*

1. 805 ft^2 2. 14.8 cm^2 3. $10\frac{7}{16} \text{ in}^2$

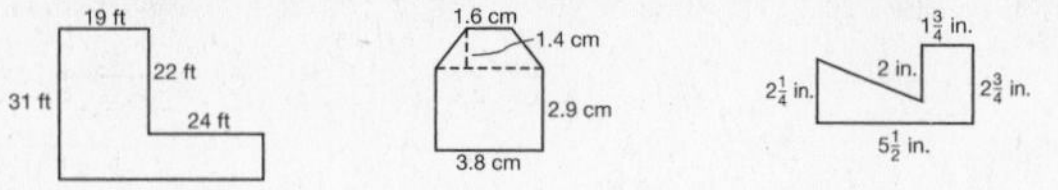

Find the missing side lengths in each pair of similar figures. *[Lesson 7-9]*

4. $t =$ 72 $u =$ 75 5. $v =$ 30 cm $w =$ 40 cm 6. $x =$ 52 $y =$ 36 $z =$ 48

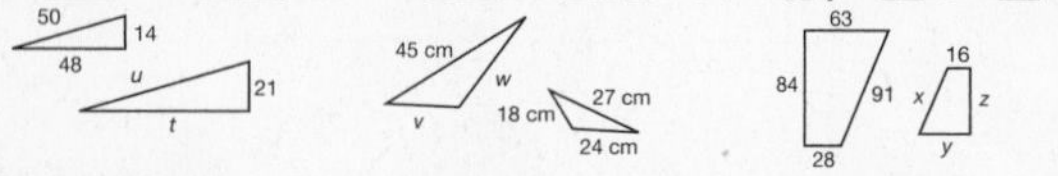

Write each fraction or decimal as a percent. Where necessary, use a repeating decimal to help express your percent. *[Lesson 8-2]*

7. 0.67 67% 8. 0.045 4.5% 9. $\frac{3}{20}$ 15% 10. $\frac{17}{25}$ 68%

11. $\frac{5}{6}$ $83.\overline{3}\%$ 12. $\frac{3}{50}$ 6% 13. $\frac{5}{8}$ 62.5% 14. $\frac{2}{5}$ 40%

Find the area of the circle, given its diameter or radius. Use $\pi \approx 3.14$, and round answers to the nearest tenth. *[Lesson 11-7]*

15. 113.0 ft^2 16. 298.5 in^2 17. 961.6 m^2

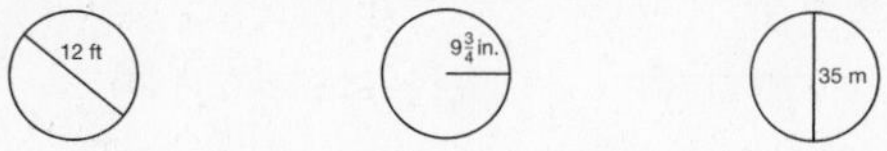

For each group of figures, identify all lettered polygons that are translations of the shaded polygon. *[Lesson 11-9]*

18. B, D 19. D 20. C

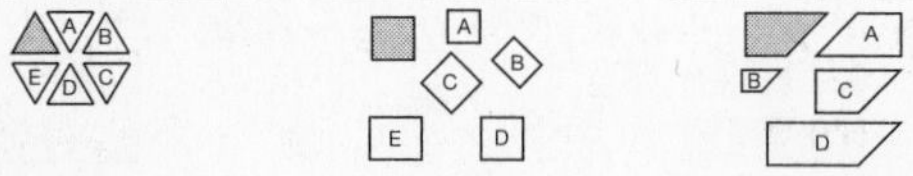

Name ______________________

Practice 12-1

Counting Methods

Use the Counting Principle to find the number of outcomes in each situation.

1. Magazine subscriptions: 4 magazines, 3 subscription lengths. How many choices? 12
2. Jeans: 3 colors, 6 waist sizes, 10 lengths. How many choices? 180
3. Computers: 3 motherboards, 3 hard drives, 4 monitors. How many choices? 36
4. Stereos: 5 receivers, 3 CD players, 4 types of speakers. How many systems? 60
5. Dinner: 4 main courses, 3 side dishes, salad with one of 6 dressings. How many choices? 72
6. You are taking a multiple-choice test. Each of the 2 questions has 4 choices (A, B, C, and D).
   a. Make a tree diagram to show the possible outcomes for the answers for this test. How many outcomes are there? 16

   Possible answer:

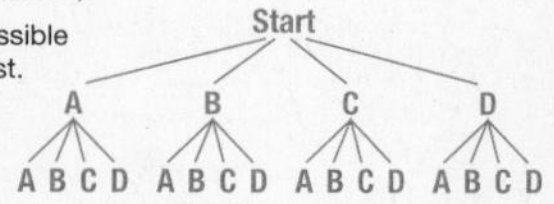

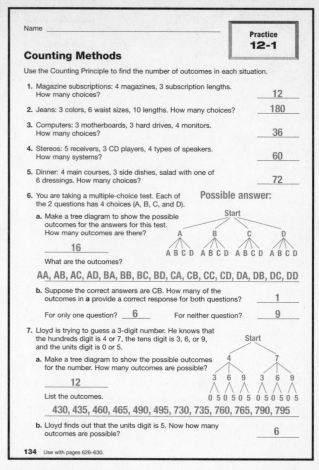

   What are the outcomes?

   AA, AB, AC, AD, BA, BB, BC, BD, CA, CB, CC, CD, DA, DB, DC, DD

   b. Suppose the correct answers are CB. How many of the outcomes in **a** provide a correct response for both questions? 1

   For only one question? 6 For neither question? 9

7. Lloyd is trying to guess a 3-digit number. He knows that the hundreds digit is 4 or 7, the tens digit is 3, 6, or 9, and the units digit is 0 or 5.
   a. Make a tree diagram to show the possible outcomes for the number. How many outcomes are possible? 12

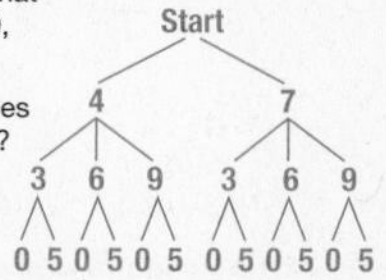

   List the outcomes.

   430, 435, 460, 465, 490, 495, 730, 735, 760, 765, 790, 795

   b. Lloyd finds out that the units digit is 5. Now how many outcomes are possible? 6

Name ______________________

Practice 12-2

Arrangements

Give each factorial product.

1. 6! 720 2. 2! 2 3. 4! 24 4. 5! 120
5. 1! 1 6. 9! 362,880 7. 8! 40,320 8. 12! 479,001,600
9. Every morning Harold feeds his dog, takes a shower, eats breakfast, and reads the newspaper. In how many different orders can he do these tasks? 24
10. Matt, Nat, and Pat are having a swimming race. List all the possible orders in which they can finish the race.

    Matt, Nat, Pat; Matt, Pat, Nat; Nat, Matt, Pat; Nat, Pat, Matt; Pat, Nat, Matt; Pat, Matt, Nat
11. Sandra displays her collection of compact discs on a shelf. Use factorial notation to give the number of ways she can arrange her discs if she has:

    a. 5 discs 5! b. 15 discs 15! c. 34 discs 34! d. 182 discs 182!
12. List all of the possible ways to order the letters in the word MATH (without repeating letters).

    AHMT, AHTM, AMHT, AMTH, ATHM, ATMH, HAMT, HATM, HMAT, HMTA, HTAM, HTMA, MAHT, MATH, MHAT, MHTA, MTAH, MTHA, TAHM, TAMH, THAM, THMA, TMAH, TMHA
13. Keith must choose a 3-letter password for a computer account. He can use any of the 26 upper-case letters of the alphabet, but he cannot repeat letters. How many passwords are possible? 15,600
14. Jarita is making a simple jigsaw puzzle for her very young cousin. She plans to arrange the shapes shown in a row. How many ways can she arrange the shapes? (The shapes are not to be rotated.) 720

15. The president, vice president, secretary, and treasurer of a school club are lining up for a photograph. In how many different orders can they line up? 24

Name ______________________

Practice 12-3

Choosing a Group

Decide whether or not order matters in each situation. Write *Yes* or *No*.

1. Choosing the digits in a lock combination Yes
2. Choosing 5 books to check out from the library No
3. Electing the president, vice president, and secretary of a club Yes
4. Choosing 5 club members to serve on a committee No

You plan to paint a clay pot. The hobby store offers appropriate paints in 6 colors. How many different ways can you choose the colors for your design if you plan to use:

5. Two colors? 15 6. Three colors? 20 7. Five colors? 6
8. At the video store, you've selected 4 videos you want to watch, but you only have time to watch 2 of them. How many ways can you select 2 of the 4 videos? 6
9. Abe, Bo, Cal, Duc, and Eve are student council members. Two of them need to meet with the school principal today.

   a. How many different ways are there to choose two of these students? 10

   b. List the possibilities.

   Abe and Bo, Abe and Cal, Abe and Duc, Abe and Eve, Bo and Cal, Bo and Duc, Bo and Eve, Cal and Duc, Cal and Eve, Duc and Eve
10. A bakery makes 3 kinds of bread: white, whole what, and nine-grain. You want to buy 2 different loaves. How many ways can you make your selection? 3
11. You have 3 extra tickets for a concert. How many ways can you choose 3 of your 5 best friends to go with you? 10
12. **History** In 1849, President Zachary Taylor chose 7 men as cabinet members. How many ways could Taylor choose 2 cabinet members with whom to consult about a particular issue? 21

Name ______________________

Practice

Section 12A Review

Use the Counting Principle to find the number of outcomes in each situation.

1. Books: 5 authors, 4 books by each author. How many choices? 20
2. Shirts: 6 styles, 3 sizes, 5 colors in each style. How many choices? 90
3. Bookcases: 3 widths, 2 heights, 4 kinds of wood. How many choices? 24
4. The employee cafeteria at a certain company offers a choice of a sandwich, casserole, or quiche for lunch. Each lunch includes soup or salad. Make a tree diagram to show the possible meals.

   Possible answers:

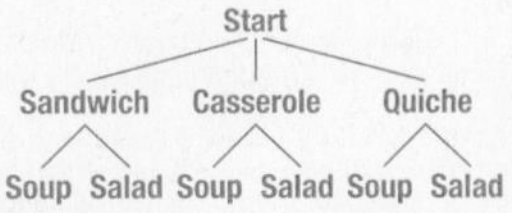

   How many possibilities are there? 6

Give each factorial product.

5. 3! 6 6. 7! 5,040 7. 9! 362,880 8. 5! 120
9. You and some friends are at a Chinese restaurant that offers 6 dishes. How many ways can you select 3 of the dishes to share? 20
10. You are taking a test and the instructions say, "Answer 2 of the next 5 questions." How many different ways can you select 2 questions to answer? 10
11. How many different four-number license plates can be made from the digits 1–5 if:
    a. digits can be repeated 625 **b.** digits cannot be repeated 120
12. At a grooming parlor, 6 dogs need to be put into 6 cages. How many different ways can this be done with only one dog per cage? 720
13. One sunny day in Houston, Texas, the First Interstate Bank Plaza building cast an 81-ft shadow and the Transco Tower cast a 75-ft shadow. The Transco Tower is 900 ft tall. How tall is the First Interstate Bank Plaza? *[Lesson 7-9]* 972 ft
14. The largest sundial in the world is located in Orlando Florida. It has the shape of a circle with diameter 37.2 m. Find the area of the sundial. *[Lesson 11-7]* About 1086 m^2

Name ______________________

Practice 12-4

Odds and Fairness

Name the possible outcomes for each experiment.

1. Spinning the spinner shown

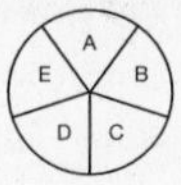

   A, B, C, D, E
2. Selecting a coin from a bag of quarters, dimes, and nickels
   Quarter, dime, nickel
3. Rolling a number cube and flipping a coin at the same time
   1-heads, 1-tails, 2-heads, 2-tails, 3-heads, 3-tails, 4-heads, 4-tails, 5-heads, 5-tails, 6-heads, 6-tails

Give the odds of each event.

4. Getting a 3 or a 6 on a roll of a number cube 2 : 4 or 1 : 2
5. Getting a vowel on a spin of the spinner in Exercise **1** 2 : 3
6. Choosing a yellow M&M® from a bag containing 5 yellow M&M's and 8 red M&M's 5 : 8

The game of Rummikub® contains 13 red tiles, 13 blue tiles, 13 black tiles, 13 orange tiles, and 2 jokers. The red, blue, black, and orange tiles are numbered 1–13. If you choose one Rummikub tile, what are the odds that it is:

7. Orange? 13 : 41 8. A prime number? 24 : 30 or 12 : 15

For each game described, give each player's odds of winning. Then tell whether the game is fair.

9. Spin the spinner in Exercise **1**. Tad gets a point for an A, B, or C. Jill gets a point for a D or E.
   Tad's odds: 3 : 2 Jill's odds: 2 : 3 Fair? No
10. Roll a number cube. Ed gets a point for a 1 or 2. Fred gets a point for a 3 or 6. Gwen gets a point for a 4 or 5.
    Ed's odds: 1 : 2 Fred's odds: 1 : 2 Gwen's odds: 1 : 2 Fair? Yes

Name ______________________

Practice 12-5

Probability

Give the probability of each event as a fraction, a percent, and a decimal.

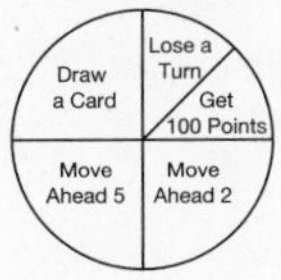

1. Spinning "Draw a Card" on the spinner shown
   $\frac{1}{4} = 25\% = 0.25$
2. Spinning "Get 100 Points" on the spinner shown
   $\frac{1}{8} = 12.5\% = 0.125$
3. Drawing a green marble from a bag containing the following marbles:
   a. 21 green **b.** 5 black and 7 white **c.** 3 green, 7 yellow
   $1 = 100\% = 1.0$ $0 = 0\% = 0.0$ $\frac{3}{10} = 30\% = 0.3$
4. **Social Studies** The circle graph shows the percent of the population of Arizona that lived in its five largest cities in 1990. What is the probability that a randomly selected resident:

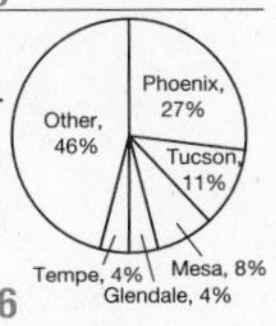

   a. Lives in Phoenix? **b.** Does *not* live in Phoenix?
   $\frac{27}{100} = 27\% = 0.27$ $\frac{73}{100} = 73\% = 0.73$
   c. Lives in Tempe, Mesa, or Glendale? $\frac{4}{25} = 16\% = 0.16$
5. Complete the table.

Probability of event	$\frac{1}{3}$	$\frac{4}{5}$	$\frac{1}{6}$	$\frac{3}{8}$	$\frac{7}{10}$	$\frac{3}{4}$
Probability that event does not happen	$\frac{2}{3}$	$\frac{1}{5}$	$\frac{5}{6}$	$\frac{5}{8}$	$\frac{3}{10}$	$\frac{1}{4}$
Odds of event	1 : 2	4 : 1	2 : 10	3 : 5	7 : 3	12 : 4

Give the probability that corresponds to each of the odds. Express each answer as a fraction in lowest terms.

6. 5 : 7 $\frac{5}{12}$ 7. 8 : 2 $\frac{4}{5}$ 8. 21 : 21 $\frac{1}{2}$ 9. 16 : 20 $\frac{4}{9}$
10. 24 : 1 $\frac{24}{25}$ 11. 44 : 56 $\frac{11}{25}$ 12. 35 : 15 $\frac{7}{10}$ 13. 27 : 81 $\frac{1}{4}$

Assume you are drawing the first tile in a Scrabble® game. Use the table on page 653 of your textbook to find each probability. Express each as a percent.

14. *P*(W) 2% 15. *P*(Not an A) 91% 16. *P*(E, F, or G) 17%

Name ______________________

Practice 12-6

Experimental Probability

The tally shows the results for several rolls of two number cubes.
a. Use the sheet to find the experimental probability of each event.
b. Use the figure on page 655 of your textbook to find the theoretical probability of each event. Give your answers as fractions in lowest terms.

1. Rolling a 2 **a.** $\frac{1}{50}$ **b.** $\frac{1}{36}$
2. Rolling a 3 **a.** $\frac{3}{50}$ **b.** $\frac{1}{18}$
3. Rolling a 5 **a.** $\frac{3}{25}$ **b.** $\frac{1}{9}$
4. Rolling a 7 **a.** $\frac{7}{50}$ **b.** $\frac{1}{6}$
5. Rolling an 8 **a.** $\frac{9}{50}$ **b.** $\frac{5}{36}$
6. Rolling a 10 **a.** $\frac{3}{50}$ **b.** $\frac{1}{12}$
7. Rolling an 11 **a.** $\frac{1}{25}$ **b.** $\frac{1}{18}$

Roll	Frequency
2	1
3	3
4	4
5	6
6	8
7	7
8	9
9	5
10	3
11	2
12	2

A speck of dust lands on the grid shown. What is the probability that it:

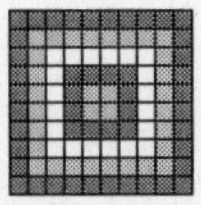

8. Lands on the dark shaded area? $\frac{12}{25} = 48\% = 0.48$
9. Lands on the light shaded area? $\frac{8}{25} = 32\% = 0.32$
10. Lands on the unshaded area? $\frac{1}{5} = 20\% = 0.2$

In a coin toss game, you earn points for landing on the shaded figures. Assume coins land randomly in the large square. What is the probability that a coin:

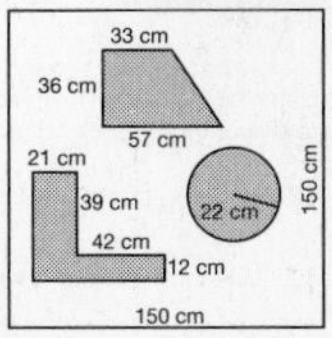

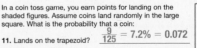

11. Lands on the trapezoid? $\frac{9}{125} = 7.2\% = 0.072$
12. Lands on the circle? $\approx 6.75\% = 0.0675$
13. Lands on the "L" shape? $\frac{7}{100} = 7\% = 0.07$
14. During the 1994–1995 basketball season, the Charlotte Hornets won 50 out of 82 games. Based on these results, what is the experimental probability that the Hornets will win a game? Express your answer as a percent. About 61.0%

Name ______________________

Practice 12-7

Independent and Dependent Events

Tell whether the events are dependent or independent.

1. A coin toss landing tails and a number cube coming up 5 — Independent
2. Sunshine in Boston, Massachusetts, and sunshine in Hartford, Connecticut — Dependent
3. Drawing a blue Rummikub® tile, then drawing a red tile (after replacing the first tile) — Independent

Exercises 4–6 refer to tossing a coin, then spinning the spinner shown. Find each probability.

4. *P*(coin landing heads and spinning a 5) $\frac{1}{14}$
5. *P*(coin landing heads and spinning a prime number) $\frac{2}{7}$
6. *P*(coin landing tails and spinning a 3, 4, 5, 6, or 7) $\frac{5}{14}$

Exercises 7–9 refer to rolling a green number cube, then rolling a red number cube. Find each probability.

7. *P*(rolling a green 3 and a red 2) $\frac{1}{36}$
8. *P*(rolling a green 4 and a red prime number) $\frac{1}{12}$
9. *P*(rolling a green number less than 6 and a red number greater than 3) $\frac{5}{12}$
10. A set of Scrabble® tiles includes 12 E's and 9 I's out of 100 tiles. Suppose you draw a tile, and then draw another tile without replacing the first.
   a. Are the two tile draws dependent or independent events? Dependent
   b. What is the probability that the first tile is an E and the second tile is an I? $\frac{3}{275} = 1.0\overline{9}\% = 0.01\overline{09}$
11. Some role-playing games use dice with different numbers of sides. You roll a four-sided die (numbered 1 to 4) and then a ten-sided die (numbered 1 to 10). What is the probability that the first number is greater than 1 and the second number is less than 7? $\frac{9}{20} = 45\% = 0.45$

Name ______________________

Practice

Section 12B Review

Name the possible outcomes for each experiment.

1. Spinning a spinner whose 7 sectors are labeled with the days of the week
   Sun., Mon., Tues., Wed., Thu., Fri., Sat.
2. Tossing a coin twice Heads-heads, heads-tails, tails-heads, tails-tails

Give the odds of each event.

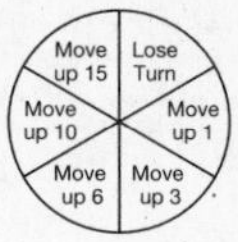

3. Spinning "Move Up 3" on the spinner at the right 1 : 5
4. Drawing an A, B, or C from a set of Scrabble® tiles (There are 9 A's, 2 B's, and 2 C's out of 100 tiles.) 13 : 87

A box contains 7 yellow, 3 green, and 4 blue pencils. Give the probability of each event as a fraction, a percent, and a decimal. (Round percent and decimal answers to two digits if necessary.)

5. *P*(blue) $\frac{2}{7} \approx 29\% = 0.29$
6. *P*(yellow) $\frac{1}{2} = 50\% = 0.5$
7. *P*(not blue) $\frac{5}{7} \approx 71\% = 0.71$
8. *P*(not yellow) $\frac{1}{2} = 50\% = 0.5$
9. If you select two pencils from the box, what is *P*(green, then yellow)? Assume you do not put the first pencil back. $\frac{3}{26} \approx 12\% = 0.12$

Tell whether the events are dependent or independent.

10. Getting an even number on the first roll of a number cube, then getting an even number on the second roll — Independent
11. Getting a face card on the first draw from a deck of playing cards, then getting a face card on the second draw (The first card is not replaced. A deck of 52 cards has 12 face cards.) — Dependent
12. Refer to the spinner in Exercise **3.** If you spin the spinner twice, what is the probability that you move up 6 or more on the first spin, and then lose a turn? $\frac{1}{12} = 8.\overline{3}\% = 0.08\overline{3}$
13. **Geography** Bulgaria has 220 miles of coastline. This is 200 miles less than three times Romania's coastline. How much coastline does Romania have? *[Lesson 10-11]* 140 mi
14. A shelf is $\frac{1}{2}$ in. thick, 10 in. wide, and 48 in. long. Find the volume of the shelf. *[Lesson 11-4]* 240 in^3

Name ______________________

Practice

Cumulative Review Chapters 1–12

Find the area of each figure. *[Lessons 5-8, 5-9]*

1. 336 m^2 2. $16\frac{7}{8}$ in^2 3. 13.92 cm^2 4. 57 ft^2

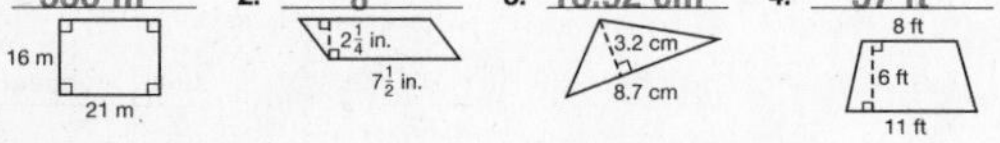

Solve each problem. If necessary, round answers to the nearest tenth. *[Lessons 8-5, 8-6]*

5. 84% of 365 is what number? 306.6
6. 23% of what number is 17? 73.9
7. 65 is what percent of 127? 51.2%
8. 863 is 128% of what number? 674.2

Solve each equation. Check your solution. *[Lesson 10-11]*

9. $\frac{m}{16} + (-5) = 4$ $m =$ 144
10. $6g - 43 = 35$ $g =$ 13
11. $\frac{t}{-4} + 31 = -8$ $t =$ 156
12. $5y + 123 = 68$ $y =$ −11

Find the surface area and volume of each polyhedron or cylinder. Where necessary, use $\pi \approx 3.14$ and round answers to the nearest tenth. *[Lessons 11-3, 11-4, 11-8, and 11-9]*

13. $SA =$ 79.2 m^2, $V =$ 45.5 m^3
14. $SA \approx$ 2,725.5 ft^2, $V \approx$ 10,462.5 ft^3
15. $SA \approx$ 471 in^2, $V \approx$ 696.0 in^3

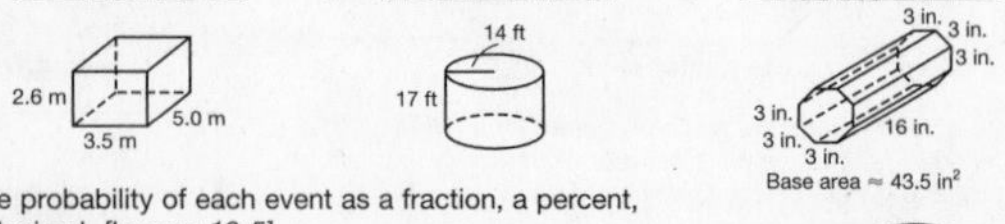

Give the probability of each event as a fraction, a percent, and a decimal. *[Lesson 12-5]*

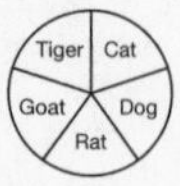

16. Spinning "Dog" on the spinner shown $\frac{1}{5}$, 20%, 0.2
17. Rolling a number less than 5 on a number cube $\frac{2}{3}$, $66.\overline{6}\%$, $0.\overline{6}$
18. Drawing a yellow marble from a bag containing the following marbles:
   a. 9 red — 0 = 0% = 0.0
   b. 6 red and 4 yellow — $\frac{2}{5}$ = 40% = 0.4
   c. 12 yellow — 1 = 100% = 1.0